PROBLEM SOLVING STRATEGIES

CROSSING THE RIVER WITH DOGS

AND OTHER
MATHEMATICAL
ADVENTURES

TED HERR
KEN JOHNSON

KEY
CURRICULUM
PRESS

2512 MARTIN
LUTHER KING JR. WAY
P.O. BOX 2304
BERKELEY
CALIFORNIA
94702

AUTHORS

Ted Herr
Roseville High School
Roseville, California

Ken Johnson
Sierra College
Rocklin, California

EDITOR

Dan Bennett
Key Curriculum Press
Berkeley, California

FIELD TESTERS

Christine Arum and Barry Chapelle, Jefferson H.S., Portland, OR
Keith Calandri and Brad Kincaid, Luther Burbank H.S., Sacramento, CA
Bob Daniel, Centaurus High School, Lafayette, CO
Steve Ganong, Tandem School, Charlottesville, VA
Gary Haas, Tokay H.S., Lodi, CA
Bob Licht, Portland Lutheran School, Portland, OR
Sue Loube, Grant's Pass H.S., Grant's Pass, OR
Don McGinnis, Thompson School District, Loveland, CO
John McMillen, St. Andrews School, Bethesda, MD
Barbara Olmstead, Long Trail School, Dorset, VT
Barb Saxe, Bear River H.S., Grass Valley, CA
Susan Smith, Suffield H.S., Suffield, CT
Jay Swartz, Norwell H.S., Norwell, MA
Reanee Wall, Eads H.S., Eads, CO
LaVeda Ward, Magnolia Senior H.S., Magnolia, AK

Printed in the U. S. A.   10 9 8 7 6 5 4 3   95 96 97 98 99   ISBN 1-55953-068-5

Contents

0 INTRODUCTION   1

1 DRAW A DIAGRAM   9

2 SYSTEMATIC LISTS   25

3 ELIMINATE POSSIBILITIES   43

4 MATRIX LOGIC   67

5 LOOK FOR A PATTERN   109

6 GUESS AND CHECK   139

7 SUBPROBLEMS   171

8 UNIT ANALYSIS   193

9 SOLVE AN EASIER RELATED PROBLEM   223

10 PHYSICAL REPRESENTATIONS   **257**

       ACT IT OUT
       MAKE A MODEL
       USE MANIPULATIVES

11 WORK BACKWARDS   **293**

12 VENN DIAGRAMS   **315**

13 ALGEBRA   **349**

14 FINITE DIFFERENCES   **379**

15 OTHER WAYS TO ORGANIZE INFORMATION   **415**

16 OTHER WAYS TO CHANGE FOCUS   **433**

       CHANGE YOUR POINT OF VIEW
       SOLVE THE COMPLEMENTARY PROBLEM
       CHANGE THE REPRESENTATION

17 OTHER FORMS OF SPATIAL ORGANIZATION   **455**

       USE A GRAPH
       SCALE DRAWING

Foreword

S INCE 1980, when the yearbook of the National Council of Teachers of Mathematics sparked a general resurgence of interest in teaching problem solving, a great many attempts have been made to incorporate this elusive set of skills into the curriculum. Many early responses to this goal involved simply adding a chapter at the end of existing texts, calling it "Problem Solving," and adding a few non-routine problems throughout. The cynical view is that the authors added something to make their books pass for the new look; a more charitable view is that the authors simply did not understand how difficult a task it is to teach problem solving.

In contrast, the authors of this text treat problem solving very seriously indeed. They understand that teaching problem solving to a student is not just an add-on skill, like teaching the long-division algorithm, or even displaying a collection of techniques, but rather involves getting in and tinkering with the very way that the student structures reality. Seen in this light, it is clear that teaching problem solving is a difficult business which needs lots of time to do well.

In this useful book, Johnson and Herr have managed to present a broad set of strategies in an accessible way. Each strategy starts with an interesting problem followed by a dialogue which examines different ways of solving the problem with this one strategy. An appealing set of problems provided at the end of the chapter provides excellent practice for internalizing the strategy and gives a good sense as to its range of utility. It will be a rare student—or teacher—who does not gain much of use from the book.

There are three features of the book which I found particularly appealing. First is the variety and interest of the examples. There are problems which arise in real life—such as when should you leave for the airport—and problems which are useful in other courses—such as converting from one system of units to another—and some simply fun problems. Each set of problems illustrates the strategy under discussion and gives a good indication of its power.

Second, the authors provide examples which validate different approaches. One of my more vivid memories when I taught problem solving was the student who came up at the end of one class when four different solutions had been displayed by participants and confessed, "I never knew there was more than one way to solve a problem." Too many students can get all the way through high school without ever coming to realize that mathematics is not just a collection of methods to be memorized, but a structure which allows many paths to success. Johnson and Herr should help remedy this outdated and dangerous view that there can be only one way to solve a problem.

Finally, I enjoyed the dialogues which suggest various approaches to the problems in a non-threatening way. This technique offers a good intermediate ground between no direction whatsoever and the voice of authority with which most books of mathematics are invested. Real students do have different ideas and different approaches and the wise teacher will both cherish and exploit this diversity. The wiser teacher will cherish even wrong approaches and let the class find out why they are wrong.

As the twentieth century comes to an end, it is clear that we need more mathematically competent people, a description which requires more than people who can recite familiar formulas or solve standard problems. We need people who can intuitively reach for the strategies in this book and apply them in a broad range of situations. In short, we need people who know what to do when they don't know exactly what to do.

Tom Sallee
Professor of Mathematics
University of California, Davis

Acknowledgments

THE SUPPORT for this book has come in many forms, from computer equipment to inspiration to trusting us. The authors wish to publicly thank those who helped in some of those ways: Randall Charles, Lisa DaValle, Gary Haas, Kerry Harrigan, Holly Herr, Joe Herr, Jennifer Johnson, Lucille Johnson, Rick Johnson, Steve Legé, Ed Patriquin, Steve Rasmussen, Tom Sallee, The Northern California Math Project, and the students enrolled in the problem-solving courses at Luther Burbank High School (Sacramento) and Sierra College.

We owe thanks to our colleagues who were sources for some of these problem ideas. You'll recognize some familiar themes and classic problems (many with new twists) from the lore of the problem-solving community. It would be impossible to even guess at—much less acknowledge—a source for each of those problems. But we're grateful to be in a profession that values sharing ideas.

A special acknowledgment is reserved for Judy Kysh, director of the Northern California Math Project. Her insight and leadership are part and parcel of her ability to foresee years ago what many of us are struggling to understand today. She brought together the people and ideas that opened our eyes to a different way of teaching.

And finally thanks to our children, Daniel and Gary Johnson and Alyse, Jeremy, and Kevin Mason-Herr.

This book is dedicated to our wives, Janie Johnson and Allyson Mason-Herr.

Letter to the Student

THIS TEXT is written for a math class that will likely be different from any other math class you have encountered. It will require you to solve problems, write, and think. Though you may know some students who have gotten through a math class without really understanding the material, that won't happen in this one. You will understand what you are doing and you will have to explain your reasoning either in writing or to other students.

The basis of this class is the teaching and learning of strategies that people in the world of work utilize when solving problems. You will develop specific problem-solving strategies, communication skills, and attitudes. You will also learn to experience pleasure in doing math problems. Challenging problems, often referred to as puzzles or brain teasers, have long been a source of entertainment for many people. Learning problem-solving strategies will also help you on the SAT and other standardized tests. Those tests are often more a test in problem solving than in traditional mathematics.

You will be asked to solve some tough problems. Through persistence and talking with other students, you will be able to solve most of them. When you are confronted with an especially difficult problem, don't give up. Remember the things you are taught, such as drawing diagrams, asking other people, looking at notes, trying other approaches, and so on. You will learn these techniques in this course.

You will be expected to talk to your classmates! Your teacher will tell you to get help from one another. Not all of the learning that will

◀ *You'll meet greater challenges and have more fun problem solving when you work together with others.*

take place is "book learning." Part of what you will be expected to learn is how to work with one another. Even students considered "the smartest" by many of their peers have found that they learn better by working with other people. These communication skills will help you through a lifetime.

Though this letter implies that you will learn, you of course realize that learning doesn't just happen. What you get out of this class will depend on how much you are willing to invest. You have a chance here to take an active role in your education.

Our wish for you, going beyond the usual "good luck" message, is that you will apply yourself to the point of excelling. Enjoy the journey!

Answers to Questions that Students Usually Ask

THERE ARE probably many questions in your mind about what this course on problem solving is going to be about. First, let us tell you what it is not going to be. It is not going to be like any math course you have ever had, nor is this book going to be like any math book you have ever read. For one thing, we think the book is going to be readable, which is rare for a math book.

In some other classes, you may get to work together in groups. But your main source of information and instruction is probably the teacher. This class is going to be very different. There will not be a *main* source of information. Rather, you will learn from your teacher, your fellow students, and the book in roughly equal shares. Your teacher and the book will teach you the new strategies. You will present problems to the class as a whole on the board.

WHAT IS PROBLEM SOLVING?

Problem solving has been defined as what to do when you don't know what to do. In previous math classes, you have often had specific examples to follow on most exercises. An *exercise* essentially asks you to repeat back a method you have learned on a similar example. A *problem* is much more difficult, as you don't usually have a preconceived notion as to how to solve it.

In this class you will learn general, wide-ranging strategies for solving problems. These strategies, many of them popularized by G. Polya's classic book *How to Solve It*, are applicable to a large scope of problems. Many of the problems you do in this class will be unique. You won't have a recipe to follow. You won't have seen a similar example in class. To solve the problems, you will employ these broad heuristic strategies. Many times, your original approach to a problem will not work. When this happens, you must recognize its ineffectiveness and try something else. Persistence in solving problems will pay off. You will get frustrated by many of the problems presented, but you must persevere. Sometimes it helps to put a problem aside and let your subconscious work on it. You may find yourself solving problems in your sleep. Don't give up on a problem.

WHY SHOULD WE WORK TOGETHER WITH OTHER STUDENTS? CAN'T WE LEARN JUST AS WELL ON OUR OWN?

You will have lots of opportunities to work with other students in this class. You should also get together with other students outside of class. When you work with other students, you are free to make conjectures, ask questions, make mistakes, and express your ideas and opinions. You do not have to worry about being criticized for your thoughts or your wrong answers. You won't always proceed down the correct path. Support each other, question each other, make another person explain what you don't understand, and make sure the other members of your group understand, too. If others in your group make mistakes, don't berate them, just help them to see why they are wrong.

HOW SHOULD WE STUDY? HOW SHOULD WE READ THE BOOK?

The book is organized into chapters, with each chapter introducing a new problem-solving strategy. Each chapter presents several problems in the text. You are asked to solve each problem, then read the sample solution. To get maximum benefit from this book, you should work the problem before reading the solution. Even if you were successful at solving the problem, read the solution anyway, because it may bring up some points you had not thought of, or it may solve the problem in a different way than you did. If you don't have time to solve each of the text problems, just read the problem and the solution. Though this will not be as valuable as trying the problems yourself, you will get something out of reading the solutions. The worst case would be to not read the book at all. Be willing to read this text slowly and carefully. It does not read like a novel; rather you must read each sentence and understand it before you go on.

WHAT OTHER PROBLEMS WILL WE DO BESIDES THE ONES IN THE TEXT?

At the end of each chapter is Problem Set A. These problems can always be solved by the strategy that was presented in that chapter. Some of them may also be solvable by some previously learned strategy. However, you should probably try to solve them with the chapter's strategy, as you are trying to learn the new strategy. To get more benefit from the course, you should also attempt to solve many of the problems in several different ways.

Beginning in Chapter 3, there is a Problem Set B following Problem Set A. Set B problems can be solved using any strategy that has been previously learned, and it's left to you to pick an appropriate strategy. These problems are harder than the problems in Set A. In fact, toward the end of the book, many of these problems are very difficult. The problems in Set B are intended to be used as week-long assignments to be turned in. They act as tests, although they are not tests in the traditional sense. You may work with other students on these problems, although each person will turn in his or her own problem set. You need to explain how you solved the problem, as well as what your answer is. You will usually write between one-half of a page and two pages for each problem. That is why there are only five problems in each Problem Set B. We estimate that each Problem Set B will take between five and seven hours of work.

In other math classes, your grade in the course depends on how well you do on tests. Many people have test anxiety and do not perform as well as they could on exams. A common complaint is, "I study so hard, do all my homework, spend hours and hours on this class, but then I blow the test and get a lousy grade." That won't happen in this class. If you spend those hours and hours in this class, you should get a very good grade, as there are no in-class tests.

WHAT IS THE ROLE OF THE TEACHER IN THIS CLASS?

In most classes, the teacher is the final authority to tell you whether you are right or wrong. Your teacher in this class will play that role at times, such as in grading your weekly problem sets. However, there will be many times when the teacher will not play that role. During student presentations, there may be days when several people get different answers. A natural student reaction at this point would be to ask the teacher who is right. The teacher should let you make up your own minds. The groups can discuss which answer they think is correct and why. Explaining why is a very important part of this class. When you stop relying on the teacher to verify your work, you will become a more powerful problem solver. Learn to evaluate your own work and the work of others carefully.

SOME COMMENTS ON ANSWERS

When you turn in written work, your answers to each problem should be written out in a sentence. Don't expect the teacher to dig through your work to find your answer.

Think carefully about what your answer means, and make sure that the form of the answer makes sense and is reasonable, given the circumstances of the problem. If the answer to a question calls for a certain number of people, for example, and your answer is a fraction or a decimal, think carefully about what your answer should be to the question. Does it make sense to round up, round down, or leave it the way it was? Try the following problem, for example.

THE VANS

There are 25 people going on a trip and each van has a capacity of 7 people.

Some people might think the answer is 3 $\frac{4}{7}$ vans. Your answer depends on the full question. Here are some possible questions for the van problem:

a. How many vans will be needed to transport all 25 people?

b. How many vans can be filled to capacity?

c. How many vans will have to be filled to capacity?

d. What is the average number of people in a van?

e. Must any van have seven people in it?

f. How many more people could fit in the vans that will be required?

Anyway, the answer to each of these questions is different, even though the problem is the same. The difference is in the question asked. Furthermore, since the problem set up may appear to be 25 divided by 7, only one of the questions approximates the division problem. Having a unit that is generally considered indivisible (vans or people) as opposed to a divisible unit (pizzas) makes the answer to the arithmetic reasonable only if the reasonableness extends to the units. In other words, no matter what arithmetic is done to the numbers in this problem, the answer must still apply to human beings going somewhere in vans. Keep these issues in mind when working problems.

This book is meant to be enjoyed. Have fun!

Some Introductory Problems

DURING THIS course you will learn many problem-solving strategies and use them to solve lots of different problems. In this chapter, we present problems for you to solve with whatever strategy you wish. You will get an opportunity to present your solutions to some or all of these problems to a small group or to the whole class. We picked problems for this chapter that could be solved with a variety of different methods. You may wish to solve each problem several times, each time solving it in a different way. The solutions to these problems are not presented here.

1. SOCCER GAME

At the conclusion of a soccer game featuring 11 players on each team, each member of the winning team "gave five" to (slapped hands with) each member of the losing team. Each member of the winning team also gave five to each other member of the winning team. How many fives were given?

2. ELEVATOR

The capacity of an elevator is either 20 children or 15 adults. If 12 children are currently on the elevator, how many adults can still get on?

3. MATH CLUB

There are eight more girls than boys in the high school math club. The club has a total of 44 members. How many boys and how many girls are there?

4. DUCKS AND COWS

Farmer Brown had ducks and cows. One day she noticed that the animals had a total of 12 heads and 32 feet. How many of the animals were ducks and how many were cows?

5. STRANGE NUMBER

If you take a particular two-digit number, reverse its digits to make a second two-digit number, and add these two numbers together, the sum will be 121. What is the original number?

draw a diagram

YOU KNOW the old saying, "A picture is worth a thousand words." Many people would probably agree with that statement. However, most people do not realize just how powerful a picture can be. A diagram has certain advantages over verbal communication. A diagram can show positional relationships far more easily and clearly than a verbal description. Some people talk to themselves or to others in order to clarify ideas in their own minds. A diagram can serve the same purpose for ideas that lend themselves to visual representations. The intent of this chapter is to improve your diagramming abilities and show the ways in which a diagram can help you elucidate your ideas. You will likely discover that a diagram often helps you clarify a problem and interpret it correctly.

At times a diagram acts as the main communication medium; at other times it plays a supporting role by enhancing another medium. One of the best examples of a diagram in the professional world is a blueprint. An architect expresses ideas concisely in a form that leaves little to interpretation. Where needed, words are added in order to spell out details that are not evident on the blueprint. A blueprint illustrates one of the strengths of a diagram: the ability to present the "whole picture" immediately.

Much problem solving revolves around information and how it is organized. When you draw a diagram, you organize the information in a spatial manner, which then allows the visual part of your brain to become more involved in the problem-solving process.

In this first chapter, you will see the value of diagrams in solving a variety of problems.

◀ *Diagrams help computer engineers visualize the relationships among different parts of their computer systems.*

Solve this problem by drawing a diagram.

A new basketball league was formed in which each of the teams will play three games against each of the other teams. There are seven teams: the Antelopes, the Bears, the Cubs, the Dusters, the Eagles, the Foxes, and the Goats. How many games will be played in all?
Do this problem carefully before continuing on.

Many different diagrams could be used to solve this problem. In fact, this problem could also be solved by methods that do not involve diagrams. Throughout this book you will return to the same problem in different chapters and solve it by different strategies. The solutions in this chapter involve diagrams. If you solved this problem without a diagram, try solving it again with a diagram. You will become a better problem solver in two ways: by solving lots of different problems, and by solving the same problem in lots of different ways.

As you work through the book, many different problems will be presented. In order to get maximum benefit from this book, you need

to solve each of these problems before reading on. You gain a lot by solving problems, even if your answers are incorrect. The process that you use to solve each problem is what you should concentrate on.

Reading on, you will see a solution process which is attributed to a student. The people mentioned in the text are real students who took a problem-solving class at Luther Burbank High School in Sacramento, California. In that class, the students presented their solutions on the board. The teacher (one or the other of the authors of this book) allowed many different students to present solutions, as we felt that the other students would greatly benefit from seeing many different approaches to the same problem. The teacher did not judge each student's solution in any way. Rather, each member of the class was asked to examine each solution that was presented, and decide which approach or approaches were valid or perhaps better.

In this book, we have tried to recreate the same atmosphere. The book sometimes presents several different approaches to each problem but will not, for the most part, judge the solutions. We encourage you to make up your own mind about the quality of the approach. You may have been led to believe that there is always one right way and many wrong ways to do problems. This statement couldn't be further from the truth. There are many right ways, and you are encouraged to try to solve the problems in this book in more than one way.

Rita solved the Modern Basketball Association problem as follows.

Each team is represented by a letter; *A* through *G* to stand for Antelopes, Bears, etc. She drew a diagram with each team represented by a labeled dot.

Next she drew a line from *A* to *B* to represent the games played between the Antelopes and the Bears. Then she drew a line from *A* to *C* to represent the games played between the Antelopes and the Cubs.

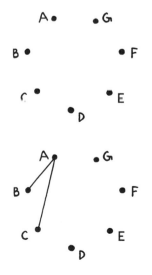

Then she continued drawing the
lines for the Antelopes. When she
had connected *A* to *G*, she was done
with the Antelopes games.

Next she began drawing the lines
for the Bears. The games the Bears
play against the Antelopes are already
represented by the line between *A*
and *B*, so the first line drawn for the
Bears is from *B* to *C*.

She continued drawing lines to
represent the games that *B* plays
against the rest of the league. (Except
of course, for the games against the
Antelopes, which were represented
with the first line drawn.)

Then she continued drawing lines to represent the whole league.
Each time, the first line drawn is from the host letter to the next letter.
For example, from the Antelopes she drew lines from *A* to *B*, *A* to *C*, *A*
to *D*, and so on. From the Bears she drew lines from *B* to *C*, *B* to *D*, *B*
to *E*, and so on.

From *C* she drew lines to *D*, to *E*, to
F, and so on through the league.
When she finally got to the Goats,
there were no more lines to be drawn
because the games with each previous
team in the league against the Goats
had already been represented with
a line.

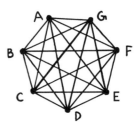

She then counted the lines. There were 21. She multiplied by 3
because each line represented three games, and the answer was 63
games.

Finally, Rita went back to make sure she answered the question that was posed. The question was "How many games were played?" "Sixty-three games were played" answers that question.

Melody solved this problem as shown below. She also used *A, B, C, D, E, F,* and *G* to represent the Antelopes, Bears, etc. She put the letters in a row and drew lines from each team to the next team. She also started by drawing all of the lines from *A*, and then all of the lines from *B*, etc. She also drew 21 lines and counted 63 games.

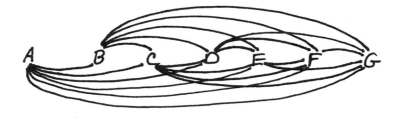

THE MODEL TRAIN

Jenny's model train is set up on a circular track. There are six telephone poles evenly spaced around the track. It takes the engine of her train 10 seconds to go from the first pole to the third pole. How long would it take for the engine to go the entire distance around the track?
Solve the problem carefully before reading on.

The quick and easy answer is 20 seconds. Obviously, if the engine can go from the first pole to the third pole in 10 seconds, that is three poles, which apparently is halfway around the track. So it takes the engine 2 times 10, or 20 seconds to go all the way around the track. Unfortunately, this answer is wrong. The correct answer becomes apparent when we look at a diagram. Dustin's diagram is shown at right.

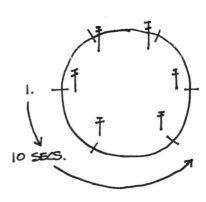

Dustin explained that the train went one-third of the way around the track in 10 seconds, not halfway around the track. So the train went around the entire track in 3 times 10 seconds, or 30 seconds.

Phong had another way of looking at the diagram. He drew the same diagram, but he interpreted it differently. "If it takes 10 seconds to go from the first pole to the third pole, then it takes 5 seconds to go from the first pole to the second pole. So it take 5 seconds to go from pole to pole, and as there are six poles, it would take 30 seconds to go all the way around the track."

Pete thought of the problem the same way as Phong, but didn't draw a diagram. Unfortunately, he got the answer 25 seconds, because the lack of a diagram caused him to neglect the fact that the train must return from the sixth pole to the first pole.

~~~~~

The diagram helped. By using the diagram, you should have been able to get the correct solution. If you were able to get the correct solution without drawing a diagram, think back: you probably had a mental picture of the train track. So even if you didn't actually draw a diagram, you probably had a picture of the scene in your mind.

Do you get the picture? Research has shown that most good problem solvers draw diagrams for almost every problem that they do. Do not be stubborn! Do not resist drawing a diagram under some pretense; just draw it!

ALIEN INVADERS

Sam, Mamie, Ralph, and Gail are all skilled at the video game Alien Invaders. Gail scores consistenly higher than Ralph. Sam is better than all of them, and Mamie is better than Ralph. Who is the better player, Gail or Mamie?

Use the clues to solve the problem before reading on.

Jamie drew the following diagram. The height of each person represents his or her relative skill. The tall figures are more skilled than the short figures. (Jamie is very tall and thus thinks that tall people are good at video games.) As you can see from her diagram, Sam is the best, followed by Mamie, Gail, and Ralph. So Mamie is better than Gail.

Kurt drew the following diagram. In his diagram, the size of the head represents video game prowess, with larger heads being better. (Kurt has a very large head, so he thinks that large-headed people are good at video games.) As you can see from his diagram, Sam is the best, followed by Gail, Mamie, and Ralph. So the answer to the question is that Gail is better than Mamie.

Rena drew the diagram shown to the right. Her diagram was drawn showing each relationship that was given in the problem with an arrow pointing from one person to another. The arrow indicates that the person from where the arrow begins is better at Alien Invaders than the person at which the arrow is pointing. If no arrow is drawn, then no relationship is given.

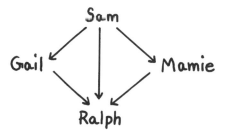

Rena's diagram makes it clear that the question can't be answered because there is no way of establishing a comparison between Mamie and Gail.

Curly dug his own swimming pool by hand with a shovel. He figured he needed a pool because digging it was hard work, and he could use it to cool off after working on it all day. He also planned a rectangular concrete deck around the pool that would be 6 feet wide at all points. The pool is rectangular and measures 14 feet by 40 feet. What is the area of the deck?

As usual, solve this problem before continuing.

Drawing a diagram helps to show the correct dimensions of the deck and pool, which together are twelve feet longer and twelve feet wider than the pool alone.

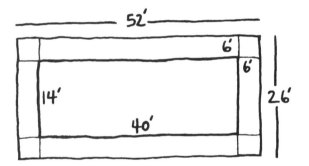

Rajesh drew the following diagram.

The diagram helps show the difficult parts of the problem. Some people solve the problem incorrectly by finding the perimeter of the pool and deck together and multiplying by the width of the deck.

26 feet + 52 feet + 26 feet + 52 feet = 156 feet
156 feet × 6 feet = 936 square feet

That approach over counts the corners.

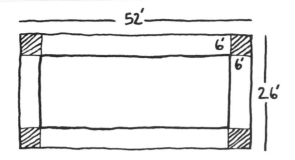

Some students solved this problem by computing the area of the deck along the sides and adding in the corners. Rajesh took this approach.

Length 40 ft.	Deck Width x 6 ft.	Two Lengths x 2	= 480 sq. ft.
Width 14 ft.	Deck Width x 6 ft.	Two Sides x 2	= 168 sq. ft.
Corners 6 ft. x 6 ft.		x 4	= 144 sq. ft.
		Total	792 sq. ft.

Other students took the corners out and attached them to either the pool-deck length or width.

May's diagram showing the corners attached to the length is shown below.

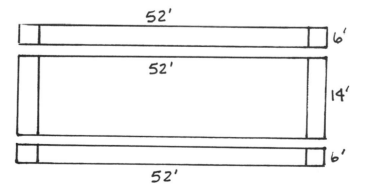

She calculated the area as follows.

52 ft × 6 ft = 312 sq ft
312 sq ft × 2 = 624 sq ft for extended lengths
14 ft × 6 ft = 84 sq ft
84 sq ft × 2 = 168 sq ft for widths
total = 624 sq ft + 168 sq ft = 792 sq ft

Still others solved this by computing the area of the walk and pool rectangle, then subtracting the area of the pool, leaving the area of the deck. Hung took this approach.

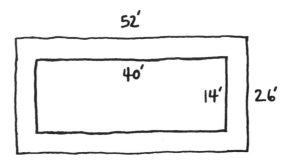

Area of entire figure = 52 ft × 26 ft = 1352 sq ft
Area of pool alone = 40 ft × 14 ft = 560 sq ft
Area of deck = 1352 ft – 560 ft = 792 sq ft

Farmer Ben has only ducks and cows. He can't remember how many of each he has, but he really doesn't need to remember. He does know that he has 22 animals, which is his age. He also remembers that those animals have a total of 56 legs, which is his father's age. Assuming that each animal is normal, how many of each does Farmer Ben have?

Stop, do the problem, and then read on.

Bill drew the following diagrams:

O O O O O O O O O O O
O O O O O O O O O O O

"These 22 circles represent the 22 animals. First, I made all of the animals into ducks." (Bill is not much of an artist, so you just have to believe that these are ducks.) "I gave each animal two legs because ducks have two legs."

"Then I converted the ducks into cows by drawing extra legs. The ducks alone had 44 of the 56 legs initially, so I drew 12 more legs (six pairs) on six ducks to turn them into cows. So there are 6 cows and 16 ducks."

Of course, Ben might have a problem when his father turns 57 next year.

Problem Set A

Solve each problem by drawing a diagram. You must draw a diagram.

1. WORM JOURNEY

A worm is at the bottom of a 12-foot wall. Every day it crawls up 3 feet, but at night it slips down 2 feet. How many days does it take the worm to get to the top of the wall?

2. THE UPS AND DOWNS OF SHOPPING

Roberto is shopping in a large department store with many floors. He enters the store on the middle floor from a skyway, and immediately goes to the credit department. After making sure his credit is good, he goes up three floors to the housewares department. Then he goes down five floors to the children's department. Then he goes up six floors to the TV department. Finally, he goes down ten floors to the main entrance of the store, which is on the first floor, and leaves to go to another store down the street. How many floors does the department store have?

3. FOLLOW THE BOUNCING BALL

A ball rebounds one-half the height from which it is dropped. The ball is dropped from a height of 160 feet and keeps on bouncing. What is the total vertical distance the ball will travel from the moment it is dropped to the moment it hits the floor for the fifth time?

4. FLOOR TILES

How many 9-inch-square floor tiles are needed to cover a rectangular floor that measures 12 feet by 15 feet?

5. COUNTING ON NINJA TURTLES

Joanne sets up her Ninja Turtles in a big circle with each turtle spaced an equal distance from its neighbors. She then proceeds to count them in order around the circle. Unfortunately, she loses track of where she started before she finishes counting. But she realizes that she can still figure out how many turtles are in the circle by noticing that the sixth turtle is directly opposite the seventeenth turtle. How many Ninja Turtles are in the circle?

6. DANGEROUS MANEUVERS

Somewhere in the Mojave desert, the army set up training camps named Arachnid, Feline, Canine, Lupine, Bovine, and Thirty-nine. Arachnid is 15 miles from Canine. Bovine is 12 miles from Lupine. Feline is 6 miles from Thirty-nine. Lupine is 3 miles from Canine. Bovine is 9 miles from Thirty-nine. Bovine is 7 miles from Canine. Thirty-nine is 1 mile from Arachnid. Feline is 11 miles from Lupine. No other pairs are connected by roads.

Answer each question. What is the shortest route from …

Feline to Bovine?

Lupine to Thirty-nine?

Canine to Feline?

Arachnid to Lupine?

Canine to Thirty-nine?

Lupine to Bovine?

Arachnid to Feline?

7. RACE

Betty, Cathy, Isabel, Lani, Alma, and Ursula ran an 800-meter race. Alma beat Isabel by 7 meters. Betty finished 12 meters behind Ursula. Alma finished 5 meters ahead of Lani but 3 meters behind Ursula. Cathy finished halfway between the first and last person. In what order did they finish? Indicate the order and the distances between each girl.

8. A WHOLE LOTTA SHAKIN' GOIN' ON!

If six people met at a party and all shook hands with one another, how many handshakes would be exchanged?

9. HAYWIRE

Recently a telephone system in a major manufacturing company went haywire. For several days, the system would only complete certain calls over certain sets of wires. Therefore, in order to get a message to someone else, an employee of this company would have to call another employee to start the message on a route to the person it was for. As best as can be determined, these are the connections: Cherlondia can call Al and Shirley. (This means that she can call them, but neither Al nor Shirley can call Cherlondia.) Al can call Max. Wolfgang can call Darlene and Darlene can also call Wolfgang back. Sylvia can call Dalamatia and Henry. Max can get calls only from Al. Carla can call Sylvia and Cherlondia. Shirley can call Darlene. Max can call Henry. Darlene can call Sylvia. Henry can call Carla. Cherlondia can call Dalamatia.

How would you route a message from …

Cherlondia to Darlene?

Carla to Max?

Sylvia to Wolfgang?

Henry to Wolfgang?

Shirley to Henry?

Max to Dalamatia?

Cherlondia to Sylvia?

Dalamatia to Henry?

How have you used diagrams in other classes?

Time	Destination	Route	Airline	Flight	Status
9:40	PARIS	SIBERIAN ROUTE	AIR FRANCE	AF 270	ON TIME
12:00	SEOUL		KOREAN AIR	KE 704	
13:00	LOS ANGELES	TRANSPACIFIC	NORTHWEST	NW 25	
13:00	NEW YORK		UNITED	UA 803	
13:05	CHEJU		KOREAN AIR	KE 714	
13:30	RIO DE JANEIRO		VARIG	RG 830	
13:55	NEW YORK	TRANSPACIFIC	NORTHWEST	NW 17	
13:55	HONOLULU	TRANSPACIFIC	NORTHWEST	NW 9	
13:55	SEOUL		NORTHWEST	NW 10	
13:55	ZURICH	POLAR ROUTE	swissair	SR 186	
14:00	LOS ANGELES		UNITED	UA 807	
14:30	WASHINGTON D.C.	TRANSPACIFIC	NORTHWEST	NW 3	
14:30	MINNEAPOLIS	TRANSPACIFIC	NORTHWEST	NW 27	
14:35	TAIPEI		NORTHWEST	NW 2	
14:40	FRANKFURT	POLAR ROUTE	Lufthansa	LH 650	
14:40	NEW YORK		UNITED	UA 801	
14:50	MANILA		NORTHWEST	NW 4	
14:55	ROME		Alitalia	AZ 786	

2

systematic lists

Leslie has 25 cents in her pocket, but does not have a quarter. If you can tell her all possible combinations of coins she could have that sum to 25 cents, she will give you the 25 cents.

As always, solve this problem before continuing.

MANY PEOPLE will start this problem in the following manner: "Let's see, we could have five nickels, or two dimes and one nickel. We might have 25 pennies. Oh yeah, we could have ten pennies, one dime, and one nickel. Perhaps we could have … "

As you can see, this is an extremely inefficient way of doing this problem. It could take forever to figure out all the ways to make 25 cents, and you would probably never be sure that you had all the ways.

A better way to solve this problem is to make a systematic list. A systematic list is exactly what the name implies: a list generated through some kind of system. The system should be clear enough so that the person making the list can quickly verify its accuracy. It should also be possible for another person to understand the system and verify it without too much effort.

Many systematic lists feature labeled columns with the information given in the problem. In this case, label the columns dimes, nickels,

◀ *Airline schedules are systematic lists that help travelers find information easily and quickly.*

and pennies. Then fill in the columns with combinations of coins that add up to 25 cents.

Brooke started the list with two dimes, the maximum number of dimes Leslie could have. She then continued by choosing the maximum number of nickels possible. In each row, she dropped the number of nickels by one. She filled in the pennies column by figuring out how many pennies she needed to add to her dimes and nickels to make 25 cents.

Dimes	Nickels	Pennies
2	1	0
2	0	5
1	3	0
1	2	5
1	1	10
1	0	15

and so on

After exhausting the ways to use two dimes, Brooke continued with one dime and again started with the maximum possible number of nickels, which was three. She then let the nickels column decrease by one each time, leaving the dimes at one.

The completed list appears to the right and includes the zero-dimes possibilities. Finish your list before reading on.

Dimes	Nickels	Pennies
2	1	0
2	0	5
1	3	0
1	2	5
1	1	10
1	0	15
0	5	0
0	4	5
0	3	10
0	2	15
0	1	20
0	0	25

Brooke's is not the only systematic list that will solve this problem. Heather used the system which follows. Figure out her system by looking at the first few lines. Then do the rest by yourself before looking at the rest of her solution.

Heather explained her system like this. "I started with the most number of pennies, which was 25. Then I let the pennies go down by fives, and filled in the nickels and dimes to make up the difference."

Pennies	Nickels	Dimes
25	0	0
20	1	0
15	2	0
15	0	1
10	3	0
10	1	1
5	4	0
5	2	1
5	0	2
0	5	0
0	3	1
0	1	2

Making a systematic list falls into the broad category of organizing information. The first chapter concerned drawing diagrams, which is a way of organizing information in a spatial manner. Making a systematic list is a way of organizing information in a chart. Many of the strategies you will explore later in this book involve organizing information in some sort of a chart. You will also learn more strategies that require you to organize information in a spatial manner.

One of the important things to keep in mind is that there may be more than one correct approach to solving a problem. You can see this is often true with systematic lists. There are many different systems that can produce a solution to a given problem. You may have used a list that was different from the two presented here. Any list is fine as long as you have a system that you understand and can use effectively. If you ever find that your original system is too confusing, simply change to another system.

Just as there may be more than one way to solve a problem using the same strategy, very often you will find that there is more than one strategy that can work to solve a given problem. Last chapter you solved the Modern Basketball Association problem with a diagram.

Solve the Modern Basketball Association problem again without referring back to the diagram solution. This time, use a systematic list.

A new basketball league was formed in which each team will play three games against each other team. There are seven teams: the Antelopes, the Bears, the Cubs, the Dusters, the Eagles, the Foxes, and the Goats. How many games will be played in all?

Do this problem carefully before continuing. This time solve it by using a systematic list.

John happens to be a basketball player and is always interested in the matchups. In the Modern Basketball Association problem, there were seven teams, which John quickly assembled in pairs of teams for games.

ANTELOPES vs. CUBS	CUBS vs. DUSTERS
BEARS vs. GOATS	GOATS vs. ANTELOPES
FOXES vs. ANTELOPES	CUBS vs. GOATS
DUSTERS vs. EAGLES	BEARS vs. ANTELOPES
CUBS vs. GOATS	FOXES vs. EAGLES
EAGLES vs. BEARS	DUSTERS vs. GOATS
CUBS vs. GOATS	CUBS vs. ANTELOPES
EAGLES vs. DUSTERS	DUSTERS vs. BEARS
BEARS vs. EAGLES	GOATS vs. EAGLES

Is John's list systematic? Are all possible match-ups represented? Are there omissions or possible duplications?

Instead of trying to verify the accuracy of John's non-systematic list, look at Monica's systematic list on the left.

AB
AC
AD
AE
AF
AG

She started with the Antelopes. Monica abbreviated Antelopes and all of the other teams with the first letter of their names. AB represents a match-up between the Antelopes and the Bears.

Next, Monica listed the opponents for the Bears (but she did not include the Antelopes, as she had already covered the matchup between the Antelopes and the Bears).

BC
BD
BE
BF
BG

She continued by listing the opponents in order for each remaining team.

```
CD    DE    EF    FG
CE    DF    EG
CF    DG
CG
```

The whole list is shown below.

```
AB    BC    CD    DE    EF    FG
AC    BD    CE    DF    EG
AD    BE    CF    DG
AE    BF    CG
AF    BG
AG
```

The system Monica used is easy to understand and the solution is easy to verify. There are patterns to developing the list and patterns that should be evident to someone checking the list. To answer the question: each pair of teams played 3 games against one another, so multiply 3 times the 21 different pairs, and the answer is still 63 games.

If you compare this solution to the diagram solution to this problem, you will see that the lines representing games were drawn in a systematic fashion so as not to confuse either the solver or the reader. Diagrams are often very systematic. A system does not have to incorporate a list, but can be anything that involves doing something in an organized way.

PENNY'S DIMES

Penny has 25 dimes. She likes to put them in three piles with an odd number of dimes in each pile. In how many ways could she do this? Work this problem before continuing on.

Randy solved this problem by making a systematic list. He made three columns entitled pile 1, pile 2, and pile 3. He started with 1 dime in the first pile, and 1 dime in the second pile. This left 23 dimes for the third pile. Then he again put 1 in the first pile, and increased the second pile by 2 while decreasing the third pile by 2. He continued in this way as shown at right.

Pile 1	Pile 2	Pile 3
1	1	23
1	3	21
1	5	19
1	7	17
1	9	15
1	11	13
1	13	11

At this point, Randy needed to decide whether or not 1, 13, 11 is a repeat of 1, 11, 13. The basis for his decision might have been that 13 in one pile and 11 in the other is the same as 11 in one and 13 in the other. (The piles are indistinguishable.) Randy apparently felt that the piles are indistinguishable, and therefore these two possibilities are the same. This will, of course, save him a lot of work and make the list a lot shorter. So he eliminated 1, 13, 11. The next possibility would be 1, 15, 9, but this is a repeat of 1, 9, 15. So he concluded that he exhausted the possibilities for 1 in the first pile.

Randy started over again with 3 in the first pile.

Randy crossed out 1, 13, 11 as shown to the right. He also crossed out 3, 1, 21. Why? Look at the second entry in the list. It was 1, 3, 21, which is the same as 3, 1, 21. Therefore he must start with 3 in the second pile as well as in the first pile. This sets up a pattern, where the second pile will always start with the same number of dimes as the first pile.

Pile 1	Pile 2	Pile 3
1	1	23
1	3	21
1	5	19
1	7	17
1	9	15
1	11	13
~~1~~	~~13~~	~~11~~
~~3~~	~~1~~	~~21~~
3	3	19

To the right is Randy's complete list. Note that the first pile changed to the next higher number at the points where the second pile equaled the third pile or the second pile was two less than the third pile. This was done to avoid repeating a combination. Also note that the list is complete, because the next possibility after 7, 9, 9 would be 9, 9, 7, which is a repeat. There are 16 ways to form the piles of dimes.

Pile 1	Pile 2	Pile 3
1	1	23
1	3	21
1	5	19
1	7	17
1	9	15
1	11	13
3	3	19
3	5	17
3	7	15
3	9	13
3	11	11
5	5	15
5	7	13
5	9	11
7	7	11
7	9	9

You can solve this problem differently, and we encourage you to experiment with other systems. One possible system would begin with 23 dimes in the first pile. You can also make the assumption that the three piles are distinguishable, which leads to a much longer list and has 78 possibilities.

On a famous episode of Star Trek, Captain Kirk and the gang played a card game called Phisbin. This problem concerns a game called Frisbin. The object of the game is to throw three Frisbees at three bins that are set up on the ground about twenty feet away. If the Frisbee lands in the largest bin, 1 point is scored. If the Frisbee lands in the medium sized bin, 5 points are scored. If the Frisbee lands in the smallest bin, 10 points are scored. Kirk McCoy is playing the game. If all three of his Frisbees land in bins, how many different total scores can he make?

Make a systematic list for this problem before reading on.

You can make essentially two different types of systematic lists for this problem. We show an example of each below.

Derrick set up columns headed 10 points, 5 points, 1 point, and total. He chose the maximum number of 10-point throws, 3, and then 2, 1, and 0. He adjusted the 5-point and 1-point throws accordingly so that there were always three throws.

10 PTS.	5 PTS.	1 PT.	TOTAL
3	0	0	30
2	1	0	25
2	0	1	21
1	2	0	20
1	1	1	16
1	0	2	12
0	3	0	15
0	2	1	11
0	1	2	7
0	0	3	3

Kirk McCoy can make 10 total scores.

Notice the system. The 10-point column starts on the highest possible number and then decreases by one. It stays on one number as long as it can. The 5-point column goes through a similar process: it starts on the highest possible number and decreases by one each time. The 1-point column makes up the difference.

Derrick was undoubtedly able to make this list very quickly. Also note that a person seeing the list for the first time can immediately follow the system.

Julian used a different method, shown below. He titled the columns with the number of the throw. Then he wrote down the points for each throw. What system did Julian use?

Throw 1	Throw 2	Throw 3	Total
10	10	10	30
10	10	5	25
10	10	1	21
10	5	5	20
10	5	1	16
10	1	1	12
5	5	5	15
5	5	1	11
5	1	1	7
1	1	1	3

Julian let the first throw be a 10 as long as he could and adjusted the other two throws. The list came out in exactly the same order as Derrick's list, but the approach was different. This way was easier to add up to get the total scores. Note that he did not have to rearrange the throws in a different order because it would not have changed the total score possibilities. In other words, 10, 10, 5 is the same as 10, 5, 10 or 5, 10, 10.

What system did Emily use in this list?

Throw 1	Throw 2	Throw 3	Total
10	10	10	30
5	5	5	15
1	1	1	3
10	10	5	25
10	10	1	21
5	5	10	20
5	5	1	11
1	1	10	12
1	1	5	7
1	5	10	16

Emily grouped together the situations where all three throws landed in the same bin. Then she grouped the situations where two throws landed in the same bin. Then she wrote the possibility where all three landed in different bins.

AREA AND PERIMETER

A rectangle has an area of 120 square centimeters. Its length and width are whole numbers. What are the possibilities for the length and width? Which possibility gives the smallest perimeter?

Work this problem before continuing.

Tuan explained his reasoning on this problem as follows. "I read that the area of the rectangle was 120 square centimeters. The first thing I did was to draw a picture of a rectangle."

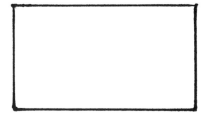

"I had no idea whether this rectangle was long and skinny, or shaped like a square. But I did know that the area was supposed to be 120 square centimeters. So I made a list of whole numbers that could be the sides that multiplied to 120."

WIDTH	LENGTH	AREA
1 cm	120 cm	120 cm^2
2 cm	60 cm	120 cm^2
3 cm	40 cm	120 cm^2
4 cm	30 cm	120 cm^2
5 cm	24 cm	120 cm^2
6 cm	20 cm	120 cm^2
8 cm	15 cm	120 cm^2
10 cm	12 cm	120 cm^2

"I knew I was done at this point, because the next possible factor of 120 is 12, and I already used 12 for the length. A 12 cm by 10 cm rectangle is the same as a 10 cm by 12 cm rectangle turned on its side. I saw no need to list it twice. I also realized that neither 7 nor 9 would work for the width, because they don't divide evenly into 120.

"Now I had to answer the other question, which was which possibility gives the smallest perimeter. I knew that the perimeter of a rectangle is the distance around the rectangle, so I needed to add up the length and width. But this would only give me half of the perimeter, so I would have to double the sum of the length and width. I added the perimeter column into the chart."

WIDTH	LENGTH	AREA	PERIMETER
1 cm	120 cm	120 cm^2	242 cm
2 cm	60 cm	120 cm^2	124 cm
3 cm	40 cm	120 cm^2	86 cm
4 cm	30 cm	120 cm^2	68 cm
5 cm	24 cm	120 cm^2	58 cm
6 cm	20 cm	120 cm^2	52 cm
8 cm	15 cm	120 cm^2	46 cm
10 cm	12 cm	120 cm^2	44 cm

"Now from my chart I can see that the 10 cm by 12 cm rectangle gives an area of 120 cm² with the smallest perimeter of 44 cm."

For an English assignment, you are to choose three of the following books to read: To Kill a Mockingbird, All Quiet on the Western Front, The Stranger, Huckleberry Finn, *and* A Midsummer Night's Dream. *How many different sets of three books can you choose?*

Do this problem before continuing on.

Li solved this problem by making a systematic list. "I decided to abbreviate the names of the books so that I wouldn't have to write out the whole name each time. I used TKM, AQWF, TS, HF, MND. Then I just made a list. I made my list by letting TKM stay in front as long as it could, and rearranged the other four books into the remaining two spots. Once I had all of the combinations that include TKM, I dropped it from the list. Then I used AQWF in the first spot. Finally I used TS in the first spot, but by that time there was only one more way to do it. There are ten ways altogether."

TKM	AQWF	TS
TKM	AQWF	HF
TKM	AQWF	MND
TKM	TS	HF
TKM	TS	MND
TKM	HF	MND
AQWF	TS	HF
AQWF	TS	MND
AQWF	HF	MND
TS	HF	MND

Jim solved the problem with a different systematic list. "I just made columns for the different books, and then I checked off three in each row. There are ten ways."

	TKM	AQWF	TS	HF	MND
1	X	X	X		
2	X	X		X	
3	X	X			X
4	X		X	X	
5	X		X		X
6	X			X	X
7		X	X	X	
8		X	X		X
9		X		X	X
10			X	X	X

Making a tree diagram is another way of making a systematic list. A tree diagram is a systematic list in the form of a diagram that looks like the branches of a tree.

David solved the previous problem and was then interested in knowing how many ways he could read a particular group of three books. He solved the problem with a tree diagram.

"I learned how to do tree diagrams in eighth grade and I really like them. It's sort of a combination diagram and systematic list. The first branch of the tree is which book I read first. Then the next branch of the tree is which book I read next. In the second branch I didn't repeat the book that was read in the first branch. Finally, the third branch is the book that has yet to be read."

This is David's diagram of the different orders he could read the three books TKM, AQWF, and TS.

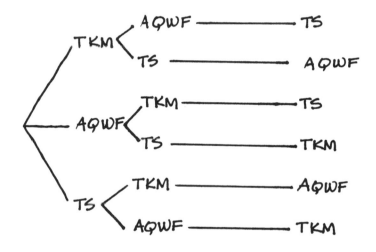

"I realized that there would be six ways for each entry in the original list. So I multiplied six and ten to get 60 ways if the order in which I read the books made a difference."

You can solve some systematic-list problems with tree diagrams. Sometimes, however, the tree diagram is too confusing or too cumbersome. You will need to decide when a tree diagram may be appropriate or possibly easier than a standard systematic list.

~~~~

As you work through this book, one major challenge you will face will be choosing an appropriate strategy. Often you will find that the best strategy is the first strategy you chose, but there will be times when you will have to experiment with different strategies to see which one is most effective. There will also be times when you will need to use two or more strategies in conjunction to solve a difficult problem. The most important thing to know about problem solving is that most problems can be solved. Persistence in trying different strategies will pay off. As you solve more and more difficult problems, your confidence in your abilities will increase.

PROFESSIONAL PROBLEM-SOLVING PROFILES

Joe uses systematic lists to solve problems in his job. He programs computers for the Bank of America. Computer failures occur in any system. They can occur because of problems in the hardware, the software, the power supply, or user actions. Part of Joe's job as a programmer is dealing with the system failures of one particular system and network of terminals. At the time of a failure, one of the things he does is to get a computer memory dump—a printout of whatever is in the computer's memory at the time. He then checks to see what program was being used, the time of failure, and then a number of registers (certain items of memory set up by the program). He must check each of these things in a systematic way so that he is sure that he has covered all possibilities. He also looks for a pattern, as he will compare a number of system failures with each other to see if there are certain types of data that reoccur. In order to do this, he also prepares histograms to show the frequency of certain data at the time of a system error. In this way, in one particular instance, he was able to detect that the hardware was not handling negative numbers correctly. Having found a pattern of a high number of system failures with negative numbers in certain memory cells, Joe could see that a problem existed with the negative numbers. (Remember that there could be many causes for one type of system failure, and that there was a good chance that various problems caused the system failures.) Joe then ran tests of the system using negative numbers in order to force system failures. His tests worked; the system failed, and he rewrote software in order to detect and handle potential system failures.

Another example of systematic lists was provided by Jennifer, an accountant. Jennifer uses systematic lists in a few ways. She receives lists of deposits and checks that are all written in random order. Jennifer must separate checks and deposits, and then organize checks by check number and deposits by date.

Another way in which she uses systematic lists is when she is working on a client's tax return. The client has a whole list of investments. She must separate investments by category: stocks, mutual funds, and savings accounts. Then for each category she must subcategorize: interest, dividends, and capital gains or losses of stock sales. Some of these categories may have further subcategories as well. For instance, capital gains and regular dividends are subcategories of dividends.

Problem Set A

Solve each problem by making a systematic list.

1. CARDS AND COMICS

Charmaign has $6.00 she wants to spend on comic books and superhero cards. Comic books cost 60 cents each and deluxe packages of superhero cards cost $1.20 each. List all of the ways Charmaign can spend all of her money on comic books and/or superhero cards.

2. FREE CONCERT TICKETS

Alexis, Bart, Chuck, and Dariah all called in to a radio show to get free tickets to a concert. List all the possible orders in which their calls could have been received.

3. IT SURE IS TOUGH TO GET AN APARTMENT THESE DAYS

In leasing an apartment for one year, the management company offered two payment plans. One was designed to have a low entry cost; the other was designed to have more gradual price increases.

PLAN A
12-month lease
$400 first month
$30 per month increase
  each month

PLAN B
12-month lease
$500 first month
$15 per month increase
  each month

Which plan costs more for just the ninth month of tenancy?
Which plan costs more for the entire 12 months?

4. STORAGE SHEDS

Andre's company makes rectangular storage sheds. They make them from aluminum side panels with measurements of 8 feet, 10 feet, 12 feet, and 15 feet. One possible shed measures 10 feet by 10 feet. Another possible shed measures 12 feet by 15 feet. List all the possible sheds.

5. MAKING CHANGE

Ms. Rathman has nickels, dimes, and quarters. In how many ways can she make change for 50 cents?

6. FINISHED PRODUCT

The product of two whole numbers is 360 and their sum is less than 100. What are the possibilities for the two numbers?

7. KYLE CRAVES CANDY

The corner convenience store sells candy in 5-cent, 10-cent and 15-cent packages. List all of the ways Kyle can spend 40 cents or less on candy.

8. CAREERS

At the end of this chapter, two professionals, Joe and Jennifer, were profiled. They both use systematic lists in their jobs. Find and interview a relative or friend who uses systematic lists or diagrams in their career.

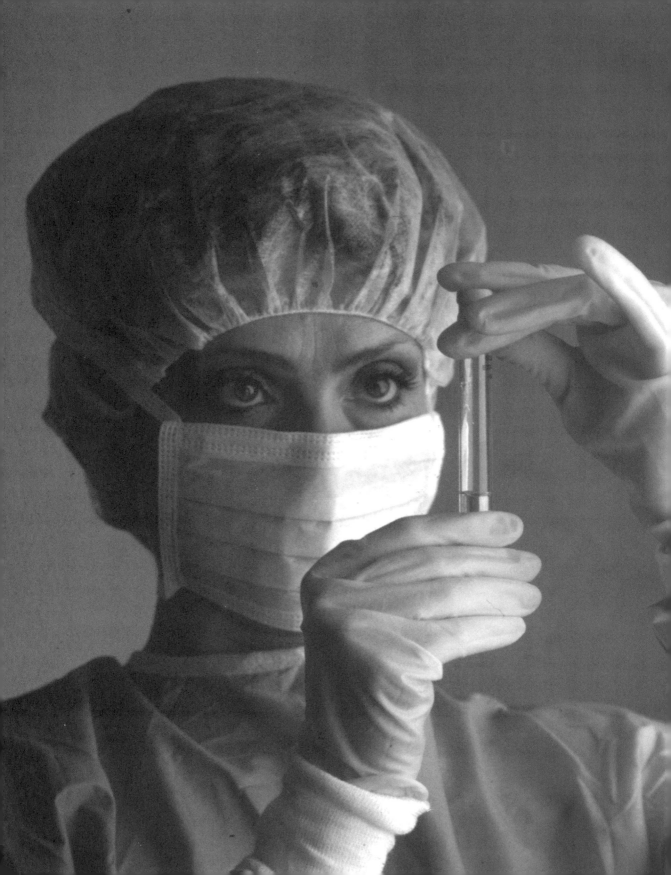

3

eliminate possibilities

Al: Well, his alibi checked out. It can't be Jerry who put the arsenic in the deceased's soup.

Betsy: Yeah, but who? We checked out everybody that went to the estate that day: the letter carrier, the gardener, the cook, the chauffeur, even the butler, though it was his day off. That eliminates everybody. I don't know who else it could be.

Al: I don't know. There has to be something ... someone we overlooked.

I T SOUNDS like a tough case for Al and Betsy. They've been working hard on it for at least 10 minutes, and must wrap it up in the next 47 minutes. Their show has just been canceled and there's no possibility for a two-part show.

Al and Betsy were busy eliminating possibilities before they were eliminated from the airwaves ... possibly forever.

~~~~~

Eliminating possibilities is a powerful problem solving strategy. Sherlock Holmes used this strategy quite extensively. In his words, "Once you have eliminated the impossible, then whatever is left, no matter how improbable, must be the solution." This chapter will explore some mathematical problems involving eliminating possibilities.

◀ *Health care professionals must do tests to eliminate possibilities when diagnosing an illness.*

The following is a canned game. It never actually took place, though you probably realize that every day, all over America, real people are acting out very similar scenes.

I'm thinking of a number between 1 and 100 inclusive. You may ask whatever questions you like, and I will respond with yes or no answers. In order to keep the game fair, I will always respond truthfully.

Question	Response
Is it 13?	No
Is it > 50?	Yes
Is it 62?	No
Is it > 75?	Yes
Is it Odd?	No
Is it 83?	No
Is it < 85?	Yes
Is it < 80?	Yes
Is it 76?	No
Is it 78?	Yes

Examine the questions that were asked in this game. Which questions were worthwhile and which were essentially wasted?

The early questions asking if the number was 13 or 62 were clearly not much help. They only eliminated one number from consideration. On the other hand, the question "Is it greater than 50?" eliminated 50 numbers. That was a very useful question. Likewise, the questions about whether the number was greater than 75 and whether it was odd were very useful as they eliminated a lot of possibilities. The question "Is it 83?" was clearly wasted, as by that time it had already been established that the number was not odd. When trying to eliminate possibilities, it helps to remember those possibilities that have already been eliminated.

Solve the following problem by eliminating possibilities:

Three brothers each arranged to spend an evening with women that none had ever met before. They each wanted to show off how suave and debonair they could be, so each formed a plan.

By coincidence, each brother decided to buy a box of candy at the same store, and each one bought tickets at the same computer ticket outlet.

Andy bought honey-based candies, as he wanted to show what a sweet guy he could bee. Tooley bought chews, as he wanted to show that he wouldn't accept just anybody—he was a choosy guy. Marty bought nuts without realizing the message it could send.

When it came time to leave, each brother grabbed a wrong candy box and ticket envelope. None of them took the candy or the tickets that belonged to him. Each took the tickets of one brother and the candy of the other. To make things short, Andy didn't have Marty's candy, and you'll have to figure out the rest.

Do this problem before continuing.

To solve this problem, Kim drew the diagram below and then began to eliminate possibilities. Kim's diagram showed the candy and ticket possibilities for each brother. "I drew the diagram like this because it was given that each brother had the candy that belonged to one brother and the tickets belonging to the other."

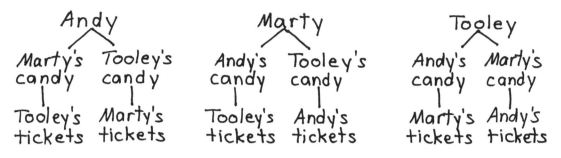

Kim went on to explain her reasoning. "It was given that Andy did not have Marty's candy. So I crossed out the possibility that Andy had Marty's candy and Tooley's tickets. Therefore, Andy must have Tooley's candy. This also means that Andy must have Marty's tickets, since each brother had the candy that belonged to one brother and the tickets belonging to the other. Since Andy has Tooley's candy, Marty can't be the one with Tooley's candy, so Marty must have Andy's candy. Then for Tooley it is evident that he doesn't have Andy's candy, thus he has Marty's candy (the only candy left, as all other possibilities have been eliminated)."

Andy

~~Marty's candy~~   Tooley's candy

|

~~Tooley's tickets~~   Marty's tickets

Marty

Andy's candy   ~~Tooley's candy~~

|

Tooley's tickets   ~~Andy's tickets~~

Tooley

~~Andy's candy~~   Marty's candy

|

~~Marty's tickets~~   Andy's tickets

"Determining who has which candy automatically determines who has which set of tickets. So the answers are: Andy has Tooley's candy and Marty's tickets, Marty has Andy's candy and Tooley's tickets, and Tooley has Marty's candy and Andy's tickets."

Penny's favorite coin is the dime, as we saw in the last chapter. Since we last saw Penny, she has spent some of her dimes and acquired some more, so she does not know how many she has now, although she knows it is fewer than 100. One day she was arranging them on her desk in different ways. She found that when she put them into piles of two, there was one left over. When she put them into piles of three, there was one left over, and the same thing happened when she put them into piles of four. She then tried putting them in piles of five, and found that there were none left over. How many dimes does Penny have?

Work this problem before continuing. (By the way, there is more than one correct answer.)

There are five clues given in this problem. They are:

1. When divided by 2, the remainder is 1.

2. When divided by 3, the remainder is 1.

3. When divided by 4, the remainder is 1.

4. When divided by 5, the remainder is 0.

5. There are fewer than 100 coins.

This problem will clearly demonstrate that it's important to consider all possibilities before eliminating some. A group of students—Marli, James, Dennis, and Troy—solved the problem this way.

James: Let's start with the first clue. I will list all of the numbers that give a remainder of one when divided by 2. (James wrote down the list below.)

$$1, 3, 5, 7, 9, 11, 13, 15, 17, 19, 21, 23, 25, 27, 29, 31, 33, 35, 37, 39 \ldots$$

Marli: (interrupting him) Wait a minute, this can be done more efficiently. I like your list because it is systematic, but I think we can improve it. Instead of just considering one clue at a time, I think we can compress this by using two of the clues from the beginning.

Dennis: Good idea, Marli. Let's try using clues 1 and 2.

Troy: I think we should use clues 4 and 5 instead.

Dennis: Why not 1 and 2?

Troy: I chose 4 because it has the smallest number of numbers attached to it, and 5 because it is so easy. So here is a list of all of the numbers less than 100 that are divisible by 5. (Troy then wrote the list below.)

5,10,15,20,25,30,35,40,45,50,55,60,65,70,75,80,85,90,95

James: Now we can go back and reconsider clue 1. My initial list showed us that these numbers are all odd. Since we are trying to eliminate possibilities, let's cross off all of the even numbers in Troy's list. (He did so.)

5, ~~10,~~ 15, ~~20,~~ 25, ~~30,~~ 35, ~~40,~~ 45, ~~50,~~ 55, ~~60,~~ 65, ~~70,~~ 75, ~~80,~~ 85, ~~90,~~ 95

Marli: Now let's continue on through the clues. Clue 2 allows us to cross off any number that is not one greater than a multiple of 3.

Dennis: Say what?

Marli: Let me explain that more clearly. The clue says, "When she put them in piles of three, there was one left over." That means, if you divide the number of dimes by three, the remainder would be one. So we have to keep everything that is one more than a multiple of three.

Dennis: Oh, I see. That means we have to eliminate everything that is not one more than a multiple of three.

James: I don't get it. Can you give me an example?

Marli: Okay. For example, 5 is two more than a multiple of three, so it can be crossed off. Fifteen is a multiple of 3, so it can be crossed off also. On the other hand, 25 cannot be crossed off because 25 is one more than 24, which is a multiple of 3. (There would be one left if we divided 25 dimes into eight piles of three.) So we can eliminate the multiples of 3 (15, 45, 75) and numbers that are 2 more than a multiple of 3 (5, 35, 65, 95). (She crossed off those numbers in the revised list.)

$$\cancel{5}, \cancel{15}, 25, \cancel{35}, \cancel{45}, 55, \cancel{65}, \cancel{75}, 85, \cancel{95}$$

Troy: This leaves us with 25, 55, and 85. Finally, we apply clue 3, which has us cross off any number that is not one greater than a multiple of 4. That means we can cross off 55 because it's three more than a multiple of 4 (since $52 = 4 \times 13$).

James: That move leaves us with the numbers 25 and 85. Each of these satisfies all of the clues. Which is the correct answer?

Marli: I guess we can't tell for sure.

This problem has more than one possible answer. You may have been led to believe that all math problems have only one answer. That is probably true in most standard math courses, but it won't necessarily be true in this book. This book mirrors life in that respect: there won't always be a single correct answer, just as there won't be a single correct approach to finding an answer. Every time you finish doing a problem, you should ask yourself if you have the only answer or if there are others to consider. On this problem we did warn you that there would be more than one answer. But watch out! We may not always warn you.

~~~~

Eliminating possibilities falls into the major category of organizing information. After organizing the information presented in the problem, you can eliminate certain possibilities. It often helps to consider the possibilities in a systematic fashion, as in the last problem. There are also aspects of guess and check in this strategy. (Guess and check will be explored more fully in Chapter 6.)

The next problem involves eliminating possibilities and maybe a little bit of guessing. Doing math problems for pleasure may seem strange, but many people have enjoyed problems like this over the years. Problems such as these are sometimes called cryptarithmetic.

Emil and Olive lived on a farm with their father, Gordon. One day, Emil asked his father, "Dad, what happened to that cat we used to have?" Olive overheard this, and said, "Yeah, and we used to have a horse too."

Gordon replied, "That tomcat and that old nag were no use. I traded them for our new goat."

Emil said, "Hey, that sounds like a good cryptarithmetic problem. Come on, Olive, let's go see if we can solve it."

Each letter stands for a different digit, 0 through 9. No two letters stand for the same digit.

TOM + NAG = GOAT

Determine which digit each letter represents.

Do this problem before reading on.

A class of students presented many solutions on the board. Several of their solutions follow.

Here's how Jonathan began solving the problem. "I started off realizing that G had to be 1, because it is impossible to have two three-digit numbers add up to something more than 2,000. Even if the numbers were 999 + 999 the answer would be 1998. So G has to be 1. So I wrote down 1 under G."

"Then I was stuck. I wasn't really sure what to do next, so I sort of started guessing numbers. I looked at O next, and finally figured out that it had to be zero, since in the tens place, O + A = A."

"Then I just sort of guessed numbers that added up to 10 for T and N. I picked 7 and 3 and everything worked out. M turned out to be 6 and then I just picked A to be 4."

Here's how Jerri worked it out, "I did the same thing as Jonathan, but I picked a different set of numbers for T and N. I used 6 and 4. Then it works out like this."

```
    T O M
   ⑥ 0 ⑤
 + N A G
   ④ ⑨ 1
  G O A T
  1 0 ⑨ ⑥
```

"But then I realized that A could be anything not used. So I got a few other solutions too."

```
   T O M        T O M        T O M        T O M
   6 0 5        6 0 5        6 0 5        6 0 5
 + N A G      + N A G      + N A G      + N A G
   4 ② 1        4 ③ 1        4 ⑦ 1        4 ⑧ 1
  G O A T      G O A T      G O A T      G O A T
  1 0 ② 6      1 0 ③ 6      1 0 ⑦ 6      1 0 ⑧ 6
```

Jack tried a chart. "I did the same things that Jonathan and Jerri did, but I realized that the choice of T and N could be anything that added up to 10. Also, the choice of T automatically picked N. I came up with this chart."

```
N:  1  2  3  4  5  6  7  8  9
T:  9  8  7  6  5  4  3  2  1
```

"I eliminated the 1, 9 and 9, 1 combinations because we already know that 1 is G. Also eliminate the 5, 5 combination because two different letters can't stand for the same digit."

```
N:  2  3  4  6  7  8
T:  8  7  6  4  3  2
```

"Now remember that we already know that T is one greater than M. So I added M into the chart."

```
N:  2  3  4  6  7
T:  8  7  6  4  3
M:  7  6  5  3  2
```

"The last possibility of N = 8 and T = 2 has been eliminated since if T were 2, M would have to be 1, but this is impossible since G = 1 and two different letters cannot represent the same digit.

"So the chart shows all of the possibilities for T, N, and M. This problem has five possible correct solutions. Actually this represents five families of solutions, because it turns out that A can be any digit not assigned to the other letters in the problem, as Jerri already explained."

Adrianne's contribution was, "I didn't get as far as Jack did, but I did notice that O could possibly have been 9. If there was a carry from the ones column, it is possible that O is 9."

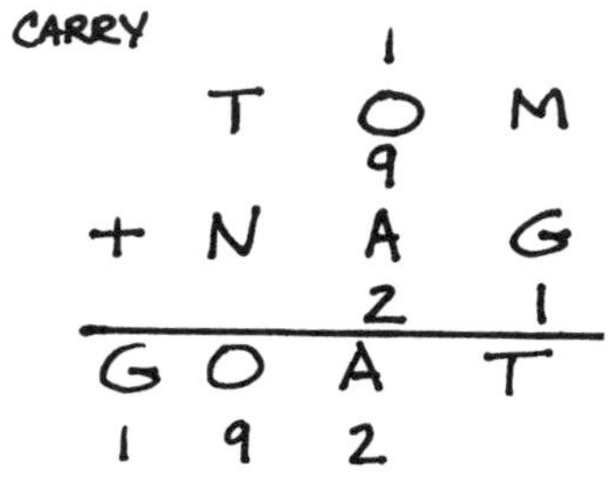

CARRY

```
           1
       T   O   M
           9
    +  N   A   G
           2       1
    ─────────────────
       G   O   A   T
       1   9   2
```

"But then I realized this was impossible. If O was 9, then the ones column would have had to carry. This means that M would have to be 9, since G is already 1 and you would need 9 more to cause the carry. But that would mean M and O were both 9, and that's impossible."

Khue noticed, "Another reason that O can't be 9 is because in GOAT, the number would have to be 19 hundred something. But that is impossible too, since the only way that GO can be 19 is if T + N adds to 19. Even with a carry from the tens column, T and N would both have to be 9 and that is, of course, impossible."

In summary, there are many possible solutions to this problem. When you solve a problem, you should pursue alternative solutions unless you are sure that none exist.

Try your hand at this next problem. It is a rather famous problem and has one and only one correct solution.

The story goes that a young man away at college needed some extra cash. He sent his mother this plea. He wanted his mother to send the amount indicated by the sum.

SEND + MORE = MONEY

Just as before, each letter stands for one of the digits 0 through 9 and there is only one letter for any one digit. How much did the young man want? (You may assume that there is a decimal point between N and E, as the mother is probably not willing to send ten thousand or so dollars to her son on request.) Work this problem before continuing.

This problem is very complicated, as is the explanation. Read through it very slowly and try to work it out at the same time on a piece of paper. Don't be afraid to reread sections of the explanation several times.

The first conclusion to draw is that M = 1, by the same reasoning that T was 1 in the previous problem: the maximum of S + M is 17, which means M cannot be larger than 1. Also note that the maximum sum of two four digit numbers is 9999 + 9999 = 19,998, so M must be 1. Since M = 1, and S + M = MO, S has to be 9 without a carry from the hundreds column, or S has to be 8 with a carry from the hundreds column. In either case, O has to be zero. This is because 1 + 9 + (a carry) would mean MO was equal to 11, but O can't be 1 since M is 1. Therefore O = 0. At this point, the solution looks as shown on the right.

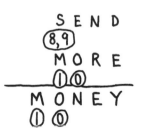

Now look at the hundreds column: E + 0 = N. Clearly, anything plus 0 is equal to the same number. Therefore, since E and N cannot be the same number, there must have been a carry from the tens column. The maximum carry is 1, so E + 1 = N.

Since S is either 8 or 9, E and N can't be 8 and 9 respectively, so the maximum value for E is 7, which makes 8 the maximum value for N.

Therefore, the hundreds column can't carry over to the thousands column, so in the thousands column, S must be 9. Now the solution looks like this, including the carries.

Recall that E + 1 = N. In the tens column N + R = E. Since E is N − 1, then N + R = N − 1. Note this would make R = ⁻1, which doesn't make sense. But it is possible that N + R > 10. In this case N + R = 10 + E. Recall E = N − 1. So N + R = 10 + N − 1 and thus R = 9. But this is impossible because S is already 9, so there must be another alternative. Therefore, R must be 8 and there must be a carry from the ones column. Up to this point, the solution looks like this.

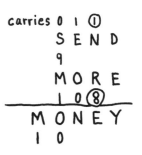

Now note that D + E in the ones column must carry. So D + E = 10 + Y. The smallest that Y can be is 2, since 1 and 0 are already taken. Therefore D + E has to be at least 12. The possibilities are listed at right. Notice that 8 and 9 are not listed for D and E as they are already taken by R and S.

D: 6 7 7 5
E: 7 6 5 7
N: 8 7 6 8
Y: 3 3 2 2
Recall that E + 1 = N.

Which possibilities are valid? The first and last possibilities must be eliminated since N would be 8, and 8 is already taken by R. The second possibility is eliminated since D and N would both be 7. Therefore the third possibility is correct and the solution is as shown at right.

carries 0 1 1
  S E N D
  9 5 6 7
  M O R E
  1 0 8 5
 M O N E Y
1 0 6 5 2

The question asked how much the young man wanted. Assuming that there is a decimal between the N and E, he wanted $106.52.

~~~~~

The next problem requires a mixture of the strategies of make a systematic list and eliminate possibilities. Many problems cannot be solved with only one strategy. As you work farther into the book, there will be more overlap of strategies and a number of problems that may require several strategies to solve.

The problem is tough. It is also a little tricky. Take your time and be sure you consider all possibilities before eliminating some.

DOWNTOWN DELI

Seymour owns his own business. He puts together deli sandwiches, which he wraps to retain freshness and distributes to several convenience stores for re-sale. One of his favorites is the Sausage and Meatball combo, but it has a very low distribution. In fact, there are only three stores that take delivery of the Sausage and Meatball: two Fast Stop stores and one Circle B store. One morning, Seymour suffered an unfortunate accident. He slipped on the floor and banged his head. He seemed to be fine, except once he was out on his delivery route, he couldn't remember which streets the three Sausage and Meatball stores were on. The streets were numbered from 1st street up to 154th street. Fortunately, he remembered that the Fast Stop stores were on streets whose numbers added up to 50. He also remembered that the Circle B store was two streets away from one of the Fast Stop stores. And he also remembered that he considered the Sausage and Meatball combination to be his "prime" favorite, as all three stores were on prime-numbered streets. Unfortunately, that wasn't enough information. He called his friend Gus and, well, let's keep this short by saying Gus remembered Seymour having told him the product of the streets the stores were on, but Gus could only remember the last digit of the product. This proved to be enough for Seymour, who promptly double-parked, whipped out a pencil, made a systematic list, and eliminated possibilities to find the answer.

Now it's your turn to re-create Seymour's heroics.

Richard solved this problem as shown. He first considered the streets that the Fast Stop stores could be on. He made a systematic list of all of the pairs of odd numbers that add to 50. He used odd numbers since even numbers cannot be prime. (The exception to this is 2, but 2 would be paired with 48, which is obviously not prime.)

Even though he knew some of the odd numbers weren't prime, he listed them all anyway because he wanted to be careful not to accidentally eliminate any possibilities before he considered them.

FS #1	FS #2
1	49
3	47
5	45
7	43
9	41
11	39
13	37
15	35
17	33
19	31
21	29
23	27
25	25

Next he eliminated all of the numbers that are not prime. He eliminated 1, 49, 45, 9, 39, 15, 35, 33, 21, 27, 25, and the numbers they were paired with (even if they were prime). He then considered the remaining pairs in either order, since either order is possible.

FS #1	FS #2
3	47
47	3
7	43
43	7
13	37
37	13
19	31
31	19

Next he added the third number. The Circle B store is two streets away from one of the Fast Stop stores, but we don't know which store, nor in which direction. Since he already listed the first two stores in either order, he doesn't have to worry about which store is which. But he does need to worry about which direction the Circle B store is from the Fast Stop store. This means that the third number is either two more or two less than the second number.

FS#1	FS#2	CB
3	47	45
3	47	49
47	3	1
47	3	5
7	43	41
7	43	45
43	7	5
43	7	9
13	37	35
13	37	39
37	13	11
37	13	15
19	31	29
19	31	33
31	19	17
31	19	21

However, Richard only needed to consider third numbers that are prime. For example, the first set of two numbers is 3 and 47. The two possible third numbers are 45 and 49, but neither of these numbers is prime, so he didn't have to consider them. He eliminated all of the third numbers that were not prime, which left him with the list at right.

FS#1	FS#2	CB
47	3	5
7	43	41
43	7	5
37	13	11
19	31	29
31	19	17

Now consider the last clue. Once Gus told Seymour the last digit of the product of the three numbers, he was able to figure out the answer. Richard does not know the product, but it is enough for Richard to know that if Seymour knew the product, Seymour could figure it out. See if you can figure out the answer before reading on.

The last digit of the product has been added to the chart. Note Richard only needed the last digit of the product. For example, $47 \times 3 \times 5 = 705$ ends in 5. Actually, Richard didn't really multiply the numbers out, he just figured out what the last digit would be.

In $7 \times 43 \times 41$ for example, $7 \times 3 \times 1 = 21$, which ends in 1, which is the last digit of the product of $7 \times 43 \times 41$.

FS #1	FS #2	CB	Last Digit
47	3	5	5
7	43	41	1
43	7	5	5
37	13	11	1
19	31	29	1
31	19	17	3

Richard noticed that 3 appears in the list only once, while 5 appears twice and 1 appears three times. So since Seymour deduced the combination after hearing the last digit of the product, that must mean that the last digit is 3, or else he would not have been able to figure it out without more information. So Richard concluded that the streets are numbered 31, 19, and 17. This means that the Fast Stop stores are located on 31st and 19th streets, with the Circle B store on 17th street.

One of the key points in this problem occurs in a lot of puzzle problems. You did not have all the information that Seymour had. However, it was enough to know that if Seymour had the information, then Seymour could solve the problem. This bit of knowledge allows you to solve the problem too.

～～～

Within the category of eliminate possibilities there is a substrategy that helps determine what can be eliminated. This is known variously as "indirect proof" in formal mathematics, or "proof by contradiction." In this book we will call it "seeking contradictions." As you saw earlier, you will often seek contradictions in solving word arithmetic problems. The substrategy of seeking contradictions will also show up quite a bit in the chapter on matrix logic.

The strategy of seeking contradictions is useful in the famous truth teller and liar problems. Variations of this problem have been around for years. Solve it by seeking contradictions.

Jim tells lies on Fridays, Saturdays, and Sundays. He tells the truth on all other days. Freda tells lies on Tuesdays, Wednesdays and Thursdays. She tells the truth on all other days. If they both said, "Yesterday I lied," then what day is it today?

Solve this problem before continuing.

Danyell solved this problem by seeking contradictions. First she set up a chart of days of the week and the two liars.

	MON	TUE	WED	THUR	FRI	SAT	SUN
JIM	T	T	T	T	L	L	L
FREDA	T	L	L	L	T	T	T

"Assume that today is Monday. Both people tell the truth on Monday, so the statement, 'Yesterday I lied,' must be true for both. But yesterday was Sunday, and only Jim was lying yesterday. Since Freda told the truth on Sunday, her statement is false. This is the contradiction we were seeking, because Freda is supposed to tell the truth on Monday. So today is not Monday.

"Assume today is Tuesday. Jim is telling the truth, so when he says, 'Yesterday I lied,' it is supposed to be true. But yesterday was Monday and Jim tells the truth on Monday. So today can't be Tuesday. A similar argument can be made for Wednesday and Thursday. A similar argument can also be made in Freda's behalf on Saturday and Sunday.

"Finally, assume today is Friday. Since Jim lies on Friday, his statement, 'Yesterday I lied,' is false. That works, because on Thursday, Jim tells the truth. Now consider Freda. She tells the truth on Friday, so her statement 'Yesterday I lied,' must be the truth, since she lies on Thursday. So I concluded that today is Friday, having reached contradictions for every other day."

Eliminating possibilities (and seeking contradictions) is a valuable problem-solving strategy. By considering all the possibilities (sometimes by making a systematic list) and eliminating the obviously incorrect ones, you can narrow in on the right answer. Sometimes, as in crime solving, not all the possibilities can be eliminated right away. However, many can be eliminated quickly, allowing the detectives to concentrate their efforts on the remaining suspects.

You will probably begin noticing that you use this strategy already in daily life—for example, when you decide what to have for dinner or what to watch on TV. If you make a conscious effort to eliminate possibilities when faced with certain problems, your problem-solving skill will increase.

Problem Set A

1. SQUARE ROOTS

The square root of 4356 is an integer. Without a calculator, determine what that integer is by eliminating possibilities. Do the same for 8464.

2. HOW MANY LINES?

Sam counted the lines of a page in his book. Counting by threes gave a remainder of 2; counting by fives also gave a remainder of 2; and counting by sevens gave a remainder of 5. How many lines were on the page?

3. EGGS IN A BASKET

If the eggs in a basket are removed two at a time, one egg will remain. If the eggs are removed three at a time, two eggs will remain. If the eggs are removed four, five, or six at a time, then three, four, and five eggs will remain, respectively. If they are taken out seven at a time, however, no eggs will be left over. Find the smallest number of eggs that could be in the basket.

4. DARTBOARD

Juana threw five darts. The possible scores on the target were 2, 4, 6, 8, and 10. Each dart hit the target. Which of these total scores are you certain is not possible? 38, 23, 58, 30, 42, 31, 26, 6, 14, 15.

5. FIND THE NUMBER

If you multiply the four-digit number *abcd* by 4, the digits get reversed. That is, $abcd \times 4 = dcba$. Find *abcd*. (*a*, *b*, *c*, and *d* are all different digits.)

6. WOW WOW, SO COOK!

Denée was having an argument with her roommate, Frankie, about whether or not Frankie was capable of cooking. Finally, after a while, she said, "Wow, wow, so cook!" Frankie, who was a math teacher, noticed that what Denée said might be a cryptarithm. She sat down to work on it while Denée ended up cooking dinner. Each letter stands for a different digit. Hint: K = 9.

```
    W O W
    W O W
  +   S O
  -------
  C O O K
```

7. NELSON + CARSON = REWARD

There was a story in the old West about two famous outlaws named Nelson and Carson. Their wanted poster indicated that if someone caught up to both of them and brought them in for trial, there would be a substantial reward. Amazingly, it turned out that their wanted poster was a great cryptarithm. All who saw the poster realized this and spent their time solving the puzzle rather than looking for Nelson and Carson. When Nelson and Carson heard all the ruckus about their wanted poster, they too tried the problem. Unfortunately, they weren't too bright and ended up visiting their local sheriff for a clue. He told them that N = 5, and then he arrested them. They solved the problem during the time they spent in jail.

Each letter stands for a different digit. Find the digits that the other letters represent.

```
    N E L S O N
  + C A R S O N
  -------------
    R E W A R D
```

8. THE THREE SQUARES

Three cousins, Bob, Chris, and Phyllis, were sitting around watching football on TV. The game was really boring, and so they started talking about how old they were. Bob (the oldest) noticed that they were all between the ages of 11 and 30. Phyllis noticed that the sum of their ages was 70. Chris (the youngest) burst out, "Gee, if you write the square of each of our ages, all of the digits from 1 to 9 will appear exactly once in the digits of the three squares." How old was each person?

9. TO TELL THE TRUTH

Puzzle books often contain puzzles involving people or creatures who are either liars or truth tellers. You no doubt know from experience, for example, that many talking dogs are notorious liars. Imagine that you have just encountered three talking dogs, and you ask them if they are liars or truth tellers. Dog 1 says something that you do not understand. Dog 2 says, "He said he was a truth teller." Dog 3 says, "Joe is lying." You then ask, "Which one of you is Joe?" Dog 2 says, "I am the only Joe." Dog 3 points to Dog 1 and says, "He is the only Joe." Determine whether each dog is a liar, a truth teller, or whether it can't be determined.

10. RANKINGS

Thuy (the tallest) is older than Miguel (the lightest). Jerel (the oldest) is shorter than Nick (the heaviest). No one has the same rank in any category. For example, if someone is the second tallest, he can't be the second heaviest or the second oldest. Rank the four boys in each category: age, height, and weight.

11. CONNECTIONS

Where have you used any of the strategies learned so far in your daily life outside of school?

Problem Set B

1. THE SIDEWALK AROUND THE GARDEN

We have a 17-by-20-foot garden. We want to pour cement for a sidewalk 3 feet wide around the garden. To make the forms for the cement, we will need to buy some 2-by-4-inch lumber. How many feet of 2-by-4-inch lumber will we need just for the perimeter of the walk? (Consider both the inside and outside perimeter.)

2. A NUMBER OF OPTIONS

Dusty Rhodes is planning to buy a new dirt bike. The different options available are:

1. She can choose either regular tires or extra heavy duty tires.

2. She can choose to get plastic, vinyl, cloth, or leather for the seat.

3. She has a choice of paint colors: Bad Brown, Sick Silver, or Grease Black.

In how many different ways can she order her new bike?

3. GOOD DIRECTIONS?

I stopped at a street corner and asked for directions to Burger Jack. Unfortunately, the person I asked was Larry Longway, whose directions are guaranteed to be too complicated. He said, "You are now facing north. Go straight for 2 blocks. Turn left. Go straight for 1 block. Turn right. Go straight for 3 blocks. Turn right. Go straight for 5 blocks. Turn right. Go straight for 3 blocks. Turn left. Go straight for 1 block. Turn right. Go straight for 4 blocks. Turn left. Go straight for 2 blocks. Turn left. Go straight for 1 block. Turn left. Go straight for 5 blocks and you are there." By the time I arrived, I was out of breath and Burger Jack was closed. Give the directions for the shortest path from my original spot to Burger Jack.

4. HIGH SCORERS

The five starters for the Seaside Shooters scored all of the team's points in the final basketball game of the season. Regina Reporter's notes were accidentally destroyed later on. Fortunately, she had taped some interviews with the players, but only a few quotes seemed relevant to the scoring when she played them back. She knew the final score was 95-94. Determine from the players' observations how many points each scored.

Kellene: Everybody's totals were odd.

Sara: Donna was fourth highest with 17 points. I scored 12 more points than Kellene.

Martina: Kellene and I scored a total of 30 points. I outscored her.

Heather: The last digit in everybody's score was different.

Donna: Our highest scorer had 25 points.

5. WAYS TO SCORE

Eighteen points are scored in a football game by the Chicago Bears. How many different ways can this occur? Points are scored as follows: safety is 2 points; field goal is 3 points; touchdown is 6 points; point after touchdown (PAT) is 1 point. (Note: A PAT cannot be scored unless a touchdown is scored first.)

4 matrix logic

S OCIETY VALUES logical thinking. Logical thinking helps in dealing with other people. Decisions reached logically are often held in higher esteem than decisions made emotionally. Arguments based on emotion could be discounted or disdained by some people. Logical arguments are more readily accepted.

A logical argument basically starts at some point and moves to another point by way of ordered steps. The argument needs to be developed in a sequential fashion, or others will not give it credence. A man might tell his daughter that she should go to the dentist because it looks like rain. This statement probably seems absolutely crazy to someone who doesn't know that she left her umbrella at her dentist's office last week. The conclusion that she should go to her dentist's office is correct; however, it appears to be ridiculous without evidence of the logical thinking behind it.

One way to improve your logical reasoning is to solve logic problems. Most grocery and discount variety stores carry magazines that are full of logic problems. (Dell is one publisher of such magazines.) Logic problems also show up occasionally in other puzzle magazines, such as *Games*. Logic problems are fun and challenging, and solving them will improve your reasoning ability. The basic idea of logic problems is to match up items in various categories. For example, you might be asked to match up first and last names of a list of people, along with each person's favorite food, favorite color, and pet owned. Another problem might ask you to match up each person's name with a kind of car and occupation. Generally speaking, the problems get harder as more people or more categories are added.

Most of these problems can be solved by a chart or table that we

◀ *Printers use matrix logic to match different types of jobs with the equipment available in order to meet tight deadlines.*

will call a matrix. The matrix serves to organize the information in the problem in a useful way. This type of matrix can be used to solve other types of problems in life, such as problems involving scheduling. The matrix facilitates eliminating possibilities, which is an important strategy for solving logic problems.

An example of a matrix logic table is shown below. This matrix could be used on a problem that matches up names (John, Phil, Mary, and Alice) with pets (dog, cat, bird, and fish). Your task would be to match each person with the pet owned.

FIRST NAMES

		John	Phil	Mary	Alice
P E T S	dog				
	cat				
	bird				
	fish				

The chart is used for two things. When a possibility is eliminated, an X is marked in the chart signifying this. For example, suppose it was determined that John did not own the dog. (How to determine this will be discussed later.) You would then place an X in the chart in the square that matches John and dog. Suppose also that you determined that Mary did not own the bird. You could place an X in the square that matches up Mary and bird.

FIRST NAMES

		John	Phil	Mary	Alice
P E T S	dog	X			
	cat				
	bird			X	
	fish				

The other basic mark in the chart is one that shows a definite connection. An X shows something that is not correct. An O shows a connection that is correct. (Some people use the words yes and no instead of X and O. Other people use other symbols.) For example, suppose you determined that Alice owned the fish. You would then place an O in the square that matches up Alice and fish. In addition to an O, however, you can also put in a lot of X's. A more or less standard feature of logic problems is the one-to-one correspondence between things. Each person owns one pet. So, if Alice owns the fish, then nobody else does. Therefore you can place X's in the rest of the fish row. Also, if Alice owns the fish, then she owns no other pet, so you can place X's in the rest of Alice's column. And, of course, any previously determined information remains. Note: the text will call attention to information that has been added since the previous matrix by showing circles around new marks.

FIRST NAMES

PETS		John	Phil	Mary	Alice
	dog	X			⊗
	cat				⊗
	bird			X	⊗
	fish	⊗	⊗	⊗	◎

At this point in this problem, suppose you were then able to deduce that Phil did not own the dog. You would place an X in the Phil-dog square.

FIRST NAMES

PETS		John	Phil	Mary	Alice
	dog	X	⊗		X
	cat				X
	bird			X	X
	fish	X	X	X	O

This would help tremendously. A glance at the chart shows that neither John, Phil, nor Alice owns the dog. Therefore, Mary must own the dog. You can therefore

FIRST NAMES

PETS		John	Phil	Mary	Alice
	dog	X	X	⊚	X
	cat			⊗	X
	bird			X	X
	fish	X	X	X	O

place an O in the Mary-dog square and an X in the Mary-cat square (since Mary owns the dog, she can't own the cat).

Now all that remains is to determine who owns the cat and who owns the bird. There would have to be some way to determine this, and that would finish the problem.

Just how do you determine these various connections and eliminations? Each problem has a set of clues for you to read. After you read them carefully, you'll be able to deduce these connections. Consider the next problem.

FAVORITE SPORTS

Ted, Ken, Allyson, and Janie (two married couples) each has a favorite sport. The sports are running, swimming, biking, and golfing. Determine from the following clues who likes which sport.

1. *Ted hates golf: he agrees with Mark Twain that golf is nothing but a good walk spoiled.*
2. *Ken can't run around the block, and neither can his wife.*
3. *Each woman's favorite sport is featured in a triathlon.*
4. *Allyson bought her husband a new bike for his birthday for use in his favorite sport.*

Work this problem before continuing.

First, set up the matrix logic chart by drawing a grid. Next, label the top and left side with the categories given in the problem. The categories in this problem are names and sports. This chart shows sports on top and names on the left side, but it could have been set up the other way. If there were more categories, then more charts would be needed. (You will see examples of this later.)

		SPORTS			
		running	swimming	biking	golf
NAMES	Ted				
	Ken				
	Allyson				
	Janie				

Jason solved the Favorite Sports problem this way.

"First I set up my chart, with the names on the side and the sports up on top. Then I read through the clues. The first clue said that Ted didn't like golf. So that eliminated Ted from being the golfer. I put an X in the Ted-golf square. I also put a 1 next to this X to show that I had eliminated this possibility by using clue 1.

"The second clue said that Ken can't run around the block. So I figured that Ken wasn't the runner, and I put an X_2 in the Ken-running space. It also said Ken's wife wasn't the runner, but I didn't know who his wife was so I left this clue alone for now.

"The third clue said that the women like sports that are featured in the triathlon. The only sport in the list that isn't featured in the triathlon is golf, so I put X_3's in the Allyson-golf and Janie-golf squares."

SPORTS

	running	swimming	biking	golf
Ted				$\otimes_1$
Ken	$\otimes_2$			
Allyson				$\otimes_3$
Janie				$\otimes_3$

(NAMES)

"This meant that Ken was the only one who could like golf. So I put an O in the Ken-golf space. This also meant that Ken couldn't like any of the other sports. So I put X's in the Ken-swimming and Ken-biking squares."

SPORTS

	running	swimming	biking	golf
Ted				X_1
Ken	X_2	$\otimes$	$\otimes$	$\bigcirc$
Allyson				X_3
Janie				X_3

(NAMES)

"Next I read clue four. It said Allyson's husband likes biking. This meant that Ted had to like biking, since he was the only man left once I knew Ken liked golf. So Ted likes biking and is Allyson's husband. So I put an O in the Ted-biking space. This meant that Ted could not be the runner or the swimmer, so I put X's in the Ted-running and Ted-swimming spaces. (The Ted-golf space already had an X in it.) I also put X's in the Allyson-biking and Janie-biking spaces, since if Ted was the bicyclist, then nobody else could be."

SPORTS

		running	swimming	biking	golf
N	Ted	⊗	⊗	Ⓞ4	X₁
A M	Ken	X₂	X	X	O
E	Allyson			⊗	X₃
S	Janie			⊗	X₃

"Now I had to figure out who was the runner and who was the swimmer. But I didn't have any more clues. I read through all the clues again. Clue number 2 said that Ken's wife couldn't run around the block. I had skipped that clue at the time, but now I thought I could use it. I know that Allyson bought her husband a bike, and her husband turned out to be Ted. This means that Ken is married to Janie, so Janie is the one who can't run around the block. (Substitute the name Janie for Ken's wife in clue 2.) So I put an X in the Janie-running space. This leaves Allyson as the runner and Janie as the swimmer."

SPORTS

		running	swimming	biking	golf
N	Ted	X	X	O4	X₁
A M	Ken	X₂	X	X	O
E	Allyson	Ⓞ2,4	⊗	X	X₃
S	Janie	⊗	Ⓞ	X	X₃

"The answers are: Allyson is the runner, Janie is the swimmer, Ted is the bicyclist, and Ken is the golfer. The chart really helped to solve this problem."

We want to add some other ideas to Jason's write-up on this problem.
First, though most people schooled in social sciences and psychology will tell you to think positively, that's the wrong attitude for this kind of problem. (For personal problems, yes, do think positively. On

matrix logic problems, don't.) You need to "think negatively." Negatives help eliminate possibilities. Notice that this strategy is based on things that cannot be, so you must think in a negative way in order to eliminate as many possibilities as you can.

Second, you should start listing the things that you know as soon as you know them and make additional marks on the chart. As soon as you know that Ted and Allyson are married to one another, start a list with "Ted – Allyson (married)" or maybe put a little heart symbol by their names on the chart so that you can remember it easily. On a problem this simple, it's not a big deal. However, on a more difficult problem, it definitely can be an asset to list such connections carefully. A list like this will be referred to as an "adjunct list."

Finally, Jason had to reread a clue while solving this problem. He skipped the clue about Ken's wife, and later came back to it when he knew who Ken's wife was. Rereading clues is helpful in solving matrix logic problems.

~~~~~

Now consider a problem with more categories. Suppose the problem asked you to match up first names (Bob, Sara, Rick, Jane), favorite color (blue, red, white, green), and the state each is from (South Dakota, Missouri, New Jersey, and Texas). How many matrices would you need?

Each category must be matched up with each other category. There must be a chart that matches each of the categories to each of the other categories. A good way to see how many charts are needed is to make a diagram. Put the different categories around in a circle, and draw lines between the categories. This will tell you how many charts you need and what each chart should be.

So there will be one chart for matching names with colors, one for matching names with states, and one for matching colors with states. A good method of chart organization is as follows. Put the first category down the left side. Put the next category on the top. Put the third category in two places: under the first category and to the right of the second category. You will see examples of four or more categories later in the chapter.

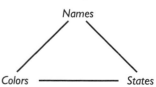

This is the chart for colors, states, and names.

		FAVORITE COLOR				STATE			
		Blue	Red	White	Green	SD	MO	NJ	TX
FIRST NAME	Bob								
	Sara								
	Rick								
	Jane								
STATE	SD								
	MO								
	NJ								
	TX								

After setting up the chart, you would then use the clues to solve the problem. Some problems can be solved just from careful reading of the clues. But most matrix logic problems require a number of different techniques, or substrategies. Some of these substrategies (rereading clues and making adjunct lists) were mentioned in the solution to the Favorite Sports problem earlier. The rest of the chapter will develop a few more substrategies, briefly outlined with partial problems, and then present full problems for practice.

One substrategy is called "bouncing" or "cross-correlating." Examine the following chart to see the way the information has been gathered so far.

		FAVORITE COLOR				STATE			
		Blue	Red	White	Green	SD	MO	NJ	TX
FIRST NAME	Bob		X						X
	Sara		X						X
	Rick		X						X
	Jane	X	O	X	X	X	X	X	O
STATE	SD								
	MO								
	NJ								
	TX								

As you can see from the preceding chart, Jane's favorite color is red. Jane is also from Texas. The third chart matches colors to states, and there are no marks on it yet. But if you take the information from the right-hand chart (Jane-Texas) and follow it back to the first chart, you meet up with Jane-red. Then follow the line down to the Texas-red square (meaning the person from Texas likes red) and fill in the chart.

A logician might say, "Jane likes red, Jane is from Texas, therefore, the person from Texas likes red." The last part is shown on the following chart.

		FAVORITE COLOR				STATE			
		Blue	Red	White	Green	SD	MO	NJ	TX
F I R S T N A M E	Bob		X						X
	Sara		X						X
	Rick		X						X
	Jane	X	O	X	X	X	X	X	O
S T A T E	SD		⊗						
	MO		⊗						
	NJ		⊗						
	TX	⊗	◎	⊗	⊗				

This is called "bouncing" because if you threw a ball from the right-hand chart along the Jane row, it would come to the Jane-red box and then it could bounce down to the appropriate Texas-red box. This is also called "cross-correlating" as you are correlating the items from two separate areas and crossing them in a place and in a way that makes sense and is useful.

Another way to accomplish the same thing would have been to list the facts as they become known.

The information discussed above should be written down as soon as it is obtained.

NAME	COLOR	STATE	
Jane	red		from left-hand chart
Jane		Texas	from right-hand chart

Of course, there is a more efficient way to do this.

NAME	COLOR	STATE
Jane	red	Texas

The strategy of bouncing or cross-correlating described above will be referred to as using positive information. This strategy can also be employed with negative information, although it is a bit more confusing. Consider the following chart. (Since this is not a real problem, the chart does not contain the previously worked out information.)

		FAVORITE COLOR				STATE			
		Blue	Red	White	Green	SD	MO	NJ	TX
F I R S T	Bob	X		X		O	X	X	X
	Sara					X			
N A M E	Rick					X			
	Jane					X			
S T A T E	SD								
	MO								
	NJ								
	TX								

From the right-hand chart it is evident that Bob is from South Dakota. From the left-hand chart, it is plain that Bob does not like blue or white. Therefore the person from South Dakota (Bob) does not like blue or white. So X's can be placed in the South Dakota-blue and South Dakota-white squares in the lower chart. This is called bouncing or cross-correlating with negative information.

		FAVORITE COLOR				STATE			
		Blue	Red	White	Green	SD	MO	NJ	TX
F I R S T	Bob	X		X		O	X	X	X
	Sara					X			
N A M E	Rick					X			
	Jane					X			
S T A T E	SD	X		X					
	MO								
	NJ								
	TX								

The next problem features three charts, cross-correlating with both positive and negative information, and an adjunct list.

OUTDOOR BARBECUE

Tom, John, Fred, and Bill are friends whose occupations are (in no particular order) nurse, secretary, teacher, and pilot. They attended a church picnic recently, and each one brought his favorite meat (hamburger, chicken, steak, and hot dogs) to barbecue. From the clues below, determine each man's name, occupation, and favorite meat.

1. Tom is neither the nurse nor the teacher.

2. Fred and the pilot play golf together. The burger lover and the teacher hate golf.

3. Tom brought hot dogs.

4. Bill sat next to the burger fan and across from the steak lover.

5. The secretary hates golf.

Work this problem before continuing.

Millissent and Tami worked on this problem.

Mill: First we need to set up one of those matrix logic charts.

Tami: That's right. We need three charts. One for names-occupations. One for names-meats. And one for meats-occupations.

(Tami drew the chart below.)

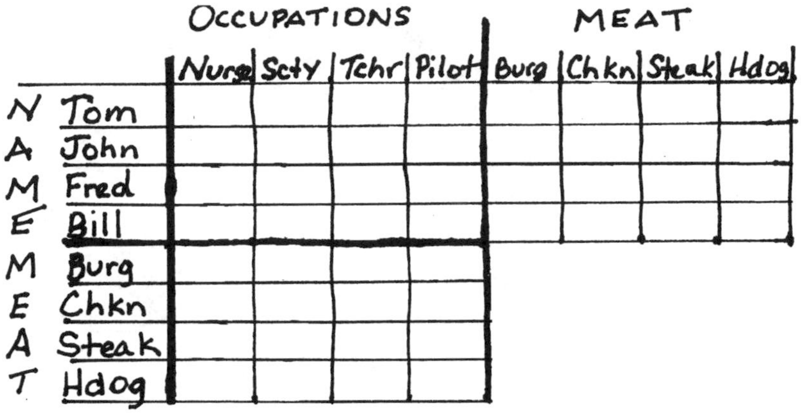

		OCCUPATIONS				MEAT		
		Nurse	Scty	Tchr	Pilot	Burg	Chkn	Steak	Hdog
N	Tom								
A	John								
M	Fred								
E	Bill								
M	Burg								
E	Chkn								
A	Steak								
T	Hdog								

Mill: Now let's read the clues and start eliminating. The first clue says that Tom is neither the nurse nor the teacher. So put X's in the Tom-nurse and Tom-teacher boxes.

Tami: Let's put little 1's next to the X's so we know we eliminated a square because of clue 1.

Mill: OK. Now the next clue says that Fred and the pilot play golf together. That means that Fred is not the pilot, so put an X_2 in the Fred-pilot space.

Tami: And then the burger lover and the teacher hate golf. So X_2 in the burger-teacher box.

Mill: Maybe we should start one of those adjunct lists.

Tami: What are those?

Mill: When you have other things referred to in the clues, it helps to list them separately. So here we have two people who play golf and two people who don't. So we make a list of this.

(She wrote down the adjunct list below.)

<u>Golfers</u>

Fred

pilot

<u>Non-Golfers</u>

burger

teacher

Tami: Oh, I see. Maybe we can use this later too. Wait a second. Fred can't like burgers or be the teacher.

Mill: How come?

Tami: Fred likes golf and the burger lover and the teacher don't. So Fred can't be either one of them. Put an X_2 in the Fred-burger and Fred-teacher spaces.

Mill: That's right. And by the same reasoning we can cross off pilot-burger also.

		OCCUPATIONS				MEAT			
		Nurse	Scty	Tchr	Pilot	Burg	Chkn	Steak	Hdog
N	Tom	(X₁)		(X₁)					
A	John								
M	Fred			(X₂)	(X₂)	(X₂)			
E	Bill								
M	Burg			(X₂)	(X₂)				
E	Chkn								
A	Steak								
T	Hdog								

Tami: OK, let's go on. Clue 3 says "Tom brought hot dogs." That's easy. Put an O in the Tom-hot dog space.

Mill: And X's in the rest of that row and column, since Tom couldn't have brought anything else and nobody else brought hot dogs. But watch out, don't put X's past the bold lines by accident.

		OCCUPATIONS				MEAT			
		Nurse	Scty	Tchr	Pilot	Burg	Chkn	Steak	Hdog
N	Tom	X_1		X_1		(X₃)	(X₃)	(X₃)	Ⓞ
A	John								X_3
M	Fred			X_2	X_2	X_2			X_3
E	Bill								X_3
M	Burg			X_2	X_2				
E	Chkn								
A	Steak								
T	Hdog								

Mill: Now I think we can do some of that bouncing with negative information we learned about. We know that Tom brought hot dogs. We also know that Tom is not the nurse or the teacher. So the nurse and teacher didn't bring hot dogs. So put an X in the nurse-hot dog and teacher-hot dog spaces.

		OCCUPATIONS				MEAT			
		Nurse	Scty	Tchr	Pilot	Burg	Chkn	Steak	Hdog
N	Tom	X_1		X_1		X_3	X_3	X_3	O
A	John								X_3
M	Fred			X_2	X_2	X_2			X_3
E	Bill								X_3
M	Burg			X_2	X_2				
E	Chkn								
A	Steak								
T	Hdog	⊗		⊗					

Tami: That was good, Millissent. The next clue says Bill is not the burger fan or the steak lover since he was sitting in different spots from them. So X_4 in Bill-burger and Bill-steak.

Mill: Look, we can fill in that Bill must be chicken now. All the other possibilities are eliminated. Bill brought chicken, so nobody else could have brought chicken. Cross off the rest of the chicken column.

Tami: That gives us John brought burgers, and Fred brought steak.

Mill: Great, one of our charts is done.

		OCCUPATIONS				MEAT			
		Nurse	Scty	Tchr	Pilot	Burg	Chkn	Steak	Hdog
N	Tom	X_1		X_1		X_3	X_3	X_3	O
A	John					⊚	⊗	⊗	X_3
M	Fred			X_2	X_2	X_2	⊗	⊚	X_3
E	Bill					⊗₄	⊚	⊗₄	X_3
M	Burg			X_2	X_2				
E	Chkn								
A	Steak								
T	Hdog	✗		✗					

Mill: Now we can do some more of that bouncing or cross-correlating with negative information. Look across Fred's row. Fred is the steak lover and isn't the teacher or the pilot, so the steak lover is not the teacher or the pilot. So put X's in the steak-teacher and steak-pilot spaces.

Tami: And that gives us the teacher is chicken.

Mill: It also gives us the pilot is hot dog after we cross off the rest of the chicken row and teacher column.

		OCCUPATIONS				MEAT			
		Nurse	Scty	Tchr	Pilot	Burg	Chkn	Steak	Hdog
N	Tom	X_1		X_1		X_3	X_3	X_3	O
A	John					O	✗	✗	X_3
M	Fred			X_2	X_2	X_2	✗	O	X_3
E	Bill					X_4	O	X_4	X_3
M	Burg			X_2	X_2				
E	Chkn	⊗	⊗	⊚	⊗				
A	Steak			⊗	⊗				
T	Hdog	✗	⊗	✗	⊚				

Tami: Now let's do some bouncing with positive information. We know that Tom likes hot dogs. We also know that the pilot likes hot dogs. So Tom must be the pilot. So put in an O in the pilot-Tom space.

Mill: Great, Tami. We can do the same thing with Bill. We know Bill likes chicken, and the teacher likes chicken. So Bill must be the teacher.

		OCCUPATIONS				MEAT			
		Nurse	Scty	Tchr	Pilot	Burg	Chkn	Steak	Hdog
N	Tom	X_1	⊗	X_1	Ⓞ	X_3	X_3	X_3	O
A	John			⊗	⊗	O	X	X	X_3
M	Fred			X_2	X_2	X_2	X	O	X_3
E	Bill	⊗	⊗	Ⓞ	⊗	X_4	O	X_4	X_3
M	Burg			X_2	X_2				
E	Chkn	X	X	O	X				
A	Steak			X	X				
T	Hdog	X	X	X	O				

Mill: We're almost there. The last clue says the secretary hates golf. How are we supposed to use that?

Tami: We can use that. Remember that adjunct list we made before. Let's look at that again, with the new information we have gained so far.

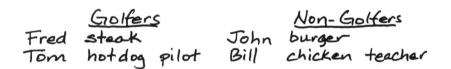

Golfers
Fred   steak
Tom   hotdog   pilot

Non-Golfers
John   burger
Bill   chicken   teacher

Mill: OK, so the secretary hates golf. That means the secretary can't be Fred, so it has to be John.

Tami: Right, and so Fred is the nurse. Great job.

		OCCUPATIONS				MEAT			
		Nurse	Scty	Tchr	Pilot	Burg	Chkn	Steak	Hdog
N	Tom	X_1	X	X_1	O	X_3	X_3	X_3	O
A	John	Ⓧ	Ⓞ	X	X	O	X	X	X_3
M	Fred	Ⓞ	Ⓧ₅	X_2	X_2	X_2	X	O	X_3
E	Bill	X	X	O	X	X_4	O	X_4	X_3
M	Burg	Ⓧ	Ⓞ	X_2	X_2				
E	Chkn	X	X	O	X				
A	Steak	Ⓞ	Ⓧ	X	X				
T	Hdog	X	X	X	O				

Tami: Let's be sure to answer the question.

Mill: OK.

Tom	hot dogs	pilot
John	burgers	secretary
Fred	steak	nurse
Bill	chicken	teacher

~~~~

Another strategy that you can employ in this type of problem is to rewrite the clues as you develop more information. Earlier we looked at a partial problem involving people, states, and favorite colors. Suppose you have already determined that the person from New Jersey's favorite color is green. Consider the clues.

1. The person whose favorite color is green went to the movie with Sara and the person whose favorite color is white.

2. The person from New Jersey is not Bob.

Since you know that the person from New Jersey's favorite color is green, the clues become:

1. The person whose favorite color is green (person from New Jersey) went to the movie with Sara and with the person whose favorite color is white.

2. The person from New Jersey (green) is not Bob.

This allows you to mark off two more squares in the chart: first, that the person from New Jersey is not Sara, and then, from the second clue, that Bob's favorite color is not green.

This method is generally referred to as substitution. The strategy of substitution gives results that are very similar to the cross-correlating with negative information strategy. In the Outdoor Barbecue problem earlier, clues 1 and 3 allowed some cross-correlating with negative information.

1. Tom is neither the nurse nor the teacher.

3. Tom brought hot dogs.

Earlier, in Millissent and Tami's solution, they cross-correlated with negative information. The same objective could be accomplished with substitution. Tom brought hot dogs. So the first clue reads, "The person who brought hot dogs is neither the nurse nor the teacher." This allows you to cross off hot dogs-teacher and hot dogs-nurse.

It is a good idea to learn both of these techniques, as one may work when the other doesn't.

Still another useful strategy is that of combining clues. Look for something that the following two clues have in common:

3. Bob, the person from New Jersey, and the person who likes blue love going to the movies each week.

4. Jane does not like the movies.

Both clues deal with people going to the movies. By combining these two clues, we see that Jane could not be one of the people who went to the movies, therefore she is not from New Jersey and she is not the person who prefers blue.

Millissent and Tami used this technique in the Outdoor Barbecue problem. Instead of making an adjunct list of golfers, they could have simply combined clues 2 and 5.

2. Fred and the pilot play golf together. The burger-lover and teacher hate golf.

5. The secretary hates golf.

These two clues could be combined and substitution could be used as well. At this point in the problem they already knew that John was the burger-lover. So John and the teacher hate golf. The secretary hates golf too, so since the secretary and the teacher can't be the same person, the secretary must be John.

One word of caution when combining clues—make sure you don't have too many people in the problem to allow this type of conclusion. Clue 2 in Outdoor Barbecue shows four people: Fred, the pilot, the burger-lover, and the teacher. Everybody in the problem is included somewhere in this clue. If the Outdoor Barbecue problem had concerned five people instead of four, there might have been three people who hated golf (hard to imagine) and the secretary and the burger-lover could have been different people.

Consider these clues.

7. The person from South Dakota and Rick like dinners out.

8. The person who likes blue likes dinners out.

Does this mean that the person who likes blue is either Rick or the person from South Dakota? No it doesn't. These clues could be referring to three different people. On the other hand (again working with the same four people from this fake problem) consider these clues.

7. The person from South Dakota and Rick like dinners out.

8. The person who likes blue likes dinners out.

9. Bob and Sara hate dinners out.

Reading these clues, five people appear to be mentioned: the person from South Dakota, Rick, the person who likes blue, Bob, and Sara. There are, however, only four people in the problem. Therefore, two of the people mentioned are actually the same person. There are two people who like dinners out and two people who don't. So clue 8 refers to one of the two people from clue 7.

Another way to handle these clues about dinners out would be to make an adjunct list.

~~~~

A comment about the introductions to problems. Some introductions tell you exactly who all the people are and what you are supposed to find. Example: "Len, Howard, and Raymond are a grocer, chemist, and model and have dogs named Clio, Fido, and Spot. Match each man's name, job, and dog." Other problems have introductions that are a little bit more vague. Example: "Three men (one is named Len) each have a different job (one is a model). Each also has a dog (one's name is Fido). From the clues below, determine each man's name, job, and dog." In this case, you would have to read the clues to find the names of the other men, the names of the other dogs, and the other occupations. You would then fill in that information in your matrix.

Another subtle point about introductions is that they sometimes hide pieces of information. Example: "Ivan and three friends (one is a mechanic) like different sports ... " From this first sentence we can see the problem concerns four people, one of whom is named Ivan. They will apparently have different jobs. The mechanic is not Ivan, because the mechanic is referred to as one of Ivan's friends. So you can cross off the Ivan-mechanic square.

The next problem features many of the techniques that have been discussed so far.

? COLLEGE APPLICATIONS

Four high school friends (one was named Cathy) were about to go to college. Their last names are Williams, Burbank, Collins, and Gunderson. Each enrolled in a different college (one was a state college). From the clues below, determine each person's full name and the college he or she attended.

1. *No student's first name begins with the same letter as her or his last name. No one's first name ends with the same letter as the end of her or his last name.*

2. *Neither Hank nor Williams went to the community college.*

3. *Alan, Collins, and the student who went to the university all live on the same street. The other student lives two blocks away.*

4. *Gladys and Hank live next door to each other.*

5. *The private college accepted Hank's application, but he decided that he could not afford to go there.*

The first thing that must be done is to determine the other three names and colleges. The first names Hank, Alan, and Gladys are mentioned in clues 2, 3, and 4 respectively. Community college, university, and private college are mentioned in clues 2, 3, and 5.

Rochelle's chart for this problem appears below.

		LAST NAMES					COLLEGES			
		Wlms	Bbnk	Clns	Gdsn	CC	State	Univ	Priv
FIRST NAMES	Hank								
	Alan								
	Gladys								
	Cathy								
COLL	CC								
	State								
	Univ								
	Priv								

Rochelle explained her solution to this problem.

"I made my chart and then I read the clues. The first clue said that the first letter of the first and last name could not be the same, and the last letter of the first and last name could not be the same either. So I went through each first name and compared the first and last letters with the different possible first and last letters of the last names. Hank started with an h and ended with a k. So his last name could not be Burbank because that ended with a k. Alan's last name could not be Gunderson because it ended with an n. Gladys's last name could not be Gunderson because it started with a G, nor could it be Collins or Williams because of the endings. Cathy's last name could not be Collins because it started with a C. I put X_1's in all these spaces to signify they were eliminated by clue 1.

"This meant that Gladys was Burbank, as that was the only last name left for her. So I put an O in the Gladys-Burbank space, and X's in the rest of the Burbank column. In the blank space in the chart I started writing down partial results."

		LAST NAMES				COLLEGES			
		Wlms	Bbnk	Clns	Gdsn	CC	State	Univ	Priv
FIRST NAME	Hank		X_1						
	Alan		X		X_1				
	Gladys	X_1	O	X_1	X_1				
	Cathy		X	X_1					
COLL	CC								
	State								
	Univ								
	Priv								

known results:
Gladys Burbank

"Next I read the second clue. Hank and Williams did not go to the community college. I could obviously put X_2's in the Hank-CC space and the Williams-CC space. However, since Hank and Williams were referred to as two people, I knew that Hank's last name could not be Williams. So I also put an X_2 in the Hank-Williams space. (Sorry, all you country-western fans.)

"Reading the next clue, I saw that Alan and Collins did not go to the university, since the clue refers to three people that live on the same street. I also knew that Alan was not Collins."

		LAST NAMES				COLLEGES			
		Wlms	Bbnk	Clns	Gdsn	CC	State	Univ	Priv
FIRST NAME	Hank	(X_2)	X_1			(X_2)			
	Alan		X	(X_3)	X_1			(X_3)	
	Gladys	X_1	O	X_1	X_1				
	Cathy		X	X_1					
COLL	CC	(X_2)							
	State								
	Univ			(X_3)					
	Priv								

known results:
Gladys Burbank

"Looking at the chart, I saw that Alan had to be Williams, because that was the only space left. I put an O in the Alan-Williams space. This meant I had to put an X in the Cathy-Williams space. But that meant that Cathy was Gunderson, which forced Hank to be Collins. So now I knew all the first and last names. I wrote all this down in my known results space."

		LAST NAMES				COLLEGES			
		Wlms	Bbnk	Clns	Gdsn	CC	State	Univ	Priv
F I R S T	N A M E	Hank							
		X_2	X_1	◎	⊗	X_2			
		Alan							
		◎	X	X_3	X_1			X_3	
		Gladys							
		X_1	O	X_1	X_1				
		Cathy							
		⊗	X	X_1	◎				
C O L L	CC	X_2							
	State								
	Univ			X_3					
	Priv								

known results:
Gladys Burbank
Hank Collins
Alan Williams
Cathy Gunderson

"At this point I had some definite connections. I reread the second and third clues and used substitution. Since I knew that Hank was Collins and Alan was Williams, the second clue read 'Neither Hank (Collins) nor Williams (Alan) went to the community college.' This allowed me to cross off the Collins-community college and the Alan-community college spaces. I put $X_{2,3}$'s in those spaces.

"Clue 3 now read, 'Alan (Williams), Collins (Hank), and the student who went to the university all live on the same street. The other student lives two blocks away.' I now knew that Williams and Hank did not go to the university. So I put $X_{2,3}$'s in those spaces also."

		LAST NAMES				COLLEGES			
		Wlms	Bbnk	Clns	Gdsn	CC	State	Univ	Priv
F I R S T	N A M E	Hank							
		X_2	X_1	O	X	X_2		$(X_{2,3})$	
		Alan							
		O	X	X_3	X_1	$(X_{2,3})$		X_3	
		Gladys							
		X_1	O	X_1	X_1				
		Cathy							
		X	X	X_1	O				
C O L L	CC	X_2		$(X_{2,3})$					
	State								
	Univ	$(X_{2,3})$		X_3					
	Priv								

known results:
Gladys Burbank
Hank Collins
Alan Williams
Cathy Gunderson

"Then I read clue 4. It said Gladys and Hank live next door to each other. Combining this with clue 3 (in substituted form), Hank Collins and Alan Williams live on the same street as the student who went to the university and the other student lives two blocks away. So Gladys must be the student who went to the university since Gladys clearly lives on the same street as Hank. I put an O_4 in the Gladys-university space, and then since Gladys's last name is Burbank, I also put an O_4 in the Burbank-university space. (Cross-correlating with positive information.) This filled in a whole bunch of X's for university, Burbank, and Gladys. When I finished filling in all those X's, I saw that Cathy Gunderson went to the community college."

		LAST NAMES				COLLEGES			
		Wlms	Bbnk	Clns	Gdsn	CC	State	Univ	Priv
FIRST NAME	Hank	X_2	X_1	O	X	X_2		$X_{2,3}$	
	Alan	O	X	X_3	X_1	$X_{2,3}$		X_3	
	Gladys	X_1	O	X_1	X_1	(X_4)	(X_4)	(O_4)	(X_4)
	Cathy	X	X	X_1	O	(O)	(X)	(X_4)	(X)
COLL	CC	X_2	(X_4)	$X_{2,3}$	(O)				
	State		(X_4)		(X)				
	Univ	$X_{2,3}$	(O_4)	X_3	(X_4)				
	Priv		(X_4)		(X)				

Known results:
Gladys Burbank—Univ.
Hank Collins
Alan Williams
Cathy Gunderson—CC

"Now all I had left to figure out was whether Hank or Alan went to the state college or the private college. The last clue said that Hank did not go to the private college. So Alan must have gone to the private college and therefore Hank went to the state college."

		LAST NAMES				COLLEGES			
		Wlms	Bbnk	Clns	Gdsn	CC	State	Univ	Priv
FIRST NAME	Hank	X_2	X_1	O	X	X_2	(O_5)	$X_{2,3}$	(X_5)
	Alan	O	X	X_3	X_1	$X_{2,3}$	(X_5)	X_3	(O_5)
	Gladys	X_1	O	X_1	X_1	X_4	X_4	O_4	X_4
	Cathy	X	X	X_1	O	O	X	X_4	X
COLL	CC	X_2	X_4	$X_{2,3}$	O				
	State	(X_5)	X_4	(O_5)	X				
	Univ	$X_{2,3}$	O_4	X_3	X_4				
	Priv	(O_5)	X_4	(X_5)	X				

So the answers are:

Hank Collins – state college

Alan Williams – private college

Gladys Burbank – university

Cathy Gunderson – community college

The completed chart contained quite a few subscripts on the X's and O's indicating the clue number that allowed Rochelle to place them in the matrix. These subscripts are useful for two reasons. First of all, if you make a mistake in solving a problem, you will have to do part of the problem over again. The subscripts give you a clue as to what information you already had before you made the mistake. Without them, you would have to start the whole problem over again. With them, you can probably just erase a few marks and start from the spot where the mistake occurred. Second, the subscripts are extremely useful for recreating your thinking on the problem after you finish solving it. If all you had were X's and O's in the matrix, you would have to do the problem again in order to explain your reasoning. The subscripts remind you why you placed each X and O in the matrix, and thus make your explanation easier to write.

~~~~

Sometimes it helps to mark the labels with additional information. This might be information that appears in an adjunct list. Another way of using this information is by making a mark next to the labels on the chart. In this example, consider these clues from the partial problem discussed earlier, paying attention to each person's gender.

5. The person from Missouri sold his skis.

6. The person who likes blue gave birth last month.

From these clues it is evident that the person from Missouri is male (sold *his* skis), and the person who likes blue is female (gave birth). This information can be marked in the chart. Notice that the names Bob and Rick are marked male (M); Sara and Jane are marked female (F).

Having identified a couple of the labels as being either male or female does help immediately in eliminating some boxes.

		FAVORITE COLOR				STATE			
		Blue (F)	Red	White	Green	SD	MO (M)	NJ	TX
F I R S T N A M E	Bob (M)	X_6							
	Sara (F)						X_5		
	Rick (M)	X_6							
	Jane (F)						X_5		
S T A T E	SD								
	MO (M)	$X_{5,6}$							
	NJ								
	TX								

Notice what was eliminated in the above chart. In the first name-state chart, although we know the person from Missouri is male, this does not determine who it is. Rather, it precludes a couple of people from being from Missouri (the women). Remember, "think negatively."

Next, in the first name-favorite color chart, we can conclude that neither Bob nor Rick prefers blue—that color is assigned to a woman.

In the state-favorite color chart, although we do not know yet all of the genders, we can determine that the person who likes blue (by our label we now know it is a woman) is not from Missouri (who we know is male).

Be careful with certain names. In this problem, it is pretty clear that Bob and Rick are men and Sara and Jane are women. However, some problems deliberately use names that could be either gender. For example, if a problem concerned four people named Kelly, Pat, Sam, and Chris, it would not be clear what gender they were. Figuring out the gender may turn out to be an important part of doing the problem. On the other hand, if a problem concerned members of a culture that you were not familiar with, you would have no way of determining gender by using the names. The moral of the story is beware of assuming anything.

With that warning on assumptions, we will consider one more substrategy: making an assumption. Making an assumption is tricky. In keeping with the idea of "thinking negatively," the most important part of making an assumption is proving your assumption incorrect. This strategy works only if you can prove that you made an incorrect assumption. The solution to the problem below employs this substrategy.

COAST TO COAST

Four women live in different cities. One of the cities is San Francisco. Determine which city each woman lives in:

1. The women from Charleston and Gainesville and Riana are not related.
2. Wendy and the woman from Provo are cousins.
3. Neither Phyllis nor Wendy is from the west coast.
4. Ann is from a coastal city.

	NAMES			
	Ann	Phyllis	Wendy	Riana
SF		X_3	X_3	
Gain	X_4			X_1
Chrl				X_1
Provo	X_4		X_2	

C I T I E S

The clues allow us to make X's in the chart above. Now assume that Riana is from Provo. If she is from Provo, then she is not from San Francisco, so Ann must be from San Francisco. You already know that Wendy is from either Charleston or from Gainesville. Reread the clues to look for a contradiction. Clue 2 says that Wendy and the woman from Provo are cousins. Since we assumed that Riana is from Provo, that means that Wendy and Riana are cousins. But clue 1 says that the women from Charleston and Gainesville and Riana are not related. Since Wendy is from either Charleston or Gainesville, clue 1 means she should not be related to Riana. But Wendy and the woman from Provo (who we assumed to be Riana) are cousins, according to clue 2. This is a contradiction which arose from an assumption. So our assumption that Riana is from Provo is false. (And proving an assumption wrong is cause for celebration: Hooray!) Therefore Riana is not from Provo.

Knowing that Riana is not from Provo allows you to mark off that box.

NAMES

		Ann	Phyllis	Wendy	Riana
C I T I E S	SF		X_3	X_3	
	Gain	X_4			X_1
	Chrl				X_1
	Provo	X_4		X_2	⊗

That now allows the conclusion that Riana is from San Francisco, and the matrix chart will solve everything else from this point on.

NAMES

		Ann	Phyllis	Wendy	Riana
C I T I E S	SF	⊗	X_3	X_3	◎
	Gain	X_4	⊗	◎	X_1
	Chrl	◎	⊗	⊗	X_1
	Provo	X_4	◎	X_2	X

The issue of who is related to whom should be checked again at this point. The women from Gainesville and Charleston are Wendy and Ann, and they are unrelated to Riana. Wendy's cousin is Phyllis (the woman from Provo) so that works.

This strategy can be very dangerous. If your assumption does not produce a contradiction, then it proves nothing. Before making an assumption, you may want to mark every known connection in the chart with pen. Then from the point you make the assumption, mark all further connections in light pencil. If you ascertain that the assumption is wrong, then that's great. If no contradictions surface, then you can erase all pencil marks and your earlier connections will still be preserved in pen.

Making an assumption should be regarded as a last resort. Don't do it unless you are completely stuck on the problem and need to try something drastic. The other substrategies explored earlier should be used first. Most logic problems do not require any assumptions to be made.

~~~~~

Many logic problems feature more people or more categories. For example, if you were given a problem that asked you to match up first names, last names, jobs, and cities, you would first have to determine how many charts to use in your matrix. A diagram, as shown earlier, can help.

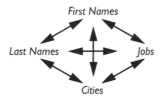

There must be a chart that matches each category with each other category. From the diagram, you can see you need the following charts.

First names and last names

First names and jobs

First names and cities

Last names and jobs

Last names and cities

Jobs and cities

You could have also made a systematic list matching two of the categories at a time. Setting the matrix up is also an important facet of solving the problem. Examine the matrix below. Note that each category will have as many entries as there are people.

	1st nm	Lst nm	Cities	Jobs
1st nm				
Lst nm				
Cities				
Jobs				

This is certainly too many charts. You don't need charts that match up first names with first names, or any other chart that matches up a category with itself. Consider the matrix below.

	1st nm	Cities	Jobs
Lst nm			
Cities			
Jobs			

This matrix is definitely an improvement, but it still has too many charts. We do not need to match a city's name to the same city's name, nor is the jobs-matched-with-jobs chart necessary. It also has two charts that match up jobs with cities. The following matrix is really useful.

	1st nm	Jobs	Cities
Lst nm			
Cities			
Jobs			

Note that the order of cities and jobs has been reversed on the top line. Having cities and jobs in a different order on the top than on the left is a way to make the matrix turn out really nicely. In general, choose one category for the top left. Choose another for the left top. The rest of the categories need to be repeated both on the top and on the left side. If you want the matrix to come out nicely, order the categories carefully.

Draw a matrix for a problem matching first names, jobs, hair color, eye color, and height.

This problem would need ten charts: names-jobs, names-hair, names-eyes, names-height, jobs-hair, jobs-eyes, jobs-height, hair-eyes, hair-height, and eyes-height

A typical matrix might look like this:

	Name	Hair	Eyes	Height
Jobs				
Height				
Eyes				
Hair				

Be sure to experiment a little bit with your matrices so that they will be really functional before you completely draw them. Use graph paper to make the lines easier to draw. And, of course, the substrategies discussed earlier apply equally well to problems with more than three charts.

Solving logic problems can improve your reasoning ability. The problems must be solved step by step, and this process is similar to making arguments based on logic. They are also fun and challenging, as all those people who buy problem-solving magazines have discovered. Enjoy the challenge.

Problem Set A

1. **CLASS SCHEDULES**

The master schedule for River High School appears below. The •'s indicate the period(s) in which a class is offered. All students must take the classes marked with *'s. The other classes are electives.

	1	2	3	4	5	6	7
*English	•		•			•	
*Math		•		•	•		
*Science			•	•			
*PE	•	•			•		
History		•					•
Drama			•				
Typing						•	•
Band	•						
*Lunch				•	•		

a. Make up a schedule for Jill. She wants to take Band and History as her electives. She needs Lunch 5th period because the science club meets then.

b. Make up a schedule for Tom. Tom wants to take Drama and Typing. He would like to have Lunch 4th period, but he doesn't care that much.

c. Make up a schedule for Leanne. Leanne wants to take Band and Drama.

d. Make up a schedule for Mea. Mea wants to take History and Typing.

e. Part 1: Jose wants to take Drama and History. Figure out his schedule.

Part 2: Jose had his schedule all figured out, but when he went to sign up for first period PE, he found out that the class was closed. The other two periods of PE were still open, however. What should he do?

Part 3:   After making a new schedule that he wasn't too happy with, Jose found out that the school was opening a new 6th period Science class. Now what should he do?

2.   **THE FISHING TRIP**

Several friends take a fishing trip every year. Each year they have a contest to see who catches the heaviest fish. The loser has to pay for all of the junk food they eat on the trip. (Second and third places are also expected to chip in token amounts.) Determine their standings in this year's contest by the following clues. By the way, in the tradition of fishing trips, everything quoted here is a falsehood.

Marta: Larry was first.

Sally: Marta beat Woody.

Woody: I beat Sally.

Larry: Woody was second.

3.   **CABINET MEMBERS**

The President was discussing some politics with the Vice President and three of her cabinet members: the secretaries of state, education, and treasury. Determine which woman (one is named Norma) holds which job.

Paula said, "Ms. President, I don't think the secretary of state knows what she is talking about. I think our foreign policy has really deteriorated lately."

(The secretary of state shook her head. So did the Vice President.)

The secretary of the treasury said, "I agree with Paula. We haven't even talked to Japan lately."

The Vice President jumped in. "Will you two leave Inez alone? She is doing a fine job."

Georgianne, who had been silent so far, finally said, "Okay, let's get on to something else."

The secretary of education said, "I'm sorry, Inez. Nothing personal."

Colleen said, "I'm sorry too, Inez. I guess we just got carried away."

Inez replied, "That's OK. I know we've all been under a lot of stress lately."

Determine the name and position of each person in this conversation.

4. VOLLEYBALL TEAM

Three friends—Elaine, Kelly, and Shannon—all start for their college volleyball team. Each plays a different position: setter, middle blocker, and outside hitter. Of the three, one is a freshman, one a sophomore, and the other a junior. From the clues below, determine each woman's position and year in school.

1. Elaine is not the setter.

2. Kelly has been in school longer than the middle blocker.

3. The middle blocker has been in school longer than the outside hitter.

4. Either Kelly is the setter or Elaine is the middle blocker.

5. MUSIC PREFERENCES

Two men (Jack and Mike) and two women (Adele and Edna) each like a different type of music (one likes jazz). Their last names are Mullin, Hardaway, Richmond, and Higgins. From the clues below, find each person's full name and favorite type of music.

1. Hardaway hates country-western music.

2. The classical music lover said she'd teach Higgins to play the piano.

3. Adele and Richmond knew the country-western fan in high school.

4. Jack and the man who likes rock music work in the same office building.

5. Richmond and Higgins are on the same bowling team. There are no men on their team.

6. SUSPECTS

The police department arrested four suspects—two men and two women—on suspicion of petty theft. The sergeant on duty who processed the suspects was having a bit of a bad day. He produced this list of suspects and descriptions.

Robin Wilde: scar on left cheek

Cary Steele: purple hair

Pat Fleece: tall and blonde

Connie Theeves: birth mark on left wrist

When the list of suspects and descriptions landed on the arresting detective's desk, he was furious.

He immediately went to the sergeant and said, "Paul, you might be having a bad day, but this list is full of mistakes. The first and last names are all mismatched. And none of the descriptions go with either the first or last name they are listed with. Do you think you can fix this?

The sergeant replied, "Sorry, Dick. I am having a bad day. But I think I need a little bit more information."

The detective answered, "OK, Paul. Here's some more info. Connie has purple hair to match her purple high tops. The men are Steele and Fleece. A woman has the scar. Do you think you can straighten this mess out now?"

The sergeant now determined the first and last names of each suspect, as well as their descriptions. You work it out too.

7. ANNIVERSARIES

Three couples are good friends. At a dinner party one night, they discovered that their anniversaries were in different months—May, June, and July. They also discovered that they had each been married a different number of years—11, 12, and 13. From the clues below, match up each husband (one is Pete) with each wife (one is Lorna), the month of their anniversary, and the number of years each has been married.

1. Jorge and his wife have three kids. Their anniversary is not in July. They have not been married as long as Tori and her husband.

2. Nylia and her husband have four kids. Their anniversary is in June. They have been married longer than Ahmed and his wife.

8. WRITE YOUR OWN

Try to write your own matrix logic problem. Or write a problem that can be solved with any previously learned strategy.

Problem Set B—Introducing the Family Family

THE PHONE NUMBER

Ed, the eldest son of the Family family, met a new girl named Candy at school at the beginning of his senior year. He really liked her and so, of course, wanted her phone number. She wouldn't tell him at first, but he persisted. He knew the first three digits were 492 because the town was so small that everyone had the same telephone prefix. Finally, one day in Physics class, she handed him a piece of paper with several numbers on it.

"The last four digits of my phone number are on this page," she explained.

3257   4682   8824   0626   4608
    8624   4632   6428   8604   8428
8064   3195   8420   4218   8240
    7915   6420   4602   2628   4178
3281   2804   4002   4826   0846
    4718   4680   6402   0428   2406

Ed protested, "But there must be 30 numbers here."

Candy laughed, "That's right. But I will give you some clues. If you really want my number, you'll figure it out."

Ed said, "OK, shoot. I'm ready."

Candy said, "Here are the clues.

1. All of the digits are even.

2. All of the digits are different.

3. The tens digit is less than the other digits.

4. The sum of the two larger digits is ten more than the sum of the two smaller digits."

Ed frantically worked away and tried to figure out which number it was. He looked up with only a few minutes left in the period. "I don't have enough information," he protested.

They were walking out after the bell rang. She said, "OK, I'll tell you the sum of all the digits." She whispered the information in his ear.

"Thanks," Ed said, because this gave him enough information to figure it out. "I'll call you tonight."

What was her phone number?

2. **A WORTHY SUITOR**

Lisa, the eldest daughter in the Family family, is a junior at the same high school that her brother attends. Ed told her about the incident with the phone number and she decided that she might use something similar sometime. Her opportunity came the next day when Ernie asked her for a date. She liked Ernie, but she couldn't resist a good puzzle. So she decided to test Ernie's puzzling skill.

"OK, Ernie, I'd like to go out with you, but I need to see if we're compatible puzzlers. You can discern that there are five ways to add up four even positive numbers (not including zero) and get a sum of 16."

Ernie replied, "Oh sure, I can do that." And he whipped out a paper and pencil and wrote down:

$$2 + 2 + 2 + 10 = 16$$
$$2 + 2 + 4 + 8 = 16$$
$$2 + 2 + 6 + 6 = 16$$
$$2 + 4 + 4 + 6 = 16$$
$$4 + 4 + 4 + 4 = 16$$

Lisa said, "Good job. Now, if you can do this problem, I'll go out with you. How many ways are there to add up six even positive numbers (again, not including zero) to get a sum of 26?"

Ernie did it. You do it too.

3. **THE SPORTING EVENTS**

Papa Family just got a new job at the recreation department. His first task is to schedule the playing field for the afternoons of the upcoming week. His first priority in scheduling is to make his three children—Ed, Lisa, and Judy—happy. They are all supposed to have games of their various sports during this week after school. He also wants to make his wife (Mama Family) happy. She is taking a golf class that needs to use the field. Use the information below and help Papa figure out the schedule that will satisfy the desires of the members of his family.

1. The only days available are Monday, Tuesday, Thursday, and Friday.

2. Lisa wants to watch the baseball game, but she has play rehearsal after school on Tuesday and Thursday.

3. Lisa and Judy have no interest in seeing each other play, because they have been in a big fight recently due to the fact that Judy likes Ernie too, and he asked Lisa out.

4. One daughter wants her ultimate Frisbee event to precede the soccer game and the golf class, because soccer players and golfers tear up the field.

5. Ed is going to visit colleges on the weekend, and wants to get an early start immediately after school on Friday.

4. THE BILLBOARD

Ed, the eldest child of the Family family, went to work for an advertising company after school and on Saturdays. For his first assignment he hired himself to create a billboard. The billboard will be 20 feet high and will proclaim his love for Candy (the girl, not the sweets). He decided that each letter should be 2 feet high, and that there will be a one-half foot space between the bottom of one line and the top of the next line. In addition, he wants $1\frac{1}{2}$ foot borders at both the top and bottom of the billboard. How many lines of words can Ed fit on the billboard?

5. THOSE AMAZING NAMES

Papa Family was sitting at the kitchen table one day, looking at a piece of paper with his children's names written on it.

The paper read:

LISA

JUDY

EDWARD

He said to Mama Family, "You know, the names of our kids almost make one of these cryptarithm word arithmetic problems."

Mama said, "Let me see." She looked at the paper. "Papa, you forgot, Ed's name is Eduard with a U, not a W. And Lisa's name is really Elisa, but we don't call her that much anymore since she got in high school and decided that Lisa is prettier. And don't you remember about Judy's name? It's really Ajudy."

"Oh yeah," Papa said. "I forgot about that. The nurse came into the delivery room and said, 'Well, what do we have here, a Kathy?' and you said, 'No—a Judy.' What a surprise when the birth certificate actually had 'Ajudy' written on it."

Mama said, "Look, Papa, if you use their real names, it does work as a word arithmetic problem."

She wrote down:

$$\begin{array}{r} \text{E L I S A} \\ + \text{A J U D Y} \\ \hline \text{E D U A R D} \end{array}$$

Together, she and Papa solved it in a few minutes. Can you? Each letter stands for one of the digits 0 to 9 and no two letters stand for the same digit.

5

look for a pattern

THE STUDY of mathematics is often called the study of patterns. Patterns show up everywhere. In everyday life, there are thousands of patterns: wallpaper, traffic, automobile design, weekday afternoon TV schedules, arrangements of cabinet doors, pool tiles, fence links. In problem solving, patterns can repeat and extend indefinitely. Recognizing patterns and extending them are problem-solving skills that will be developed in this chapter.

Finding patterns is extremely useful in real life. Detectives look for patterns of behavior in order to determine the type of person who is committing a crime. They also attempt to link similar crimes together in order to strengthen the existing evidence. People involved in research need to be able to detect patterns in order to isolate variables and reach valid conclusions. A child uses patterns to learn about the world. For example, children learn to differentiate between positive and negative behavior as they recognize patterns in their parents' reactions.

Finding patterns is also a good problem-solving strategy. It enables you to reduce a complex problem to a pattern and then use the pattern to derive a solution. Often the key to finding a pattern is to organize information. Organizing information is one of the three major areas that will be discussed in this book.

This chapter starts with sequences in math. A sequence is simply a string of numbers tied together with some sort of consistent rule (or set of rules) that determines the next number in the sequence.

Consider this sequence: 3, 7, 11, 15, ___, ___, ___, ___.

The rule appears to be adding 4 to each number to generate the next term in the sequence: 3, 7, 11, 15, **19**, **23**, **27**, **31**.

◀ *A fabric designer looks for patterns that are aesthetically pleasing. Looking for patterns is also a powerful method for solving problems in mathematics.*

Theoretically, the sequence could also be continued by repeating the first four numbers: 3, 7, 11, 15, **3, 7, 11, 15**.

For the purposes of this text, the repeating pattern is declared null, void, illegal, invalid, unconstitutional, unpatriotic, immoral, corrupt, and not at all nice. In other words, don't take the cheap way out on these. Find the pattern and apply it to find subsequent numbers in the sequence.

The following are examples of sequences in math.

SEQUENCES

Find the pattern and predict the next four terms. Then write a sentence explaining your pattern.

1. *1, 2, 4, ____, ____, ____, ____*
2. *1, 3, 5, 7, ____, ____, ____, ____*
3. *1, 6, 11, 16, ____, ____, ____, ____*
4. *1, 4, 9, 16, ____, ____, ____, ____*
5. *1, 3, 6, 10, ____, ____, ____, ____*
6. *3, 6, 5, 10, 9, 18, 17, 34, ____, ____, ____, ____*
7. *77, 49, 36, 18, ____ (the sequence ends there)*

Solve the above problems before continuing on.

The first sequence illustrates an important point. Here are two possible answers with rule explanations.

a. 1, 2, 4, **8, 16, 32, 64** (Double each number to get the next term in the sequence.)

b. 1, 2, 4, **7, 11, 16, 22** (Add one higher number each time. It starts off as "add 1," then "add 2," then "add 3," and so on.)

As you can see, there is more than one reasonable, correct answer to this sequence. Each answer follows a *consistent* rule. Therefore, from this point on, you must check your answers with extreme caution. Those who come up with the same answer as the authors are obviously geniuses. Those who have different answers, double-check to make sure that you are applying your rule in a consistent manner. It is quite possible that some of these sequences have more than one verifiable correct answer. There may also be different patterns to arrive at the same answers (see numbers 2 and 4 below).

These are the common answers, although you may be able to justify a different set of answers.

2. 1, 3, 5, 7, **9, 11, 13, 15**, ...

3. 1, 6, 11, 16, **21, 26, 31, 36**, ...

4. 1, 4, 9, 16, **25, 36, 49, 64**, ...

5. 1, 3, 6, 10, **15, 21, 28, 36**, ...

6. 3, 6, 5, 10, 9, 18, 17, 34, **33, 66, 65, 130**, ...

7. 77, 49, 36, 18, **8** (No further terms)

See if you can decipher the patterns that you didn't get—before you read the explanations below.

2. 1, 3, 5, 7, 9, 11, 13, 15, ...
Here the pattern is clearly odd numbers. But there are many ways to explain it:

a. The pattern is the odd numbers.

b. Add two to the previous number to get the next number.

c. Take the number of the term, double that number and subtract 1. For example, the third term is 5. If we double the term number 3 and subtract 1, we get $2 \times 3 - 1 = 5$. The eighth term is 15, because $2 \times 8 - 1 = 15$.

3. 1, 6, 11, 16, 21, 26, 31, 36, ...
To get the next number, add 5 to the previous number. $1^{st}, 6^{th}, 11^{th}$, and so on.

4. 1, 4, 9, 16, 25, 36, 49, 64, ...
Most people see this pattern in one of these ways:

a. To get the next number, add an odd number. To get the number after that, add the next odd number. Continue in this way, adding successive odd numbers. So first we add 3, then 5, then 7, etc., always adding the next odd number.

b. To get the next number, begin by adding 3 to the first number, and then add 2 more than you added last time: 1^{+3}, 4^{+5}, 9^{+7}, 16^{+9}, 25^{+11}, ...

(Note: this is essentially the same as adding successive odd numbers, but is seen in a slightly different way.)

c. The sequence is the sequence of square numbers. So the first number is 1×1 or 1^2. The second number is 2^2. The third number is 3^2. The fourth number is 4^2, and so on.

Note: These numbers are called "square" because you can form squares out of them.

$1^2 = 1$ $2^2 = 4$ $3^2 = 9$ $4^2 = 16$ $5^2 = 25$

The pattern of adding odd numbers can also be seen in this diagram of squares. In each successive diagram, the bottom and right sides of the square have been added. The number of dots required is always the next odd number.

$1^2 = 1$ $2^2 = 4$ $3^2 = 9$ $4^2 = 16$ $5^2 = 25$

5. 1, 3, 6, 10, 15, 21, 28, 36, ...

Start by adding 2 to the first number. Then add 3. Then add 4. Each time, add 1 more than you added last time: 1^{+2}, 3^{+3}, 6^{+4}, 10^{+5}, and so on. This sequence is often referred to as the triangular numbers, because you can form triangles out of them. In each successive diagram, you are adding one more dot than you added to the last term to make the next bottom row.

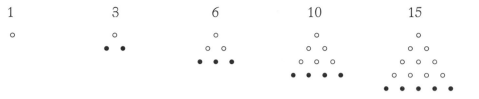

| 1 | 3 | 6 | 10 | 15 |

6. 3, 6, 5, 10, 9, 18, 17, 34, 33, 66, 65, 130, ...

This is a different kind of a pattern. First we multiply the first number by two to get the next number. Then to get the next number we subtract 1. Then we again multiply by 2. Then again subtract 1. We continue in this way, alternately multiplying by 2 and subtracting 1. So 2×3 gives 6. Then $6 - 1$ gives 5; $5 \times 2 = 10$; $10 - 1 = 9$. After that, $9 \times 2 = 18$ and $18 - 1 = 17$. The pattern continues in this way.

7. 77, 49, 36, 18, 8 (No further terms)

This is a very strange pattern. It doesn't fit much of what we have done so far. This illustrates the need to be mentally flexible when dealing with patterns. This time, we treat the digits in the number as separate numbers and multiply them together. So $7 \times 7 = 49$. Then $4 \times 9 = 36$. Then $3 \times 6 = 18$. Then $1 \times 8 = 8$, and the pattern is over. You might try to make up a problem like this, starting with a two-digit number, and see if you can come up with a longer sequence.

Patterns can be used to solve problems. After you find the pattern, the solution is easier to derive. Patterns can reduce the difficulty of complex problems.

There is a joke among radio broadcasters about the number of people who start leaving Dodger Stadium in the seventh inning of baseball games. One evening, during a particularly boring baseball game in which the Dodgers were trailing by six runs after six innings, the fans began to leave at a record pace. After the first out in the top of the seventh inning, 100 fans left. After the second out, 150 fans left. After the third out, 200 fans left. The pattern continued in this way, with 50 more fans leaving after each out than had left after the previous out. The ridiculous thing was, the Dodgers tied up the game in the bottom of the ninth inning, and people still kept leaving early. The game lasted ten innings (the Dodgers lost anyway), and the pattern continued through the bottom of the tenth inning. How many fans left early?

Work this problem before continuing.

Chemene wrote the following solution.

"My first reaction was, 'Holy cow, there won't be any fans left at the end of the game.' But after the panic subsided I was ready. And as I thought about my visit to Dodger Stadium a few summers ago when we visited L.A., I realized that the problem was probably accurate. Anyway, I made a chart."

Inning	Out	Fans leaving	Fans who've left so far
top 7th	1	100	100
top 7th	2	150	250
top 7th	3	200	450
bot 7th	1	250	700
bot 7th	2	300	1000
bot 7th	3	350	1350
top 8th	1	400	1750
top 8th	2	450	2200

"At this point, I realized that this was going to take forever and there had to be a more efficient way. After I thought about it a little more, I realized from the top of the seventh inning to the bottom of the tenth, there were going to be 24 outs. So on my next chart, I just counted outs instead of writing the inning too. This was my next chart."

Out	Fans leaving	Fans who've left so far
1	100	100
2	150	250
3	200	450
4	250	700
5	300	1000

"At this point, I realized I could do this in a different way. I made a third chart. This time I set up the chart so that I could read down to get the total number of fans leaving after each out. I broke up each out into the 100 fans that leave every time, plus the 50 more fans that leave for each out after the first out. For example, after the fourth out, 250 fans had left. This breaks down into $100 + 50 + 50 + 50$, which is the way it is shown in the chart below. For each successive out, I just added in another row of 50 fans leaving from then until the end."

Out #	1	2	3	4	5	6	7	...	Total
Base fans leaving	100	100	100	100	100	100	100	...	2400
Additional fans leaving		50	50	50	50	50	50	...	1150
Additional fans leaving			50	50	50	50	50	...	1100
Additional fans leaving				50	50	50	50	...	1050

"To get the totals on the right, I just multiplied. There were 24 outs of 100 people leaving. Then 23 outs of 50 people leaving. Then 22 outs of 50 people leaving, etc. I then totaled up the amount at the side, which, of course, showed a pattern after the first 2400. (1150 + 1100 + 1050 + 1000 + …) I then totaled up the subtotals to get my answer. So 16,200 people left early. But that includes the people who left after the last out, which technically isn't early. If we don't include the 1250 people who left right after the last out, then 14,950 people left early."

Chemene realized that her first few attempts would have worked but would have taken forever. She didn't hesitate to abandon one chart in favor of another. Her third chart clearly showed a pattern, which she used to solve the problem.

~~~~~

All of the work in this chapter deals with some sort of sequence which shows a pattern. These next problems are sequences taken from algebra. They are models of functions. A function assigns an output to each input. There is a consistent rule in each problem that turns the input number into the output number. For example, consider the following function. Take the input number, multiply it by 5, and then add 4. This would produce the table of values shown to the right. If 8 were the input, what would be the output?

IN	OUT
0	4
1	9
2	14
3	19
4	24

It is usually quite easy to use the rule for a function to figure out the table of values. It is another matter to start with the table of values and figure out the rule for the function. Patterns can help you do this.

Determine the rule for each of the functions shown below. Then fill in the outputs for the inputs 5 and 895.

IN	OUT	IN	OUT	IN	OUT	IN	OUT
M	?	N	?	P	?	Q	?
0	5	0	0	0	-3	0	0
1	6	1	2	1	-1	1	-1
2	7	2	4	2	1	2	-2
3	8	3	6	3	3	3	-3
4	9	4	8	4	5	4	-4
5	?	5	?	5	?	5	?
895	?	895	?	895	?	895	?

Hint: If you can't figure out what the rule is, simply treat each problem as if it were a sequence written vertically. Note: These are four separate problems.

In each of these problems, the pattern you're looking for depends on the term. In the first one, the pattern could have been written as a sequence:

5, 6, 7, 8, 9, __, __, __, __

In order to find the next four terms, you simply add one to each previous term:

$5^{+1}, 6^{+1}, 7^{+1}, 8^{+1}, 9^{+1}$, __, __, __, __

So the next numbers are 10, 11, 12, 13, and so on.

Written in this chart form, however, you may see it more as a rule relative to a certain term. When M is 2, the output is 7. When M is 4, the output is 9. Adding 5 to the input seems to work. A little thought shows you that this works all the time. Set up in this form, determining the answer for an input of 895 would be fairly easy: $895 + 5 = 900$. The difference between the two methods becomes more apparent on the more difficult patterns.

M	?
0	5
1	6
2	7
3	8
4	9

The outputs for N are just twice N, so the rule is $2N$. The output for 895 is 1790.

The problem involving P is the most difficult of these. If you extend this chart and compare it to the chart from the previous problem, you might notice that the ? column almost keeps up with twice the P column.

P	?	N	?
0	-3	0	0
1	-1	1	2
2	1	2	4
3	3	3	6
4	5	4	8
5	7	5	10
6	9	6	12
7	11	7	14

A quick glance shows that the output column for N is 3 more than the output column for P. So the rule for P is output $= 2P - 3$. Note that both functions have in common that the output numbers successively increase by 2. The output for $P = 895$ is $2(895) - 3 = 1787$.

The rule for the last problem is quite obviously change the sign of the number. So the output for $Q = 895$ is $^-895$.

Jamie wanted to buy a rabbit. She had always liked the Easter bunny when she was a kid, so she decided to raise some bunnies of her own. She went to the store with the intention of buying one rabbit, but she ended up with two newborn rabbits, a male and a female. She named them Patrick and Susan. Well, rabbits being what they are (rabbits), it is fairly impossible to have just two rabbits for an extended period of time. She bought them on April 1, 1991, which happened to be the day after Easter that year. On June 1, she noticed that Patrick and Susan were now the proud parents of two newborn rabbits, again one male and one female. She named these new arrivals Thomas and Ursula.

On July 1, Patrick and Susan again gave birth to a male and female rabbit. She named these Vida and Wanda.

On August 1, Patrick and Susan again gave birth to a male and a female. But Jamie was really surprised to see that Thomas and Ursula also gave birth to a male and a female. Allyson was running out of names, so she didn't bother giving them any.

On September 1, Patrick and Susan gave birth to a male and a female, and so did Thomas and Ursula, and so did Vida and Wanda. (Actually, Vida was no longer Vida and Thomas was no longer Thomas. Jamie was worried about maintaining a diverse genetic pool among her bunnies, so she traded the original Thomas and Vida to other breeders and named their replacements with the same names.)

Jamie also noticed a pattern. A pair of rabbits was born. Two months later they bred a pair of rabbits, and continued to breed a pair of rabbits every month after that. Jamie wondered, "If this keeps up, how many rabbits am I going to have on April 1 of 1992?"

Do this problem before continuing on to the next page.

Four students—whose names just happened to be Pat, Sue, Tom, and Ula—worked on this problem.

Pat: Wow, this is weird, these rabbits have the same names as we do.

Tom: Let's try and do this problem, okay? We don't need to know whether the rabbits are named after us.

Pat: I just thought it was interesting.

Ula: How are we going to do this? I'm totally confused.

Sue: Let's try making a systematic list.

Pat: Okay, let's see, we've got adult rabbits and baby rabbits.

Sue: Yeah, but we also have teenage rabbits. Like after Thomas and Ursula were born on June 1, they didn't have babies until August 1. So in July, they were just teenagers.

Ula: Let's get all this down in a chart. Then maybe we can find a pattern.
  (Ula began writing a chart.)
  All numbers represent pairs of rabbits.

Month	Adults	Teenagers	Babies	Total
April	0 pr	0 pr	1 pr	1 pr

Tom: That's great, Ula. Okay, so in May, Patrick and Susan grow to be teenagers. And then in June they become adults and they have babies: Thomas and Ursula. And in July they have more babies.

Month	Adults	Teenagers	Babies	Total
April	0 pr	0 pr	1 pr	1 pr
May	0	1	0	1
June	1	0	1	2
July	1	1	1	3
August	2	1	2	5

Sue: Wait, how did you get August?

Ula: Well, in August, Thomas and Ursula grew up to be adults, and they had babies. So did Patrick and Susan.

Pat: Who are the teenagers?

Tom: Vida and Wanda. They were babies in July, so they are teenagers in August.

Pat: Oh, I think I see a pattern. The adults is the same number as the babies, because each pair of adults has a pair of babies.

Sue: Yeah, and the ones who are babies this month become teenagers next month.

Ula: Right. And the adults are whoever were adults last month plus whoever were teenagers last month.

Tom: I think we can figure this out now.

Month	Adults	Teenagers	Babies	Total
April	0 pr	0 pr	1 pr	1 pr
May	0	1	0	1
June	1	0	1	2
July	1	1	1	3
August	2	1	2	5
September	3	2	3	8
October	5	3	5	13
November	8	5	8	21
December	13	8	13	34
January	21	13	21	55
February	34	21	34	89
March	55	34	55	144
April	89	55	89	233

Tom: I think we are done. Allyson has 233 pairs of rabbits on April 1 of the next year. Great job, guys.

Sue: Wait a second. I see a pattern here. Look down the total column. You just have to add the two numbers above it to get the next number.

Pat: What?

Tom: I see what she means. Look at the top of the total column. The first two numbers are 1 and 1. The next number is 2 which is 1 + 1. The next number is 3 which is 1 + 2. The next number is 5 which is 2 + 3. Then look, 8 is 3 + 5. So just add the two numbers above to get the next number.

Ula: Neat. And look, the same thing happens in all of the other columns, but starting later. And the numbers in each column are the same: 1, 1, 2, 3, 5, 8, 13, 21, 34, …

Pat: Wow, that's cool. I think this sequence has a name. The Liberace sequence, maybe?

Ula: I think it's the Fibonacci sequence. It's named after some Italian guy.

Tom: I guess when you think you're done, maybe you're not. It's kind of neat to look back and find the pattern. With that pattern it would be really easy to keep going.

Sue: Yeah, but let's not. But we might see that pattern again someday.

This problem illustrates the efficacy of finding a pattern. The group found a pattern in what was going on, but they didn't catch the number pattern until they were all done. And Tom is right, it's always good to look back at your work and notice things you might have missed, and to make sure your answer is reasonable.

~~~~~

The Fibonacci sequence is named after thirteenth-century mathematician Leonardo of Pisa (ca. 1180–1250), who worked under the name Fibonacci. The sequence that bears his name shows up in some surprising places in nature. For instance, if you count the two sets of spirals on a pinecone, you will always get consecutive Fibonacci numbers. A pinecone might have eight spirals going in one direction and thirteen in the other direction, for example. The same thing also happens in sunflowers, pineapples, cacti, and other plants. You can probably find information about Fibonacci in an encyclopedia or a history of mathematics book.

FIBONACCI SEQUENCES

Find the next four values of each of these sequences.

1. 2, 2, 4, 6, 10, 16, 26, ___, ___, ___, ___

2. 1, 3, 4, 7, 11, 18, 29, ___, ___, ___, ___

3. 3, 1, 4, 5, 9, 14, ___, ___, ___, ___

4. 1, 2, 3, 6, 11, 20, 37, ___, ___, ___, ___

5. ___, ___, ___, ___ 16, 25, 41, 66, 107

Work the above sequences before continuing.

1. 2, 2, 4, 6, 10, 16, 26, **42**, **68**, **110**, **178**, ...

   This is an ordinary, straight Fibonacci sequence where you add two numbers to find the next one in the sequence. This one started with a "seed" of 2, 2.

2. 1, 3, 4, 7, 11, 18, 29, **47**, **76**, **123**, **199**, ...

   The second one also is found by adding two numbers together. In this case it started with a "seed" of 1, 3. This is often referred to as the Lucas sequence.

3. 3, 1, 4, 5, 9, 14, **23**, **37**, **60**, **97**, ...

   This sequence was produced by reversing the seed of the previous sequence. Again, by adding two numbers, each of the next terms was developed.

4. 1, 2, 3, 6, 11, 20, 37, **68**, **125**, **230**, **423**, ...

   This sequence turns out to be a variation. The seed in this case was 1, 2, 3, and then three numbers were added to produce the fourth. This could easily be mistaken for a "sum of two numbers" Fibonacci sequence, as the first two numbers in the seed add up to equal to the third.

5. **5**, **2**, **7**, **9**, 16, 25, 41, 66, 107, ...

   Again, this one is based on adding two numbers, but the process is reversed because the seed and the next two numbers are missing. However, it's not too difficult to reverse the process and find the missing numbers.

Find the next four terms of these sequences.

1. 2, 3, 5, 9, 17, 33, ____, ____, ____, ____
2. 1, 5, 13, 29, 61, 125, ____, ____, ____, ____
3. 1, 4, 13, 40, 121, 364, ____, ____, ____, ____

Find the next four terms of each of these sequences before continuing.

In order to solve the first sequence, write the difference between each pair of numbers: that is, the number you have to add to a term to get the next term.

2^{+1}, 3^{+2}, 5^{+4}, 9^{+8}, 17^{+16}, 33, ___, ___, ___, ___

The difference between each pair of numbers shows an exponential sequence. The sequence shows up very well if you place one above the other.

1	2	4	8	16					
1,	3,	5,	9,	17,	33,	___,	___,	___,	___

The top row is a pure exponential sequence; the one below is the same thing, but with 1 added to each term: 2, 3, 5, 9, 17, 33, **65, 129, 257, 513**.

≈≈≈

Sequence 2 is also related to an exponential sequence. It becomes evident by looking at the differences.

1^{+4}, 5^{+8}, 13^{+16}, 29^{+32}, 61^{+64}, 125, ___, ___, ___, ___

Again, the powers of 2 show up: 1, 2, 4, 8, 16, 32. In this case, however, the first two terms of the sequence have been truncated. By placing one series over the other, we get:

4	8	16	32	64					
1,	5,	13,	29,	61,	125,	___,	___,	___,	___

By extending the sequence of differences out a few more terms, it becomes more obvious.

4	8	16	32	64	128	**256**	**512**	**1024**	**2048**
1,	5,	13,	29,	61,	125,	**253,**	**509,**	**1021,**	**2045**

So, evidently this sequence is 3 less than the exponential sequence of powers of 2.

~~~~

Approach sequence 3 in the same manner, by taking a look at the differences (written as sums) between terms in the sequence.

$$1^{+3}, 4^{+9}, 13^{+27}, 40^{+81}, 121^{+243}, 364, \underline{}, \underline{}, \underline{}, \underline{}$$

In this case, the sequence of differences looks suspiciously like powers of 3. You can continue the sequence using the pattern:

$$\ldots, 364^{+729}, \mathbf{1093^{+2187}}, \mathbf{3280^{+6561}}, \mathbf{9841^{+19683}}, \mathbf{29524}$$

The actual rule for the nth term of the sequence is difficult to derive.

RETURN OF THE HOWLING DOGS

Shawna liked to jog late at night. One night she noticed an unusual phenomenon: as she jogged, dogs would hear her and bark. After the first dog had barked for about 15 seconds, two other dogs would join in and bark. And then in about another 15 seconds, it seemed that each barking dog would "inspire" two more dogs to start barking. Of course, long after Shawna passed the first dog, it continued to bark, as dogs are inclined to do. After about 3 minutes, how many dogs were barking (as a result of Shawna passing the first dog)?

Work this problem before continuing.

Joan solved the Return of the Howling Dogs problem.

"This sounds like my neighborhood, every night, all night long. I started out by trying to draw a diagram of what was going on. It was a mess."

ROVER (DOG #1)

"The biggest problem seemed to be that the first dog doesn't just stop, but continues barking and continues inciting more dogs into stupid barking frenzies. And every other dog that starts barking also incites new dogs to bark.

"The second time I tried this problem, I decided to try to organize the problem into a chart. This was far more successful. The first dog barks and causes the other two to bark. The first dog continues barking and causes two more to bark (under the "3rd set of barkers") and then the first dog continues to bark and causes two more to bark (under the "4th set of barkers") and so on. The first row shows the original dog and the two dogs every 15 seconds that he or she inspires."

1ST BARKER	2ND SET BARKERS	3RD SET BARKERS	4TH SET BARKERS	5TH SET BARKERS
1	2	2	2	2

"Then I had to figure out a way to record the dogs that were inspired to bark by the dogs Rover inspired. See, the first two dogs that Rover inspired are, in turn going to inspire other dogs to bark every 15 seconds. Those two dogs will each inspire two new dogs every 15 seconds after they start barking. So four new dogs start barking each 15 seconds. I recorded this in the second row. It shows the first two dogs inspired by Rover (circled before the colon), and the four dogs that take up barking every 15 seconds thereafter that are inspired by those same two second-round barkers."

1ST BARKER	2ND SET BARKERS	3RD SET BARKERS	4TH SET BARKERS	5TH SET BARKERS
1	2	2	2	2
	(2:)	4	4	4

"So the chart now shows the original dog, Rover, and the dogs inspired by Rover in the first row, and it shows the set of four dogs that Dot and Spot inspired every 15 seconds. Dot and Spot themselves are shown circled at the beginning of the second row; their sets of 'inspired followers' are the 4's that follow them.

"Now the third row. There were two dogs inspired by Rover and 4 inspired by Dot, and Spot in the third set of barkers. These six dogs will each inspire two dogs every 15 seconds from then on. The third row lists these six dogs (circled in front of the colon) and the twelve dogs they inspire every 15 seconds thereafter.

"Similarly, the fourth row starts with 18 dogs (2 + 4 + 12) that inspire 36 dogs thereafter."

1ST BARKER	2ND SET BARKERS	3RD SET BARKERS	4TH SET BARKERS	5TH SET BARKERS
(1:)	2	2	2	2
	(2:)	4	4	4
		(6:)	12	12
			(18:)	36
				(54:)

TOTAL DOGS BARKING: $1 \, ^{+2}$ $3 \, ^{+6}$ $9 \, ^{+18}$ 27

"The totals column actually adds the circled numbers before the colon. At the start, there is just Rover. After one generation, there are Rover, Dot, and Spot, for a total of three dogs barking. After the next generation, there are Rover, Dot, Spot, and six more dogs for a total of nine. Those 9 then get 18 more riled up for a total of 27 barking dogs. Each of those gets 2 more dogs excited apiece, or 54 dogs plus those 27 makes 81.

"Then I looked for a pattern. The sequence of total barking dogs is 1, 3, 9, 27, 81. These were the powers of 3: 3^0, 3^1, 3^2, 3^3, 3^4, and so on.

"After 3 minutes, there are twelve 15-second intervals. So not only is it 3^0 for the original Rover, but you must also take 3^{12} for the 12 intervals. There are now 531,441 dogs barking.

"By the way, this answer may seem completely unbelievable and unreasonable to you. However, if you've been around my neighborhood at night, you would probably think the answer was pretty close to reasonable, if not dead-on."

Loc had a different way of setting up the chart for this problem to find a pattern. He organized his chart as shown below. The dogs barking column refers to the number of dogs that were barking at the beginning of the round. The new dogs barking refers to the dogs that start barking during that round, and the total dogs barking is the number of dogs that are barking at the end of the round. The total dogs barking for one round becomes the dogs barking for the next round.

Time	Round	Dogs Barking	New Dogs Barking	Total Dogs Barking
0	0	0	1	$1 = 3^0$
:15	1	1	2	$3 = 3^1$
:30	2	3	6	$9 = 3^2$
:45	3	9	18	$27 = 3^3$
1:00	4	27	54	$81 = 3^4$

So Loc also concluded that at the end of the 3 minutes, which would be 12 rounds, there would be 3^{12} dogs barking.

Alysia and Melissa and Dante and Melody loved milk. They convinced their older brother, Mark, who did all the shopping, to buy them each their own gallon of milk because they each liked it so much. They all put their names on their gallons. One day, they were all really thirsty and each took ten drinks according to a different system. Alysia started by drinking half of the milk in her container. Then she drank one-third of what was left. Then she drank one-fourth of what was left, then one-fifth, and so on.

Melissa started by drinking one-eleventh of her milk, then one-tenth of what was left, then one-ninth of what was left, and so on.

Dante started by drinking one-half of his milk, then two-thirds of what was left, then three-fourths of what was left, then four-fifths, and so on.

Melody started by drinking one-half of her milk, then one-half of what was left, then one-half of what was left, and so on.

After each had taken ten drinks, how much milk remained in each container?

Work this problem before continuing.

Bimiljit answered the problem in this way.

"This problem seemed a little tough. I examined Melody's usage first as it seemed to be the easiest. I made a chart and looked for a pattern. Example: On the second drink, she drank one-half of the remaining half, which is one-fourth of the whole container. This leaves her with one-fourth of the whole container."

Drink #	Amount drunk	Amount remaining
1	$\frac{1}{2}$	$1 - \frac{1}{2} = \frac{1}{2}$
2	$\frac{1}{2} \times \frac{1}{2} = \frac{1}{4}$	$\frac{1}{2} - \frac{1}{4} = \frac{1}{4}$
3	$\frac{1}{2} \times \frac{1}{4} = \frac{1}{8}$	$\frac{1}{4} - \frac{1}{8} = \frac{1}{8}$

"The pattern for the amount remaining was pretty obvious ($1/2$, $1/4$, $1/8$, $1/16$, etc.), so I looked at each denominator as a power of 2, and it turned out it matched up completely with which drink she was working on. (Like $1/8$ is $1/2^3$ after the third drink.) So after ten drinks, Melody would have $1/2^{10} = 1/1024$ of her milk left. That's not very much.

"I then tried to make the same kind of chart for Alysia, as her's seemed to be the next easiest. On her second drink, she drinks $\frac{1}{3}$ of the remaining half. This is $\frac{1}{6}$ of the whole container. Subtracting $\frac{1}{6}$ from $\frac{1}{2}$ gives $\frac{1}{3}$ left in the container after two drinks."

Drink #	Amount drunk	Amount remaining
1	$\frac{1}{2}$	$1 - \frac{1}{2} = \frac{1}{2}$
2	$\frac{1}{3} \times \frac{1}{2} = \frac{1}{6}$	$\frac{1}{2} - \frac{1}{6} = \frac{1}{3}$
3	$\frac{1}{4} \times \frac{1}{3} = \frac{1}{12}$	$\frac{1}{3} - \frac{1}{12} = \frac{1}{4}$
4	$\frac{1}{5} \times \frac{1}{4} = \frac{1}{20}$	$\frac{1}{4} - \frac{1}{20} = \frac{1}{5}$

"I couldn't believe how easy this pattern was once I saw it. The numerator is 1 and the denominator is one more than the drink number. The tenth drink would leave $\frac{1}{11}$ of the milk remaining.

"Next I tried doing Melissa's. Hers seemed to be a little harder."

Drink #	Amount drunk	Amount remaining
1	$\frac{1}{11}$	$1 - \frac{1}{11} = \frac{10}{11}$
2	$\frac{1}{10} \times \frac{10}{11} = \frac{1}{11}$	$\frac{10}{11} - \frac{1}{11} = \frac{9}{11}$
3	$\frac{1}{9} \times \frac{9}{11} = \frac{1}{11}$	$\frac{9}{11} - \frac{1}{11} = \frac{8}{11}$
.		
.		
.		
10	$\frac{1}{2} \times \frac{2}{11} = \frac{1}{11}$	$\frac{2}{11} - \frac{1}{11} = \frac{1}{11}$

"The pattern wasn't hard to see: it keeps going down by $\frac{1}{11}$. But the end was hard to figure out. I figured out that the pattern for the numerator goes 10, 9, 8, 7, 6, 5, 4, 3, 2, 1. So after ten drinks, she would have $\frac{1}{11}$ of her milk left. The amazing thing was that it was the same as Alysia's.

"Dante's seemed like the hardest. But the chart and pattern finding was working so well, I just kept at it."

Drink #	Amount drunk	Amount remaining
1	$\frac{1}{2}$	$1 - \frac{1}{2} = \frac{1}{2}$
2	$\frac{2}{3} \times \frac{1}{2} = \frac{1}{3}$	$\frac{1}{2} - \frac{1}{3} = \frac{1}{6}$
3	$\frac{3}{4} \times \frac{1}{6} = \frac{1}{8}$	$\frac{1}{6} - \frac{1}{8} = \frac{1}{24}$
4	$\frac{4}{5} \times \frac{1}{24} = \frac{1}{30}$	$\frac{1}{24} - \frac{1}{30} = \frac{1}{120}$
5	$\frac{5}{6} \times \frac{1}{120} = \frac{1}{144}$	$\frac{1}{120} - \frac{1}{144} = \frac{1}{720}$

"This pattern was much harder to find. I couldn't see any pattern at all in the amount he drank. But the denominators of the amount remaining looked strangely familiar: 2, 6, 24, 120, 720. Then I remembered where I had seem them. Those are the numbers that show up in factorials. You know, like 5! (5 factorial) is $5 \times 4 \times 3 \times 2 \times 1 = 120$. But the denominator of each one was actually the factorial of the next number. So after three drinks, he had $1/4! = 1/24$ of his milk left. And after five drinks, he had $1/6! = 1/720$ left. So after ten drinks he was going to have $1/11! = 1/39916800$ of his milk left. Wow, that isn't much at all. Those factorial things sure get big fast.

"So the answers are, Alysia and Melissa each had $1/11$ of their milk left. Dante had $1/39916800$ of his left, and Melody had $1/1024$ of hers left. I can see why Mark bought them each their own gallon."

Bimiljit was successful on this problem for many reasons. The main reason was because she was unafraid of the problem and continued to persist to solve it. She found many patterns in the problem. The reason the patterns appeared to show up so easily is that she was organized with her thinking and her chart made the patterns fairly obvious.

~~~~~

Looking for and finding a pattern is a very effective problem-solving strategy. The key to finding most patterns is to organize the information in some sort of chart or table so that the patterns jump out at you. Patterns fall into the major category of organizing information. Patterns turn up in many places. Keep your eyes open for them.

Problem Set A

1. SEQUENCE PATTERNS

Write the next three numbers in each sequence and explain your pattern.

    a. 2, 5, 10, 17, …

    b. 64, 32, 16, 8, 4, …

    c. 5, 10, 9, 18, 17, 34, 33, …

    d. 1, 3, 7, 13, 21, …

e. 2, 3, 5, 9, …

f. 1, 5, 13, 26, 45, 71, …

g. 1, 2, 6, 24, 120, 720, …

2. AIR SHOW

In order to keep the spectators out of the line of flight, the Air Force arranged the seats for an air show in a "V" shape. Kevin, who loves airplanes, arrived very early and was given the front seat. There were three seats in the second row, and those were filled very quickly. The third row had five seats, which were given to the next five people who came. The following row had seven seats; in fact, this pattern continued all the way back, each row having two more seats than the previous row. The first twenty rows were filled. How many people attended the air show?

3. RECTANGULAR DOTS

Continue this pattern (rectangular dots). How many dots are there in the thirty-fourth figure?

4. PENTAGONAL NUMBERS

In the text you dealt with triangular numbers and square numbers. The previous problem was about rectangular numbers. This problem is about pentagonal numbers. Find the pattern and determine how many dots would be in the seventeenth figure.

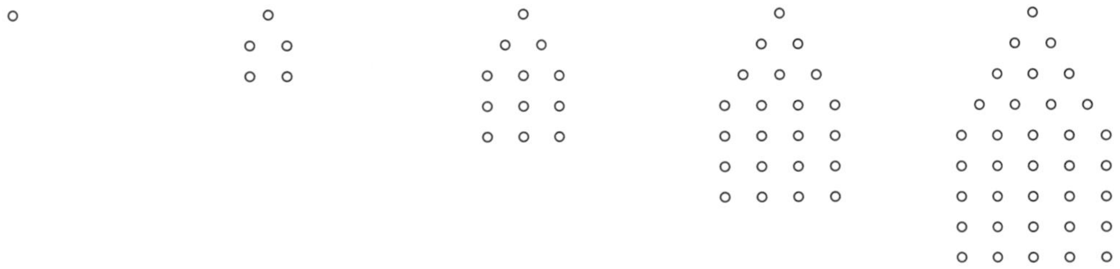

What is the units digit of 2 to the 57th power?

Determine the rule for each function. Then fill in the outputs for the other inputs shown.

IN	OUT		IN	OUT		IN	OUT
R	?		S	?		T	?
0	-6		0	-1		0	1
1	-5		1	4		1	2
2	-4		2	9		2	5
3	-3		3	14		3	10
4	-2		4	19		4	17
5	?		5	?		5	?
712	?		63	?		895	?

The chart below is a spreadsheet. The numbers in each column are reached by doing some operation on the numbers in the x and y columns. For example, Column C is the result of multiplying the number in the x column by 3. So in row 1, $x = 1$. Multiplying 1 by 3 gives the answer 3 that appears in the C column. Similarly, in row 4, $x = 5$. Multiplying 5 by 3 gives 15, which appears in the C column.

The rules for some columns involve only one of the numbers x or y. The rules for other columns involve both x and y.

Determine the rules that generate the numbers in the A, B, D, E, F, and G columns.

	x	y	A ?	B ?	C $3x$	D ?	E ?	F ?	G ?
1.	1	3	4	2	3	5	-1	7	-6
2.	2	1	3	-1	6	5	3	6	-2
3.	3	5	8	2	9	11	1	11	-10
4.	5	-1	4	-6	15	9	11	7	2
5.	-2	0	-2	2	-6	-4	-4	1	0
6.	0	4	4	4	0	4	-4	7	-8
7.	4	5	9	1	12	13	3	12	-10

8. BEES

A male bee is born from an unfertilized egg, a female bee from a fertilized one. So, in other words, a male bee only has a mother, while a female bee has a mother and a father. How many ancestors does a male bee have total going ten generations back? (Try drawing a diagram to help organize this.)

9. PASCAL'S TRIANGLE

The triangle below is called Pascal's Triangle. Find a pattern that will produce the next row. Then copy the triangle and fill in the next four rows.

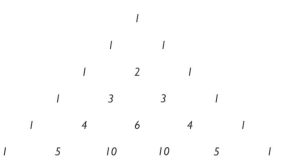

10. OTHER PATTERNS IN PASCAL'S TRIANGLE

Look for other patterns in Pascal's Triangle. Write down three other patterns.

11. COIN FLIPS

Pascal's Triangle shows up in the solution of many problems. Consider the next problem and how Pascal's Triangle may help solve it.

One coin may be flipped in two ways, either heads or tails. Two coins may be flipped in four ways.

HH	HT	TH	TT

Make a list of all of the ways that three coins can be flipped.

Make a list of all of the ways that four coins can be flipped.

What does this have to do with Pascal's Triangle?

Could Pascal's Triangle help you figure out the number of ways for five, six, seven, or more coins?

12. REFLECTION

At this time we would like you to reflect on what you have learned thus far in this course. Have you learned new techniques for problem solving or become better at strategies you already were familiar with? Have you enjoyed working with other students? What have you liked best about the course so far? What have you liked least? Do you use any of these strategies outside this course?

Problem Set B

1. GOLF MATCH

Clark, Chris, Doug, and Diana are standing on the first tee of their favorite golf course about to begin a best-ball of partners match. (A best-ball match pits two golfers against the other two golfers.) They are standing in a square, with two partners standing next to each other on the cart path facing the other two partners standing next to each other on the grass. This standing arrangement is typical of the beginning of a golf match. They shake hands and then they throw a tee in the air and let it hit the ground. Whoever it points to will tee off first. Clark is standing diagonally opposite Diana. Chris is facing the person whose name begins with the same letter as the person who will tee off first. Partners tee off one after the other. Who will tee off second?

2. LEGAL EAGLES

There are exactly five parking spaces along the front side of the law offices of Stetson, Neumann, Ostrom, Savidge, and Schoorl. The colors of the lawyers' cars are blue, tan, black, silver, and burgundy. Match up the owners with the color of their cars and their parking spaces. Then determine the gender of Neumann.

1. Ostrom does not own the silver car.

2. The woman who parks in the fifth space owns the burgundy car.

3. Stetson owns the black car.

4. Schoorl parks her car in the middle space.

5. There are cars parked on both sides of Neumann's car.

6. Ostrom parks his car on one end, but the man who owns the blue car does not.

7. A woman parks in space number 4.

3. COMIC OF THE MONTH

I subscribe to the "Comic of the Month" club. Each month I can buy any number of the 48 titles offered by the club. The first month I bought five comics for $3.07. The second month I bought two comics for $1.72. The next month I bought six of the club offerings for $3.52. In May I bought three more for a charge of $2.17. The club charges a handling fee and then a fee for each comic. How much would it have cost to buy all 48 titles at the same time?

4. RUDY'S CLOTHES RACK

Rudy examined his rack of clothes (five shirts and four ties), trying to decide what combination to wear. His five shirts included three solids and two patterns. His three solid-color shirts were blue, green, and white. One of his two pattern shirts was a blue-and-green print, and the other was a red-and-white stripe. He needed to match a shirt with a tie. In ties he had white, blue, and yellow in solid colors, along with a green-and-blue striped one. Rudy has his own rules of good taste, which include that you don't wear two solids of the same color; and if you wear a pattern, match it with a solid of one of the main colors of the pattern. Given those conditions, what is the probability that Rudy will pick out a combination that includes blue?

5. ROO AND TIGGER

Roo and Tigger decided to have a race. Their race course was 100 feet up and back (200 feet total). Roo could make three jumps of 2 feet each in the same time that Tigger could make two jumps of 1 yard each. Who won the race and by how much?

guess and check

GUESS AND CHECK—even the name sounds bad. It sounds like something your math teachers tried for years to get you to stop doing. When you learn the strategy and start to use it, it even feels like cheating. But it's not. It's a powerful tool for solving problems. When somebody figured out that a sand wedge is a great way to escape a sand trap on a golf course, it may have felt like cheating to the first people using it. (Some people use a hand wedge, which is definitely cheating.) Now sand wedges are an accepted part of golf, and no one feels it is cheating to use them.

The strategy of guess and check serves an analogous function in math. It isn't cheating and it really helps! It is tremendously effective in giving you a place to start. Guess and check helps you understand the problem. It can lead to solutions very quickly. And, as you will see in the algebra chapter, it even helps set up an algebraic equation (if that's the goal). In this chapter, however, you will not use algebra at all.

Why guess and check? Certainly guessing is nothing new to most people. Students have been guessing at answers for years. Some have even bothered to check their answers. So it would seem that the strategy of guess and check would arise naturally in most people's educational experience. Unfortunately, that is not the case. While it is true that most people have flirted with this strategy, they probably have not seen its power. The strength of the guess and check strategy comes from organizing the information in the problem into a useful form. You'll evaluate your guesses in a systematic way, enabling you to advance to more refined guesses.

Guess and check is not only a strategy, it is also an attitude. When guessing and checking, you must first believe that you can solve the

◀ *A string musician tunes an instrument by checking its pitch, guessing how much to tighten or loosen a string, and checking it again, constantly refining the guesses to zero in on the pitch.*

problem, even if you don't understand it well at the outset. Then, through your organization and your persistence, you will work toward a solution.

The strategy is loose on one hand, and highly structured on the other. When you draw a diagram, you do something specific that allows you to solve the problem. During elimination, you examine possibilities and get rid of as many as you can, as quickly as you can. With guess and check, you guess, and then add, multiply, subtract, divide (nothing unusual), and you check your answer. The heart of guess and check is not simply the operations on numbers. In fact, the heart is not so much a heart as it is a skeleton: a surrounding structure that holds the strategy together. What guess and check is and stands for is organizing the way you guess to reach the answer. Anybody can guess without being taught. Anybody can check answers without being taught. Not everybody has learned to unite the two into a problem-solving tool. That is simply what guess and check is—a tool for organizing information in such a way that this information becomes more useful to you and more powerful in your hands.

The focus of this chapter is for you to learn this powerful strategy called guess and check. Plus you also get a real-life, "How-guess-and-check-saved-the-day-and-changed-the-rest-of-my-life" story later.

SATURDAY AT THE "FIVE AND DIME" GARAGE SALE

Sandy held a garage sale during which she charged a dime for everything, but accepted a nickel if the buyer bargained well. At the end of the day, she realized she had sold all twelve items and raked in a grand total of 95 cents. She only had dimes and nickels. How many of each did she have?

Do this problem before continuing. Even if you think you can write an equation for it, don't. Do it by guessing a possible answer and checking to see if it is correct. Make another guess, check it, and so on.

The correct answer is seven dimes and five nickels. Let's go through this using guess and check. As you will see, the method demonstrated here will not just be random guesses, but will be a very organized procedure.

The following is provided by Kasidra, who gave us a "thought-process" narration on how to solve this problem.

"First, make a guess. I usually guess five because there are five fingers on my right hand. If I ever end up on an uninhabited island and need to do guess and check, I can always check my hand to see what I should guess first. Unless, of course, an alligator bites off one of my fingers.

"Five whats? Five dimes. Or five nickels. It really doesn't matter. I'll make it dimes. Next, set up a chart to keep track of the guesses. This is very important—this is not simply guess and guess, it is guess, check, and refine your guess. In order to do this well, you must have an organized chart."

Dimes
5

"Not bad for a first guess, but somehow I think this should all be expanded. If she had sold 12 items in all, then the number of coins she had must be 12. So if I guess 5 dimes, she must have 7 nickels to make 12 coins."

Dimes	Nickels
5	7

"Well, that looks a little better, but there must be more to this problem. I've got to figure out a way to see if this guess is correct. I need to know how much these coins are worth, because the problem says she has 95 cents. Expand the chart again."

Dimes	Nickels	Value of Dimes	Value of Nickels
5	7	$.50	$.35

"Now this chart is beginning to look like it leads somewhere. This slow process is not devised simply to frustrate people. Part of the point of using guess and check is that you often don't know where a solution is heading even if you have a good approach to solving the problem. I'm developing this chart as I go, rather than using a predetermined format. If the chart appears to be working, I'll keep it. If the chart appears to be failing, I'll get rid of it and start again.

"Here's the next improvement on my chart. I need to know the total value of these coins."

Dimes	Nickels	Value of Dimes	Value of Nickels	Total Value
5	7	$.50	$.35	$ .85

"Now get ready for the mega-action on the chart. I add in the rating column to tell me how the guess compares to the right answer of 95 cents. This particular guess has a total of 85 cents, which is less than 95 cents. The answer is low, so I rate the guess as 'low.'"

Dimes	Nickels	Value of Dimes	Value of Nickels	Total Value	Rating
5	7	$.50	$.35	$ .85	low

"Now that I appear to have completed the chart, I evaluated my first guess for accuracy. The guess was wrong, and note that the guess gave us a result that was too low. I will continue to guess, and use the previous guess as a guide. I will increase the number of dimes to raise the total value."

Dimes	Nickels	Value of Dimes	Value of Nickels	Total Value	Rating
5	7	$.50	$.35	$ .85	low
8	4	$.80	$.20	$1.00	high

"The next guess was wrong too, but I did manage to have the results of that guess come out just a little too high. The first guess was too low, the second was too high. Let's try something in-between to see how that comes out. My next guess needs to be between five dimes and eight dimes."

Dimes	Nickels	Value of Dimes	Value of Nickels	Total Value	Rating
5	7	$.50	$.35	$ .85	low
8	4	$.80	$.20	$1.00	high
7	5	$.70	$.25	$ .95	right

"Fortunately, I came up with the right answer on the third guess. The first guess allowed me to make a reasonable second guess; the first two guesses allowed me to modify and then make what turned out to be a correct guess for the problem.

"Finally I checked the problem for the question that was asked. The question asked how many dimes and how many nickels Sandy had. I always state my answer in a sentence, as I wouldn't want to count on the teacher finding my right answer in the chart. So the answer is Sandy had seven dimes and five nickels.

"In short, what I did was:

1. I started by making a guess.

2. I followed my guess through to a reasonable conclusion.

3. I evaluated the guess.

4. I modified and guessed again.

5. When I got a correct guess, I checked to see what the question was, and I answered it in a sentence.

"The chart, it is important to note, was nothing sacred. It was made up as I went and designed to fit the needs of that particular problem. I also didn't clutter the chart with a lot of unnecessary detail. I did my computations in my mind or on scratch paper."

Thank you, Kasidra.

~~~~~

Along with the points that Kasidra made, another major point that needs to be discussed is that wrong guesses are just steps on the way to solving the problem. Many people resist guess and check at first because of the fear of being wrong. Apparently this fear was drummed into us in red ink by all of our teachers in school. When an answer was wrong, it was marked up with red pen. When it was right, it was left alone. So many of us became fearful of the red pen that our primary aim was to avoid being wrong. Sometimes, the best way to avoid being wrong was to skip the problem. The suggestion here is that wrong answers just help you to find the right answers, and are an important part of the journey. So guess. It may take you fifty guesses to reach the right answer, but at least you are on your way. It is far better to guess and be wrong than not to guess at all.

Here's another problem to guess and check on.

FARMER JONES

Farmer Jones raises ducks and cows. She tries not to clutter her mind with too many details, but she does think it's important to remember how many animals she has, and how many feet those animals have. She thinks she remembers having 54 animals with 122 feet. How many of each type of animal does Farmer Jones have?

Do this problem before continuing.

Here's the way Vanessa solved this problem.

Ducks	Duck Feet	Cows	Cow Feet	TOTAL Feet (122)	Check
20	40	34	136	179	high
10	20	44	176	196	high
40	80	14	56	136	high
50	100	4	16	116	low

"At this point, I knew the answer must be somewhere between 40 ducks and 50 ducks, since 40 ducks gave a high result, and 50 ducks gave a low result. The other interesting thing was my second guess. My first guess was too high, so I guessed a smaller number the second time. This actually gave me more total feet, so I was guessing in the wrong direction. I thought this was strange, but then I realized that ducks had fewer feet than cows, so decreasing the number of ducks would increase the number of cows and add more feet.

"I continued guessing and checking numbers between 40 and 50."

Ducks	Duck Feet	Cows	Cow Feet	TOTAL Feet (122)	Check
20	40	34	136	179	high
10	20	44	176	196	high
40	80	14	56	136	high
50	100	4	16	116	low
45	90	9	36	126	low
47	94	7	28	122	right

"Of course, whenever you work a word problem you should give your answer in words: There are 47 ducks and 7 cows."

There is more than one way to set up a chart. Vanessa's chart was set up as follows.

The chart might have also been set up as.

Ducks	(Cows)	(Duck Feet)	Cow Feet	Total Feet (122)	Check

The columns "Cows" and "Duck Feet" have been reversed, and that might help keep in mind that the ducks and cows have to add up to 54.

Still another way to set up the chart is the following.

Ducks	Duck Feet	(Cow Feet)	(Cows)	Sum of Animals (54)	Check
20	40				

Following the guess of "20 ducks" through this chart, since there is a total of 122 feet, there must be 82 cow feet, as 40 feet are used up on ducks.

Ducks	Duck Feet	Cow Feet	Cows	Sum of Animals (54)	Check
20	40	82			

Since there are 82 cow-feet, at 4 per cow that comes out to 20.5 cows (dividing by four). This gives a total of 40.5 ducks and cows which is low because there are supposed to be 54 animals.

Ducks	Duck Feet	Cow Feet	Cows	Sum of Animals (54)	Check
20	40	82	20.5	40.5	low

There is nothing sacred about how the chart is set up. You are encouraged to set up the chart in a way that is meaningful to you. If it works, great, but if it doesn't work you have to be willing to scrap it and start again. However, some kind of chart is very helpful in keeping the work organized and will lead to a solution.

Here's another problem to hone your new found skills on.

ALL AROUND THE PLAYING FIELD

The perimeter of a rectangular playing field is 504 yards. Its length is 6 yards shorter than twice its width. What is its area?

Solve this problem before continuing. You might find that a diagram is helpful as well as guess and check.

Brad's solution:

"First I drew a picture of a rectangle to represent the field. I figured I had to guess the width and length. It seemed like it was easier to guess the width, so then I could double it and subtract 6 for the length. I put my guesses on my diagram as well as in my chart.

"This problem essentially breaks down into two problems: first find the dimensions and then find the area using the dimensions. (Breaking a problem down into several subproblems will be the subject of the next chapter.) I decided to worry about the dimensions first, and after I got them right, I would get the area. My diagram helped me realize that the perimeter of a rectangle is twice the width plus twice the length so that you be sure and go around the whole figure."

Width	Length	Twice Width	Twice Length	Perimeter (504)	Rating
100	194	200	388	588	high
60	114	120	228	348	low
80	154	160	308	468	low
90	174	180	348	528	high
85	164	170	328	498	low
87	168	174	336	510	high
86	166	172	332	504	right

"I couldn't believe how many guesses it took me to get the right answer. My diagram was getting really cluttered with all the eraser marks. I actually ended up drawing new rectangles about every third guess to make it easier on my eraser.

"Finally, after all those guesses, all I had to do was multiply the length times the width (86 yards × 166 yards) to get 14,276 square yards for the area, which answers the question."

One of the things that you'll notice about Brad's work is that he "bracketed" the answer. He found something too low (width of 60) and something too high (width of 100) and then went right in-between in order to try to narrow it down some more. The guess of 80 yards revealed that 80 was too low, and he continued working between 80 and 100.

He also guessed the obviously smaller number (the width). Guessing the smaller number generally helps by limiting the range of possible numbers and also allows you to multiply and add to get another number rather than dividing or subtracting.

One other thing to notice about Brad's work is that he drew a diagram and found it to be helpful. He also was willing to draw several diagrams when his original one got too messy. As mentioned in the diagrams chapter, many people resist drawing a diagram. However, those who do go to the extra trouble (about 5 seconds worth) find that it pays off in increased understanding.

Dan has twice as much money in nickels as he does in quarters. He has 33 coins in all (all nickels and quarters). How much money does he have?
As usual, work this problem before continuing.

Before reading the solution, make sure that you interpreted the problem as twice as much monetary value in nickels as in quarters, not as "twice as many nickels as quarters." The distinction is huge, and you may need to work the problem again before continuing.

Nathan and Adrian really liked guess and check a lot—so much so, in fact, that they nicknamed themselves Gus and Chuck. These nicknames stuck for several years, although most people had to employ a guess and check strategy to determine which boy answered to which nickname. Gus and Chuck approached the problem this way.

Gus: Let's set up a chart. These coin problems are all the same. We need a nickels column, a quarters column, a value quarters, value nickels, and a total value column.

Quarters	Nickels	Value of Quarters	Value of Nickels	Total Value	Rating
5	10	$1.25	$.50	$1.75	?

Chuck: Wait a minute, Gus. You've got this all wrong. It says, the value of the nickels is twice the value of the quarters. And you left out the bit about 33 coins. If it said the number of nickels was twice the number of quarters, it would be 11 quarters and 22 nickels. But it doesn't say that. So we need to start over.

Gus: You're right, Chuck. How about this?

Quarters	Value of Quarters	Nickels	Value of Nickels	Total Coins	Rating
20	$5.00	15	$.75	35	?

Chuck: That's not bad, but I think it's too inconvenient to check that way. Let's try this.

Quarters	Nickels	Total Coins	Value of Quarters	Value of Nickels	Rating
10	23	33	$2.50	$1.15	too high

Gus: What does too high mean?

Chuck: It means we have too many quarters. The nickels are supposed to be worth twice as much money as the quarters. So we need fewer quarters and more nickels. But we have to keep guessing so that we have 33 coins all the time.

Gus: OK, so if we guess 5 quarters we would need 28 nickels to make it 33 coins.

Quarters	Nickels	Total Coins	Value of Quarters	Value of Nickels	Rating
10	23	33	$2.50	$1.15	too high
5	28	33	$1.25	$1.40	too high
2	31	33	$.50	$1.55	too low
3	30	33	$.75	$1.50	right

Gus: Wow, that wasn't so bad. So Dan had 3 quarters and 30 nickels. Was that the question?

Chuck: No, the question was how much money does he have? This adds up to $2.25. So Dan had $2.25.

Again, note that Gus and Chuck were willing to start over several times. The magical, wonderfully perfect chart will not necessarily show up the first time you try a problem. Don't be afraid to discard your first approach in favor of a more efficient one. And sometimes you may find you want to go back to your first approach again.

Gus and Chuck were also not afraid to be wrong. Their first few guesses could not have been right since they did not even match some of the conditions in the problem. But those guesses were an important part of the solution process, and without their willingness to be wrong, Gus and Chuck may have just given up and called themselves stuck.

Mewa solved this problem with a diagram. "It occurred to me that if you were going to have twice as much money in nickels then quarters, then you needed to have 10 nickels for every quarter. I knew this because 10 nickels is 50 cents and one quarter is 25 cents, so that would be twice as much money in nickels as in quarters. So I drew a diagram of 10 nickels and 1 quarter."

"That was eleven coins. So for thirty-three coins I needed to have three of those diagrams. Since I figured that out, I didn't even bother drawing the diagram. So Dan has 30 nickels and 3 quarters, which gives him $2.25."

FERDIE'S ROLLER COASTER

Ferdie was excited. Tonight was the night of the big party, and Ferdie had been practicing his opening lines all week. However, as soon as Ferdie got to the party, 20 of the girls at the party left. There now remained two boys for each girl. This made Ferdie extremely bummed. A lot of the other boys got bummed too, so 20 of the boys left too (probably to look for the 20 girls). There were now three girls for each boy. This made Ferdie happy. How many boys and girls were at the party when Ferdie got there?
Solve this problem before continuing.

This is Robert's contribution to the solution of this problem.

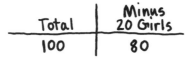

Total	Minus 20 Girls
100	80

This chart is pretty confusing, and one of the reasons for that is the word "Total." It's hard to tell what "Total" means here.

Here is his second try:

Start (Boys)	(Girls)	Minus 20 Girls (Boys)	(Girls)
50	50	50	30

And now his third try:

End (Boys)	(Girls)	Before 20 Boys Leave (Boys)	(Girls)	Check
1	5	21	5	Nope—has to be a 3:1 boy:girl ratio. This is a 4.2:1 ratio.
10	50	30	50	Nope—this is a 0.6:1 ratio.
5	20	25	20	Nope—this is a 1.25:1 ratio.

"This problem was getting me totally frustrated. I first started guessing wildly, with no idea of what I should be guessing. This last chart I made looks like it has potential, but it seems like it could take forever because I am guessing two things. I thought by starting at the end and working backwards, it might help. However, even though I am a little less confused, it seems like I'll never be done."

At this point, Rickey came over to help Robert. After Robert had shown Rickey everything he had tried so far, Rickey came up with a good suggestion. "Why don't you try guessing starting from the middle?"

Robert said, "I don't understand what you mean."

Rickey said, "Let me show you." He drew this chart.

Start		Middle		End	
Boys	Girls	Boys	Girls	Boys	Girls
		50	25		

Rickey said, "See? Start guessing in the middle and then work backwards to the beginning (have the 20 girls come back) as well as working forwards to the end (have the 20 boys leave). But make the middle guess have the right ratio of two boys for each girl."

Robert said, "Oh, I see. So for 50 boys and 25 girls in the middle, there would be 50 boys and 45 girls at the start and 30 boys and 25 girls at the end. But how do I check to see if it's right? Oh, wait, don't tell me. I just have to check to see if the ratio of girls to boys at the end is 3:1."

Rickey said, "Right. Go to it."

Start		Middle (Guess Here) 20 Girls Leave		End 20 Boys Leave		End Ratio
Boys	Girls	Boys	Girls	Boys	Girls	Girl:Boy
50	45	50	25	30	25	.66:1
60	50	60	30	40	30	.75:1
30	35	30	15	10	15	1.5:1
20	30	20	10	0	10	10:0
		25	12.5			
26	33	26	13	6	13	2.2:1
24	32	24	12	4	12	3:1

Robert said, "Finally. But at least this way, by always guessing the middle numbers and making sure that the boys-to-girls ratio was always 2:1, I saw that I was going to get there eventually. My second guess went the wrong way, since the ratio got further away from 3:1 instead of closer. And I made that other guess of 25 boys to 12.5 girls. That didn't seem like it would help too much, because you couldn't have half of a girl. Actually, if I had carried that guess all the way out, I could still have learned something. This was a pretty tough problem, but guess and check really helped a lot. Working backwards part of the way helped too.

"It was also nice to have a second brain working on it. It's funny, even though we've worked together quite a bit in this class, I still feel somewhat resentful when someone comes over to work with me. But working together with someone almost always helps me think more clearly. I hope I get over this attitude of resentment. It's weird that I would feel that way anyway, because I love working in groups."

Note: Robert's guesses that were finally successful partially employed the strategy of working backwards. This is a very powerful strategy and will be discussed more fully in a later chapter. Also note that Robert at one point made a guess that was worse than his previous guess. This often happens in guess and check. It is sometimes very difficult to figure out whether a particular guess is too high or too low.

When this occurs, use your next guess to help you. Consider the direction your results are going. If a guess gets you closer to the correct result, you've changed in the right direction. If, on the other hand, you're getting farther from the correct result, make your next guess in the opposite direction.

Robert also made some comments about groups. Some people resent the idea that they might require a second brain to solve a problem. Their perception is that they are somehow not smart enough to reach the solution on their own. But this resentment usually passes quickly as the group works toward a solution. While it is probable that you can eventually solve most problems alone, it is very beneficial to have the input of other people. The solution is usually achieved more quickly. It is also helpful to see how other people think, as this insight makes you a better thinker.

Studies have shown that the number-one reason people are fired from jobs is the inability to work with other people. Some people actually seek positions where they can work alone. Unfortunately, this attitude makes it very difficult to advance much beyond simple jobs with little responsibility. The really good, responsible jobs require lots of people contact. You will also need to work together with people in other areas of life. A family needs to communicate and cooperate to function smoothly. Successful social organizations need lots of volunteers working together. Good friendships are based on communication. Working with others is a skill that cannot be overemphasized. You should seek out opportunities to work with others as much as possible. Problem solving is a good opportunity to practice your cooperative behaviors.

Cloe is two years less than four times as old as Zeke. Cloe is also one year more than three times as old as Zeke. How old is each?
Work this problem before reading on.

Bart worked this problem using guess and check and came up with the following solution.

CLOE'S AGE	ZEKE'S AGE
5	?

Bart remarked: "To find Zeke's age, I would have to add 2 years on to Cloe's age and then divide by 4, giving 1 $^3/_4$, so in other words Zeke isn't even 2 yet. This would be fine, except that the other part of the problem meant I had to add more to the chart."

CLOE'S AGE	ZEKE'S AGE
5	1 $\frac{3}{4}$

"Computing Zeke's age the other way ('Cloe is also 1 year more than 3 times as hold as Zeke.'), I came up with Zeke being 1 $^1/_3$ years old. I was encouraged that these two numbers at least came out close to one another, but it wasn't the right answer because they weren't the same.

"I decided to change my chart because it was too hard to calculate Zeke's age if I had Cloe's age. It would be much easier to calculate Cloe's age if I guessed Zeke's age."

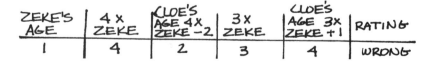

ZEKE'S AGE	4 X ZEKE	CLOE'S AGE 4 X ZEKE −2	3 X ZEKE	CLOE'S AGE 3 X ZEKE + 1	RATING
1	4	2	3	4	WRONG

At this point, Bart said he knew the third column and the fifth column had to be equal because they both represented Cloe's age. But he really didn't know if having a 2 in one column and a 4 in the other meant he needed to make his guess higher or lower. "However," he noted, "there are a lot more ages higher than Zeke's than there are lower, so I'll start guessing some higher ages."

To continue:

ZEKE'S AGE	4 × ZEKE	CLOE'S AGE 4× ZEKE −2	3 × ZEKE	CLOE'S AGE 3× ZEKE +1	RATING
1	4	2	3	4	WRONG
2	8	6	6	7	CLOSER
4	16	14	12	13	HIGH (3RD COL. HIGHER THAN 5TH)
3	12	10	9	10	JUST RIGHT!

"Zeke is 3 years old and Cloe is 10."

Reconsider some of the things Bart did that made him successful on this problem.

1. He wasn't afraid to guess.

2. When things didn't go quite right, he was willing to back up and start again. He continued using the method of guess and check, but changed how he went about making his guesses and the organization of his chart.

3. He guessed smaller numbers and worked up to bigger numbers. (Originally he guessed Cloe's age, but found it was too hard, so he changed to guessing Zeke's age.)

4. He kept working until he found an answer.

Work the following problem using guess and check.

Working alone, Mona can paint a room in 4 hours. Working alone, Lisa could paint the same room in 3 hours. About how long should it take them to paint the room if they work together?

Work this problem before reading on. The answer shown will be to the nearest tenth of an hour.

Aimee approached the problem like this. "The key is knowing that each of them gets a certain part of the room painted in each hour. Mona can paint one-fourth of the room in one hour, whereas Lisa can paint one-third of the room. I used my calculator on this, so I set it up as Mona doing .25 rooms each hour, and Lisa doing .33 rooms each hour. I know .33 is a little bit off, but I knew, if I needed to, I could go back and make it more accurate after I got close to the answer. Knowing the work rate, I can calculate the part of the room painted by multiplying. For example, using Mona's work rate, if she works 5 hours she will paint 1.25 rooms (.25 times 5). To check, I want the total painted to equal one, as that represents one room painted."

Her chart looked like this:

Guess (Hours)	Amount Mona Paints	Amount Lisa Paints	Total Painted	Rating
5	1.25	1.65	2.90	high
2	.5	.66	1.16	high
1	.25	.33	.58	low
1.5	.375	.495	.87	low
1.8	.45	.594	1.044	high
1.7	.425	.561	.986	low
1.75	.4375	.5775	1.015	high

"Since we were looking for the answer to the nearest tenth, I figured I was done because 1.7 was too low and 1.75 was too high. Anything in between those two numbers would still round off to 1.7 anyway, so it wasn't important to know the answer to any more decimal places. Who knows, they could have stopped to get a Coke, and that makes your answer completely wrong anyway. So, I'm done. Mona and Lisa painted for approximately 1.7 hours."

Aimee stated very succinctly the dilemma of producing an exact answer. In a real sense, her answer would probably be wrong anyway because of the inexact nature of the problem as presented.

Carlos also worked the problem, and took a slightly different approach.

"I worked on this problem for a little bit using fractions. I saw that if they worked for one hour, Mona painted $1/4$ of the room and Lisa painted $1/3$ of the room. After a few guesses, I realized that I could just add the $1/4$ and $1/3$ together to get how much they painted together in one hour. So I added them and got $7/12$. So they did $7/12$ of the room in one hour. This would mean they would paint $14/12$ of the room in two hours. So it wouldn't take them two hours to paint the whole room.

Hours	Mona Work Rate	Lisa Work Rate	Mona Work Done	Lisa Work Done	Total Work Done
1	$\frac{1}{4}$	$\frac{1}{3}$	$\frac{1}{4}$	$\frac{1}{3}$	$\frac{7}{12}$
2	$\frac{1}{4}$	$\frac{1}{3}$	$\frac{2}{4}$	$\frac{2}{3}$	$\frac{14}{12}$ (or $1\frac{1}{6}$)

"It suddenly occurred to me that to make $^7/_{12}$ of a painted room come out to one whole room, I had to multiply by the reciprocal of $^7/_{12}$. This is where I realized that I didn't have to spend the rest of my life adding fractions to find the answer. I knew that when I multiplied through by $^{12}/_7$, the total work done column would have to come out to 1."

Hours	Mona Work Rate	Lisa Work Rate	Mona Work Done	Lisa Work Done	Total Work Done
$\frac{12}{7}$	$\frac{1}{4}$	$\frac{1}{3}$	$\frac{3}{7}$	$\frac{4}{7}$	$\frac{7}{7} = 1$

"I don't know if I ever would have guessed 1 $^5/_7$. But that has to be the answer: 1 $^5/_7$ hours."

~~~~~

This problem is one of a type that is popular in many algebra textbooks. Those people who recognize this type of problem probably also remember the gut-wrenching feeling of not being able to set up the algebraic equation. Guess and check is a useful tool for developing algebraic equations in situations where an equation is desirable. This will be explored more in a later chapter.

NEXT TRAIN EAST

A train leaves Roseville heading east at 6:00 a.m. at 40 miles per hour. Another eastbound train leaves at 7:00 a.m. on a parallel track at 50 miles per hour. What time will it be when the two trains are the same distance away from Roseville?

Do not read on until you've worked this problem.

This is a typical problem from algebra class. In algebra class you were taught to set up a rate-time-distance chart and choose a variable and write an equation. The problems also broke down into three types: same-direction problems, opposite-directions problems, and round-trip problems. You probably had to memorize three different equations for the three different types. Many students get frustrated by these problems and come to hate them because they are unable to master these equations.

Guess and check can be a life saver in algebra class. Guess and check helps get the student started with the problem, and then obviously helps lead to a solution. As you will see in the algebra chapter in this book, guess and check also helps you to set up the equation in cases where the teacher requires an equation or the guessing is just becoming too tedious and a faster way is needed.

Jerel encountered this problem in algebra class. "I hate these rate-time-distance problems. I never could figure out what the equation was, so I just skipped them. When the teacher asked me why, I just said 'I don't do rate-time-distance problems. Some people don't do windows, I don't do those kind of word problems.' But then one of my friends taught me guess and check. What a great method! I'll never fear a word problem again.

"This problem was kind of tough. I knew how fast the trains were going, but I didn't know how long they had been traveling and how far they went. I figured I should guess their times, and then I would be able to figure out how far they went. So I started to set up a chart."

6:00 TRAIN TRAVEL TIME	7:00 TRAIN TRAVEL TIME
10 HOURS	10 HOURS

"I wrote down 10 hours for each train, and then I tried to figure out how to check to see if this was right. After I read the problem again, I realized that the time for the 7:00 train had to be one hour less because it left an hour later. So I changed my guess, and then I figured out how fast and how far they each went."

"I then wanted to put the distances on my chart, but I was running

6:00 TRAIN TRAVEL TIME	7:00 TRAIN TRAVEL TIME	6:00 TRAIN SPEED	7:00 TRAIN SPEED
10 HOURS	9 HOURS	40 MPH	50 MPH

out of room. My friend taught me that one guess should fit on one line of my paper. If it had to go in two lines, it was too confusing. He said to make the titles smaller and use more lines for them. So I crossed out that chart and started over."

6:00 TRAIN TIME	7:00 TRAIN TIME	6:00 TRAIN SPEED	7:00 TRAIN SPEED	6:00 TRAIN DIST.	7:00 TRAIN DIST	RATING
10 HRS.	9 HRS.	40 MPH	50 MPH	400 MI	450 MI	?

"I had no idea if that guess was high or low. That's another thing my friend taught me. Sometimes you can't tell whether your first guess is high or low. So he said to make another guess in one direction, and then carefully analyze it and figure out if you are better or worse off than you were before. This is sometimes hard to do, but it is good advice and I try to follow it. I decided that this guess was too low, so I guessed more hours."

6:00 TRAIN TIME	7:00 TRAIN TIME	6:00 TRAIN SPEED	7:00 TRAIN SPEED	6:00 TRAIN DIST.	7:00 TRAIN DIST	RATING
10 HRS.	9 HRS.	40 MPH	50 MPH	400 MI	450 MI	?
14 HRS.	13 HRS.	40 MPH	50 MPH	560 MI	650 MI	WORSE

"I decided that this next guess was worse, because the miles for the two trains got further apart. Then it occurred to me why. In my first guess, the early train had gone 400 miles and the later train had gone 450 miles. Since the later train had already passed the early train, the time must be less. This was what my friend meant when he said really analyze the guess to see which way it is off. So I made my next guess lower than 10, not just lower than 14, because 10 had been too high in the first place. My next guess turned out too low because the later train hadn't caught up yet. I got it on my fourth guess."

6:00 TRAIN TIME	7:00 TRAIN TIME	6:00 TRAIN SPEED	7:00 TRAIN SPEED	6:00 TRAIN DIST.	7:00 TRAIN DIST	RATING
10 HRS.	9 HRS.	40 MPH	50 MPH	400 MI	450 MI	?
14 HRS.	13 HRS.	40 MPH	50 MPH	560 MI	650 MI	WORSE
3 HRS.	2 HRS.	40 MPH	50 MPH	120 MI	100 MI	LOW
5 HRS.	4 HRS.	40 MPH	50 MPH	200 MI	200 MI	RIGHT

"So it will be 11:00 a.m. when the two trains are the same distance away from Roseville. That's another thing my friend told me, make sure you answer the question. Like this question could have been, 'How far away are the two trains from Roseville when the later train catches up?' That answer would be 200 miles. My friend told me to watch out for questions like that, and make sure I answer them. Boy, I love guess and check. It sure has saved my bacon a few times."

Liz solved this problem in a different way. "I drew a diagram of the two trains going in the same direction, one leaving an hour later than the other."

"Then I made a list of the times and how far away each train was from Roseville at each of those times."

"I also noticed a pattern here. The difference between the two trains

Time	Distance of First Train	Distance of Second Train	Difference Between Distances
7:00	40 mi	0 mi	40 mi
8:00	80 mi	50 mi	30 mi
9:00	120 mi	100 mi	20 mi
10:00	160 mi	150 mi	10 mi
11:00	200 mi	200 mi	0 mi

went down by ten miles each hour. That's because the second train goes ten miles per hour faster. Eleven o'clock answers the question."

HOW-GUESS-AND-CHECK-SAVED-THE-DAY-AND-CHANGED-THE-REST-OF-MY-LIFE (AS TOLD BY HOLLY)

Holly works for a law firm in San Francisco as the office manager and bookkeeper. As with most law firms, they tried to keep smart people hanging around, as it usually helps. One of those smart people is Holly.

Holly is no sluff when it comes to math. She graduated from Cornell University with a major in math. On one particularly fateful day, however, much of that math education failed her. It wasn't the education's fault, nor was it her fault. It's just that she had yet to be exposed to guess and check.

The problem she encountered on that day was a tax-payment problem. The law firm's partners used a profit-sharing account in order to reduce their personal taxes and to provide more benefits and finances for their deserving employees. It was Holly's responsibility to determine the amount of each partner's income that needed to be contributed to the profit-sharing fund.

By no accident, this fund was set up in such a way that the partners could benefit by reducing their own personal taxes legally (based on the amount of their contributions to the profit-sharing account). This, of course, was limited by an equation given by the Internal Revenue Service. It was limited by a percentage of the highest personal income of the partners (which could not be determined until the profit-sharing funds had been taken out). Of course, one of the ways to figure out how much profit-sharing money to take out was to know the personal income of the partners. Yet this could not be determined until the profit-sharing money was taken out. Thus we had a "tax and law" version of the old question: "Which came first, the chicken or the egg?" In this case, which came first, the determination of personal income or the declaration of profit-sharing amounts?

Two things that Holly considered were her employers' financial well-being and her own financial well-being. She was trying to lawfully maximize the partners' personal income. She was also trying to maximize the size of the profit-sharing account, as she was a direct beneficiary of that fund.

Part of the objectives were mutual. By maximizing the legal contribution, she not only reduced each of the partners' incomes (and thereby their taxes), but also managed to maximize her own income.

One of the complicating factors was that the social security tax is a tiered type of tax. The deduction is not simply a set portion of one's income, but it also depends on what plateau(s) that income has reached.

Holly worked on the problem all afternoon. Other people in the office helped her but they were not able to reach a solution. Holly then took the problem home with her, and spent a few more hours on it. She did not reach an answer, though she had a reasonably good estimate of the percent of the partners' income that should go toward the profit-sharing account.

For those familiar with algebra, Holly's equations boiled down to a very complicated quadratic equation. (There were initially three equations and three unknowns.) It was one that appeared solvable using the quadratic formula. However, due to the amount of manipulation involved in first producing and then solving the equation, a large amount of error was introduced through calculator rounding and limited decimal capacity.

She then called her son. She gave him the equation parameters, and after about 45 minutes of fooling with the equations, he called her back to report an answer that he didn't trust. Indeed, his calculator answer was sufficiently different from her calculator answer that they declared a mistrial. (Never mind—they simply decided neither answer could be trusted at this point.)

They decided to use guess and check instead of algebra. They programmed a computer to guess possible solutions and check them. After about 15 minutes of programming and 45 seconds of run time, the computer produced an answer. The answer also turned out to be readily verifiable, which is something that the previous answers were not. (Especially since the previous answers were close, but wrong.)

~~~~

It is relatively common for problems to be difficult when worked with normal algebraic methods. These problems can often be solved with guess and check. But guess and check is not the normal algebra taught. It should be. It works when algebra doesn't, and builds algebraic concepts when you are learning algebra. As a problem-solving strategy, it needs to be applied when appropriate. Guessing and checking does not perform miracles, but it does organize things in such a way that you can make information more useful. It is up to you, though, to take advantage of the strategy. It is like any tool—in the right hands it does a lot of work. Used improperly, it won't do the job it was designed to do.

The key points to remember are:

1. Start guessing—as you work through a guess, you'll learn more about the problem.

2. Keep your work organized—guess and check helps by organizing information. You will defeat it (and yourself) if you fail to keep your guesses organized.

3. Be ready to start again—as you learn more by working through guesses, one of the things you could learn is that your first approach was not productive.

4. Start with smaller numbers and build up to bigger numbers.

Guess and check is a tremendously powerful strategy. Keep the above points in mind, and you will enjoy great success.

Problem Set A

1.   DIMES AND QUARTERS

Annette has five more dimes than quarters. The total amount of money she has is $3.30. How many of each coin does she have?

2.   MARKDOWN

Jenny bought ski gloves that were marked down 30 percent to $24.01. What was the price of the gloves before the markdown?

3.   TAX

The cost of a basketball was $15.54, including 7.25% sales tax. How much of that cost was the price of the basketball, and how much was the tax?

4.   REFINANCING

Covell's home-mortgage payments are about $900 per month. He is going to refinance the loan, which will cost him about $2500 in fees, and the new payments will be $830 per month. How long will it take him before the new loan starts saving him money?

5.   NEW CONTRACT

"Bullet Train" Benson was negotiating a new contract with his team. He wanted $700,000 for the year and an additional $1800 for every game he started. His team, who BT was convinced was out to cheat him, was offering $5000 for every game started, but only $600,000 base salary. How many starts would he need to make in order to make more with the team's offer?

6.   CHECKING ACCOUNT

Javier received a letter from his bank recently concerning his checking account. Under his current plan, each check he writes costs 15 cents, and there is a monthly fee of $1.60. Under the proposed new plan, each check he writes will cost 12 cents, and there will be a monthly fee of $2.75. What is the minimum number of checks Javier must write monthly in order to make the new plan cost him less than the old plan would?

7. WEIRD NUMBER

If you take a certain two-digit number and reverse its digits to get another two-digit number, then add these two numbers together, their sum is 132. What is the original number?

8. BASEBALL CARDS

Rita has two more than three times the number of baseball cards that Ben has. If Rita gave Ben 12 of her cards, they would each then have the same number of cards. How many cards did Rita start with?

9. STAMPS

Charlie put $1.29 postage on a package he sent his sister. He used 16-cent stamps and 7-cent stamps exclusively. How many of each type of stamp did he use?

10. A BUNCH OF CHANGE

Plato has 58 coins in nickels, dimes, and quarters. The number of nickels is three less than twice the number of dimes. The total value of the coins is $7.40. How many of each type of coin does Plato have?

11. BOYS AND GIRLS

There are 9 boys to every 10 girls in a particular high school. There are 2622 students at the school. How many girls are there?

12. HOW OLD ARE RONNIE AND ALAN?

Ronnie's age plus the square of Alan's age is 2240. Alan's age plus the square of Ronnie's age is 1008. How old are Ronnie and Alan?

13. TRAVELING TO MOM'S HOUSE

Joan got on her bike and went for a ride. She rode at a speed of 16 miles per hour from her house to her sister's house in another city. The two women then got in a car and traveled at a speed of 50 miles per hour to their mother's house. The total distance from Joan's house to her mother's house is 315 miles, and Joan traveled for 8 hours. How far is it from Joan's house to her sister's house?

14. RIDING A HORSE

Hilary went riding in the hills. At one point, however, her horse stumbled and was hurt. Hilary left the horse and walked back home to call her vet. Hilary figures the horse walks about twice as fast as she does. If her horse was hurt about 8 miles in, and the whole trip took 4 hours total, how fast does Hilary walk?

15. FARGO

Tiffany drove from her home to Fargo, North Dakota, in 2 hours. On the way back, she drove 48 miles per hour and it took her 14 minutes longer. At what speed did she drive on the way to Fargo?

16. TELEPHONE SOLICITOR

Keiko is a telephone solicitor. She has only been able to convince 18% of her calls to donate. If she gets 12 of the next 30 to donate, she'll barely break 25% for the day. She will make about 30 more calls. How many calls has she made so far today?

17. EQUAL VOLUME

A box manufacturing company makes rectangular boxes with a square base. Their most popular box is 27 inches wide by 27 inches long by 12 inches high. Two employees in the company's research and development department are experimenting with increasing the volume of the box. Malcolm is experimenting with increasing the height and leaving the base alone. Rosa is experimenting with increasing the sides of the base and leaving the height the same. They were comparing notes one day, when Malcolm said to Rosa, "Wow, when you increased the base side by this number, it gave you a volume increase that was exactly the same as the volume increase I got when I increased the height by the same number that you increased the base." What was that number?

18. **FREE THROWS**

Gail's free-throw percentage so far this season is .875. If she makes only 13 of her next 20 free throws, her percentage will drop to .860. How many free throws has Gail made this season?

Problem Set B

1. **DAILY ROUTINE**

Aji has an argument with his daughter. She says, "You do the same darn thing every day." Aji does go fishing every day, but contends that every day is different because he does things in a different order each day. Before he leaves shore in his rowboat: he gets fresh bait, checks the weather, and adjusts his seat cushion. Out in the water: he eats his fruit, puts the meat on his sandwich, drinks his apple juice, and eats his sandwich. Back at shore after tying his boat to the dock: he takes the fishing pole in his right hand, and the ice chest in his left hand. Then he finally heads back home to have the same argument with his daughter. For how many days could Aji do things in a different order before he has to repeat the order of some prior day? Is there any easy way he could double the number of days in his cycle?

2. **AFTER THE FOOTBALL GAME**

A group of students went to their favorite restaurant after the football game one Friday night. They all ordered from the menu and forgot to tell the server to give them separate checks. The bill totaled $27, including the tip. They decided to split the bill evenly and figured out how much each of them owed. But then three people said they had no money. The rest of the people had to each chip in 45 cents extra to cover the tab. How many people were in the group?

I hate cats. It seems like cats hate me too. I wonder why. My neighbor, Madeleine, loves cats. She seems to attract them in bunches: especially alley cats, tabby cats, and manx cats. I knew she already had three alleys, five tabbies, and two manx cats, when more of each kind began to show up on her doorstep in March. The alley cats showed up first on the first. One showed up on the first, and one new one showed up every day for the rest of the month. The tabby cats began to show up on the fourth. Two showed up on the fourth, and two new ones showed up every day for the rest of the month. Not to be outdone, the manx cats showed up on the sixth. Four of them came on the sixth, and four new ones came every day for the rest of the month. How many cats did Madeleine have at the end of the month?

4. STOCK MARKET

Ms. Edwards and three other high school students decided to pretend to invest in the stock market. They all chose one big-name stock to invest in, and each invested $1,000 of pretend money. After one month, they bought the Wall Street Journal to see how they did. It turned out that three of the girls came out ahead, and the other girl lost money. From the clues below, determine the full name of each girl, what stock she "invested" in, and how much each girl made or lost.

1. Two people made more money than the girl who invested in IBM.

2. Ms. Kortright did not invest in AT&T, but the girl who did made the most money.

3. Denise made $700, which made her the big winner.

4. Ms. McDonald lost $300 and Tina made $200.

5. Nita did not invest in Xerox.

6. The girl who invested in Ford was the only one who lost money.

7. Luann, who is neither Ms. Kortright nor Ms. McElhatton, made $300 less than Denise.

Seymour, the census taker, came to the house of Larry Longway and asked for the ages of the three children living in the house. Because Larry does not believe in giving information away easily, he gave Seymour the following clues. The clues were given one at a time. After each clue Seymour really tried to figure it out. If he couldn't figure it out, he then asked for another clue.

Clue 1: The product of their ages is 72.

From this clue Seymour tried, but could not figure out the ages.

Clue 2: The sum of their ages is the same as today's date.

Seymour knew what the date was, but he still could not figure out the ages.

Clue 3: The oldest child loves to eat at Burger Jack.

From this clue, Seymour was able to figure out the ages of the children.

What are the children's ages?

New plant
economic impacts
Engineering
1. Cost
2. Cost
Environmental
1. Impact
testing

7

subproblems

U P T O **this** point all the strategies considered in this book have involved organizing information in some way. Drawing a diagram organizes information in a spatial manner. All of the other strategies presented thus far (such as making a systematic list, or guess and check) have involved organizing information in some sort of a chart or list. The method of solution was usually readily apparent after the information is organized.

The strategy of subproblems is different. It involves organizing your plan of attack. You need to change your focus away from the problem that is asked, and instead concentrate on achieving a subgoal. Subproblems fit into the major strategy we call changing focus.

Use the strategy of subproblems on problems for which a solution method is not readily apparent. The Scholastic Aptitude Test (SAT) is full of problems of this type. A simple example will illustrate this concept.

If $3x - 1 = 17$, what is $2x - 4$?

In order to solve this problem, you must first solve for x in the equation $3x - 1 = 17$, then substitute the value of x into the expression $2x - 1$. Note that you couldn't answer the question until you solved for x first. This is called a subproblem: a mini-problem that must be solved before answering the original question.

Some problems have many subproblems. In order to attack these kinds of problems, it is helpful to list the subproblems before starting to solve the problem. The list then becomes the plan of attack. Each subproblem can then be solved in turn to reach a solution to the problem. Making a list of subproblems can focus your thinking. If you

◀ *Any large, real life project, like developing a power plant, is broken down into subproblems that may be divided again into smaller subproblems which must be solved to attain the overall goal.*

decide that you need help with the problem, the list of subproblems helps you determine exactly where you need help.

Solving a problem by using subproblems is much like crossing a river using stepping stones. If the river were very wide, it would not be possible to jump all the way across it. But by going across on stepping stones, a person can make it all the way across the river. The strategy of subproblems is exactly the same. It is often not possible to do the entire problem at once (jumping across the whole river), but by doing subproblems (the stepping stones) you can achieve your goal of solving the problem (getting across the river).

The first problem contains some simple subproblems. List the subproblems and solve them before reading on. It is helpful to list each subproblem as a question.

LITTLE GREEN APPLES

How many apples, each weighing 2 ounces, will be needed to balance three 2-pound weights?
Do this problem before continuing on.

A typical student-teacher conversation about this problem might go something like this. This student has never heard of the strategy called subproblems, although, as you will see, he understands the strategy quite well.

Student: I need help on this problem.

Teacher: Well, what don't you understand?

Student: I don't understand any of it.

Teacher: Well, show me what you've tried.

Student: I threw it away.

Teacher: Why did you throw it away?

Student: My answer didn't match the one in the back of the book.

Teacher: Can you remember anything that you did?

Student: Yeah. First I figured out the number of apples in one pound, and that was eight because there are 16 ounces in a pound and an apple weighs 2 ounces.

Teacher: That's right.

Student: Then I figured out that there were 6 pounds, because the problem said there were three weights, each weighing 2 pounds.

Teacher: That's right too. I thought you said you didn't understand anything about this problem.

Student: Well, I didn't get the answer right.

Teacher: But so far you have understood the problem completely. Go on, what did you do next?

Student: Since 8 apples weighed 1 pound, and there were 6 pounds, I multiplied 8 times 6 and got 64 apples. But that was wrong, so I threw it away.

Teacher: You multiplied 8 times 6 and got what?

Student: I got 64. Oh no, it's 48. Thanks. See ya.

This conversation illustrates two things. First—and probably most important—the student really understood the subproblem process for finding the solution, but felt that since he had not gotten the "right answer," all of his work was meaningless. This reaction couldn't be further from the truth. He made only one minor mistake in one of the many subproblems that he found and solved. Second, had the student understood the concept of subproblems, he could have shown the teacher his work, including all of the stated subproblems. The teacher would have quickly been able to determine that the student understood the whole process. The teacher would also have been able to quickly tell the student that his only mistake was in multiplication, and assure the student that his reasoning was perfect, and only his mechanics were flawed.

Debbie solved the apples problem like this. First she listed the subproblems as shown below. You will note that Debbie's subproblems are the same ones used by the student in the prior conversation. But Debbie knows that it is very helpful to write the subproblems down, rather than just think about them. Writing them down focuses her thinking and gives her a written plan of attack. Instead of trying to find the answer to the original question, she concentrates on finding and then solving the subproblems that will lead to the final answer.

1. How many ounces are in a pound?

2. How many apples does it take to make 1 pound?

3. How many pounds are in three 2-pound weights?

4. How many apples will balance three 2-pound weights?

After she listed the subproblems, solving them proved to be easy.

1. How many ounces are in a pound? A pound has 16 ounces. (To some people this is not really a subproblem because they already know and can recall how many ounces are in a pound. Other people consider it a real problem and need to look up the answer.)

2. How many apples are needed to make 1 pound? Since there are 16 ounces in 1 pound and an apple weighs 2 ounces, 8 apples will weigh 1 pound.

3. How many pounds are in three 2-pound weights? Six pounds. Again, not much of a subproblem, but it still must be thought about.

4. How many apples will balance three 2-pound weights? Since 8 apples will weigh 1 pound, and together the weights equal 6 pounds, 48 apples will weigh 6 pounds and will balance the three weights.

Note: The fourth subproblem is actually a restatement of the original problem. The subproblems up to this point lead in the direction of the original problem.

Guille used a different set of subproblems.

1. How many ounces are in a pound?

2. How many pounds are in three 2-pound weights?

3. How many ounces are in three 2-pound weights?

4. How many apples will balance three 2-pound weights?

The solution of these subproblems will indicate a rather different approach to the problem.

1. How many ounces are in a pound? 16 ounces.

2. How many pounds are in three 2-pound weights? 6 pounds.

3. How many ounces are in three 2-pound weights? Since there are 16 ounces in a pound and there are 6 pounds, that makes 96 ounces.

4. How many apples will balance three 2-pound weights? An apple weighs 2 ounces, so dividing 96 by 2 gives 48 apples in 96 ounces.

Notice that the answer is 48 apples either way (isn't it nice when you get the same answer both times you do a problem?), but the two girls approached the problem differently. There is often more than one set of subproblems that will solve a problem.

⌃⌃⌃⌃

Breaking the original problem down into subproblems is a very effective strategy. Problems that may appear to be difficult are often much easier once broken into subproblems. Listing the subproblems gives you a plan of action. The list also helps you to identify the known information and what needs to be figured out.

Three quarts of water are needed to water 1 square foot of lawn. How many gallons of water will be needed to water a lawn that measures 30 feet by 60 feet?

List the subproblems and answer the question before proceeding.

E-Chung wrote the following list of subproblems.

1. How many square feet are in the lawn?

2. How many quarts are needed to water the entire lawn?

3. How many quarts are in a gallon?

4. How many gallons are needed to water the entire lawn?

Note: these could have been listed in a different order, with the only requirements being that number 1 must precede number 2, and number 4 must be last.

By listing the subproblems, he has clearly laid out the plan of attack. The solution to the problem now seems relatively trivial. In fact, the hardest part of using this strategy is figuring out what the subproblems are. Once you know what you have to solve, the actual solving is usually fairly easy. The subproblems don't all have to appear like magic at the same time, well worded and in the correct order. In fact, it is likely that you will get a mix of a couple of different approaches to the problem, and they might be in the wrong order. Part of solving the problem will be arranging them in the right order. However, this task may be almost automatic, as a subproblem is in the wrong order only if its solution depends on the answer to another subproblem. And then it should be obvious that you need another answer before you can continue with the subproblem at hand.

This is how E-Chung solved the subproblems he had listed.

1. How many square feet are in the lawn? Since the lawn is 30 feet by 60 feet, the area of the lawn is $30 \times 60 = 1800$ square feet.

2. How many quarts are needed to water the entire lawn? One square foot of lawn requires 3 quarts of water. So 1800 square feet of lawn would require $3 \times 1800 = 5400$ quarts of water.

3. How many quarts are in a gallon? Four quarts are in 1 gallon. (Again, this may not be much of a subproblem.)

4. How many gallons are needed to water the entire lawn? The whole lawn needs 5400 quarts. There are 4 quarts in a gallon. Dividing 5400 by 4 gives 1350 gallons to water the entire lawn.

This problem could also be solved by the following set of subproblems. This is the set of subproblems that Romina used.

1. How many gallons does it take to water 1 square foot of lawn? Three quarts is three-fourths of a gallon for 1 square foot of lawn.

2. What is the area of the lawn? The area is 1800 square feet.

3. How many gallons does it take for the entire lawn? Since each square foot of lawn requires three-fourths of a gallon, and the area of the lawn is 1800 square feet, $(^3/4) \times 1800 = 1350$ gallons.

You should have noticed by now that there is often more than one set of subproblems that can solve a given problem.

THE CAR BARGAIN

Paul went into the local new car lot to buy a car. He knew the kind of car he wanted, as his friend Barbara (often called Bar) Gain had bought the same car the day before. Barbara got a 30% discount on the car, which listed at $15,000. The salesperson offered Paul the $15,000 car at a 20% discount instead. When Paul protested the salesperson offered an additional 10% off the 20% discounted price. This offer satisfied Paul and he bought the car, convinced he had paid the same price as Barbara. Had he?

Solve this problem before continuing.

Pragnesh wrote this list of subproblems.

1. What is 30% of $15,000?

2. How much did Barbara pay for the car?

3. What is 20% of $15,000?

4. What is the sale price that Paul protested?

5. What is 10% of this new price?

6. What is the final price that Paul paid for the car?

7. Who paid more and by how much?

8. How many subproblems do I have to write before the teacher is satisfied?

Again, listing the subproblems gives Pragnesh a plan of attack. Solving the subproblems does not seem too hard, even though the original problem looked rather formidable.

1. What is 30% of $15,000? Thirty percent of $15,000 is $4,500. This represents the amount of money that Barbara saved.

2. How much did Barbara pay for the car? Barbara paid $15,000 less her discount of $4,500, for a net price of $10,500.

3. What is 20% of $15,000? The first discount that the salesperson offered Paul was 20%. Twenty percent of $15,000 is $3,000.

4. What is the sale price that Paul protested? The original sale price that Paul was offered was $15,000 less $3,000, for a net price of $12,000.

5. What is 10% of this new price? The new sale price would be $12,000, so 10% of this is $1200.

6. What is the final price that Paul paid for the car? The discounted $12,000 price less $1200 is $10,800.

7. Who paid more and by how much? Barbara paid $10,500 and Paul paid $10,800, so Paul paid $300 more. He shouldn't have been so happy.

8. How many questions do I have to write before the teacher is satisfied? Eight is probably enough, unless the teacher is having a rotten day.

~~~~~

Percent problems are often very confusing, and listing the subproblems is very helpful in understanding what is going on. A given percentage of different amounts is never the same amount. For example, suppose a baseball player has made hits 40% of the time. (This is a .400 batting average.) Is this player one of the greatest who ever lived or is he some fluke? Well, it depends on how many times he has been at bat. Suppose he just came up from the minor leagues and has only five at bats. If he has made hits 40% of the time, that gives him two hits. Big deal. But suppose he has played all season and has 500 at bats. Now, if he has made hits 40% of the time, that gives him 200 hits. That is a big deal and he will undoubtedly go to the Baseball Hall of Fame if he can do that consistently every season. Forty percent in both cases, but very different results. Percentages serve as comparisons, but you have to be careful. Sometimes you end up comparing apples with oranges and so the comparison can be basically worthless.

The capacity of an elevator is either 20 children or 15 adults. If 12 children are currently on the elevator, how many adults can still get on?

List the subproblems and solve this problem. This problem can also be solved by drawing a diagram, so you might want to try that method also.

Solve this problem before continuing.

There are many sets of subproblems that you could use to solve this problem. To be correct, your set does not have to match any of the various sets shown. But of course, to be correct, your set has to work. Some of those shown do not.

A class presented this problem on the board. Justin wrote his work on the board as shown below.

$$\frac{15}{20} = \frac{x}{12}$$

$$20x = 180$$

$$x = 9$$

"I figured this problem out with a proportion. I got $x = 9$ so there are 9 adults."

Renita took a different approach. "I wrote down some subproblems. I figured that I should use subproblems, since that is what we have been working on. They were:

1. How many adults are equivalent to one child?

2. How many children can still fit on the elevator?

3. This is equivalent to how many adults?

"This seemed like it would work, so I solved my subproblems."

1. How many adults are equivalent to one child? "Since 20 children are equivalent to 15 adults, one child is equivalent to $^{15}/_{20}$ or $^{3}/_{4}$ of

an adult. That seems to be about right, as kids are smaller than adults."

2. How many children can still fit on the elevator? "There are 12 children on the elevator right now. Since the elevator can hold 20 children, there is room for 8 more children."

3. This is equivalent to how many adults? "Since one child is equivalent to $3/4$ of an adult, 8 children is equivalent to $(3/4) \times 8 = 6$ adults. So six more adults can get on the elevator."

"I didn't get the same answer that Justin got. I think he messed up, but I'm not sure. I think what I did was right."

Lupe explained who was correct. "Justin is way wrong. I did it the same way he did, but he only solved one of the subproblems. He just figured out that 12 children is equivalent to 9 adults. So you could take the 12 children out of the elevator and replace them with 9 adults. But that means that six more adults can get on. So Renita and I are right, and Justin is wrong."

Tim solved this problem with a drawing as shown at right. "I didn't see this as subproblems, I saw it as a diagram. The drawing on the left represents the elevator filled with children, and the drawing on the right represents the elevator filled with adults. Notice that four children take up the same amount of space as three adults. So if 12 children are already on the elevator (taking up $3/5$ of the available space) 6 adults ($2/5$ of the available space) can still get on."

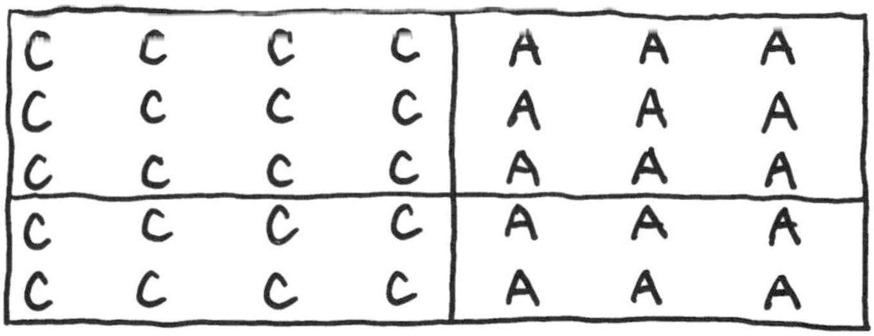

"Mixture problems" are some of the most confusing problems a person faces in algebra. When you understand the strategy of subproblems, however, you find that these problems are actually quite straightforward. Probably what makes them so confusing in algebra is the troublesome equations you are given with which to solve them. The origin of a mixture-problem's equation is difficult to make sense of, so you try to memorize the equation setup. This in turn leads to all kinds of mistakes.

The following two problems are mixture problems. The first one does not require any use of algebra to solve.

PAINT

A mixture is 25% red paint, 30% yellow paint, and 45% water. If 4 quarts of red paint are added to 20 quarts of the mixture, what is the percentage of red paint in the new mixture?

List subproblems and solve this problem before reading on.

Were you confused by this problem? Did all of the mixture-problem algebra demons come rushing out of the closet of your mind? After you recovered (did you recover?), were you able to write down some subproblems?

Melanie and Kirk were working on this problem.

Melanie: Arghh, I hate mixture problems. I could never do them in algebra class.

Kirk: Me neither. I get all mixed up. Let's try it with these subproblem things.

Melanie: Okay, I'm game. What do we need to know?

Kirk: What, er, hmm … How about, what is the percentage of red paint in the new mixture?

Melanie: Good, genius. That's the question. Can we figure that out right now?

Kirk: Well, what do we need to know to figure it out? Boy, this problem is making me see red.

Melanie: We need the amount of red paint in the final mixture and the total amount of paint in the final mixture so we can divide, and get the percentage.

Kirk: Yello, that's good. Let's start writing these down. (He wrote down these subproblems.)

1. How many quarts of red paint will be in the new mixture?

2. How many quarts of paint will be in the new mixture?

3. What percentage of the new mixture is red paint?

Melanie: Okay, let's figure these out. How much red paint is there in the final mixture? How do we figure that out? We don't even know how much paint there is in the original mixture.

Kirk: You're right, that's another subproblem. I'll add it to the list. (He added it on top of the others and renumbered.)

1. How many quarts of red paint are in the original mixture?

2. How many quarts of red paint will be in the new mixture?

3. How many quarts of paint will be in the new mixture?

4. What percentage of the new mixture is red paint?

Kirk: Okay, I think we're in business now. The original mixture is 25% red. Since there are 20 quarts in the original mixture, 25% of 20 = 5 quarts of red paint in the original mixture.

Melanie: Great. Okay, so in the new mixture there will be the original five plus the four that were added, and that makes nine.

Kirk: Now we've got things stirred up. Our next subproblem is how many quarts of paint are in the new mixture. Well, that's redily apparent. It's 24. We started with 20 and we just added 4.

Melanie: And finally, we just have to divide to find the percentage of red paint in the final mixture. So $^9/_{24} = .375$. So that's 37.5% red. We did it. These subproblems made this problem not so bad.

Kirk: Yeah. Let's go paint the town.

Note: You could also figure the new percentages of yellow paint and water in the same fashion. If you were unable to solve this problem before, figure out the percentages of yellow paint and water by yourself before going on.

〰〰〰

The next problem should bring up more of those ghosts from Algebra I. Solve this problem by using a combination of subproblems and guess and check. (You could use algebra, but try solving this problem without it.)

CHOCOLATE MILK

Augustus is trying to make chocolate milk. So far he has made a 10% chocolate milk solution (this means that the solution is 10% chocolate and 90% milk). He has also made a 25% chocolate milk solution. Unfortunately, the 10% solution is too weak and the 25% solution is way too chocolatey. He has a whole lot of the 10% solution, but he only has 30 gallons of the 25% solution. How many gallons of 10% solution should he add to the 25% solution to make a mixture that is 15% chocolate? Augustus is sure it will be absolutely perfect.

Solve this problem before continuing on.

Pak loves guess and check. Pak would solve every problem by guess and check if he could. So he wanted to guess and check. His solution is a combination of guess and check and subproblems. He started by listing some subproblems.

1. How much chocolate is in the 30 gallons of 25% solution?
   25% of 30 = 7.5 gallons of chocolate in the 30 gallons of solution. This also means that there are 22.5 gallons of milk in the 30 gallons of solution.

Then Pak was stuck. He didn't know any other subproblems. So he decided to try his favorite strategy, guess and check. He didn't know what to guess, so he adopted the strategy of guessing the answer to the question. The question asked how many gallons of 10% solution need to be added. So Pak began to set up his chart.

Gallons of 10% Solution
5

But Pak didn't know what to write next. Then he realized that there was another subproblem lurking here. If he guessed 5 gallons of 10% solution, he needed to know how much chocolate it contains. So he added to his chart. He also created columns for the information he already had.

Gallons of 10% Solution	Gallons of Choc in 10% Soln	Gallons of 25% Solution	Gallons of Choc in 25% Soln
5	0.5	30	7.5

Now he had to determine how to check his guess. He realized that this problem involved more subproblems.

2. How much chocolate is in the new mixture (for that guess)?

3. How many gallons of solution are in the mixture (for that guess)?

4. What percentage of the new mixture is chocolate (for that guess)?

He added three more columns to his chart.

Note: The percentage of chocolate in the total mixture column was computed by dividing the total gallons of chocolate by the total gallons of the mixture and changing to a percent. For example, in the first guess, 8 gallons of chocolate divided by 35 gallons of mixture is $8/35 \approx .228 = 22.8\%$. Truncate percentages to a tenth of a percent. Also note that the third and fourth columns always remain the same as they contain the information given.

Gallons of 10% Solution	Gallons of Choc in 10% Soln	Gallons of 25% Solution	Gallons of Choc in 25% Soln	Total Gallons of Choc	Total Gallons of Mix	% of Choc in Tot Mix	Rate
5	0.5	30	7.5	8	35	22.8%	high
30	3	30	7.5	10.5	60	17.5%	high
50	5	30	7.5	12.5	80	15.6%	high
100	10	30	7.5	17.5	130	13.4%	low
60	6	30	7.5	13.5	90	15%	right

So the answer is Augustus needs to add 60 gallons of the 10% solution.

Pak's attempt to bracket the answer didn't succeed too well as his first three guesses were too high. He was very willing to guess much larger numbers, which aided him in reaching the answer (quite quickly).

This is another problem in which strategies overlap. We will visit this problem again in the algebra chapter and discuss where those nasty equations from Algebra I come from.

Cheryl solved this problem in a completely different way. Her solution involves a different subproblem.

"This would have been really easy if they wanted a 17.5% solution 'cause that would be halfway between the 25% solution and the 10% solution. That would mean you needed the same amount of each solution. So you would need 30 gallons of the 10% solution. Of course, it's not 17.5%, it's 15%.

"But that brought to mind a needed subproblem: what does the ratio have to be between the 10% solution and the 25% solution?

"I noticed that 15% was one-third of the way from 10 to 25, so I think I only need to add in a small amount of the 10% mix to create the 15% mix.

"In terms of how close 10% is to 25%, the 15% mix asked for is only one of three parts of the way. Or better yet, if you break down into 10%-15%, 15%-20%, and 20%-25%, getting 10% up to 15% is one part close to 10% and two parts close to 25%. Here's a diagram to show what I mean."

"Fifteen percent is one of three parts of the way toward 25% from 10%. So there's one part on the left and two on the right. That means you have to keep this 1:2 ratio when you mix the solutions together. I at first thought it had to be one part of the 10% mixed with two parts of the 25%, but that would actually make the blend closer to the 25%, so I knew I had it backwards.

"Therefore, the right answer is a 2:1 ratio of the weak stuff to the strong stuff; he already has 30 gallons of strong chocolate milk. In a 2:1 ratio, you need to add twice as much as you've already got, so twice 30 is 60. So he needs 60 gallons of the 10% solution."

Cheryl looked at this problem with a different perspective, and thus found that she needed an unusual subproblem. The ratio of the two liquids was the key to her solution. Her diagram helped her find that ratio and solve the problem.

~~~~

The strategy of subproblems is very useful for solving complicated problems. A problem may often look impossible when you first see it. However, after you break it down into subproblems it may seem quite easy. Listing the subproblems focuses your thinking and enables you to see more clearly what you know, what you don't know, and what you can figure out. It is a very powerful strategy.

Problem Set A

Solve each problem by first listing all of the subproblems and then solving the subproblems in turn to answer the question.

1. COFFEE

How many ounces of coffee can be bought for $1.11 if 2 pounds cost $5.92?

2. SHARING EXPENSES

Five students held a party. They agreed to share the expenses equally. Leroy spent $14 on drinks. Alex spent $3 on paper plates. Kulwindor spent $7 on decorations. Max spent $9 on snacks. Bobbi spent $2 on envelopes and paper to send invitations out, and she also spent $5.80 in postage. Who owes money to whom?

3. AIRPLANE SEATS

On an airplane that was two-thirds full, 20% of the passengers were boys, one-fourth of the passengers were women, one-eighth of the passengers were girls, and there were 68 men. How many seats are on the plane?

4. SIX SQUARES

The picture shows six equal squares. The total area is 54 ft². What is the perimeter?

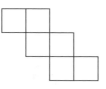

5. SHADED AREA

Find the shaded area in the figure. The large figure is a square, and each arc is one-fourth of a circle.

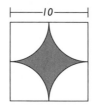

6. SAVINGS PLAN

A woman saves 10% of her salary every month. Her company has fallen upon hard times, so her monthly salary has just been decreased (what a drag!) from $3600 to $3000. The woman decides to save the same dollar amount each month, even though her salary was reduced. What percent of her new salary will her savings be now?

7. TEST AVERAGE

Mr. Howard's first period class of 40 students averaged 96% on a recent test. His second period class of 20 students averaged 90% on the same test. What was the combined average for both classes?

8. CAR TRIP

If Clarence drives 60 miles per hour it will take him 3 hours to drive to Concordia. How many minutes longer will it take to make the trip if he drives 50 miles per hour?

9. TEST TRACK

A certain car that is being tested by its manufacturer uses its entire fuel supply in about 38 hours when idling. The same car, when driven at 60 miles per hour on a test track, uses about three-and-a-half times as much fuel per hour as it does when idling. If the engine has been idling for 10 hours and the car is then run at 60 miles per hour, how much longer will the car run before it uses up all of its fuel?

10. BOX

The area of the top of a rectangular box is 324 in², the area of the front of the box is 135 in², and the area of the end is 60 in². What is the volume of the box?

11. STYROFOAM CUP

Find the volume of a styrofoam cup. The diameter of the top is 3 inches. The diameter of the base is 2 inches. The height is 4 inches.

12. RED ROAD

In right triangle RED, angle R is the right angle. Point O is on segment ER and point A is on segment ED. Segment OA is perpendicular to segment ED. $EA = 6$, $AD = 14$, $ER = 16$. Find the area of quadrilateral $ROAD$.

Problem Set B

1. WHO WEIGHS WHAT?

Devon, Frank, Fua, Morris, and Pedro belong to the same workout gym. The gym rules prohibit the staff from giving out personal information about their clients. However, each of the five guys said just enough that you can figure out their exact weights. (Do this quickly, as after the workout, Morris and Devon are going to an "all you can eat" buffet.)

Devon: Pedro weighs 18 pounds more than me. None of us weighs over 200.

Frank: My weight is divisible by 7. Morris weighs 12 pounds more than me.

Fua: I am the fourth heaviest. Pedro's weight is a prime number.

Morris: I'm heavier than Pedro. Devon is the lightest.

Pedro: Morris's weight is divisible by 10. The five of us together total exactly 840 pounds.

2. FAMILY DAY

Incredibly Huge Motors is planning an employee and family day at the baseball park. They have reserved 6000 seats with the ball club. Each section at the ballpark has 15 seats in each row, and is 18 rows deep. How many sections does the ball club need to set aside for the IHM employees and family?

3. CARROT JUICE

Bill, a health food enthusiast, is mixing concoctions in his basement. He has invented a new drink that needs to be 40% carrot juice (and 60% other stuff). He has been to the store and found some concentrated carrot juice (60% carrot juice) and his neighbor Clara (who decided one day that she doesn't like carrot juice that much anymore) has contributed 80 quarts of 12% carrot juice. How many quarts of the concentrated carrot juice does he need to add to the 80 quarts of weak juice to produce his perfect drink with 40% carrot juice?

Most Hrunkla lived in giant, 12-story apartment houses, and their homes were large square rooms bounded on four sides by corridors. Each room had a single door which opened halfway along a corridor. On even-numbered floors, the doors opened onto the east corridor; on odd-numbered floors, the doors opened onto the north corridor. At each intersection of corridors, there was something like an elevator that could be ridden up or down. Half of the corridors had moving belts on the floor, and no self-respecting Hrunkla would walk if he could ride one of these belts. The belts were so arranged that those on floors 1, 5, and 9 ran to the east; those on floors 2, 6, and 10 ran to the south; those on floors 3, 7, and 11 ran to the west; and those on floors 4, 8, and 12 ran to the north. Describe how a Hrunkla who lived on floor 10 could use these moving belts and elevators to visit a friend who lived in the room directly below his.

(This problem reprinted from *Make it Simpler* by Carol Meyer and Tom Sallee © 1983 Addison-Wesley Publishing Company.)

5. NIGHTMARES

Elmo was having some bad, recurring nightmares. He was having a nightmare about 19 witches casting 19 spells each on him (and these recurred every 19 days). He was also having nightmares every 13 days about 13 black cats crossing his path. He had a bad week in April, when on the night of Friday, April 5, he had the nightmare about the 19 witches casting their 19 spells. The very next night, he had the nightmare about the 13 black cats. Elmo knows he can handle these nightmares when they occur from time to time, but he is really worried about them both occurring on the same night. Do they ever occur on the same night by the end of the year, and if so, on what date?

8

unit analysis

U NIT ANALYSIS involves dealing with measuring units very carefully in order to produce a correct answer. People often ignore units in normal math class computations, such as finding the area of some region, but they are a necessary component of the problem and the answer. An answer is not complete unless it contains the correct units.

For example, suppose your boss asked you to find out how much fence you would need to enclose the company parking lot. You do the necessary research and respond by saying you need 145 to do the job. So your boss goes out and buys 145 yards of fence material. Unfortunately, you meant she needs 145 feet of fence material. You may end up searching for another job.

Unit analysis falls into the broad category of organizing information. By keeping the units in the problem organized, especially the numerators and denominators of fractions, you can solve many problems simply by making the units turn out correctly.

This chapter will contain several different sections that use units in different ways.

UNIT CONVERSIONS

This section will start off nice and easy. People are always having to convert units of measure. We change measurements made in feet to inches. We change time given in hours to minutes or days to describe shorter or longer intervals.

As you know, there are different size units of measure. For example, you can measure length in inches, feet, yards, miles, or even light years: whichever is appropriate for a given situation. There are also

◀ *Unit analysis is often used by chemists and physicists when they want to check that they've set up their calculations correctly.*

different systems of measurement: the English system used in the ex-English colony the United States, and the metric system used everywhere else. More and more metric measurements are being used in the United States, so gradually we see the change from English to metric taking place. When the full conversion takes place, parts of this chapter will be outmoded. Until then, as long as there are both math students and math teachers, these problems will exist as real-life applications of unit conversions.

Relax. There's no need to rush into this. The first conversion is changing feet to yards. (This is not at all like changing socks to feet.)

How many feet are there in 7 yards? The answer is easy, unless you don't know that there are 3 feet in every yard. Knowing this gives the answer "21 feet."

For the purposes of the rest of this chapter, we will introduce you to a style of solving this problem through a technique of canceling units. Consider the fraction below.

This fraction has a value of 1. The numerator is equal to the denominator. But what is so important about 1? Imagine this. Take your shoe size and multiply it by 1. Do you still have the same shoe size? This simple experiment should remind you that something can be multiplied by 1 without changing its value. This concept is key to being able to do unit conversions.

Consider again the question, "How many feet are there in 7 yards?" Another way to solve the problem is to multiply by 1, in this case a very particular form of 1.

$$7 \text{ yards} \quad \times \quad \frac{3 \text{ feet}}{1 \text{ yard}}$$

In order to solve this problem, however, "7 yards" needs to have a denominator of one.

$$\frac{7 \text{ yards}}{1} \quad \times \quad \frac{3 \text{ feet}}{1 \text{ yard}}$$

By canceling the "yards" with "yards" in the problem (yes, this is legal), and multiplying 7 by 3, the solution is:

$$\frac{7 \; \cancel{\text{yards}}}{1} \times \frac{3 \; \text{feet}}{1 \; \cancel{\text{yard}}}$$

You may be surprised to see that doing the problem this way gives the correct answer. This chapter is based on the concept of multiplying by 1 in various forms.

You should also analyze what type of unit is involved in each problem, though this may not seem important right now. The last problem dealt with distances. The next problem deals with time. It applies the concept of multiplying by 1 to a problem with more steps.

How many minutes are there in 5 days?

Start with the 5 days, change days to hours, then change hours to minutes.

$$\frac{5 \; \cancel{\text{days}}}{1} \times \frac{24 \; \cancel{\text{hours}}}{1 \; \cancel{\text{day}}} \times \frac{60 \; \text{minutes}}{1 \; \cancel{\text{hour}}}$$

The units all conveniently cancel, except for the minutes. Multiplying takes care of converting the units. The solution is 7200 minutes. This kind of problem can be done rather simply by multiplying, without all of the canceling. In the above case, the solution is $5 \times 24 \times 60 = 7200$. On such a straightforward example, the answer is obviously correct (though incomplete without the units). However, there are numerous examples that are not so obvious, such as the following:

Francisco ran 8 miles. Being a football fan, Francisco wondered how many times he had run the equivalent of a full football field (100 yards).

In order to solve this, you should multiply 8 by 5280, divide by 3 and then divide by 100. Do you believe it? Examine this problem done using the canceling units approach.

$$\frac{8 \; \cancel{\text{miles}}}{1} \times \frac{5280 \; \cancel{\text{feet}}}{1 \; \cancel{\text{mile}}} \times \frac{1 \; \cancel{\text{yard}}}{3 \; \cancel{\text{feet}}} \times \frac{1 \; \text{football field}}{100 \; \cancel{\text{yards}}}$$

Doing all of the canceling and then multiplying reduces the problem to:

$$\frac{42{,}240 \text{ football fields}}{300}$$

All that needs to be done to finish the problem is to divide 42,240 by 300. The answer is 140.8 football fields. So Francisco ran the length of a football field about 141 times.

The first approach to solving the problem was "multiply 8 by 5280, then divide by 3, and divide by 100." It turns out to be correct. If you are still resisting the canceling units technique, ask yourself. "Which of the two solutions is more readily verified to be correct? Or which solution could I easily explain to another person?"

The types of units involved above were distances. (Obviously, but keep your head in this for the instance where it becomes more complicated later.)

~~~~

English units are not the only ones that can be converted. Consider the measure of length in the metric system: meters. How many centimeters are there in a dekameter?

"Kind hearts don't use dirty crummy manners." A strange sentence to find in the middle of doing a problem in the middle of a book on problem solving. There must be some purpose to it suddenly appearing out of the blue. The sentence is easily memorized, and thus, is a useful mnemonic device. It helps the memorizer to remember the relative units of the metric system.

Kind	Hearts	Don't	Use	Dirty	Crummy	Manners
Kilo	Hecto	Deka	Unit	Deci	Centi	Milli

So having used the mnemonic to memorize the chart, what does the chart mean?

Kilo	Hecto	Deka	Unit	Deci	Centi	Milli
1000	100	10	1	.1	.01	.001

Each unit is 10 times as large as the one to its right. The spot marked unit refers to the basic unit of measure in the metric system, whether that is length in meters, volume in liters, or mass in grams. Each unit in the chart is compared with the basic unit. So one kilometer is 1000 meters. One centigram is .01 grams. One milliliter is .001 liters.

The metric system abbreviations are quite easy to learn also. Meter is denoted with the letter m, liter is denoted l, gram is denoted g. Each prefix is denoted by its first letter, so kilo is k and centi is c, etc. The only exception to this is deka and deci. Deka is abbreviated dk while deci is simply abbreviated d. These two prefixes, along with hecto, are not very common. The most common prefixes are centi, milli, and kilo.

The other interesting thing about the chart is that as you move over one space you either multiply or divide by 10, depending on which way you are going. So return to the problem asked earlier." How many centimeters are there in a dekameter?" The deka position is three places further to the left than centi, so multiply 10 times 10 times 10 (that's 1000). So there are 1000 centimeters in 1 dekameter. It is sometimes easy to get this backwards, and say there are 1000 dekameters in 1 centimeter. To counteract this urge, think about which unit is larger. Centimeters are very small, so it takes a whole lot of them to make up one dekameter.

You can also do this problem using unit canceling.

$$\frac{1 \text{ dkm}}{1} \times \frac{10 \text{ m}}{1 \text{ dkm}} \times \frac{10 \text{ dm}}{1 \text{ m}} \times \frac{10 \text{ cm}}{10 \text{ dm}}$$

or even

$$\frac{1 \text{ dkm}}{1} \times \frac{10 \text{ m}}{1 \text{ dkm}} \times \frac{100 \text{ cm}}{1 \text{ m}}$$

or perhaps

$$\frac{1 \text{ dkm}}{1} \times \frac{10 \text{ m}}{1 \text{ dkm}} \times \frac{1 \text{ cm}}{.01 \text{ m}}$$

In all three cases, all of the units cancel except centimeters, and the arithmetic comes out 1000, so the answer is 1000 cm.

Other common prefixes in the metric system are:

micro = 1 millionth $(.000001, \text{ or } 1 \times 10^{-6})$
nano = 1 billionth $(.000000001, \text{ or } 1 \times 10^{-9})$

METRIC AND ENGLISH UNIT CONVERSIONS

Raoul had done all of the measurements perfectly. He needed a piece of wood that measured 122 centimeters by 244 centimeters. The problem was, with all of his traveling he had gotten used to the notion that if it's Tuesday, this must be Belgium. Unfortunately, it was Thursday, and he had jetted to America the night before. What size piece of wood should Raoul ask for at the local hardware store where they have never heard of the metric system?

Raoul needs some conversions, fast. Raoul, along with most of the rest of the world, is using a metric mind to deal with the English measurement system (which even the English won't use anymore).

Of course, Raoul remembered to analyze first: these are distances. Raoul recalled something from his studies of ancient measurement systems: 1 meter is approximately 3.281 feet. So let's help him out with his conversions.

$$\frac{122 \text{ cm}}{1} \times \frac{1 \text{ m}}{100 \text{ cm}} = \frac{1.22 \text{ m}}{1}$$

Now, change the meters to feet: use 1 meter = 3.281 ft.

$$\frac{1.22 \text{ m}}{1} \times \frac{3.281 \text{ ft}}{1 \text{ m}} = \frac{4.00282 \text{ ft}}{1}$$

Doing the same series of changes for his measurement of 244 centimeters, we get:

$$\frac{244 \text{ cm}}{1} \times \frac{1 \text{ m}}{100 \text{ cm}} \times \frac{3.281 \text{ ft}}{1 \text{ m}} = \frac{8.00564 \text{ ft}}{1}$$

As it turns out, it looks like Raoul needs a 4 ft by 8 ft sheet of plywood.

CONVERSION PRACTICE

Work these problems: You may use any English-to-English conversions that you want, and any metric-to-metric conversions that you want. However, the only English-to-metric conversions you may use are: 1 meter = 3.281 feet and 1 gallon = 3.79 liters

    1. Change 12 feet to meters.
    2. Change 6 meters to inches.
    3. Change 5 gallons to liters.
    4. Change 85 kilometers to miles.

Work these problems before continuing.

You might notice that the strategy of subproblems naturally shows up in these problems, as it does in most unit analysis problems. You will often find yourself unable to go directly from the unit given to the unit asked for, so you must look for intermediate steps along the way. This involves the same thought process as subproblems did.

Solution to problem 1:

Type of units: distances. In order to change feet to meters, we use 1 meter = 3.281 feet.

$$\frac{12 \text{ ft}}{1} \times \frac{1 \text{ m}}{3.281 \text{ ft}} = \frac{12 \text{ m}}{3.281} = 3.66 \text{ m}$$

The answer is rounded to the nearest hundredth.

Solution to problem 2: (distances)

These are the subproblems.

6 meters   Change meters to feet   Change feet to inches

$$\frac{6 \text{ m}}{1} \times \frac{3.281 \text{ ft}}{1 \text{ m}} \times \frac{12 \text{ in.}}{1 \text{ ft.}} = 236 \text{ in.}$$

Solution to problem 3: (volumes)

5 gallons   Change gallons to liters

$$\frac{5 \text{ gallons}}{1} \times \frac{3.79 \text{ liters}}{1 \text{ gallon}} = \frac{18.95 \text{ liters}}{1}$$

Solution to problem 4: (distances)

Tim set this up a little differently.
Change 85 kilometers to miles.

$$\frac{85 \text{ km}}{1} \left| \frac{1000 \text{ m}}{1 \text{ km}} \right| \frac{3.281 \text{ ft}}{1 \text{ m}} \left| \frac{1 \text{ mi}}{5280 \text{ ft}} \right.$$

"Then I just multiply all the numbers on the top and divide by each of the numbers on the bottom. That gave me 52.82 miles."

UNITS IN RATIOS

Units are often divided as part of a problem: Someone who drives 180 miles in 3 hours has an average speed of 60 miles per hour. Miles per hour is obtained by dividing the miles by the hours. Notice that miles per hour is a ratio of distance to time.

Here is another example of units in a ratio: Suppose a university decided to spend $99,000 on a fleet of cars for certain administrators. Determine how much money is being spent on each car.

$$\frac{\$99,000}{6 \text{ cars}} = \frac{\$16,500}{1 \text{ car}}$$

Notice that the unit here is dollars/cars. Successfully breaking this down into a relevant unit makes the problem more understandable. Now that it is broken down into a price/unit, we can start questioning the type of car purchased. Did they buy Mercedes and get a great deal? Did the university purchase Pintos at outrageously high prices, thus padding someone's profits with university money? (Lest you think this is impossible, remember the Pentagon was known to spend several hundred dollars for a hammer.) Whatever the question, a lot of the meaning of answer hinges on the price per unit.

Along those same lines, someone who spent $24 on gasoline for her car might be asked, "What was the price?" (usually given in dollars/gallon), or, "How much did you buy?" which is asking for a gallons answer. If she didn't know the price, but instead knew the number of gallons and the total amount she paid, these values could be converted into a dollars/gallon figure for comparisons to other gas stations at other times and places.

Many grocery stores now carry shelf tags that list something called "unit-pricing." Those make it easier to answer such questions as: "Should I buy the 12-ounce can of refried beans for $.59, or should I buy the 16-ounce can, which is priced at $.81?" Before these tags appeared in stores, many shoppers would spend several minutes doing mental calisthenics with pained expressions on their faces. The unit-pricing tag allows economics to become a secondary issue very quickly. Doing unit pricing on the smaller can gives us a price of 5.25 cents per ounce. The unit price of the larger can is 5.1 cents per ounce.

The larger can is clearly the better buy. The question is no longer about economics, but whether the larger can will fit the shopper's needs in terms of storage and consumption.

Occasionally, however, the shelf tag gives the information in ounces per cent. In this case, you would want to buy the can with the greater number of ounces per cent, because you would be getting more for your money.

TONI'S TRIP

Toni drove 90 miles in 2 hours and used 3 gallons of gas. You should realize there are three different types of measures here—miles, hours, and gallons—which measure distance, time, and volume respectively. How many ratios of measures are there, considering two at a time? After finding that, calculate all of the ratios you found. (Hint: There are fewer than 10 ratios.) Work this problem before continuing.

The answers 3 and 6 are both acceptable. Three is the number of combinations of two things; 6 is the answer if you wrote each combination of two things as a ratio and as a reciprocated ratio. (For example, gallons per hour and hours per gallon.)

Calculator in hand, here are the combinations and ratios we found.

1. Miles/Hour: $\dfrac{90 \text{ miles}}{2 \text{ hours}} = \dfrac{45 \text{ miles}}{1 \text{ hour}}$

2. Hours/Mile: $\dfrac{2 \text{ hours}}{90 \text{ miles}} = \dfrac{.0222 \text{ hours}}{1 \text{ mile}}$

This is equivalent to 1.33 minutes/mile, which we got by multiplying hours/mile by 60 min/1 hr in order to convert hours to minutes

3. Gallons/Hour: $\dfrac{3 \text{ gallons}}{2 \text{ hours}} = \dfrac{1.5 \text{ gallons}}{1 \text{ hour}}$

This is probably more relevant as a measure of fuel consumption in airplanes.

4. Hours/Gallon: $\dfrac{2 \text{ hours}}{3 \text{ gallons}} = \dfrac{.67 \text{ hours}}{1 \text{ gallon}}$

This would be very relevant if you wanted to know what amount of time you could drive before worrying about filling up the gas tank.

5. Gallons/Mile: $\dfrac{3 \text{ gallons}}{90 \text{ miles}} \approx .033$ gallons per mile

(one-thirtieth of a gallon/mile)

6. Miles/Gallon: $\dfrac{90 \text{ miles}}{3 \text{ gallons}} = \dfrac{30 \text{ miles}}{1 \text{ gallon}}$

This is our famous mpg as a relative measure of fuel economy in cars.

We can obviously make this more trivial or more relevant, depending on our needs and the extent of our planning. If necessary, we could change the miles to feet. We could also change the hours to minutes or seconds. Then instead of using miles per hour, we could use feet per second. Speed limit signs could be given in terms of feet per second if we changed our speedometer readings to the new standard of velocity. If the sign declared a limit of 37 feet per second, we could avoid speeding tickets by driving approximately what we now call 25 miles per hour. But there are reasons for the speed limit being given in terms of miles per hour: it is the most useful unit for most motorists. Imagine the anxiety motorists would face when trying to drive from San Francisco to Los Angeles—a stated map distance of approximately 2.1 million feet—at the designated speed limit of 75 feet per second. How long would it take them to get there? Even if they were vaguely proficient in mental math and were able to divide 2.1 million by 75, the answer of 28,000 seconds would be virtually meaningless. Contrast that with the same problem where the distance on the map is expressed in miles and the stated speed limit is expressed in miles per hour. It is approximately 400 miles from San Francisco to Los Angeles. If a motorist were going to drive approximately 50 miles per hour, how long would it take him to get there? This problem is, of course, quite easy, and the answer is quite close to the previous answer of 28,000 seconds, but this time is expressed as 8 hours.

Nolan Ryan has been clocked throwing a baseball 100 miles per hour. At that speed, how much time does the batter have to react? (How much time before the ball reaches the plate?) The pitcher's mound is 60 feet 6 inches from home plate.

Work this problem before continuing.

This problem involves feet, miles per hour (remember miles per hour is also miles/hour), miles, and seconds. The problem is stated in miles/hour, and the answer is requested in time, but the problem doesn't specify whether to give the answer in seconds or minutes (rather, fractions of a minute). When finalizing the answer, consider what form makes more sense in conveying to another person how little time the batter has to react. In order for the answer to be in its best form, it should be something that the receiving audience will best relate to.

The unit of speed in the fastball problem is given as:

$$\frac{100 \text{ miles}}{1 \text{ hour}}$$

The above looks wonderful except that miles/hour is a measure of distance over time. The answer needs to be given in terms of the number of seconds to traverse 60 feet 6 inches, or in other words, time over distance. So invert the measure given from miles/hour to hours/mile.

$$\frac{1 \text{ hour}}{100 \text{ miles}}$$

The units are showing promise as something more helpful. The next thing to do is to make a series of unit conversions. First, change hours/miles to seconds per mile. Start by changing hours to minutes. Again, note that subproblems keep popping up.

$$\frac{1 \text{ \cancel{hour}}}{100 \text{ miles}} \times \frac{60 \text{ minutes}}{1 \text{ \cancel{hour}}} = \frac{60 \text{ minutes}}{100 \text{ miles}}$$

Notice that hours in the numerator canceled with the hours in the denominator. Next, convert the minutes portion into seconds, giving seconds per mile.

$$\frac{60 \text{ minutes}}{100 \text{ miles}} \times \frac{60 \text{ seconds}}{1 \text{ minute}} = \frac{3600 \text{ seconds}}{100 \text{ miles}}$$

Now that the time units are in the form needed, the next thing to consider is the distance units. Miles will be converted into feet, since the distance between the pitcher's rubber and home plate is given as 60 feet 6 inches (from this point on, 60 $\frac{1}{2}$ feet or 60.5 feet will be used.)

$$\frac{3600 \text{ seconds}}{100 \text{ miles}} \times \frac{1 \text{ mile}}{5280 \text{ feet}} = \frac{3600 \text{ seconds}}{528,000 \text{ feet}}$$

Now it is in the form of seconds per feet. But that's not good enough. Now we need to know the number of seconds it takes to travel 1 foot (probably not very many) and then multiply by 60.5 to find the total seconds it takes to go all the way to home plate.

$$\frac{3600 \text{ seconds}}{528000 \text{ feet}} = \frac{.0068181 \text{ seconds}}{1 \text{ foot}}$$

$$\frac{.0068181 \text{ seconds}}{1 \text{ foot}} \times \frac{60.5 \text{ feet}}{1} = \frac{.4125 \text{ seconds}}{1}$$

At this point, there are not any units for the denominator. It needs to be that way so we can give the answer as seconds, not as seconds per feet, or whatever. So the ball reaches home plate in slightly less than half of a second. Would you want to bat against Nolan Ryan?

The steps in this problem could have been done all at the same time, as the following set of fractions demonstrates. As you get better at unit analysis, you will be able to carry out all of the steps at once.

$$\frac{1 \text{ hr}}{100 \text{ mi}} \times \frac{60 \text{ min}}{1 \text{ hr}} \times \frac{60 \text{ sec}}{1 \text{ min}} \times \frac{1 \text{ mi}}{5280 \text{ ft}} \times \frac{60.5 \text{ ft}}{1} = .4125 \text{ sec}$$

COMPOUND UNITS

The units we have dealt with in this chapter so far are solitary units (a single unit by itself, such as feet) or units in a ratio (such as price per gallon). Just as putting units into a ratio is a key use of units, units are also often combined into what are called "compound units."

Compound units are found a lot in physics and chemistry.

A simple example follows.

The area of a rectangle can be found by using the formula:
$A = \text{length} \times \text{width}$.

Find the area of a rectangle with length 3 feet and width 2 feet.

$$\begin{aligned} \text{Area} \quad &= \text{length} \times \text{width} \\ &= 3 \text{ feet} \times 2 \text{ feet} \\ &= 6 \text{ square feet (which also can be written feet}^2 \text{ or ft}^2) \end{aligned}$$

The unit in this problem is a compound unit: square feet. The unit started as a measure of linear distance; it is now a measure of area. The "square feet" is an integral part of the problem and answer. A square foot is a square measuring 1 foot on each side.

We could have approached this problem differently. We could work the problem again describing the dimensions of the rectangle as 3 feet by 24 inches (instead of 2 feet). This time the area would turn out to be 72 "inch-feet." This answer would make sense if you consider an inch-foot to be a strip 1 inch wide with a length of 1 foot. So 72 inch-feet would be equivalent to a rectangle that was 72 inches long by 1 foot wide, or a rectangle that was 72 feet long by 1 inch wide. Granted, these bring up very different shapes in the mind's eye. It is for this reason that we usually compute area in square units such as square feet or square inches.

Note: This answer can be converted to the previous answer by the following set of fractions.

$$\frac{72 \cancel{\text{ inch}} \text{ - feet}}{1} \quad \times \quad \frac{1 \text{ foot}}{12 \cancel{\text{ inches}}} \quad = \quad 6 \text{ feet}^2$$

The inch unit canceled out leaving the answer as square feet, and we get the same answer as before.

If we use 36 inches (instead of 3 feet) by 24 inches, then the area would be in square inches. 864 square inches. Again, we can show that this is equivalent to 6 square feet as shown below. Square inches could also be written as inch-inch.

$$\frac{864 \cancel{\text{ inch}} \text{ - } \cancel{\text{inch}}}{1} \quad \times \quad \frac{1 \text{ foot}}{12 \cancel{\text{ inches}}} \quad \times \quad \frac{1 \text{ foot}}{12 \cancel{\text{ inches}}} \quad = \quad 6 \text{ feet}^2$$

Note: To convert square inches to square feet, you don't simply divide by 12 inches. Rather, you must divide by 12 inches squared (144 square inches).

The next problem will use the idea of area combined with unit pricing that we discussed earlier. Most people have been to a pizza parlor. It is often assumed that the larger the pizza, the better the deal. This is usually the case. Analyzing pizza prices with unit analysis lets the consumer make an informed purchase. Look at the following problem.

PIZZA PRICES

Use the pizza parlor menu below to determine which cheese pizza is the best buy. All pizzas are round.

TYPE:	DIAMETER:	PRICE:
small	10 inches	$6.80
medium	12 inches	$8.50
large	14 inches	$12.60
giant	20 inches	$21.00

Work this problem before continuing.

You first must assume that all these pizzas have the same height, and therefore their weight is proportional to their area. Second, you must not fall into the trap of comparing price to diameter. The size of a pizza does not grow in proportion to its diameter. In fact, area is the important unit (again, assuming equal heights). So compare price to area and see which is the best buy. You could use either dollars/square inch or square inches/dollar. Let's use square inches per dollar.

A necessary subproblem is then to find the area of each pizza. The formula $A = \pi r^2$ gives the area of a circle. Note that the area turns out in square units, since you square the radius unit (in this case inches) before you multiply it by π. (π is unitless.) Needing the area leads to another subproblem (an easy one) of finding the radius of each pizza. Then compute the area.

Type	Diameter	Radius	Area
Small	10 inches	5 inches	25π in^2
Medium	12 inches	6 inches	36π in^2
Large	14 inches	7 inches	49π in^2
Giant	20 inches	10 inches	100π in^2

Now compute the value of square inches per dollar. Use 3.14 as an approximation for π. Round off to the nearest hundredths place.

Type	Area	Price	Area/$
Small	25π in^2	$6.80	11.54 in^2/$
Medium	36π in^2	$8.50	13.30 in^2/$
Large	49π in^2	$12.60	12.21 in^2/$
Giant	100π in^2	$21.00	14.95 in^2/$

Clearly the giant pizza is the best buy as it gives the most area per dollar. (If you instead examined price/area then you wanted the lowest $/area.) But the next best deal is the medium, which may be rather surprising. Understanding how to evaluate best buys gives consumers the opportunity to worry about other things, such as how hungry they are and whether there is room in the refrigerator for the leftovers.

Another common type of compound unit shows up in the transportation field: both as a measure of the efficiency of public transportation and in traffic safety statistics. These both deal with the compound unit passenger-miles. Traffic safety statistics are often given in terms of per billion passenger-miles. For example, you might see statistics on deaths per billion passenger-miles, accidents per billion passenger-miles, or even arrests per billion passenger-miles. We will look at some death statistics a little bit later. Bus and train companies often advertise their ability to inexpensively provide a large number of passenger-miles.

Just exactly what is a passenger-mile? It represents one passenger traveling 1 mile. For example, a car with one passenger traveling 12 miles racks up 12 passenger-miles. A car with three passengers traveling 5 miles accounts for 15 passenger-miles. (One passenger traveled 5 miles, another traveled 5 miles, and still a third traveled 5 miles.) An airplane that travels 2500 miles with 400 passengers aboard produces 1 million passenger-miles.

Cars are quite clearly an inefficient means of transportation, as they do not provide very many passenger miles because they don't carry very many people. You often see diamond lanes on busy freeways for use during rush hour. Only cars with two or more passengers can travel in the diamond lane. The diamond lanes are often empty or sparsely populated, while the adjacent lanes are stuffed with cars with only one occupant. The United States is very car-oriented, and most people are not likely to carpool or take some form of public transportation because of a weak claim of inconvenience. Other countries quite often have extensive public transportation systems which are far more efficient. Trains, buses, vans, subways, and trolleys carry many more passengers and are therefore able to supply quite a number of passenger-miles per journey in contrast to a car with only one occupant.

But what about the economics of the situation? Occasionally people drive places together and decide to share gas expenses. This type of shared transportation is subject to analysis based on various units. Public transportation can also be analyzed in this way. Buses are expensive to buy and expensive to run. They get only a few miles per gallon, especially considering that most buses in cities are run in stop-and-go conditions, where the bus has to accelerate and decelerate every few blocks. A lot of fuel is used every time a bus must be brought from zero up to 25 or 35 miles per hour. The Southern California Rapid Transit District (Los Angeles and the surrounding communities) used to address this issue by advertising that their buses averaged over 200 passenger-miles per gallon. When you can pack 40 to 70 people on a bus, it becomes a very fuel-efficient mode of transportation, despite poor gas mileage. When computing the total costs of running the bus, though, you need to consider the driver's wages and the wages of the support personnel. Again, when considered in terms of "per passenger-mile" (or in the case of an hourly wage, we could calculate on the basis of "per passenger-hour"), these costs are very low.

The next problem—a problem dealing with a carpool situation—will serve to illustrate some of these ideas.

Gerónimo and three friends drove 208 miles. Their car got 35 miles per gallon during the trip. They drove at an average speed of 50 miles per hour and the gasoline for the trip cost them $8.02. Find each of the following:

1. *Gallons of gas used*
2. *Hours*
3. *Average feet per second*
4. *Dollars per hour*
5. *Dollars per gallon*

6. *Dollars per passenger*
7. *Cents per mile*
8. *Total number of passenger-miles*
9. *Passenger-miles per gallon*
10. *Cents per passenger-mile*

Solve this problem before continuing.

Consider the questions one at a time.

1. Gallons of gas used.

   To find gallons, consider the unit "miles per gallon" that is given. We want the gallons part, but we need to get rid of the miles part. Miles are also given, however. Consider multiplying the two of them together.

   $$\frac{35 \text{ miles}}{1 \text{ gallon}} \times \frac{208 \text{ miles}}{1}$$

   Unfortunately, the miles unit would not cancel and the result would be miles²/gallon, which might make sense if you were plowing a field with a tractor, but certainly makes no sense here. But if the miles per gallon figure were inverted, miles would cancel leaving gallons.

   $$\frac{1 \text{ gallon}}{35 \text{ miles}} \times \frac{208 \text{ miles}}{1} = 5.94 \text{ gallons}$$

   Many students might set it up to cancel miles as follows.

   $$\frac{35 \text{ miles}}{1 \text{ gallon}} \times \frac{1}{208 \text{ miles}} = \frac{35}{208 \text{ gallons}} = \frac{.168}{\text{gallons}}$$

Miles would cancel as needed, but does the answer look reasonable? And take a close look at the units: They're actually 1/gallons instead of gallons. You could then take the reciprocal to get the units right and the previous answer:

$$\frac{208 \text{ gallons}}{35} = 5.94 \text{ gallons}$$

2. Hours:

June solved it this way. "This one looked like it might be similar to the gallons one, because the only way we had hours expressed in the problem was in a ratio."

$$\frac{50 \text{ miles}}{1 \text{ hour}} \quad \times \quad \frac{208 \text{ miles}}{1}$$

"All I did was look, look, look and then stare at these units. I finally saw that since I wanted hours, I had to flip the miles per hour to make hours per mile and then I could multiply and get the miles to cancel, leaving hours."

$$\frac{1 \text{ hour}}{50 \text{ miles}} \quad \times \quad \frac{208 \text{ miles}}{1} = \frac{4.16 \text{ hours}}{1}$$

3. Average feet per second:

Terrence said, "This was a piece of cake. First I converted the miles to feet, then I changed the hours to seconds.

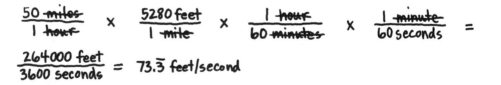

$$\frac{50 \text{ miles}}{1 \text{ hour}} \times \frac{5280 \text{ feet}}{1 \text{ mile}} \times \frac{1 \text{ hour}}{60 \text{ minutes}} \times \frac{1 \text{ minute}}{60 \text{ seconds}} =$$

$$\frac{264000 \text{ feet}}{3600 \text{ seconds}} = 73.\overline{3} \text{ feet/second}$$

4. Dollars per hour:

$$\frac{\$8.02}{4.16 \text{ hours}} = \$1.93/\text{hour}$$

5. Dollars per gallon:

$$\frac{\$8.02}{5.94 \text{ gallons}} = \$1.35/\text{gallon}$$

6. Dollars per passenger:

$$\frac{\$8.02}{4 \text{ passengers}} = \$2.005 \text{ (or } \$2.01/\text{passenger)}$$

7. Cents per mile:

$$\frac{8.02 \text{ dollars}}{208 \text{ miles}} \times \frac{100 \text{ cents}}{1 \text{ dollar}} = \frac{802 \text{ cents}}{208 \text{ miles}}$$

Which is 3.86 cents per mile (or roughly 4 cents/mile).

8. Total number of passenger-miles:

$$4 \text{ passengers} \times 208 \text{ miles} = 832 \text{ passenger-miles}$$

9. Passenger-miles per gallon:

$$\frac{832 \text{ passenger-miles}}{5.94 \text{ gallons}} = \frac{140.1 \text{ passenger-miles}}{1 \text{ gallon}}$$

10. Cents per passenger-mile:

$$\frac{802 \text{ cents}}{832 \text{ passenger-miles}} = \frac{.96 \text{ cents}}{1 \text{ passenger-mile}}$$

Or a little less than one cent per passenger-mile.

Note: Because of the carpool, this car provided a much more efficient method of transportation than if all four individuals had driven their own cars. In Problem Set A you'll find another problem illustrating this concept, and you will be asked to compare that situation with this one.

Now consider traffic safety. Which is safer: driving, taking a train, or flying? Well, most people make most trips safely, however they travel. But when there is an airplane accident, the death toll can be very high. The death toll in a single car accident is low, but there are a lot more deaths each year from auto accidents.

In 1989, two train passengers died as a result of railroad accidents. On the other hand, 213 people died in the United States in accidents involving commercial airlines. A staggering 25,614 died in car accidents. It appears that flying is far more dangerous than taking a train, and it also appears that driving is the most dangerous.

Note: Car accident deaths are probably fairly stable from year to year, but both train and plane deaths could wildly fluctuate from year to year depending on the occurrence of major accidents.

Let's put these statistics in perspective. Consider them in terms of how much these modes of transportation are used.

The most common standard for comparison is "passenger-miles." To make equitable comparisons, we need to consider these statistics in terms of the total passenger-miles produced by each mode of transportation.

During 1989, the commercial airlines produced approximately 334.2 billion passenger-miles (334,200,000,000!). The railroads produced 12.8 billion passenger-miles. Automobiles provided 2,143.9 billion passenger-miles. How do the death statistics compare now?

Write ratios showing deaths/bill pass-miles for each form of transportation.

Airlines:

$$\frac{213 \text{ deaths}}{334.2 \text{ bill pass-miles}} = \frac{.63 \text{ deaths}}{\text{bill pass-miles}}$$

Trains:

$$\frac{2 \text{ deaths}}{12.8 \text{ bill pass-miles}} = \frac{.16 \text{ deaths}}{\text{bill pass-miles}}$$

Automobiles:

$$\frac{25614 \text{ deaths}}{2143.9 \text{ bill pass-miles}} = \frac{11.95 \text{ deaths}}{\text{bill pass-miles}}$$

Evidently, automobiles are far more dangerous than either planes or trains. How many deaths per year would occur if cars had the same death rate per billion passenger-miles as trains?

$$\frac{.16 \text{ deaths}}{\text{bill p-m}} \times \frac{2143.9 \text{ bill p-m}}{1 \text{ year}} = \frac{343.02 \text{ deaths}}{1 \text{ year}}$$

When you consider that every year, on a Labor Day weekend, there will be approximately 600 to 700 traffic deaths in the United States, the safety rate of the railroads becomes even more impressive.

The next problem again combines compound units and units in ratios.

MR. ROGER'S NEIGHBORHOOD

Janice, Stephanie, Rose, and Gina are going to be paid $84.70 for cleaning up Mr. Rogers' neighborhood. They each worked 5 hours, except Rose, who was 45 minutes late. How much should each one be paid?
Work this problem before continuing.

Some people have kind and generous inclinations and would have all four girls paid the same amount—they would not want Rose to receive a lesser amount of money. These people may eventually save humanity. They probably do not go into business.

Rose contributed 4 $\frac{1}{4}$ hours of labor. Janice, Stephanie, and Gina each contributed 5 hours of labor (or 15 hours among the three), making a total of 19 $\frac{1}{4}$ labor-hours.

Note: We could also use 19:15 for 19 hours and 15 minutes. Unfortunately, this often leads to the decimal 19.15 instead of the correct decimal 19.25 for 19 $\frac{1}{4}$ hours.

Now divide:

$$\frac{\$84.70}{19.25 \text{ labor-hours}} = \$4.40 \text{ per labor-hour}$$

To find the fair share for each worker, multiply her hours by the dollars per labor-hour.

Janice, Gina, and Stephanie:

$$\frac{\$4.40}{1 \text{ \sout{labor-hour}}} \times \frac{5 \text{ \sout{labor-hours}}}{1} = \$22.00$$

Being careful with the units reveals that the unit labor-hours cancels, leaving the units as dollars.

The computation for Rose is similar.

$$\frac{\$4.40}{1 \text{ labor-hour}} \times \frac{4.25 \text{ labor-hours}}{1} = \$18.70$$

If you attempt to double-check this problem by multiplying the hourly rate times the labor-hours, the labor-hours units cancel, and the unit that is left is dollars.

$$\frac{\$4.40}{\text{\sout{labor-hour}}} \times \frac{19.25 \text{ labor-hours}}{1} = \frac{\$84.70}{1}$$

Another approach was to set up a chart like ones used in algebra classes for solving various word problems. Tom took this approach.

Name	Hours Worked	Pay Rate/Hour	Total Pay
Gina	5		
Stephanie	5		
Janice	5		
Rose	4.25		
Total	19.25		$ 84.70

"I divided the $84.70 by 19.25, giving $4.40 per hour. Then all I had to do was to multiply each girl's hours times her pay rate to come up with her total pay."

Name	Hours Worked	Pay Rate/Hour	Total Pay
Gina	5	$ 4.40	$ 22.00
Stephanie	5	$ 4.40	$ 22.00
Janice	5	$ 4.40	$ 22.00
Rose	4.25	$ 4.40	$ 18.70
Total	19.25	$ 4.40	$ 84.70

Sometimes, problems from courses such as chemistry and physics are more easily solved if you pay attention to the units involved. One of Ken's students came to him one day with a problem in his chemistry class. Even though Ken knows absolutely nothing about chemistry, he was able to assist the student in solving the problem using unit analysis. Now, it is not our intention to belittle science knowledge—quite the contrary. Using simply a unit analysis approach to solve a problem does not require any understanding of science. In fact, if you don't understand the science involved, you may make mistakes by relying strictly on unit analysis. However, if you keep careful track of units in science problems, an approach to the solution may be more readily apparent. You should use unit analysis in conjunction with knowledge of science in order to enhance further learning and understanding. Ultimately, the goal should be enhanced problem solving in all fields of science. This includes problems that arise in research, not simply textbook problems. The ideal is to improve learning and understanding by tying together all current knowledge and tools.

An example of a real-world use of unit analysis was provided by Rick, a professor of physiology at a leading university.

"In our research we are very concerned with the timing of our experiments. The computer can sample data in nanoseconds (1 billionth of a second), microseconds (1 millionth of a second), or milliseconds (1 thousandth of a second). We often have to go back and forth between these different computer sampling rates and match them with the frequency responses of the nerve cells which are in seconds, milliseconds, and microseconds. The computer sampling rate during the experiment must be configured to maximize the efficacy of the nerve activity that is being sampled. There are two types of nerve activity: low-frequency nerve activity and high-frequency nerve activity. To avoid excess computer storage of data, low-frequency nerve activity must be sampled with low computer sampling rates and high-frequency nerve activity must be sampled with fast computer sampling rates. If the nerve activity is occurring every millisecond (1 thousandth of a second), we need to set the computer sampling rate to at least 20,000 times per second. So the computer will be sampling every 50 microseconds. In this way, I am sure we will record the necessary data. If the nerve activity occurs every second, and we were to sample 20,000 times per second again, we would waste a lot of computer memory. We would get 1000 times more data points then we would need. Computer storage space is very expensive, so we must be sure that we sample at the right rate. Knowledge of the units involved is very important."

Problem Set A

1. UNIT CONVERSIONS

Convert from metric to English or from English to metric as indicated. The only metric-to-English conversions you are allowed to use are: 1 meter = 3.281 feet and 1 gallon = 3.79 liters. Of course, you may use any English-to-English conversions (such as 1 mile = 5280 feet) and any metric-to-metric conversions (such as 1 km = 1000 m).

a. 35 m to feet

b. 170 ft to m

c. 150 mi to km

d. 47 km to mi

e. 4 ft to cm

f. 87 cm to inches

g. 54 inches to mm

h. 32 mi/hr to m/sec

i. 5 gal to liters

j. 16 liters to quarts

2. CHRISTINA'S TRIP

Christina drove 116 miles in 2 hours and 15 minutes. She used 4 gallons of gas that cost her $4.76. Find each of the following.

a. mi/hr

b. mi/gal

c. $/gal

d. ft/sec

e. $/hr

f. qt/min

g. ¢/min

h. ¢/mi

i. mi/$

j. gal/hr

3. ANOTHER LONG COMMUTE

Anastoli and two friends drove 87.5 miles and got 35 miles per gallon. They drove at a speed of 50 miles per hour and the trip cost them $3.30 in gasoline. Find each of the following.

a. gallons

b. hours

c. ft/sec

d. $/hour

e. $/gallon

f. $/passenger

g. ¢/mi

h. total number of passenger-miles

i. passenger-mi/gal

j. ¢/passenger-mile

Comparing this car with Gerónimo's car from the Long Commute problem in the text, which car do you think is being used most efficiently?

4. **RULE OF THUMB**

A car driving 60 miles per hour is traveling how many feet per second? A car driving 40 miles per hour is traveling how many feet per second? A car driving 50 miles per hour is traveling how many feet per second? Find a pattern in the above examples, and come up with a rule of thumb for converting miles per hour to feet per second.

5. **PROJECTILE**

A projectile is shot in space at 150 feet per second.

a. How many miles per hour is that?

b. How many kilometers per hour is that?

6. **PAINTING CHIPMUNKS**

Alvin, Simon, and Theodore went to work helping Dave paint his house. Alvin worked 6 hours, Simon worked 1 ¼ hours less than Alvin, and Theodore worked 4 ½ hours. They were paid $61 for their work. How much should each chipmunk get?

7. READING RATE (PART 1)

If you read 15 minutes per day every day and end up reading 12 books of 200 pages each in one year, what is your reading rate in pages per minute?

8. READING RATE (PART 2)

If you increase your reading speed so that each page takes you 30 seconds fewer than it did before, and you begin reading 20 minutes per day, how many 200 page books can you now read in a year?

9. NURSING

Allyson is a nurse in the intensive care unit of a hospital. She works with units daily in administering drugs through intravenous (i.v.) tubes. A common dosage for the drug dopamine is 2 to 5 micrograms per kilogram of body weight per minute. She will put 400 milligrams of dopamine into 250 cc (cubic centimeters) of fluid and administer it into the patient through an i.v. tube. At what rate, in cc/hr, should she set the flow to achieve a dosage of 3 micrograms per kilogram per minute into a patient with a mass of 75 kg?

10. CONNECTIONS

Where have you used unit analysis in other courses or in your daily life?

Problem Set B

1. WANT A SMOKE?

Smoking has long been connected to all sorts of horrible diseases such as lung cancer, emphysema, heart disease, and others. It has been estimated that for every cigarette a person smokes, he or she loses anywhere from 10 to 15 minutes of his or her life. Assuming the worst (15 minutes of life lost for each cigarette), how much shorter would the life span be of someone who smoked two packs a day for 35 years? (Each pack contains 20 cigarettes.) Answer in years, days, hours, and minutes. (For example: 42 years, 152 days, 7 hours, and 28 minutes.)

SESAME STREET LIVE

The national touring company of Sesame Street Live visited Seattle, Washington, last year. The producers held a special promotional ticket sale for one hour. During this time, adult tickets sold for $5, junior tickets (kids aged 8 to 16) sold for $2, and children's tickets (kids aged 0 to 8) sold for the ridiculously low price of 10 cents. During this sale, 120 tickets sold for exactly $120. How many of each kind of ticket were sold during the sale?

3. **CHAIN LETTER**

Albin Digas made up the following chain letter.

Dear Friend:
This is a chain letter. Make two copies. Send the two copies and this original to three friends.

Sincerely,

Albin

Since Albin wanted to get the letter going in a big way, he made five originals and sent them out in the first mailing. If Albin's first mailing is considered the first generation, and each set of copies constitutes the next generation, how many letters will be in existence after the tenth generation is produced?

(Note: Chain letters are illegal, and—as you can see from this problem—ridiculous.)

4. **WHO WAS SNOOZING?**

One of the five senators in the defense budget committee meeting was suspected of sleeping during the meeting. It was known that only one senator had actually slept, but no one (except the five senators) knew which senator it was. The Vice President questioned the senators and they made the following statements.

Davis: The snoozer was either Rawls or Charlton.
Rawls: Neither Vongy nor I was asleep.
Charlton: Both Rawls and Davis are lying.
Bobbins: Only one of Rawls or Davis is telling the truth.
Vongy: Bobbins is a liar.

When the committee chairperson (she was not questioned) was consulted, she said that three of the senators always tell the truth and two of them always lie. Who slept in the meeting?

5. **VOLLEYBALL LEAGUE**

Use the league standings for this recreational volleyball league and the schedule for the first three weeks in order to determine which teams won each week. (By the way, the Renegades won their second match.) What happened in each of the three matches that the Buckeyes played?

STANDINGS			SCHEDULE
TEAM	WINS	LOSSES	WEEK I
Red Skeletons	3	0	Red Skeletons vs Walleyball
Bombay Bicycle	2	I	Bombay Bicycle vs Bill's Thrills
Renegades	2	I	Whine Sox vs Renegades
Sacto Magazine	2	I	Sacto Magazine vs Buckeyes
Walleyball	2	I	WEEK 2
Buckeyes	I	2	Renegades vs Sacto Magazine
Bill's Thrills	0	3	Walleyball vs Whine Sox
Whine Sox	0	3	Buckeyes vs Bombay Bicycle
			Bill's Thrills vs Red Skeletons
			WEEK 3
			Whine Sox vs Sacto Magazine
			Walleyball vs Bill's Thrills
			Red Skeletons vs Buckeyes
			Bombay Bicycle vs Renegades

9 solve an easier related problem

O N E O F the most famous legends in mathematics is that of Carl Friedrich Gauss (1777–1855). The story concerns the young Gauss in fourth grade. The teacher was in a bad mood and wanted to give the class something to do so that he could get some work done at his desk. So he gave the class an assignment: Add up all the numbers from 1 to 100. The teacher believed that this would keep the class occupied for 30 minutes. But after just a short time, Carl Gauss walked up to the teacher's desk with the answer written on his slate. Fortunately, the teacher didn't accuse Gauss of cheating, but instead asked him how he solved the problem. Before we relate the story, you should try the problem.

FROM ONE TO ONE HUNDRED

What is the sum of the first hundred whole numbers?
Work this problem before continuing.

There are many ways of approaching this problem. One way (the brute force problem-solving strategy) is to get out a piece of scratch paper or your calculator and just keep adding. A second way would be to use the constant addition feature and the memory on your calculator and just press the M+ (memory plus) key 100 times. But Carl Gauss

◀ *Riding a bicycle may seem impossibly hard at first, but mastering riding a bike with training wheels is an easier, related problem that can give a child a feel for the real thing.*

SOLVE AN EASIER RELATED PROBLEM   **223**

did not have a calculator, so he must have done it differently.

Another method is a combination of subproblems and patterns. Tori approached the problem this way.

"I decided to break the problem into subproblems. I split the 100 numbers into groups of ten, and computed the sum of each ten. Then I looked for a pattern."

$$1 + 2 + 3 + 4 + 5 + 6 + 7 + 8 + 9 + 10 = 55$$
$$11 + 12 + 13 + 14 + 15 + 16 + 17 + 18 + 19 + 20 = 155$$
$$21 + 22 + 23 + 24 + 25 + 26 + 27 + 28 + 29 + 30 = 255$$

"I quickly saw the pattern, and so I added up the sums of the ten groups of ten."

$$55 + 155 + 255 + 355 + 455 + 555 + 655 + 755 + 855 + 955 = 5050$$

"Subproblems and patterns made this problem easy. Of course, I used a calculator and Carl Gauss couldn't have had one 200 years ago."

So just what did Gauss do anyway? Let's imagine the way he might tell the story.

"When my teacher gave me this problem, I really didn't want to do it. I could tell that he was just trying to keep us busy, because we had been kind of rowdy, throwing paper airplanes and spitballs around the room. I hadn't caused any of the trouble and so I didn't feel like I should be punished. I looked around and noticed that all the other kids were busy doing the problem. They kept erasing their slates and everything. I didn't want to put up with that stuff. So I thought about it for a while. I pretended that the teacher had given us a different problem instead. I thought from 1 to 100 would take too long, so I thought about 1 to 10. I knew I could add that up no problem."

$$1 + 2 = 3 \quad 3 + 3 = 6 \quad 6 + 4 = 10 \quad 10 + 5 = 15 \quad 15 + 6 = 21 \quad \text{etc.}$$

"I got tired of this real quick. I couldn't imagine going all the way to 100. There had to be an easier way. Then it occurred to me that I didn't have to add up the numbers in that order, I could use any order I wanted. So I started playing around with the numbers. I added 1 and 5 and got 6. Then I added 2 and 4 and got 6 again. I thought that was sort of weird. I started over again. This time I added 1 and 10. That gave me 11. Then I did 2 + 9 and 3 + 8 and 4 + 7 and 5 + 6 and got 11 every time. So the sum of the whole numbers from 1 to 10 had to be 5×11 since there were 5 groups of 11.

"From this easy problem, it was immediately obvious how to do the original problem."

$$1 + 100 = 101$$
$$2 + 99 \ \ = 101$$
$$3 + 98 \ \ = 101$$
$$4 + 97 \ \ = 101$$

"... and so on. There were going to be 50 pairs of 101, so the answer was $50 \times 101 = 5050$. I walked up and told my teacher. Boy, was he impressed."

What Carl Gauss did in the eighteenth century contains a great lesson for today. If a problem seems to be too hard, make it easier. You will see a number of different ways of making a problem easier. Of course, the easier problem has to be related to the one you are doing. Gauss would not have been helped on the above problem if he thought about the problem of tying his shoe. Tying his shoe is clearly easier to do, but it is not related to the problem at hand.

~~~~~

One way to make an easier related problem is to simply replace difficult numbers in the problem with easier ones. You probably do this all the time. Suppose you were buying fast food and you only had $5.00. Instead of adding $1.59 for a hamburger, $.89 for a soda, and $1.29 for a large order of french fries, you might add easier numbers quickly in your head: $1.50 for the burger, $1.00 for the drink, and $1.25 for the fries. The estimated total is $3.75—you have enough money. If you only had $4.00 you would have to consider adding more carefully and also determine if there's any tax on the meal. Easier numbers aren't only useful for estimating. Sometimes just replacing difficult numbers with easier ones and experimenting with them to explore for reasonable answers can give you insight into how to actually solve a problem.

Our friend and mentor Tom Sallee, a professor at the University of California at Davis, who first taught both of us about problem solving, considers the easier, related problem strategy to be one of the most useful. He mentioned that there were many ways to make a problem easier and more manageable.

Here is Tom Sallee's list of common ways to make a problem easier.

1. Use a number instead of a variable.

2. Use a small or easier number in place of a more difficult one in order to develop the process for solving the problem.

3. Do a set of specific easier examples and look for a pattern.

4. Do a specific easier example and figure out an easier process that will work.

5. Change, fix, or get rid of some conditions.

6. Eliminate unnecessary information.

This chapter employs several of these ways to make a problem easier. This is a pretty difficult strategy to get the hang of. But remember, when a problem seems too hard or too confusing, look for an easier, related problem and see if that helps.

One more quote from Sallee. "Easier, related problems (abbreviated ERP) are analogous to guess and check in a funny way. In guess and check you try a number and see if it works. In ERPs you try a process and see if it works."

~~~~~

Solving an easier, related problem is another strategy that falls into the major category of changing focus. There may be some elements of organizing information involved, but the major part of the strategy is to change your focus away from the original problem to an easier, related problem. Then after solving your easier problem, decide if you have a plan for the original problem. Sometimes it is necessary to do several easier problems before going back and solving the original problem.

The clerk of Simpletown had the job of getting the materials ready for the next municipal election. There were 29 issues and candidates. In the last election, there were 28,311 registered voters, representing 18,954 households, and they voted at 14 polling places. She figures she needs about a proportionate amount of materials for this election. There are 34,892 people registered this time. How many polling places will be needed?

Work this problem before continuing.

Janeen contributed the following comments about this problem:

"This problem just totally confused me at first. I had no idea what it was all about. After I reread it a couple of times, I started to think about some way to make the problem easier. I rounded off all of the numbers and made a chart."

Polling Places: 15
Voters (last election): 30,000
Households: 20,000
Issues: 30
Voters (this election): 35,000

"I looked at these numbers and realized that the polling places and the voters had something in common: polling places are locations for voters. The numbers must be connected somehow. Since there were 30,000 voters at 15 polling places last election (by my rounded numbers), that would be 2000 voters at each polling place. The number of households would be important to an elections clerk for deciding the number of information pamphlets to send out, but probably not necessary in calculating the number of polling places needed. Besides, the only information provided for both elections is the numbers of voters for the two elections. So I ignored the information about households. I also didn't figure the number of issues mattered a whole bunch. It was probably the same as the last election, but I have no way of knowing since the problem didn't say. It actually would make a difference if there were a whole bunch more issues this time than last time as it would take someone longer to vote. But I decided to ignore that too.

"Now I needed to know how many polling places were needed for this election. I decided to keep it at 2000 people per polling place. So I just divided 35,000 by 2000 and got 17.5. So that's either 17 or 18 polling places for this election.

"Since I had a plan, I now went back to the original problem. In my easier, related problem, I came up with $^{30,000}/_{15}$ polling places is 2,000 voters per polling place. So I divided 28,311 by 14 to find out about how many voters there are per polling place in the original problem. The answer is 2022.3 (rounded). I then divided 34,892 by 2022.3 and got 17.25 polling places needed. I figured they would try to set up 17 polling places. This would be 34,892 voters divided by 17 polling places, which gives 2052.5 voters per location, which is probably no problem. And I thought it was interesting that I got basically the same answer with my easier problem."

Janeen's success on this problem can be traced to the following things she did.

1. She organized the information.

2. She simplified the numbers (take note of this).

3. She ignored all of the irrelevant information.

It is admirable that instead of panicking, Janeen got started on the problem and worked on it. The problem is complicated because it uses large numbers, and there is no direct indication that you need to divide to solve the problem. She also ignored the irrelevant information. She did this by determining relevant information and ignoring the rest. Simplifying the numbers put Janeen in a better position to analyze the problem. Janeen used the strategy called solve an easier, related problem. For Janeen, the easier, related problem was essentially:

> The clerk of Easierelatedtown had the job of getting the materials ready for the next municipal election. In the last election, there were about 30,000 registered voters, and they voted at 15 polls. She figures she needs about a proportionate amount of materials for this election. There are about 35,000 people registered this time. How many polling places will be needed?

The problem is nowhere near as complicated as before, yet is essentially the same problem. An easier, related problem can often help you decide how to proceed on a difficult problem.

Use the strategy of easier, related problems to solve the next problem.

HALLOWEEN NIGHT

Last Halloween, each goblin was to scare exactly 3 people out of every 517 in the city. They were also supposed to find 47 newts (presumably for their eyeballs) for every 912 people in the city. And for hors d'oeuvres (for the All-Spooks party), they needed to bring in 19 wings of flies for every 33 people in the city. There were 1,414,512 people in the city that night, of whom 359,278 went to some kind of Halloween party. How many newts did the goblins need to find?

Work this problem before continuing.

Did you catch the irrelevant information? What did you need to find out?

Knute solved it this way.

"First I figured out what was unnecessary information. Since the problem asked for the newts the goblins needed to bring in, I decided to focus on that. The problem said '47 newts for every 912 people in the city.' Since it talked about people in the city, I also wrote down 1,414,512 people in the city. I think everything else was irrelevant, because that should be enough for me to answer the question. I changed some of the numbers. I changed 912 people to 1000 people, because it is so easy to work with 1000. I changed 1,414,512 people to 1.4 million. I also changed 47 newts to 50 newts. That made the problem '50 newts for every 1000 people,' and '1.4 million people in the city.' So I divided 1,400,000 by 1000, which gave 1,400 (representing 1400 groups of 1000 people). I multiplied that times 50 newts (50 newts for each group of 1000 people), giving 70,000 newts. That's a lot of newts! Anyway, then I went back to the original numbers and did the same thing."

$$1,414,512 \div 912 = 1,551$$
$$1,551 \times 47 = 72,897 \ (NEWTS)$$

"It's still a lot of newts and newts' eyeballs, but it makes sense and my answer was close to the estimate."

Knute did several things very well in his solution: He estimated, he eliminated irrelevant information, he used easier numbers to make the problem easier, and he checked his answer for relevance, if any can be found in this problem. Seriously, his comments about the eyeballs indicate that he paid attention to the significance of his numerical result."

Anita took a different approach.
"This problem, once you got done throwing up and being confused, sounded a lot like the 'unit analysis' problems we used to do. I saw it in the following ways."

$$\frac{47\ newts}{912\ people} \qquad \frac{19\ fly\ wings}{33\ people} \qquad \frac{1414512\ people}{1\ city}$$

$$\frac{1414512\ people}{359278\ partyers} \qquad \frac{3\ scared}{517\ people}$$

"In unit analysis, you kind of always kept your goal in the back of your mind, so I checked the question, and it has to do with newts the goblins need to find. None of the other units were relevant. It turned out that all you really had to do was multiply and cancel units."

$$\frac{47\ newts}{912\ people} \times \frac{1414512\ people}{1\ city}$$

"The peoples units canceled, leaving newts/city (and this makes sense, too, because we needed to find out how many newts were needed for the whole city). The answer is 72,897 newts."

Anita's sense of unit analysis is correct, as this problem is set up as a set of related ratios. And the unit approach she took is sensible, even though the units are not the commonplace ones.

How many squares are there on a checkerboard? (Hint: It is more than 64).
Work this problem before continuing.

Angie and Isaac worked on this problem. Isaac is a checker player, so of course he liked this problem. They worked with squares on a piece of graph paper.

Isaac: This problem is too easy. It's 64. There are 8 squares on each side, and 8 times 8 is 64.

Angie: But that can't be right because it is too easy. Look, aren't there some other squares on this board? Like right here; if we divide the square into fourths, we have four more squares that each contain 16 of the little squares. And how about this square that has nine squares in it?

Isaac: Wow, you're right. This problem is harder than I thought.

Angie: Well, let's look at an easier problem. How could we make this one easier?

Isaac: I know, how about 3 + 5. That's an easier problem and the answer is 8.

Angie: Isaac, the easier problem has to be related to the one we're doing.

Isaac: Okay, Okay. I know, we could use a smaller square. How about 7 by 7 instead of 8 by 8?

Angie: Good idea, but that still seems too hard.

Isaac: Well, this is ridiculous. How about 1 by 1, is that easy enough for you?

Angie: Yeah, I think I can handle that. (She drew a 1 by 1 square.) How many squares are here?

Isaac: Gee, I don't know, one?

Angie: Yeah, that was a little easy. Maybe we should try something a little harder. How about 4 by 4?

Isaac: Now, wait. I think I see what you are getting at. Maybe if we go to 2 by 2 and then 3 by 3, we might find a pattern.

Angie: Yeah, Okay, let's do 2 by 2. (She drew a 2 by 2 square. A "2 by 2" means a "checkerboard" with two squares along the width and two squares along the length. See the picture below.) Well, I see four squares.

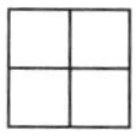

Isaac: I see five. There are obviously four little squares. But the whole picture is a square, so that makes five.

Angie: Oh yeah. Let's try a 3 by 3.

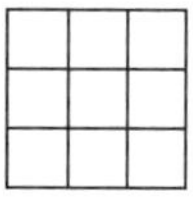

Isaac: Wow, this is getting harder. Let's see, there are nine little squares and one big square, so there are ten.

Angie: Yeah, but wait. There are also some medium-sized squares: squares that contain four squares. They are the same size as the 2 by 2 square we looked at a minute ago.

Isaac: I see them. How many are there?

Angie: Well, gee, they sort of overlap. I think there are four.

Isaac: I think so too. (He outlined them.)

Angie: Okay, so there are nine little 1 by 1 squares, four 2 by 2 squares, and one 3 by 3 square. So that is a total of 14. I think I'm seeing a pattern here.

Isaac: Me too. Can we organize this somehow?

Angie: I think so. Let's make a chart.

Isaac: What are we going to put in the chart?

Angie: Good question. Well, let's see. So far we have:

Size of "checkerboard"	Number of squares
1 by 1	1
2 by 2	5
3 by 3	14

Do you see a pattern?

Isaac: No, I don't. But that last one was interesting. Let's do a 4 by 4.

Angie: Okay. (She drew a 4 by 4 square.)

Isaac: Okay, there are obviously 16 little squares. How many 2 by 2 squares are there?

Angie: I don't know. But there is one big square.

Isaac: Come on, Angie, we've got to do this systematically.

Angie: Okay, we're looking for squares that are 2 by 2. I think there are 4. We can divide the whole square into fourths, so there are four.

Isaac: I don't think so. Last time the squares overlapped. I think that happens here too. Let's just look at the top two rows. We can put a square on the left side, one in the middle, and one on the right side. (He outlined them.)

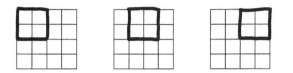

Angie: And we can do that in the second and third rows, and in the bottom row. So there are nine. I think I see a pattern here.

Isaac: I do too. I bet there are four 3 by 3 squares.

Angie: Yes, there are. (She outlined them.)

Isaac: And there is one 4 by 4 square. It seems as though the pattern is the squares. We need to organize this.

Size of Board	Number of Squares
1 by 1	1
2 by 2	4 + 1 = 5
3 by 3	9 + 4 + 1 = 14
4 by 4	16 + 9 + 4 + 1 = 30

Isaac: Oh, hey, look at this. If we reorganize this chart …

Size of Board	1 × 1 Squares	Size of Squares 2 × 2 Squares	3 × 3 Squares	4 × 4 Squares	Sum
1 by 1	1				1
2 by 2	4	1			5
3 by 3	9	4	1		14
4 by 4	16	9	4	1	30

Isaac: I see a ton of patterns.

Angie: Yea, check this out. The first column keeps on increasing: the next row is the next perfect square.

Isaac: And then it happens again in the second, third, and fourth columns.

Angie: But look at the rows, too: 14 is 1 + 4 + 9, and 30 is 1 + 4 + 9 + 16. And …

Isaac: I think we're on to something!

Angie: Great, so keep going. All we have to do is to add up all of the squares up to the size of the checkerboard. So for the original problem, which is 8 by 8, we will add up $8^2 + 7^2 + 6^2 + 5^2 + 4^2 + 3^2 + 2^2 + 1^2$.

Isaac: And the answer is (getting his calculator) 204. Great job. We could do this for any size checkerboard.

Angie: Yes, we could. I wonder if there is a formula for this?

Isaac: I bet there is. Maybe we will learn it later.

DIVISORS AND RECIPROCALS

The divisors of 360 add up to 1170. What is the sum of the reciprocals of the divisors of 360?
Work this problem before continuing.

Rori approached this problem this way.

"I can't even imagine listing all of the divisors of 360, let alone trying to find all of their reciprocals and adding them up. So there has to be an easier way. I'm a little lazy anyway, so its not hard for me to look for an easier way. I decided to change the number 360 to something smaller. Of course, I wouldn't know what the divisors of my new number added up to, but if I pick a small number, I shouldn't have any problem finding its divisors so I can add them up.

"So I picked the number 24. I picked 24 because it has a fair number of divisors, but not too many that would be hard to figure out.

"The divisors of 24 are 1, 2, 3, 4, 6, 8, 12, and 24. These add up to 60. Okay, now what? Well, let's see, the original problem asks for the sum of the reciprocals of the divisors. So I added up $\frac{1}{1} + \frac{1}{2} + \frac{1}{3} + \frac{1}{4} + \frac{1}{6} + \frac{1}{8} + \frac{1}{12} + \frac{1}{24}$. Yuck. I hate fractions. Okay, let's see, we need a common denominator. It looks like the least common denominator is going to be 24. Well, that's interesting. So change everything to 24ths."

ORIGINAL		NEW
$\frac{1}{1}$	$=$	$\frac{24}{24}$
$\frac{1}{2}$	$=$	$\frac{12}{24}$
$\frac{1}{3}$	$=$	$\frac{8}{24}$
$\frac{1}{4}$	$=$	$\frac{6}{24}$
$\frac{1}{6}$	$=$	$\frac{4}{24}$
$\frac{1}{8}$	$=$	$\frac{3}{24}$
$\frac{1}{12}$	$=$	$\frac{2}{24}$
$\frac{1}{24}$	$=$	$\frac{1}{24}$

"Then I added up all of the new fractions. I ended up adding up the numerators, which are 24, 12, 8, 6, 4, 3, 2, 1. But I did this already before. I know the sum of these numbers is 60 because these are just the factors of 24. So the answer to my easier problem is $\frac{60}{24}$. My prediction is the answer to the original problem is going to be the sum of the factors over the number. I will test this prediction on another example.

"This time I tried 10. I picked a smaller number to test my theory quickly. The factors of 10 are 1, 2, 5, 10. Adding up these numbers gives 18. My prediction for the sum of the reciprocals is $^{18}/_{10}$. I tried it."

$$\frac{1}{1} + \frac{1}{2} + \frac{1}{5} + \frac{1}{10} = \frac{10}{10} + \frac{5}{10} + \frac{2}{10} + \frac{1}{10} = \frac{18}{10}$$

"I noticed that again I just added the numerators which were the factors of the number in reverse order: 10, 5, 2, 1. So the sum of the factors is 18, and the denominator is 10, so the answer is $^{18}/_{10}$.

"Therefore, the answer to the original problem is the sum of the divisors over the number, so it is $^{1170}/_{360}$."

Rori did a few specific, easier examples and this led her to an easier process for solving the original problem. She didn't even have to actually work the original problem.

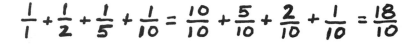

THE TEN-THOUSAND DAY WAR

If the Ten-Thousand-Day War started on a Wednesday, on which day of the week did it end?
Work this problem before continuing.

Ms. Warner's class worked this problem.

Ms. W: How should we start this problem?

Hiren: I think it's a Friday

Demick: I think it's a Tuesday.

Hiren: No, it's a Friday.

Ms. W: Wait a minute fellas. Let's have a strategy here, not just an argument. Who can suggest a strategy that might work?

Bijaya: I think we should use a systematic list. We could just write down all the days. So the first day is a Wednesday, the second is a Thursday, the third is a Friday, until we get to ten thousand.

Ms. W: Don't you think that might take a while?

Bijaya: Yeah, maybe about ten minutes.

Theresa: No way, it would take a lot longer than that. There must be an easier way.

Kapenda: What about these easier, related problems you are always talking about?

Ms. W: How would you make this problem easier?

Kapenda: Well, how about a nine-thousand-day war? Or maybe eight thousand.

Theresa: Oh, come on. That would still take forever.

Sang: How about a one-day war? Then it would end on a Wednesday, the day it started. Or how about a two-day war? Then it would end on a Thursday.

Erik: That's a good idea. I agree with Sang. But I kind of agree with Bijaya too. Let's make a systematic list, but with wars that are shorter.

Ms. W: Okay. Who would like to make the list on the board?

Karmen: I will. I love to go to the board. What should I write?

Danielle: Write what Sang said.
(Karmen writes.)

1. Wednesday

2. Thursday

3. Friday

4. Saturday

Karmen: This is going to take forever.

Ms. W: Maybe we can organize it a little differently.

Bruce: How about a calendar?

Ms. W: What do you mean?

Bruce: You know, a calendar. We can put the days of the week at the top and the numbers down below. I'll show you. (He goes to the board.)

Karmen: Hey, this is my job.

Bruce: Look, like this:

Sun	Mon	Tue	Wed	Thu	Fri	Sat
			1	2	3	4
5	6	7	8	9	10	11
12	13	14	15	16	17	18
19	20	21	22	23	24	25
26	27	28	29	30	31	32
33	34	35	36	37	38	39
40	41	42	43	44	45	46
47	48	49	50	51	52	53
54	55	56	57	58	59	60
61	62	63	64	65	66	67
68	69	70	71	72	73	74

Bruce: Hey, I'm getting tired of this.

Ms. W: Does he need to keep going all the way up to ten thousand?

Theresa: No way, that would take forever.

Hiren: See, my answer was right, it's going to be Friday.

Demick: No, it's going to be Tuesday.

Ms. W: Can anyone suggest something that might help?

Craig: I think I see a pattern.

Hy: I do too. The numbers in each row are all seven more than the numbers right above them.

Craig: Yeah. And it looks like the Tuesday column is the most significant.

Ms. W: What do you mean?

Craig: Well, all the numbers in the Tuesday column are multiples of 7. So if 10,000 is a multiple of 7, it will be a Tuesday.

Demick: (punching the buttons on his calculator) I see what Craig is saying. But 10,000 is not a multiple of 7, so it's not a Tuesday and I was wrong.

Hy: What is the closest multiple of 7 to 10,000?

Demick: Let's see. When I divided 10,000 by 7, I got 1428.571428. So if I multiply 1428 by 7, I get 9996. So the 9996th day is a Tuesday, because that's where the multiples of 7 fall.

(Bruce continues the chart on the board.)

Sun	Mon	Tue	Wed	Thu	Fri	Sat
61	62	63	64	65	66	67
68	69	70	71	72	73	74
...						
		9996	9997	9998	9999	10,000

Bruce: It's a Saturday.

Hy: You could have also looked at the remainder when you divided 10,000 by 7. The quotient was 1428 remainder 4. So count four more days from Tuesday: Wednesday is one, Thursday is two, Friday is three, Saturday is four. So it's a Saturday.

Ms. W: Great job, everybody. So the easier, related problem helped a lot, and so did making a list and looking for a pattern.

~~~~~

One of the ways that solving easier, related problems can be made more relevant is to consider learning traditional math skills. For example, change $^{12}/_{11}$ into a decimal. Students often ask, "Which number do you divide by?"

Consider this dialogue between a teacher and a student:

Student: I have to change this to a decimal. How do I punch it into my calculator?

Teacher: Think back to an easier problem. For that type of thing, I like to use $^1/_2$. How do you punch that in?

Student: I don't know. 1 ÷ 2?

Teacher: Try it!

Student: No, it's gotta be 2 ÷ 1, because you would've have said something.

Teacher: I did say something. I said "Try it." If you think it's 2 ÷ 1, try it, if you think it's 1 ÷ 2, try it.

Student: But I didn't ask about this problem. I need to know about $^{12}/_{11}$. Anybody knows $^1/_2$ is point 5.

Teacher: Yes, that's why I want you to do the division for $^1/_2$. If you get 0.5 for your answer, then you will have done it correctly and you can use that as a model for doing $^{12}/_{11}$.

Student: Oh, Okay. (a short time later) It works when I punch in 1 ÷ 2. So does that mean I punch in 12 ÷ 11?

Teacher: What do you think?

Student: I think I'm right, because if I'm wrong you would have told me.

Teacher: Okay, do what you want. Remember this when you get stuck: Think of a similar problem related to the one you're trying to solve. Pick a problem that you either already know how to do, or that you already know the answer to. Do the easier problem, and then apply what you learned to the problem you're really trying to solve.

The idea of using a simpler problem in learning mathematics can be very powerful. Knowledge of some facts, such as $^1/_2 = 0.5$, can allow a student to extend the concept to the general process of changing a fraction to a decimal. In the situation above, the student was confused about which number to divide by. By using the things he already knew, the student worked an easier, related problem and applied the knowledge back to the more difficult problem.

Another good place to use easier, related problems in math class is in working with variables and exponents. Many students have difficulty remembering the "product rule" and the "power rule" for exponents. They often confuse the two. Work these problems.

Simplify each expression:

$m^{1/8} \, m^{5/13}$ $\qquad\qquad (y^{1/3})^{6/7}$

Work this problem before continuing.

Ha, ha! Fooled you! There's no solution here! Instead, if you have any doubt about your answer, work these two problems and look for the rule to apply back to the two problems on the previous page. The first step is done for you.

$x^2 \bullet x^3$ $\qquad\qquad (x^2)^3$
$(xx)(xxx)$ $\qquad\qquad (xx)(xx)(xx)$

Now, work these problems before continuing on to the next paragraph.

We decided not to give the answer. Sorry. If you truly aren't sure what the answer is, use another problem-solving strategy: Ask somebody.

The process used in the two math class examples is similar to the process used to solve problems in this chapter. With the problems in this chapter, however, you probably don't know the answer to the easier problem that you are posing. But the fact that you are trying to solve an easy problem means that the answer to the easy problem is within your reach. After you solve the easy problem, a way to solve the more difficult problem becomes evident.

GOOD LUCK GOATS

In ancient Kantanu, it was considered good luck to own goats. Barsanta owned some goats at the time of her death, and willed them to her children. To her first born, her favorite, she willed one-half of her goats. (The will was drawn up long before her death, and was written in general terms.) To her second born, who was not the favorite, she willed one-third of her goats. And last (and in the eyes of Barsanta, the least) she gave one-ninth of her goats to her third born (the "black sheep" among goat owners).

As it turned out, when Barsanta died she had 17 goats. Barring a Solomonic approach, how should the goats be divided?

Work this problem before continuing.

This problem involves working an easier, related problem. In this case, an even number would probably work better.

Nikki approached it like this.

"Since 17 is an odd number, I decided to try a simpler number: 2. Two worked fine for the first born, but didn't work for the second born. Since it had to be divisible by 2 and also divisible by 3, I tried 6.

However, 6 didn't work well for the third born. So this time I tried 18. The weird thing was, 18 seemed to work."

$\frac{1}{2}$ of 18 is 9 (1st born)

$\frac{1}{3}$ of 18 is 6 (2nd born)

$\frac{1}{9}$ of 18 is 2 (3rd born)

Total: 17 goats distributed to children, one goat left over

"It's weird because there's one goat left over, but Barsanta didn't really have 18 goats, she had 17. So there really isn't a goat left over because it doesn't really exist. It's also weird because if you really tried to do half of 17, you'd have to cut a goat into parts, so 17 doesn't work, but 18 does work to make 17 work."

Nikki's solution is an example of changing a condition in the problem to make the problem easier. She changed the number of goats Barsanta had, and that enabled her to solve the problem.

Another way to make a problem easier is to use numbers in place of variables. Use that technique on the next problem. Problems like this are quite common on the SAT test.

AVERAGES

The average of a group of quiz scores is 31.8. There are k quiz scores in the group. The average of 10 of these quiz scores is 24.3. Find the average of the remaining quiz scores in terms of k.
Work this problem before continuing.

There are several things that are difficult about this problem. The given averages are difficult numbers and the number of quiz scores in the original group is not known. There are two things that the solver can do to make the problem easier. One has been mentioned before. Make the numbers 31.8 and 24.3 into easier numbers. Use 30 and 25 instead. So now the problem says:

The average of a group of quiz scores is 30. There are k quiz scores in the group. The average of 10 of these quiz scores is 25. Find the average of the remaining quiz scores in terms of k.

However, it is still difficult to figure out what to do. If you knew the number of test scores, the problem might seem more manageable. So make up a number for k. While you are at it, you might as well pick an easy number. Let's say there are 50 scores. So now the problem says:

The average of a group of quiz scores is 30. There are 50 quiz scores in the group. The average of 10 of these quiz scores is 25. Find the average of the remaining quiz scores in terms of 50.

It seems a little easier now, although the last sentence may not make a whole lot of sense. For now, pretend that the last sentence of the problem says, "Find the average of the remaining quiz scores." If there are 50 scores with an average of 30, then their total must be 1500. Why is that? To get an average you take the total of all the scores and divide by the number of scores.

$$\frac{\text{Total Scores}}{\text{Number of Scores}} = \text{Average}$$

For our easier, related problem we have

$$\frac{\text{Total Scores}}{50} = 30$$

The total of all the scores must be $30 \times 50 = 1500$. The next part of the problem says that the average of 10 of these quiz scores is 25.

$$\frac{\text{Total of 10 Scores}}{10} = 25$$

The total of this group must be $25 \times 10 = 250$. (Notice that this is a subproblem.)

The remaining scores must add up to $1500 - 250 = 1250$. How many scores are remaining (more subproblems)? We started with 50 scores and have already considered 10 of them. So there must be 40 scores left that add up to 1250. The average of these scores is:

$$\frac{1250}{40} = 31.25 \text{ is the the average of the remaining scores.}$$

Solving this easier, related problem gives a clue as to how to solve the original problem.

Look carefully at the numbers 1250 and 40. Where did they come from? 1250 was just 1500 – 250. But where did we get those numbers? We got 1500 by multiplying 30 (the average of all scores) and 50 (the total number of scores). We got 250 by multiplying 25 (the average of the small group of scores) and 10 (the number of scores in the small group). We got 40 by subtracting 50 (the total number of scores) minus 10 (the number of scores in the small group).

$$\frac{1250}{40} = \frac{1500 - 250}{50 - 10} = \frac{30 \times 50 - 25 \times 10}{50 - 10}$$

Now recall the original problem. The average of all scores is really 31.8, not 30. The average of a small group of 10 scores is really 24.3, not 25. And there are really k scores in the whole group, not 50. Substitute these numbers into the expression above.

$$\frac{31.8\,k - 24.3 \times 10}{k - 10} \quad \text{or} \quad \frac{31.8\,k - 243}{k - 10}$$

In this problem we used two types of easier, related problems. We replaced difficult numbers with easier numbers and we replaced a variable with a number to see what was going on. Both of these substitutions made the problem much more manageable and gave us a plan of attack. After solving the easier problems, the plan for the original problem became clear and it wasn't hard to do anymore. It was just a matter of applying the procedure learned on the easier problem to the hard problem.

~~~~

The next problem appeared in the Guess and Check chapter. This time solve it by an easier, related problem by changing some of the conditions in the problem.

A train leaves Roseville heading east at 6:00 a.m. at 40 miles per hour. Another eastbound train leaves at 7:00 a.m. on a parallel track at 50 miles per hour. What time will it be when the two trains are the same distance away from Roseville?

Work this problem before continuing.

Marla solved this with an easier, related problem.

"First, I drew a diagram of the two trains."

"Then I started thinking about it. It was obvious that the later train was gaining on the slower train 10 miles every hour. So I decided to pretend that the first train had traveled for an hour, and then stopped. The second train then left at 10 miles per hour. I thought this was the same problem. (An example of changing the conditions in the problem.) So the second train had to make up 40 miles (the distance the first train traveling at 40 miles per hour covered between 6:00 and 7:00) at 10 miles per hour. That would obviously take the second train 4 hours to catch up. So the answer is 4 hours from 7:00 (when the second train left) which gives 11:00. I then checked this. The first train goes from 6:00 to 11:00, which is 5 hours, and covers 200 miles at 40 mph. The second train goes from 7:00 to 11:00 (4 hours) and covers 200 miles at 50 mph. So both trains cover the same distance, so the answer of 11:00 must be right."

~~~~~

The next problem was first posed by G. Polya—one of the first teachers of problem solving—in his book *How To Solve It*, published in 1945.

Given any triangle, draw a square inside of it so that all four vertices of the square are on the triangle. Two of the vertices of the square should be on one side of the triangle, and the other two sides of the triangle should each have one vertex of the square.

Make the problem easier by eliminating one of the conditions. You need to draw lots of diagrams.

Work this problem before continuing.

Ronaldo and Julie worked on this problem.

Ronaldo: This problem seems really tough. How can we make it easier?

Julie: I'm not sure, let's experiment by drawing triangles and see if we get lucky.

(They drew the triangles shown below, and attempted to put the squares inside of them. They were not successful, as the inside figures did not look like squares.)

Ronaldo: This isn't working at all. We need to make this easier somehow. What did our teacher say about changing the conditions of the problem?

Julie: Yeah, she said we could make the problem easier if we changed or fixed or got rid of some conditions. I'm not really sure what she meant, though.

Ronaldo: Well, we can change the conditions and make it a triangle inside of a square. That would be really easy.

(He drew the picture below.)

Julie: I don't think that was what she meant. Maybe we can try only putting three of the vertices of the square on the triangle, and let the fourth one float around the inside or outside.

(She drew the pictures below.)

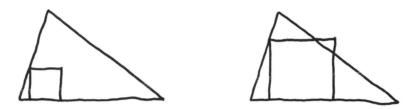

Ronaldo: I think you're onto something there, Julie. That must have been what our teacher meant. It's easy to draw just three of the vertices on the triangle. Let's agree to always put the longest side of the triangle on the bottom, and always put two of the vertices on that side.

Julie: That's a good idea. But wait, I think we should start by picking a point on the left side of the triangle. Then draw a line down to the base. Then measure that distance across the base, and then go up.

Ronaldo: But that last vertex probably won't be on the triangle. But let's do it anyway. That is relaxing a condition.

(They drew the series of pictures below.)

Julie: I think I see what is going on. All of the fourth vertices form a straight line.

Ronaldo: Yes, they do. So all we have to do is draw that line, and where it intersects the third side of the triangle, we have our fourth vertex. Then it's easy to draw the square.

(Their final picture is shown below.)

At the beginning of the chapter, we showed the following list from Tom Sallee. Next to each item in the list is the problem(s) in the text that used that method. Some problems involved more than one of these.

Common ways to make a problem easier:

1. **Use a number instead of a variable.** We used this in Averages.

2. **Use a small or easier number in place of a more difficult one in order to develop the process for solving the problem.** We used this in Simpletown Elections, Halloween Night, the math class discussion, and Averages.

3. **Do a set of specific easier examples and look for a pattern.** We used this in From One to One Hundred, How Many Squares, and the Ten-Thousand-Day War.

4. **Do a specific easier example and figure out an easier process that will work.** We used this in Divisors and Reciprocals.

5. **Change, fix, or get rid of some conditions.** We used this in Good Luck Goats, Next Train East, and Inscribed Square.

6. **Eliminate unnecessary information.** We used this in Simpletown Elections, and Halloween Night.

Using an easier, related problem sounds like an easy strategy to master, but it is actually really difficult. When confronted with a problem that seems too hard or impossible, you should remember to ask yourself the following question: "What can I do to make this problem easier?"

Problem Set A

1. **DIAGONALS**

A certain convex polygon has 25 sides. How many diagonals can be drawn?

2. **SUM OF ODDS**

Find the sum of the first 5000 odd numbers.

3. **TV TRUCK**

Theotis has to load a truck with television sets. The cargo area of the truck is a rectangular prism that measures 8 ft by 21 ft by 11 ft. Each television set measures $1\frac{1}{2}$ ft by $1\frac{2}{3}$ ft by $1\frac{1}{3}$ ft. How many sets can be loaded into the truck?

4. **POTATOES**

In order to prepare dinner in the mess hall, Jamie, who is a member of the 4th battalion of the 23rd regiment, generally used about 85 pounds of potatoes to feed the 358 people in his unit. He usually assigned three soldiers to scrub the potatoes, and it takes them just under 2 hours to complete the job. However, this next week he will need to feed about 817 people beginning at 17:30 hours, due to a special army event. When he arrived at the mess hall tent for the field exercises, he discovered 181 pounds of potatoes had been sent. He needed to send for the rest right away. How many pounds should he request, and how many soldiers does he need if he is going to have them spend about 2 hours each on scrubbing?

5. SQUARE AND HEXAGON

A square has an area of S^2. A regular hexagon has a perimeter of T. If p is the perimeter of the square and h is a side of the hexagon, then find $h + p$ in terms of S and T.

6. TWENTY-FIVE MAN ROSTER

Roger Craig, during his term as manager of the San Francisco Giants, received a strange communication from the team general manager, Al Rosen. Mr. Rosen told him to select 25 players for his roster according to this formula:

$1/2$ of the team had to be outfielders and infielders,
$1/4$ of the team had to be starting pitchers,
$1/6$ of the team had to be relief pitchers, and
$1/8$ of the team had to be catchers.

Roger was a bit confused by Al's request, yet complied anyway. How did he do it?

7. ODD AND EVEN

Find the difference between the sum of the first 500 even numbers and the sum of the first 500 odd numbers.

8. LAST DIGIT

What is the last digit in the product of:
$(2^1)(2^2)(2^3)(2^4) \dots (2^{198})(2^{199})(2^{200})$?

9. FIFTY-TWO CARD PICKUP

A deck of cards was dropped on the floor. While Amel was out of the room, Naoko picked up at least one card. She may have picked up one, all fifty-two, or any number in between. How many possible combinations are there for what she picked up?

Problem Set B

1.   COVERING THE GRID

A grid has lines at 90-degree angles. There are 12 lines in one direction and 9 lines in the other direction. Lines that are parallel are 11 inches apart. What is the least number of 12-inch by 12-inch floor tiles needed to cover all of the line intersections on the grid? The tiles do not have to touch each other. You must keep the tiles intact—do not break or cut them.

2.   TUPPERWARE PARTIES

A Tupperware party host was frustrated at her attempts to get more people to host sales parties for her. She finally offered to pay any host $25 who (a) hosted a party for her, and (b) arranged for two other friends to host parties (during the next month). To her surprise, it worked! She had 100% success (every host was able to arrange two more parties). She started with five hosts in the first month. If this continues for the entire year, how many parties will there be during the year?

3.   ADDING CHLORINE

I have a small doughboy circular swimming pool in my backyard for my kids. Last weekend, I set it up and bought chlorine to put in it. The directions on the bottle said to put in 16 fluid ounces of chlorine per 10,000 gallons of water. Of course, our pool is a lot smaller than 10,000 gallons, so I needed to figure out how much chlorine to put in. I measured the pool with my tape measure and found it to have a circumference of 27 feet 3 inches and a water height of 21 inches. I knew that the circumference of a circle was $C = 2\pi r$ and the volume of a cylinder was $V = \pi r^2 h$ (r is the radius of the cylinder and h is the height). I knew that a milliliter is a cubic centimeter. I also knew that there are 3.79 liters in 1 gallon, and 3.281 feet in one meter. How many fluid ounces of chlorine did I need to put in? (I have a measuring spoon capable of measuring to the nearest quarter of a fluid ounce.)

4. JOGGING AROUND A TRACK

Dionne can run around a circular track in 120 seconds. Basha, running in the opposite direction as Dionne, meets Dionne every 48 seconds. Sandra, running in the same direction as Basha, passes Basha every 240 seconds. How often does Sandra meet Dionne?

5. NINE POINTS

There are nine points on a piece of paper. No three of the points are in the same straight line. How many different triangles can be formed by using three of the nine points as vertices?

40 physical representations

MANY ASPECTS of mathematics were developed to solve real-life problems. Other mathematics developed as peripheral to real-life problems or even devoid of apparent real-life applications.

This chapter involves taking problems back into the real-life stage. Although few of the problems represented in this chapter may actually be "true to life," the method for solving them and for solving many real-life problems is the same: create a physical representation.

Physical representations fall into the major category of spatial organization. A physical representation is different from a diagram, however, in that you can touch the problem, not just represent it with a diagram. You gain a new perspective on the problem by using objects or people to solve it.

We begin the chapter with the most basic type of physical representation, where people are involved and walk through the problem. This is called acting it out. The second section explores using physical objects called models or manipulatives. The last section of the chapter deals with looking for ways to change a problem into a manipulatives problem. You'll see that the strategies of acting, models, and manipulatives are closely related and overlap one another. They are different ways of physically representing a problem.

Physical representations have traditionally been left out of the curriculum in most schools. This is unfortunate, as mathematics has become totally abstract to many people. When problems are represented with objects, the problems become more concrete and are more easily understood.

◀ *Architects build actual models of housing developments so they can manipulate pieces and visualize different arrangements.*

Section 1: Act It Out

O F ALL of the strategies presented in this book, this one is probably the most fun. Acting out a problem involves contact with other people and is also a very effective problem-solving strategy. Other strategies will work to solve these problems. However, acting the problem out with a small group of people works very well. There are no written explanations for the solutions of the problems in this section. The correct solution should be obvious when you act it out.

THE JACKALS AND THE COYOTES

Three jackals and three coyotes are on a trek across the Mokalani Plateau when they come to a river filled with carnivorous fish. There is a rowboat in sight, and the party decides to use it. (Both species are known for their cleverness, regardless of how much this problem exceeds reasonableness.) However, the boat is too small for any more than two of the group at a time. So they must traverse the river in successive crossings. There is one hitch, though. The jackals must not outnumber the coyotes at any time, in any place. If it happens, for example, that there are two jackals on the western bank, and only one coyote, then this problem is reduced to simple subtraction and gluttony. (The jackals will overpower, kill, and eat the coyotes.) It's okay to have an equal number of each, and it is also okay to have more coyotes than jackals in a given place. Neither situation poses a danger to the coyotes, and the coyotes do not pose a threat to the jackals. So, the trick here is to use the one small rowboat, a lot of sweat, and a little brainpower to assure the coyotes' survival while both groups cross the river.

Close the book and find some people to act this out with. You should also pick some object to be physically transported across the room as the "boat."

Parts of your solution probably involved some guess and check. It is usually wise to act out the solution to a problem before actually implementing it. In real life, you would have to be careful about using guess and check, since a wrong guess could lead to an early dinner for the jackals.

In working this problem, you should have reached several "major understandings." The first is realizing that there could only be two animals in the boat. The second is dealing with the first move: sending two coyotes over on the first trip only means death for the third coyote. The next major understanding comes after you get two coyotes and two jackals on the far side. The only thing to do is bring back one of each and then send two more coyotes over. Then finally, send the solitary jackal back to begin bringing over the other two jackals.

≋ ≋ ≋

Sometimes the critical elements of acting out a problem are the physical objects you employ. This problem exhibits that notion.

THE HORSE TRADER

Once upon a time, there was a horse-trader. One day, the horse trader bought a horse for $60. Just after noon, the horse trader sold that same horse back to the original owner for $70. He then bought it back again just before 5:00 for $80. By midnight, he managed to sell the horse back to the original owner for $90. How much money did the horse trader make or lose on this horse?

Close the book and act this problem out before continuing. You will need something to represent the horse, some play money in different denominations, and at least two people to act out the roles of the horse trader and the original owner.

Acting it out allows several people to act as verifiers—checking for mistakes and making sure that all transactions were done correctly. Part of the trickiness of this problem is identifying net financial gain and where it occurs. By having a couple of people looking out for their interests in the problem, you can verify which direction money has flowed, and how much.

Problem Set A-1

Solve each problem by acting it out.

1. THREE ADULTS AND TWO KIDS

Three adults and two kids want to cross a river using a small canoe. The canoe can carry two kids or one adult. How many times must the canoe cross the river to get everyone to the other side?

2. THE DOG, THE GOOSE, AND THE CORN

There was once a farmer who, as part of his route to town, used a rickety old boat to cross a wide river. He took his dog and went to town one day just to buy corn. However, not only did he buy some corn, but he also bought a goose that he intended to take home and use to start raising geese. (This farmer was no fool; he already had another goose.) He also knew, however, that his boat was not reliable: It could only handle himself and one of the other three things he had with him. He feared that if left alone, the dog would eat the goose or the goose would eat the corn. How could he get himself and everything else across the river safely?

3. HOOP GREETING

A group of 10 kids got together at the playground to play basketball. Before the game, every kid shook hands with each of the other kids exactly once. How many handshakes took place?

4. SWITCHING JACKALS AND COYOTES

There are three jackals on one side of a river and three coyotes on the other side. They have a boat capable of carrying two animals. At no point can the number of jackals outnumber the number of coyotes on one side of the river, or else the jackals would eat the coyotes. Each group wishes to change sides of the river. Figure out which side of the river the boat must be on, and how to manage the groups to get each animal safely to its destination.

5. THE HOTEL BILL

Three sales representatives attending a convention decided to share a room in order to take advantage of some cheaper hotel rates. The clerk at the desk charged them $60, which they paid with cash. A little while later, the clerk discovered that he had made an error; the room should have only been $55. He dispatched a bellhop with a $5 bill to deliver to the women. The bellhop was dishonest, though, and kept $2 and returned $1 to each of the three women. So each one thought that her part of the bill was $19 instead of the original $20.

When Franklin heard about this story, he did some calculations: Each woman thought she paid $19, and 3 × $19 is $57. The bellhop kept $2, so $57 + $2 = $59. What happened to the missing dollar? Is Franklin's reasoning right or wrong? Determine what happened to the missing dollar and explain your reasoning.

6. PERSIS' GIFT SHOP

Persis owns a gift shop. One day while she was opening a shipment of figurines she had just received, a stranger walked in and asked how much the figurines were. The figurines had cost Persis $6 each, but she had not decided on a price for them. She finally decided on $13 each, and the stranger promptly said he'd take one. Her new clerk accepted his traveler's check for $40 and gave him change. Persis needed more change for the register and signed the traveler's check over to the pharmacist next door, Dr. Drell. An hour later though, Dr. Drell came back over and showed her that the traveler's check was actually in French francs (worth about $8 at the time). Persis apologized and wrote the pharmacist a check to cover the difference. Who lost how much on this transaction?

7. BUCKINGHAM PALACE

At Buckingham Palace, four guards are pacing back and forth performing maneuvers. Two of the guards are wearing blue uniforms (Basil and Barry) and the other two guards are wearing red uniforms (Ralph and Randy). They are performing their maneuvers for an audience. The guards are standing in large tile squares on the floor. The tile arrangement with each guard's present location is shown below.

Basil		Barry
Ralph		Randy

One move for a guard consists of the following: He moves from his position one square in one direction (not diagonal), then turns 90 degrees and moves two squares in that direction. (Or he could move two squares first and then one square.) Each move a guard makes is in this L-shape, and he does not stop until he has finished the complete move.

So, for example, Basil could move one square south and two squares east and end up in the square directly to the north of Randy's square. No two guards may occupy the same space at the same time.

a. How many of these moves does it take for the blue guards (Basil and Barry) to change places with the red guards (Ralph and Randy)?

b. How many of these moves does it take for Basil to change places with Ralph?

Section 2: Make a Model or Use a Manipulative

IN ACTING OUT problems, people get together and assume roles in order to gain insight into the problem. Several brains may be working on the problem at once, and physical constraints become more and more apparent and more easily respected by using people in the roles. For example, a coyote (played by a person) can only be on one side of a river at a time. Using a person in the role of a coyote assures us that no laws of physics and biological existence are broken. On the other hand, working out the jackals and coyotes problem with paper and pencil could result in a coyote appearing simultaneously on both sides of the river. By having a person act the role of the coyote, normal laws of matter are respected.

Each problem in the first portion of this chapter was based on re-creating the problem and acting it out. This is a form of physical representation. Some of the problems in the previous section had people in the roles of animals (jackals, coyotes, horses, dogs, geese) and others had people in the roles of inanimate objects (such as corn).

Often, acting it out is impractical (there is no one around when you are working on the problem), too time-consuming (there are people around, but it takes a while to round them up), too embarrassing (no one will want to be the goose, for example), or too expensive (the only way you can get people to be involved in the horse trader problem is to use real money—yours—and they get to keep it, and even then you are forced to act out the part of the horse).

We now extend the abstraction one more step. Instead of using actual people to act out the problems, many of the characters in the problem will simply be represented by objects called manipulatives. The acting will be done by one person.

Reducing the jackals and coyotes to little pieces of paper has the advantage that you can solve this problem by yourself, without having to hunt up some friends capable of acting like coyotes and jackals. It has the disadvantage of having only one brain working on the problem. However, this idea of using a manipulative is one step away from actually acting it out with people. The manipulative needs to be designed to contain the critical elements of the problem, and needs to be in a form such that the problem can be worked out.

> *Solve the jackals and coyotes problem again using manipulatives. Choose something to represent coyotes and something to represent jackals. Scraps of paper with C on some and J on others work well. Coins, paper clips, or bottle caps will also work. Determine the minimum number of river crossings. Work this problem before continuing.*

A disadvantage of not having actual people is that pieces of paper tend not to contribute any creative thinking to the problem. In acting out the jackals and coyotes problem, a person playing the part of a coyote would squawk if left alone with two jackals. But a little piece of paper labeled "coyote" will probably not have much to say in its own defense.

Despite these limitations, manipulatives can be very powerful problem-solving tools. When planning a manipulatives approach, you often have to make a conscious effort to look for a way to do the problem using manipulatives. You must have a little inventiveness in you. The necessary materials are often right around you. Dimes and pennies make very good manipulatives. Not only are they different sizes and different colors, but the back side of each can be distinguished from the front side. If you are in the forest, you can always find twigs, leaves, and pebbles (to represent wolves, bears, and campers, for example). If by chance there is a piece of paper nearby (even hamburger wrappers or discarded soda cups) you can tear it up into little pieces and write labels on the pieces. The manipulatives are there for anybody existing in the real world; the trick is to think of using them and then to use them effectively. Sometimes the first manipulative doesn't work very well, so a second one takes its place.

~~~~

None of the problems thus far have involved any measurement beyond simple counting (such as counting three coyotes). Some problems may involve an element of magnitude, scale, or orientation. The physical representation needs to demonstrate this aspect, and more thought needs to go into creating the physical representation. We call such representations models.

The strategy of making a model is used in the real world extensively—though probably not nearly enough. Models are made of airplanes, cars, freeway bridges, buildings, rockets, filing cabinets, and on and on. All can be used to test designs before moving to a more advanced stage of production. Many of the problems in this book require you to build some sort of model. In some models, relative size is one of the critical elements. Other problems feature shape as the critical element. Orientation is the key ingredient in the next problem.

FOUR CONTIGUOUS STAMPS

In how many ways can four stamps be attached together?
Be sure to pay attention to the thrust of this chapter. Take care to record each configuration.
Work this problem before continuing.

The critical elements in the stamps problem were that the four items used as manipulatives had to be relatively similar in size and shape. It was also important to distinguish the top from the bottom, as stamps are usually printed all in the same direction. You should have found 19 different configurations.

Orientation is also a feature of the next problem.

LETTER CUBE

Build this cube to see what letter is opposite the letter T. Pay attention to the orientation of the letters as well.

Draw this figure on a piece of paper (graph paper works well), cut it out, and fold it to make a cube. Then write the letters on it.

Work this problem before continuing.

Problems of this type often show up on IQ tests. You are "supposed" to visualize the cube in your mind to figure out where each letter is. What the designers of the IQ test don't tell you is that spatial visualization needs to be developed. Most people aren't very good at it at first. Building a model to solve a problem like the cube problem is really helpful in developing the ability to visualize.

After cutting out and folding up your cube, you should write the letters on it in the correct orientation. The solution for the problem is easily seen to be O.

The difference between models and manipulatives is very slight. We are using the term models to describe any sort of physical representation where magnitude, scale, or orientation is involved. A problem involving quantity, directional movement, positional relationships, static relationship or number combinations in which little pieces of paper or coins could be used is a manipulatives problem. In both cases, the problems are derived from a real physical object or situation, and pushed slightly toward the abstract by the model or manipulative. In some cases, the original problem is abstract, and the model/manipulative becomes a representative physical manifestation.

~~~~

Work this next problem by using a diagram of a volleyball court and pieces of paper with the players' names on them.

THE VOLLEYBALL TEAM

The volleyball team has six players: Betty, Martha, Karen, Walt, Guy, and Steve. Put them in their positions by using the clues to get the best rotation. (From the net, there are three players in the front row and three in the back row. The server is in the back left corner.)

1. *The players must alternate by gender.*
2. *Betty is the team's best server; she should start in the serving position.*
3. *Guy and Karen are the team's setters. They must be opposite each other at all times.*
4. *Walt and Martha communicate well—it helps to put them next to each other.*
5. *Steve is an effective server. He needs to be positioned so he will rotate into the serving position quickly.*

Note: A volleyball court has six players. They rotate in a clockwise manner. (See the diagram below.)

```
┌────── BACKLINE ──────┐
│                      │
│  Srvr 1   Srvr 6   Srvr 5
│
│  Srvr 2   Srvr 3   Srvr 4
│                      │
└──────── NET ─────────┘
```

Players are considered opposite if there are three positions between them. So server 1 is opposite server 4, server 2 is opposite server 5, and server 3 is opposite server 6.

Work this problem before continuing.

In order to solve this problem, tear up little pieces of paper and write the names of each of the players on them. You could also solve this problem simply by drawing a diagram, but using manipulatives is faster and requires no erasing. Manipulatives allow you to try different possibilities quickly, without worrying whether or not they are correct.

The solution to the volleyball problem follows. If you did not get it correct, check two things: (1) Did you use manipulatives, and (2) did you go back through the clues after you thought you were done to check for compliance?

```
┌────────── BACKLINE ──────────┐
│                              │
│   Betty      Guy     Martha  │
│                              │
│   Steve     Karen     Walt   │
│                              │
└──────────── NET ─────────────┘
```

≈≈≈≈

Sometimes it helps to use little pieces of paper with numbers written on them to solve problems. In this case, the problems are abstract—they are not real-world cases that have been abstracted with numbers. Problems like the one below were popularized by a math teacher and consultant named Marcy Cook, who creates materials for use in math classes. Her puzzle books include number tiles to manipulate when solving the problems.

❓ NUMBER PUZZLE

Use the digits 0, 1, 2, 3, 4, 5, 6, 7, 8, 9, once each to fill in the blanks in this puzzle:

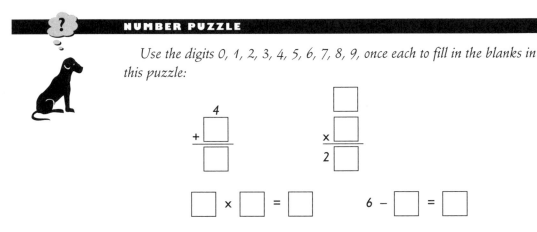

Work this problem by cutting up little pieces of paper and labeling them with the numbers 0 through 9. Then manipulate them around in the puzzle until you find a way that works. There is more than one possible solution.

There are essentially two different solutions to this problem. One of them starts with 4 + 1 = 5, and the other one starts with 4 + 5 = 9. We hope you found both solutions. (Note: Both solutions can be slightly changed by reversing the numbers in either of the last two number sentences, but those aren't really different solutions.)

~~~~~

The next problem was originally solved by using a systematic list. Solve it this time by making a systematic list in conjunction with a model.

FOOTBALL SCORES

How many ways are there to score 20 points in a football game? Use color rods to solve this problem.

Work this problem before continuing.

Color rods are made up of 1 cm cubes glued together in a line. An example of a 5 cm rod is shown below.

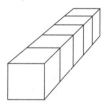

Color rods used as models can help in the formation of systematic lists of this type. Football scores can be made in the following ways. Safety–2 points, Field Goal–3 points, Touchdown–6 points, Touchdown with PAT–7 points. Let the red, light green, dark green, and black color rods represent 2, 3, 6, and 7 points respectively. Set up two orange rods (10 each) to represent 20 points. Then line up the smaller rods adjacent to the two orange rods and make them the same length.

Begin with all red rods. You can line up ten red rods next to the two orange rods as shown. This represents 10 safeties and is equivalent to 20 points. Start a systematic list to record results. Then gradually replace red rods with longer rods. Every time you take a red rod away, put it aside and don't use it anymore. Always start replacing red rods with light green ones, then dark green ones, and finally black ones.

The complete diagram and list are shown on the next page.

Point combinations (rods)	Sfts 2 pts	FG 3 pts	TDs 6 pts	TDs 7 pts
orange / orange — red red red red red / red red red red red	10	0	0	0
red red red red red / red red red red	9 reds—no			
red red red red red / red red red	8 reds—no			
red red red red red / red red lt grn / lt grn	7	2	0	0
red red red red red / red red / drk grn	7	0	1	0
red red red red red / red lt grn / lt grn	6 reds—can't make 8			
red red red red red / lt grn / black	5	1	0	1
red red red red / lt grn lt grn / lt grn lt grn	4	4	0	0
red red red red / lt grn lt grn / drk grn	4	2	1	0
red red red red / drk grn / drk grn	4	0	2	0
red red red / black / black	3	0	0	2
red red / lt grn lt grn lt grn / black	2	3	0	1
red red / lt grn / drk grn / black	2	1	1	1
red / lt grn lt grn lt grn lt grn / lt grn lt grn	1	6	0	0
red / lt grn lt grn lt grn / lt grn drk grn	1	4	1	0
red / lt grn lt grn / drk grn / drk grn	1	2	2	0
red / drk grn / drk grn / drk grn	1	0	3	0
lt grn lt grn / black / black	0	2	0	2
drk grn / black / black	0	0	1	2

There are 16 ways to score 20 points in a football game.

~~~~

Manipulatives or models can be used in other types of systematic list problems also. The Frisbin problem from the Systematic Lists chapter is another good example. They can also be used in problems where people need to line up in different orders.

The next problem could possibly be solved with matrix logic, but it would be rather confusing. The key to the problem is the position of each person at the table. Manipulatives are a good way to attack logic problems that involve positioning.

Four friends (one is named Janie) went out to dinner at a Mexican restaurant. The hostess seated them in a booth. Each ordered a different meat (one ordered pork) and each ordered a different kind of Mexican dish (one was a tostada). Use the clues below to determine what dish each person ordered, the kind of meat it contained, and where each person was sitting.

1. *The person who ordered mahi-mahi sat next to Ted and across from the person who ordered a burrito.*
2. *Ken sat diagonally across from the person who ate the fajita and across from the person who ordered beef.*
3. *The person who ordered a chimichanga sat across from the person who ordered chicken and next to Allyson.*

(For those unfamiliar with California-Mexican cuisine, burritos, fajitas, chimichangas, and tostadas are flour tortillas with various fillings such as mahi-mahi, pork, beef, and chicken.)

Work this problem before continuing.

The first twist is determining the names of the people, the dishes, and the meats ordered in the problem. This information was not stated at the beginning of the problem as usual, but hidden in the problem. By reading each clue, you can determine all of that. The names are Janie, Ted, Ken, and Allyson. The meats are pork, mahi-mahi, beef, and chicken. The dishes are tostada, burrito, fajita, and chimichanga.

The first step in a manipulative solution is to tear up pieces of paper (12 in this case) and write down the names of the people, meats, and dishes. Then read through the clues and arrange the pieces of paper as the clues would suggest. Making a "booth" manipulative is helpful for keeping track of position with respect to sides of the table.

The first clue says, "The person who ordered mahi-mahi sat next to Ted and across from the person who ordered a burrito." Something that you could do at this point is to tape the pieces of paper together in their relative positions:

	burrito
Ted	mahi-mahi

There is another possibility with this clue. It is possible that the arrangement should have been set up as:

Ted	mahi-mahi
	burrito

But this can still be accommodated by flipping over the three pieces as they are taped and writing the information on the back side.

By then taping other clues together in their relative positions, you make a set of larger manipulatives (involving two or three of the smaller manipulatives). These larger manipulatives can then be moved in a very limited number of positions, especially since some of the clues indicate positions on opposite sides of the table. By moving the large manipulatives on top of each other, you can find many contradictions, such as two people sitting in the same spot or two types of meat in the same position. For example, start with the burrito-Ted-mahi-mahi and the fajita-beef-Ken papers. Place the burrito-Ted-mahi-mahi paper on the desk, and place the other paper on top of it. There are four different ways to do this, two of which require you to turn the paper upside down and read the back sides.

1.

fajita	beef burrito	this is possible
Ted	Ken mahi-mahi	

2.

	Ken burrito	impossible, beef and mahi-mahi are
fajita Ted	beef mahi-mahi	matched with the same person

3.

Ken	
	burrito
beef Ted	fajita mahi-mahi

possible

4.

beef	fajita burrito
Ken Ted	mahi-mahi

impossible, Ted and Ken are sitting in the same seat

So at this point, there are only two possibilities. You should now superimpose the third paper, with Allyson-chimichanga-chicken on it, on top of the two possible combinations. Again, arrange it in the four ways for each combination (eight arrangements altogether). If these instructions seem difficult to read and follow, make sure that you are (a) using the manipulatives, and (b) understanding that this is precisely our point.

By taping the pieces in their relative positions, it is a lot easier to see which combinations are contradictions (and thus do not work). The Allyson-chimichanga-chicken paper won't work in any combination with number 1 above. The only combination that does work is with number 3, as shown below.

chicken Ken	
	burrito
chimichanga beef Ted	Allyson fajita mahi-mahi

You then fill in the remaining information (marked *).

Ken chicken *tostada	*Janie *pork burrito
Ted beef chimichanga	Allyson mahi-mahi fajita

Using manipulatives allows you to try different solutions very quickly. Sometimes, as in this problem, it even helps to tape the manipulatives together.

Manipulatives are also very good for solving problems involving balancing equations in chemistry. In chemistry, one of the basic problems to solve is the balancing of equations that describe what occurs in a chemical reaction. The total number of atoms of each element has to be equal before and after the reaction. A very simple example is the mix of hydrogen and oxygen molecules to form a water molecule. A molecule of hydrogen gas is symbolized by H_2 which means it contains two atoms of hydrogen. A molecule of oxygen gas is symbolized by O_2 which means it contains two atoms of oxygen. When these two gases come together they form water which is symbolized H_2O, which means it contains two atoms of hydrogen and one atom of oxygen. However, since the before and the after number of atoms have to be the same, something is wrong here. We started with two atoms each of hydrogen and oxygen and ended with two atoms of hydrogen but only one of oxygen. This reaction is not balanced. The equation form is shown below.

$$H_2 + O_2 \rightarrow H_2O$$

To balance this equation, you must add in new molecules on one or both sides of the equation to get an equal number of hydrogen atoms on each side and an equal number of oxygen atoms on each side. However, you can only add molecules that were present in the original reaction. You can't add a single atom of oxygen, because an oxygen molecule contains two atoms of oxygen. It doesn't come any other way. So by adding one or more of any of the molecules you started with to the side they started on (in other words, you can't add water H_2O molecules to the left side), you must find a way to equalize the number of each atom on each side.

One way to solve this problem is by using manipulatives. Cut out little pieces of paper and write H_2 on several of them, O_2 on several of them, and H_2O on several of them. Then put the H_2's and the O_2's on one side of your desk and the H_2O's on the other side of your desk. Pull one of each down into your work space.

Since there are two hydrogens and two oxygens on the left side and two hydrogens and only one oxygen on the right side, there clearly needs to be another H_2O on the right side. So add in another H_2O.

Now the number of oxygens is the same on both sides, but there are two few (pun intended) hydrogens on the left side. So add in another hydrogen on the left side.

Now there are 4 hydrogens and 2 oxygens on both sides, so the equation is said to balance.

Work this next one.

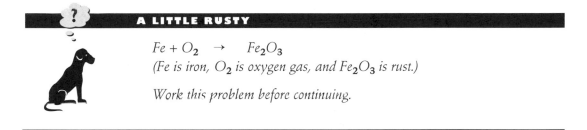

A LITTLE RUSTY

$Fe + O_2 \rightarrow Fe_2O_3$
(Fe is iron, O_2 is oxygen gas, and Fe_2O_3 is rust.)

Work this problem before continuing.

Use little pieces of paper again. Write Fe on several little pieces of paper, O_2 on several pieces of paper, and Fe_2O_3 on several pieces of paper. Then pull down one of each into your work space.

There are one atom of iron (Fe) and two atoms of oxygen on the left. There are two atoms of iron and three atoms of oxygen on the right. Add one iron on the left to make the irons balance. Add one oxygen on the left also.

Now the iron balances, but the left has one extra oxygen. So the right needs more oxygen. Add one molecule of rust (Fe_2O_3) to the right.

Now the right has four iron atoms and six oxygen atoms, while the left has two iron atoms and four oxygen atoms. So add one more O_2 and two more Fe's to the left.

Now there are four iron atoms and six oxygens on each side, so the equation is balanced.

~~~~~

Models and manipulatives are used often in the real world. Two NASA engineers recently used Tinkertoys, masking tape, lamp cord, and glue to make a model of the Hubble Space Telescope and figure out how to fix a problem occurring in outer space. One said afterward, "The moral of the story is that there is no solution that's too humble."

NASA FIXES HUBBLE'S ANTENNA

Cable blocked movement;
Tinkertoy helps engineer find solution

Associated Press

GODDARD SPACE FLIGHT CENTER, Md. – The Hubble Space Telescope, all $1.5 billion of it, was put back into working order Monday because a NASA engineer used a Tinkertoy, a lamp cord, masking tape and glue to help solve a major problem.

The telescope's No. 2 high-gain antenna, wedged in one position since Friday, was free and sending data through relay satellites.

The National Aeronautics and Space Administration expected calibration and other normal start-up work to begin by tonight and to receive its first pictures from the telescope by this weekend. "The moral of the story is that there is no solution that's too humble," said David Skillman, who built a model of the jammed antenna.

"We were faced with a problem on the telescope that involved quite intricate geometry," he said. "A number of us realized we could benefit greatly from a model. Someone suggested that even a Tinkertoy model could be useful."

He drove to a toy store Sunday afternoon and bought two boxes of the construction toy. He got the other items in a drug store and put the model together in 15 minutes with another engineer, John Decker.

The telescope has two dish-shaped high-gain antennas that are designed to transmit science data to two orbiting relay satellites at speeds equivalent to sending the contents of a 30-volume encyclopedia in 42 minutes.

The No. 2 antenna jammed on Friday when engineers were turning it left and right. Sensing something wrong and trying to prevent damage, the telescope's computer shut down the whole system. One engineer noticed that the inch-thick electrical cable on the back of the antenna was slightly out of position. With that in mind, they looked at telemetry data for signs that the cable could interfere with the counter-weights when the dish was turned to certain positions.

The model that Skillman and Decker built showed that to be the case and that, in turn, would cause the motors to work too hard and be automatically halted.

Troubleshooters had eyed the cable as a possible problem after studying photographs of the telescope while it still was on the ground and nestled in the cargo bay of space shuttle Discovery.

Data from the telescope indicated the dish's position and, said Skillman, "when we set the model to angles in the computer screen, we could see the interference in antenna parts and cable."

What they visualized with the model was matched with computer drawings at Lockheed Missiles and Space Co. in California.

Armed with that knowledge, computer commands were sent to the telescope directing exactly the way the dish should move to back out of its jam.

"The antenna moved beautifully and easily out of its problem and back to normal," said Skillman. "Many times a simple solution is the best solution."

Using models and manipulatives is a very powerful and underused strategy. We were rarely encouraged to use it in school, despite its obvious real-life application. In fact, our teachers may have discouraged its use in favor of a more abstract approach. Students may even be criticized for not being able to visualize the problem in their heads.

Sadly, many students buy this criticism and forgo the manipulative. Unfortunately, this leads to a lack of self-esteem when these type of problems become extremely difficult without the physical representation.

So don't apologize for using manipulatives and models. They are extremely helpful. You might even find yourself tearing up little pieces of paper when you take the SAT exam, as one recent Luther Burbank High School graduate did. It helped him get an 800 on the exam. Above all else, enjoy this strategy and consciously look for places to use it. The next section will help you expand your view as to when you can use manipulatives.

Problem Set A-2

8. TWO JACKALS LOSE THEIR LICENSE

Solve the jackals and coyotes problem again (all six of them start on the same side of the river), but this time only one of the jackals can operate the boat, and all three coyotes can operate the boat.

9. JACK-QUEEN-DIAMOND

Three playing cards from an ordinary deck of 52 cards lie face down in a row. There is a queen on the right of a jack. There is a queen on the left of a queen. There is a diamond on the left of a heart. There is a diamond on the right of a diamond. What are the three cards?

10. BASEBALL SEATING

A family of five, consisting of Mom, Dad, and three kids—Alyse, Jeremy, and Kevin—went to a baseball game. They had a little trouble deciding who was to sit where. Alyse would not sit next to either of her brothers. Kevin had to sit next to Dad. Mom wanted to sit on the aisle, and she didn't want to sit next to any kids, although she would sit next to her daughter if she had to. How was the seating arranged?

11. MAGIC TRIANGLE

To do this Magic Triangle, you must use the digits 1 through 6 (once each). Place one digit in each circle to make each side of this triangle have a sum of 11.

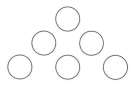

12. MAGIC SQUARE

The following is a magic square. The sum of each row is 12. The sum of each column is also 12. And the sum of each diagonal is also 12. Use the digits 0, 1, 2, 3, 4, 5, 6, 7, and 8 to find the proper location of each (there is more than one correct solution).

13. TRUE EQUATIONS

Use the digits 0, 1, 2, 3, 4, 5, 6, 7, 8, 9 to make true equations. Use each digit once.

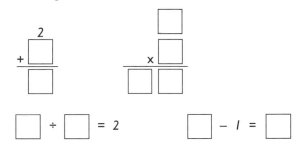

14. THREE-ON-THREE BASKETBALL

In a recreational basketball league, there were only three players on a team. Each team had a center, a forward, and a guard. The tallest on each team was the center; the shortest was the guard. The information below refers to three teams.

1. Leon and Weston are guards.

2. Horace and Ingrid play the same position.

3. Kathryn, the shortest, played her best game against Ingrid's team.

4. Horace and Leon are on the same team.

5. Jerome and Taunia are on the same team. On that team, neither is Jerome the shortest, nor is Taunia the tallest.

6. Sasha is shorter than both Weston and Horace.

Who is the forward on Kathryn's team? Who plays guard on Sasha's team? What position does Tiffany play and who else is on her team?

15. CUBIST

Three views of a cube are shown below. The cube has the five vowels A, E, I, O, U on the faces. One letter appears twice. Fill in the blank space in the last cube with the right letter in the right orientation.

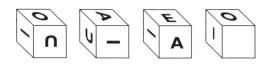

16. FOLDING CUBES

Given the diagrams below, where would you attach a sixth square so that if you cut out the figure, it would fold into a cube, if possible?

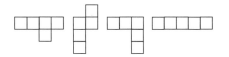

17. COED VOLLEYBALL

This volleyball team has eight players: Allyson, Cheryl, Jan, and Sue are the females; Marty, Ted, Dave, and Harold are the males. They will have six players on the court and two players off the court at any time. The two players off the court will rotate into the middle position in the back row. Players must alternate gender. Set up their beginning rotation with these constraints in mind.

1. Allyson can't be placed next to Dave or Harold because they hog the ball.

2. Sue should be by Harold because she is the best setter and he is the team's best hitter.

3. Dave should probably be next to Sue as he is the team's next best hitter.

4. Allyson prefers to play next to Ted.

5. Harold should get as much time as possible on the front row, as he is the team's best front-row player.

6. Dave is the team's best server. He should begin the game serving or be one of the first servers.

7. The weakest players are Jan, Cheryl, and Marty. They should not be placed next to one another.

Balance these equations.

$$HCl + Zn \rightarrow ZnCl_2 + H_2$$
(hydrochloric acid + zinc = zinc-chloride + hydrogen gas)

$$Na + Cl_2 \rightarrow NaCl$$
(Na is sodium, Cl2 is chloride, NaCl is sodium chloride or table salt.)

$$Al + O_2 \rightarrow Al_2O_3$$
(aluminum + oxygen gives aluminum oxide)

$$Na + H_2O \rightarrow NaOH + H_2$$
(sodium + water gives sodium hydroxide + hydrogen)

Section 3: Conversions

Work these six problems before continuing.

1. **HOLIDAY BLOCKS**

Use red and light green color rods. What are the possible totals of each color required to exactly fill this space?

2. PUNK BLOCKS

To do this puzzle, you are allowed to use exactly 13 color rods. Some can be red; the rest must be purple. How many of each are needed to exactly fill this space?

3. SPRING BLOCKS

Use only purple and yellow color rods. Make a string of purples the exact same length as a string of yellows, using one more purple than yellow.

4. TRIKES AND BIKES

Mr. Wheeler has tricycles and bicycles in his garage. He has a total of exactly 27 wheels on those vehicles. What are the possible combinations of bikes and trikes?

5. MORE DUCKS AND COWS

Janice counted total of 13 heads and 36 legs in a barnyard. She couldn't remember how many were ducks and how many were cows. Can you find out how many of each there were?

6. NEXT TRAIN EAST

A train leaves Roseville heading east at 6:00 a.m. at 40 miles per hour. Another leaves at 7:00 a.m. on a parallel track at 50 miles per hour. After how many hours will they be the same distance away from Roseville?

～～～

What you may have noticed about the last six problems is that there are really only three problems: Each one was written in two different ways. Let's go back and compare them.

In problem 1, you were asked to figure the number of red rods (two squares) and light green rods (three squares) that would fill a space that covered 27 squares. In problem 4 you were asked to use bicycles (two wheels) and tricycles (three wheels) to get a total of 27 wheels.

In problems 2 and 5 you were supposed to come up with a combination of 13 twos and fours that gave a total of 36. In the first case you were asked to fit some blocks into a space. (The area of that rectangle was 36 square centimeters; the blocks were each either 2 or 4 square centimeters.) In the next case, the twos and fours represented the number of legs on animals.

Finally, in problems 3 and 6 you were to work a train problem, involving the formula "distance = rate × time." But in problem 3, you used some manipulatives that could have represented the distances per hour in problem 6, and you used one more of one color than the other (representing traveling 1 hour longer).

The point of these pairs of problems is this: Problems can be worked in various ways. Part of what determines how you work a problem depends upon how the problem is presented. In the cases where the problem was stated in terms of manipulatives, there's an excellent chance you worked the problems in that way. Problems presented without mention of manipulatives, you probably worked in some other way.

Solving problems using manipulatives is not a common method. In some cases it is warranted, and in others it is not. One of the impediments to working problems with manipulatives is simply that people are not used to solving problems that way. Thus an unpracticed skill and strategy fails to become useful.

In order to become a better problem solver, you must look for opportunities to use manipulatives. Very few problems, be they real-world or contrived, are presented in a recognizable manipulatives form. You have to look for ways to use manipulatives on the problem.

There are certain types of problems that lend themselves easily to being adapted to manipulatives:

STATIC ARRANGEMENTS OF PEOPLE

A volleyball rotation, golf foursomes, and starting positions for softball teams are all examples of static arrangements. Also, who is sitting next to whom at a dinner table or a wedding tend to be natural manipulatives problems. In order to solve such problems, it is not necessary to have little figurines of people. Usually, all you need to do is to tear up little pieces of paper, write the names of the people on them, and draw a representation of the area in which they are to be manipulated.

For arranging the starting positions of a softball team, you would want to at least draw a baseball diamond so that you can set the pieces of paper in their relative positions. This has been done in cases where the team did not have fixed positions. Some people were strong in any position they played, others were weak in any position, and some could be weak or strong depending on the position. Having weak players on the field may not be an optimal solution, but it is true to life, and an acceptable arrangement can often be found.

DYNAMIC ARRANGEMENTS OF PEOPLE

In setting up transportation for a number of people in a few vehicles to and from various points, you can also use manipulatives. This might be done if you have people who need to be picked up from an airport after work, after shopping, before fitting tuxedos, and so on prior to a wedding. Many times in such situations there are only a few cars available, and there are many things to be done by various individuals or sets of people in various places. Again, by tearing up pieces of paper and also by setting up the locations and the vehicles (with capacity written on them), you can work out the problem in advance and make sure that everyone is taken care of.

PROBLEMS INVOLVING SPATIAL RELATIONSHIPS

Rearranging furniture is a great problem to work with manipulatives. By making a scale model of the space and the equipment/furniture needed inside that space, you can make a number of changes very quickly without risking anybody's back or toes. You can also determine how to landscape a yard in this fashion, by cutting out paper scaled to a plant's expected size at maturity. By moving around trees, bushes, fountains, or pink flamingos on a scale drawing, you can see where plants may be too crowded or where you can set up a visual focal point.

PROBLEMS INVOLVING LOGICAL CONNECTIONS

In the matrix logic chapter, we dealt with logic problems. Many of these problems can also be solved with manipulatives. By writing the names of the people and also their various characteristics on individual pieces of paper and manipulating the pieces, you can often make the logical connections. Tape even comes in handy in some cases.

PROBLEMS INVOLVING TANGIBLE NUMBERS

Rate-time-distance problems are a good example of this. Color rods or money can be used to represent different speeds or different distances or times.

ABSTRACT PROBLEMS INVOLVING NUMBERS

Little pieces of paper can be torn up to represent numbers. This technique proves useful in magic squares and other similar problems.

PROBLEMS INVOLVING ORDER

Dilyn manages a record store. Every week she receives the list of Billboard's top 200 albums. It lists the most popular albums in all categories in numerical order from 1 to 200. Dilyn wants the list in alphabetical, rather than numerical, order. So she makes a copy of the list and gives it to one of her employees. The day I visited the store, that employee was Carrie. Carrie cut the list up into 200 little strips of paper. She then alphabetized it by moving the strips around on a large counter and finally taped it back together. Dilyn told me, "We used to have a computer do this. But when the computer did it, the employees wouldn't even notice the new artists that showed up on the list. If a customer came in asking for a new record, Carrie probably wouldn't have heard of it. By doing the alphabetizing with the manipulatives every week, Carrie and my other employees stay current with the most popular artists and records. We actually had to move away from technology for the best results."

∧ ∧ ∧ ∧

A number of problems can be rewritten to reflect a bias toward (or against) being solved with manipulatives. It is no accident that math problems can be solved with manipulatives. Most math is based on real-world models. Therefore, changing problems back into real-world interpretations really isn't that big a jump.

Convert the next two problems into problems more slanted toward using manipulatives.

Malcolm used to brag that he had 11 Hondas at his estate; all were either motorcycles or cars. In all, his vehicles had 36 wheels. How many of each did he have?

My grandfather told me about the time he, his sister, and his cousins drove to the lake from his cousins' house. They took separate cars. My grandfather and his sister drove 30 miles per hour. His cousins left two hours later and drove 40 miles per hour. Both cars arrived at the lake at about the same time. What was the approximate distance from his cousins' house to the lake? Rewrite both problems before continuing.

There are many correct ways to rewrite each of these to make them slanted towards a manipulatives solution.

In Malcolm's Hondas, the critical elements are that there are 11 items, all of which have a value of two or four (two wheels or four wheels.) The total value is 36. The problem could easily be changed in the following ways.

1. The wheels become centimeters, the total is a length of 36 centimeters. The total is to be made up in groups of 2 and 4. Therefore: "String together 2-blocks and 4-blocks in the length that totals 36 centimeters. Use exactly 11 blocks."

2. The wheels become square centimeters, the total is an area of 36 cm². The total is to be made up in groups of 2 cm² and 4 cm². (We will also keep these areas in terms of rectangles, with a uniform width of 1 cm.) Therefore: "Fill in a rectangle with area 36 cm² using exactly 11 smaller rectangles, each measuring either 2 cm² or 4 cm²."

3. Use dimes and nickels. The nickels count as motorcycles, the dimes are considered cars. Since the total value is 36, which could be made up with 18 motorcycles, consider the total value to be 90 cents. (18 motorcycle-nickels times 5-cents each.) Therefore:

"Using exactly 11 coins, all either nickels or dimes, make 90 cents worth of change."

Note: You could simply act this out. Invite a number of friends over, making sure that you invite a combination of cyclists and motorists (if you are under the legal driving age, consider inviting friends with scooters and wagons). Park the vehicles in 11 parking spaces and guess and check until you have exactly 36 wheels in the 11 parking places.

In A Drive to the Lake the critical elements are the average speeds (30 and 40 mph), that both vehicles go the same distance, and that one vehicle drives 2 hours longer than another.

1. A possible rewrite is to use 3-blocks and 4-blocks, representing rate in 10 mph segments. There need to be two more 3-blocks than 4-blocks. Make strings of blocks. The string with 3-blocks needs to be the same length as the 4-block string (representing that they both drove the same distance).

2. Another way to write this for manipulatives is to say, "How many pennies would it take to balance a scale if: (a) you can only put pennies on one side in groups of 30, and on the other side in groups of 40, and (b) you have to use exactly two more groups of 30 pennies than you use of 40 pennies."

In the second approach, you could also lay the pennies out in lines, to see how many it would take to make them the same length, rather than balancing them on a scale. This approach would work even if someone wrote the problem like this:

My grandfather told me about the time he, his sister, and his cousins drove to the lake from his cousins' house. They took separate cars. My grandfather and his sister drove 28 miles per hour. His cousins left one and one-half hours later and drove 35 miles per hour. Both cars arrived at the lake at about the same time. What was the approximate distance from his cousins' house to the lake?

The concepts for writing this as a manipulatives problem are the same: Use groups of 28 and 35 pennies. There must be one and a half more groups of the 28 pennies than groups of 35 pennies. The two strings of pennies must be the same length.

~~~

You can use manipulatives to solve many different kinds of problems. You will often have to consciously look for ways to use them, as sometimes it is not at all obvious that the problem lends itself to some sort of physical representation. Be creative. Modeling is a very powerful strategy. Have fun with it, and look for ways to use it effectively.

Problem Set A-3

Make specific suggestions for modeling each of these problems. Identify the critical elements of each problem and how each would be represented in your model. Then solve the problem using your model.

19. VATS THE PROBLEM

In the back room of a scientific supply store, there are two big vats of liquid. The red one contains 10 liters of alcohol, and the black one contains 10 liters of purified water. Not thinking at all, Jimmy pours 3 liters of the alcohol into the water. Then realizing his mistake and hoping to cover it up, he pours 3 liters from the black vat back into the red vat. Each vat again has 10 liters in it. Is there more alcohol in the water, or more water in the alcohol?

20. TRAINS FROM SALT LAKE CITY

Two trains left Salt Lake City, one heading east and the other heading west. The first train is traveling at 40 miles per hour. The second train left one hour later and is traveling at 60 miles per hour. When will the two trains be 400 miles apart?

21. CATCHING REMZI

Remzi left Chicago driving west on Interstate 80 at 8:00. He usually averages about 50 miles per hour when he drives on freeways. Natasha and Jessica, who are going to the same convention, left an hour later, but were going to try to average 60 miles per hour. How long before they catch up to Remzi?

22. INCHWORM

An inchworm that is 6 inches long travels at the rate of 6 inches per minute. How long does it take it to crawl completely across a piece of paper that is 12 inches long?

23. CAN DO

Kathy, Nate, and Adam went to buy some Meadow Dew soda at Mega-Save Drug Stores. Right now, there is a special promotion sponsored by the bottler. Some of the six-packs have six sodas, but some special promotional six-packs are actually eight-packs. There are 12 packs, and 78 cans. How many of each type of pack are there?

24. SODA

Marisan reported back to her friends that she bought 288 ounces of soda. Soda comes in cans (12 oz), bottles (16 oz), and quart-bottles (32 oz). What are the possible combinations she bought?

Problem Set B

1. DECREASING NUMBERS

A number is called a decreasing number if it has two or more digits and each digit is less than the digit to its left. For example 7421, 964310 and 52 are decreasing numbers but 3421, 6642, 8, and 963212 are not. How many decreasing numbers are there?

2. WHITE SALE

Judy purchased $91 worth of sheets at a sale on Labor Day, when $1.60 was marked off every article. She returned the sheets on Thursday (she really didn't want sheets anyway), when everything was marked at regular prices. Amazingly enough, the sales clerk gave her credit with regular prices and not sale prices, so she got more than $91 worth of credit. Judy was ecstatic about this, so she immediately exchanged the sheets for towels and washcloths. In exchange for one sheet she was able to get a towel and a washcloth. (The towels, wash-cloths, and sheets were now all marked at regular prices.) She came home with 16 more articles than she had before. Since washcloths cost only $2.70, she took six more washcloths than towels. How many washcloths and towels did she buy and how much would they have cost if Judy had bought them on Saturday at sale prices?

3. KDOG TV

One of the local TV stations, KDOG, plans out the number of commercials based on what type of show is being broadcast. Each commercial is a minute long. On daytime TV they run 18 commercials every hour and then drop it down to 16 per hour for the news. (There are 8 hours every day of daytime programming, and 2 hours a day of news.) During their prime time, which is 3 hours of each day, they run 12 commercials per hour. During the late-night movies they sell commercial time really cheap and run 20 per hour. Their "other" programming, which is 5 hours per day, is done at the rate of eight commercials per hour. Late-night movies are shown 6 hours each day. For the sake of simplicity, consider all seven days to have the same number of hours of each type of programming. Find how many hours per week this station has commercials on the air.

4. THUNDER AND LIGHTNING

In a thunder and lightning storm there is a rule of thumb that many people follow. After seeing the lightning, count seconds to yourself. If it takes 5 seconds for the sound of the thunder to reach you, then the lightning bolt was 1 mile away from you. Sound travels at 331 meters/sec. How accurate is the rule of thumb? Express your answer as a percent error.

Dear Wendy,

How's my favorite daughter? Things are a little slow at the state fair today, so I thought I'd write you a letter and invite you to come visit me next week. The fair runs all this week and next, and the way things are going so far, I'm going to be pretty bored and could stand to have some visitors. My company, Hot Spas, is not going to be too happy about how slow business is.

Let me tell you where my booth is. But, you know your ol' dad, I can't just tell you straight out. There are seven booths on row 3, and I'm in one of them. On one side of me is Computer Horoscopes—their computers are beeping all the time and bugging me. The booth on the other side of me is real quiet. My friend, Ann, works for Encyclopedia Antarctica. She keeps dropping by to visit, as her booth is pretty slow too. She always comes and goes from my right, so her booth must be that way. She told me that the Slice-It-Dice-It-Veggie-Peeler booth is so popular that the vacuum sellers, who were in the booth next to Slice-It-Dice-It-Veggie-Peeler, left the fair because nobody was ever visiting them. So now there are only five booths occupied, because the ladder sellers didn't show up at all. Ann tells me that the other booth on our row is Foot Massage. She says she went to their booth and it is always really noisy with ticklish people laughing hysterically. The last time Ann visited, she was in a real grouchy mood. Seems she was promised an end booth, but they are both presently occupied. She also complained about her neighbor, Computer Horoscopes. After she left, someone actually came to see my stuff. He came from my right, and wanted to demonstrate his new Slice-It-Dice-It Peeler on my lunch.

That's it, you have enough information to come directly to my booth. See you next week.

Love,
Dad

Which booth is Wendy's dad's?

work backwards

LUCILLE AND HER FAMILY recently took a vacation to Hawaii. On the day before they left Hawaii to come home, they began planning their activities for the following day. This is Lucille's tale of the problem they faced.

"Our flight was scheduled to leave at 12:40 p.m., and we needed to return our rental car before we left. We also wanted to spend 30 minutes at the pineapple plantation. It was a 45-minute drive to the airport, with about a 10-minute detour to go to the plantation. We also considered going to the sugar cane museum. It was about 10 minutes out of the way and we planned to stay there about one hour. Based on all this information we wanted to determine when to leave our condo. We used the strategy of working backwards to solve the problem.

"We started by figuring that we needed to be at the airport 90 minutes before our flight. Since our flight left at 12:40 p.m., we subtracted an hour and a half and decided that we needed to be at the airport at 11:10 a.m. Since we had to return the rental car also, we adjusted that to 11:00 a.m. Ignoring the sugar cane museum for the moment, we figured in the time for the plantation. We subtracted the 10-minute drive and the 30 minutes we planned to stay there from 11:00 and got 10:20 a.m. Then we subtracted the 45-minute drive to the airport. This meant we had to leave at 9:35 a.m. If we subtracted the hour and 10 minutes for the sugar cane museum (10-minute detour and an hour to look around) we would need to leave at 8:25 a.m. Since we had to check out of our condominium, and we also had two little kids, we didn't think we could leave that early. So we canceled our plans to go to the sugar cane museum, and left at about 9:30 a.m.

◀ *Construction workers often work backwards from an expected completion date in order to plan their work.*

"We visited the plantation without being rushed (allowing us time to buy some pineapples and a great hat) and we still got to the airport in plenty of time. This was fortunate since I ended up arguing with the rental car agency for 30 minutes as they were trying to charge me for a minuscule dent in the passenger door. Had we not used working backwards to figure out when we needed to leave, I might have had to rush to the airplane and not had enough time to argue. This could have resulted in a large bill when I arrived home."

~~~~~~

Working backwards is another strategy that falls into the broad context of changing your focus. Most other strategies involve working through the information forwards. In order to successfully work backwards, you need to change your focus and consider the whole problem in reverse. This is a very useful strategy in certain situations. Much of algebra is based on working backwards. It is also very useful in planning schedules or agendas, as Lucille's Hawaii trip demonstrates.

One of the most difficult parts of working backwards is keeping track of the information and organizing it in a meaningful way. Although we give solutions in various formats, we encourage you to experiment with finding new ways to organize these problems.

To begin, though, we will take you through some exercises in working backwards. All of this prepares you for the rest of the chapter.

The following is a map of Wallowville. Mark is exiting the freeway and needs directions to drive to his friend's house. Write the directions and double-check them before you move on.

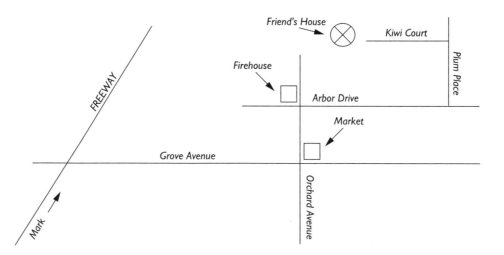

After visiting his friend, Mark is ready to leave. He needs directions to follow to get back to the freeway. *Without* looking at the map, write the directions.

There are at least two basic things that you need to do to write the directions for going back to the freeway. The first is to mention the landmarks and the street names in reverse order; the second is to do the opposite action at each juncture. Other problems might involve objects other than landmarks and street names. The process thus involves reversing the order of the objects and reversing the actions.

~~~~

Solutions to many math problems involve the same process. For example: I am thinking of a whole number between 1 and 10. I double it and come up with 12. What is my number?

Obviously, you must take my answer and divide it by 2 (giving 6) in order to reach the answer. (This is a math example of "reversing the action"—division reverses multiplication and vice versa, just as subtraction reverses addition and vice versa.)

Now consider an unknown number between 1 and 10. Multiply the number by 3. Then add 5 to the result, giving 32. What is the original number?

To find the number you must reverse the order of the "objects" and reverse the actions. The first object was the 3 (as in "multiply by") and the second object was the 5. Thus the objects to be dealt with (in reverse order) are the 5 and the 3. Now reverse each action. Instead of adding 5, subtract 5. ($32 - 5 = 27$). Reverse multiplying by 3 to "dividing by 3" ($27 \div 3 = 9$). So the original number was 9.

Lo and behold, you got the right answer. To check, work the problem forward: 9 times 3 is 27. Add 5, which gives 32.

Do these three problems:

I'm thinking of a number between 1 and 10. If I multiply by 4 and then subtract 3, my answer would be 25. What is my number?

I'm thinking of a number between 1 and 30. I add 22. I divide by 3. My answer is 12. What is my number?

I'm thinking about a number. Divide it by 2 and then subtract 1. The answer is 7 ½. What is my number?

Note: The answers to these problems can be found on pages 7, 14, and 17, respectively.

Now on to more serious endeavors.

POOR CHOICES

Half of the ballet company stayed up late watching tractor pulls on TV, the night before their debut in Carnegie Hall. Excuse me, make that half of the company plus one more. There were 13 tired dancers in all, so how many dancers were in the company?

Work this problem before continuing.

As an example for setting up the solution, follow this from line to line:

A. Half of the company
B. And one more
C. Thirteen in all

C. Thirteen in all	13
B. And one more (Actually one less as a reverse action)	12
A. Half of the company (Reverse by multiplying by 2)	24

So there are 24 dancers in the company. To check, work the problem forwards. Starting with 24 dancers, half of company were tired, which would be 12 dancers. And one more makes it 13 tired dancers in all. This checks with the information in the problem.

THE STOLEN PIGEONS

Bad Bargle snuck into Homer's pigeon loft one day. He took half of the pigeons. He decided that wasn't bad enough, so he took one more and left. Later, Homer opened the door of the loft in order to exercise his prize possessions. Half of the remaining flock flew out, leaving six inside the pen. How many pigeons did Homer have before Bad Bargle did his dirty deed?
Work this problem before continuing.

First write down the actions in the order they appear in the problem.

A. Bargle stole half of the pigeons.

B. Bargle stole one more pigeon.

C. Half of the remaining flock flew out.

D. Six were left.

Whoops. This is only half of the setup for the solution. Before you continue, note that you should read the above actions in a downward direction. In the following solution, read the left-hand column only (until specifically instructed otherwise).

Working this forwards:

A. Bargle stole half of the pigeons.

D. Bargle returned half of the original pigeon flock. (Fat chance!)

B. Bargle stole one more pigeon.

C. Bargle returned one pigeon.

C. Half of the remaining flock flew out.

B. Half of the flock flew back in.

D. Six were left.

A. Six were left.

Now you can read the right-hand column going up. These are the reverse actions, and if you read them from bottom to top, you also reverse the order.

Oops. The numbers are missing. So let's put the numbers in place using the reverse actions in the reverse order. (But all you have to do is read down. They have been reversed for you.)

D. Six pigeons remained. (6 pigeons)

C. Half of the flock flew back in. (Now there are 12.)

B. Bargle returned one pigeon (Now there are 13.)

A. Bargle returned half of the pigeons. (Fat chance!) (The flock is back to 26 birds.)

P.S. Check this by working forwards.

On Wednesday, Dad got paid. Thursday morning my brother took half the money to go open a checking account (because he was always short of money). On Friday, I needed some for a date, so I took half of what remained. Sis came along next, and took half of the remaining money. Dad then went to gas up the car and used half of the rest of his money, and wondered where it all went so fast. He only had $5 left. How much money did he start with in his wallet?

Don't forget to reverse the actions and reverse the order, and of course, don't go on until you've worked this problem.

In order, this is what happened to poor Dad.

A. He got his money from the bank.

B. Brother took half of his money.

C. I took half of what remained.

D. Sis took half of what remained.

E. He spent half of the remainder on gas.

Now it's time to reverse the order and reverse the actions. Think of a film of the entire sequence of events. Imagine watching the film run backwards. (The italicized parts are the reverse actions.)

E. At the end, the wallet has $5 in it.
Dad spent half on gas. *(He gave back the gas and got back half of his money.)*

D. The wallet now has $10 in it.
Sis took half of the remainder. *(She gave back what she had taken which was the same as what she left in the wallet since she had taken half.)*

C. The wallet now has $20 in it.
I took half for a date. *(I gave back an amount equal to what I left—$20.)*

B. The wallet now has $40 in it.
Brother took half to start his nest egg. *(Brother gave back his half of the money—$40.)*

A. The wallet now has $80 in it.
So Dad's wallet had $80 in it before all the raids took place.

As you can see, there are different ways to record the information and then use it for solving the problem. A few other ways of organizing the information will be shown in later examples. Your organization needs to help, not hinder, the process of working backwards. Be sure to experiment with your own style as you attempt the next problem and the problems that follow.

THE MAGIC TRICK

Start with a number between 1 and 10.
Multiply the number by 4.
Add 6 to the number you have now.
Divide by 2.
Subtract 5.
Tell me the number you ended with and I'll tell you the number you started with.

Two students, Glenda and Sonia, played this game. Sonia started with a number, did the arithmetic, and told Glenda that she had ended with 12. Glenda then figured out what number Sonia started with. What number did Sonia start with?
Work this problem before continuing.

Glenda found Sonia's number this way.
"I could have tried this problem with guess and check and that definitely would have worked. But I wanted to use working backwards because I thought it would be easier. First I wrote down the given information and then I worked backwards until I found the original number. I reversed the actions each time. So subtracting 5 became adding 5 as I worked backwards, and so on."

Organizing information is very important for keeping track of what you are doing. Glenda found, as many solvers have, that the most useful way to do this is to work up the page. With the information written in the original order, do your work from the bottom of the page to the top. The finished product looks something like this. Read down the right column (the actions). Then read up the left column for the numbers. This time, the reverse actions are not written in.

Start with a number between 1 and 10.

7

Multiply the number by 4.

28

Add 6 to the number you have now.

34

Divide by 2.

17

Subtract 5.

12

The result is 12.

Notice how the information and the numbers are staggered every other line. In this way one can read either down or up. It is also easy to check this way. Start with a number (7). Multiply by 4 to get 28. Add 6 to get 34. Divide by 2 to get 17. Subtract 5 to get 12. It checks.

Do this problem again, this time assuming that the final number that Julie reached was 4.

~~~~~

This idea of working up the page may seem strange, but it is used in the real world. Airline baggage tags list the airports in reverse order. The original departure point is shown on the bottom of the tag, with each successive airport on the preceding line. The final destination is shown on the top of the tag.

↑JFK	1273
↑ORD	4689
↑SFO	385

Work the next problem by writing down the information and then working backwards up the page.

Mr. Phil T. Rich left half of his estate to his wife, $30,000 to his daughter, half of what was left to his butler, half of what remained for the care of his goldfish, and the remaining $8,000 to charity. What was the value of the estate?

Work this problem before continuing.

Again, summarize the information in a column. Then work backwards from the end of the problem. Work up the page. Most of our students show the way the solution looks, and explain afterwards. This is Rewa's work on this problem.

$124,000	Start
62,000	Half of his estate to his wife;
32,000	30,000 to his daughter;
16,000	Half of what was left to his butler;
$8,000	Half of what remained for his goldfish;
0	The remaining $8,000 to charity.

Rewa explains: "Beginning at the end, he gave his last $8,000 to charity. He must have had $8,000 before that in order to give his last $8,000 to charity. Before that, he gave half of what was left to his goldfish. He must have had $16,000 so that he could give half to the fish and leave $8,000.

"Right before that he gave half of what was left to the butler, leaving $16,000. So the butler got $16,000 also. This means that the value of the estate before paying the butler was $32,000.

"Right before that, he gave $30,000 to his daughter. Since he had $32,000 left after giving money to his daughter, he must have had $62,000 (add $30,000 to $32,000) just before giving money to his daughter.

"Finally (or initially), he gave half of his money to his wife. She must have received $62,000, so there must have been $124,000 to begin with."

~~~~~

The next problem features fractions other than one-half. You might find that a diagram helps you keep track of the information.

MINTS

Three friends, returning from the movie Friday the 13th Part 65, stopped to eat at a restaurant. After dinner, they paid their bill and noticed a bowl of mints at the front counter. Sean took $\frac{1}{3}$ of the mints, but returned four because he had a momentary pang of guilt. Faizah then took $\frac{1}{4}$ of what was left but returned three for similar reasons. Eugene then took half of the remainder but threw two that looked like they had been slobbered on back into the bowl. (He felt no pangs of guilt—he just didn't want slobbered-on mints). The bowl had only 17 mints left when the raid was over. How many mints were originally in the bowl?

Work this problem before continuing.

Again, write down all of the information that occurred, in the proper order.
Start
Sean took one-third of the mints.
Sean returned four.
Faizah then took one-fourth of what was left.
Faizah returned three.
Eugene then took half of the remainder.
Eugene threw two back in the bowl.
The bowl had 17 mints left.

This problem tends to be a little confusing. You may wish to act it out with manipulatives (pennies, pieces of paper, or actual mints). You also might imagine that a movie of this incident took place. Then starting from the end, run the movie backwards. Keep in mind that you have to reverse the order and reverse the action.

Aniko solved this problem as follows. "I began at the end. There were 17 mints left in the bowl when the raid was over. Right before that, Eugene threw two back in the bowl. This means that there must have been 15 mints in the bowl before Eugene threw two back.

"Right before that, Eugene took half of the mints and left 15 in the bowl. This means that there must have been 30 mints in the bowl before Eugene took his greedy turn.

"Right before that, Faizah put three mints back in the bowl, leaving 30. So just before she put those three back, there must have been 27 in the bowl." (A common mistake is to add 3 and get 33. But think of watching this in a movie. If there were 33 in the bowl before Faizah put three back, then after she put in the three there must have been 36, which does not match what the problem says. The reverse action of Faizah putting three back is for her to take three out. So when we work backwards, we take three away from 30 which leaves 27. Then going forwards, she will put three back and 27 + 3 = 30.)

"Right before that, Faizah took one-fourth of the mints, leaving 27." (Again, a common mistake is to multiply 27 by 4. However, this is not what happened. A diagram can illustrate this. The following type of diagram, invented by Ken's student Hao Ngo, is very helpful.) "I drew a rectangle to represent all of the mints before Faizah took any."

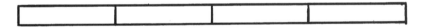

"Now, Faizah would have separated the mints into four parts, so as to take one-fourth of them. So separate the rectangle into four parts."

"Now, Faizah takes one of the parts, so cross out one of the parts."

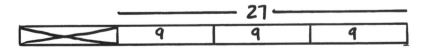

"The three parts that are left total 27 mints. This means, since the parts are all equal, that each part represents nine mints."

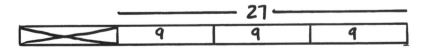

"Therefore, the part that Faizah took, which must also be equal to the other three equal parts, must also represent nine mints."

"So with four parts of nine mints each, there must have been 36 mints in the bowl before Faizah did her dastardly deed.

"Let's see if everything checks at this point. When Faizah arrives at the bowl, she finds 36 mints. She takes one-fourth of them ($\frac{1}{4}$ of 36 is 9). Now 36 − 9 leaves 27 mints in the bowl. Then she puts three back (adds 3) so 27 + 3 = 30 mints in the bowl when Faizah is done. Then Eugene takes half of the mints ($\frac{1}{2}$ of 30 is 15 and 30 − 15 = 15) which leaves 15 mints in the bowl. Then he puts two back, so there are 17 left when he is done. Everything checks thus far."

Let's pick up Rachel's solution. It shows a different way of doing the fractional parts.

"Right before Faizah, Sean returned four to the bowl. Since there were 36 mints in the bowl when Faizah got there, there must have been four fewer mints before Sean put four back. So there must have been 32 mints in the bowl before Sean's pangs of guilt.

"Right before those pangs of guilt, Sean took one-third of the mints. This means he left two-thirds of the mints in the bowl. I used algebra to find how many were in the bowl before that. I used m to represent the number of mints before Sean took one-third of them."

$$\begin{aligned}
(\tfrac{2}{3})\, m &= 32. \qquad \text{Multiply both sides by } \tfrac{3}{2}.\\
(\tfrac{3}{2})(\tfrac{2}{3})\, m &= (\tfrac{3}{2})(32)\\
m &= 48
\end{aligned}$$

"So there must be 48 mints in the beginning."
Note: You could also use a diagram as below.

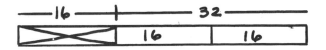

Rachel checked her work as follows. "There were 48 mints to begin with. Sean took one-third ($\frac{1}{3}$ of 48 = 16 and 48 − 16 = 32) leaving 32. Then he put 4 back, so there are 36 when he is done." Aniko's check of the rest of the problem appeared a few paragraphs back, so we are satisfied with this answer. There were 48 mints to start with.

~~~~

The work on the problem could have looked something like this.

	Start
48	
	Sean took one-third of the mints.
32	
	Sean returned four.
36	
	Faizah then took one-fourth of what was left
27	
	Faizah returned three.
30	
	Eugene then took half of the remainder.
15	
	Eugene threw two back in the bowl.
17	
	The bowl had 17 mints left.

The diagram technique or the algebraic technique are both very effective for dealing with fractional parts that were taken away in the problem. But algebra in general is not a very efficient way of solving problems of this type. For instance, if m represents the number of mints that the bowl contained to start, an algebraic equation to represent the entire problem would look like this.

$$\{[m-(\tfrac{1}{3})m+4]-(\tfrac{1}{4})[m-(\tfrac{1}{3})m+4]+3\}-(\tfrac{1}{2})\{[m-(\tfrac{1}{3})m+4]-(\tfrac{1}{4})[m-(\tfrac{1}{3})m+4]+3\}+2=17$$

Solve this equation if you don't believe working backwards is easier.

Guess and check can be used to solve many of these problems. However, since the theme of this chapter is working backwards, the solutions focus on that strategy. Getting started with a working backwards solution is a little bit harder than getting started with a guess and check solution. However, reaching the solution by working backwards is usually easier and quicker than reaching a solution by guess and check.

Problem Set A

1. LOSING STREAK

A man competing on a game show ran into a losing streak. First he bet half of his money on one question, and lost it. Then he lost half of his remaining money on another question. Then he lost $300 on another question. Then he lost half of his remaining money on another question. Finally he got a question right and won $200. At this point, the show ended and he had $1200 left. How much did he have before his losing streak began?

2. GENEROSITY

Phil Anthropist likes to give away money. One day he was feeling especially generous, so he went to the park with a wad of money. He gave $100 to a man feeding pigeons. He then gave half of his remaining money to a child licking an ice cream cone. He then gave $50 to the balloon seller. He then bought a hot dog, and paid for it with a $20 bill. "Keep the extra for a tip," he said to the hot-dog seller. Then he gave half of his remaining money to someone giving a sermon on a soapbox. At this point, he had $3 left and stuck it under the collar of a stray cat. How much money did Phil have when he started his good deeds?

3. WHAT'S MY NUMBER?

I am thinking of a number. I multiplied my number by 3, subtracted 8, doubled the result, and added 14. Then I added on 50% of what I had and subtracted 11. Then I divided by 5. After all that, I was left with 8. What number did I start with?

4. THE MALL

My sister loves to go shopping. Yesterday she borrowed a wad of money from Mom and went to the mall. She began her excursion by spending $18 on a new compact disc. Then she spent half of her remaining money on a new dress. Then she spent $11 taking herself and her friend out to lunch. Then she spent one-third of her remaining money on a book. On her way home she bought gas for $12 and spent one-fourth of her remaining money on a discount tape at the convenience store. Finally, she slipped me $2 when she got home, and gave Mom back $10 in change. Mom was furious and demanded an explanation of where the money went. What did Sis tell her? (List the items and amount spent on each item.)

5. USED CAR

A car dealership was trying to sell a used car that no one wanted. First, they tried to sell it for 10% off the marked price. Then they tried to sell it for 20% off the first sale price. Finally, they offered it for 25% off the second sale price and someone bought it for $3240. What was the original price of the car?

6. HOCKEY CARDS

Jack and Jill were admiring each other's hockey cards. Jack had quite a few cards, and Jill had some of her own. Jack was trying to impress her, so Jack gave Jill as many hockey cards as she already had. Jill then gave Jack back as many cards as he had left. Jack, not to be outdone by Jill's generosity, gave her back as many cards as she had left. This left poor Jack with no cards and left Jill with 40 cards altogether. How many hockey cards did each of them have just before these exchanges took place? (You might want to try acting this out in conjunction with working backwards.)

DONUTS

Four customers came into a bakery called Totally Excellent Donuts. The first one said, "Give me half of all the donuts you have left, plus half a donut more. The second customer said, "Give me half of all the donuts you have left, plus half a donut more." The third customer said, "Give me three donuts." The last customer said, "Give me half of all the donuts you have left, plus half a donut more." This last transaction emptied the display case of donuts. How many donuts were there to start with?

8. **GOLF CLUBS**

Ken played golf yesterday and shot 107. Considering that he normally shoots in the low 80's or high 70's, this round of golf really frustrated him. It was so frustrating that he decided to buy new golf clubs. But first he had to give his old golf clubs away. He gave half of his golf clubs, plus half a club more, to Daniel. Then he gave half of his remaining golf clubs to Gary. Then he gave half of his remaining golf clubs and half a club more to Will. This left Ken with one club (his putter), which he decided to keep. How many golf clubs did Ken start with before giving them away?

9. **WRITE YOUR OWN**

Make up a working backwards problem.

Problem Set B: The Camping Trip

These problems all concern the Family family going camping.

1. HOW MUCH DOG FOOD?

The Family family (Mama, Papa, and the three kids: Ed, Lisa, and Judy) were about to go on a camping vacation. They decided to take their five dogs with them, and they needed to know how many cans of dog food to take. They had received a free sample of dog food in the mail, and all the dogs really liked it. The cans of dog food were on sale for $1.24 and the package said that three cans of dog food would feed two dogs for one day. They were planning on going camping for eight days. How much would the dog food cost them for the eight days?

2. THE LUGGAGE RACK

The Family family were about ready to leave on their camping trip. They loaded up their van with stuff, but it was getting really full. They had all kinds of equipment, plus five dogs. (Everyone had his or her own dog.) They were trying to decide whether to take the luggage rack for the top of the van to store some of their camping gear, or whether they should just cram it all inside the van. Papa didn't want to take the luggage rack because he said their gas mileage would be worse because of the increased drag. Mama said she didn't want to be crowded inside the van, and she didn't care how much it cost, she wanted to take it. Papa said they got 20 miles per gallon with the luggage rack off, and 17 miles per gallon with it on. Their destination was 3 hours away at 55 miles per hour with the rack off, but with the rack on they could only go 50 miles per hour. Gas cost $.89 per gallon. How much more would it cost them to take the luggage rack, and how many extra minutes would it take them to get there?

3. CROSSING THE RIVER WITH DOGS

The five Family family members and their five dogs (each family member owned a dog) were hiking when they encountered a river to cross. They rented a boat which could hold three living things—people or dogs. Unfortunately, the dogs were temperamental: Each was comfortable only with its owner and could not be near another person, not even momentarily, unless its owner was present. Dogs could be with other dogs, however. The crossing would have been impossible except that Lisa's dog had attended a first-rate obedience school and knew how to operate the boat. No other dogs were that well-educated. How was the crossing arranged and how many trips did it take?

4. DON'T FEED THE ANIMALS

On the camping trip, the Family family had brought many bags of peanuts for snacks. Peanuts were everyone's favorite, and so they were well stocked. Unfortunately, the campground was quite populated by various animals that also enjoyed an occasional peanut. The first night, after the Family family went to bed, a raccoon visited their camp and ate five of the bags of peanuts they had brought. The next day, the Familys ate one-third of the remaining bags. That night, a beaver came to call, and ate two more of the bags. The next day, the Familys consumed one-fourth of the remaining bags for breakfast. Then they took the boat trip described in the previous problem, and they had to feed one bag of peanuts to each dog to get them to quiet down. That night, an elephant from a nearby zoo came to the camp and ate four bags. The next day, each member of the Family family ate one-ninth of the remaining bags. That night, a spotted owl ate half of the remaining bags. The next day, there were only four bags left. The Familys couldn't decide how to split them amongst the five of them, so they fed them to the ducks. How many bags of peanuts did the Familys bring with them on the camping trip?

5. **LOST IN PURSUIT OF PEANUTS**

On the fifth day, after the peanuts were all gone, Ed and Judy took a hike to the store to get some more peanuts. On the way back, they got lost in the middle of a big forest. The forested area they were in measured roughly 13 miles from north to south and 14 miles from east to west. When they first discovered they were lost, they were at a point that was 7 miles from the southern border and 7 miles from the eastern border of the forest. (Of course, they didn't know this or they wouldn't have been lost.) In their indecision as to whether they should walk east (towards the morning sun), west (towards the setting sun), south (from which they came), or north (because they might be wrong about the direction from which they came), they decided to walk in all four directions. They devised a plan where they would walk north first for 30 minutes. If they weren't out of the forest yet, they would then turn right and walk east for 60 minutes, then turn right again and walk south for 90 minutes, and so on, adding 30 minutes with each change of direction. (Nobody said this was a good plan.) It turns out that in the forested area, they covered about 1 mile every 30 minutes. They also decided to drop a peanut after every 100 yards, so they would be sure that they never doubled back on their tracks. They had 50 bags of peanuts with them, and there were 40 peanuts in each bag. On which side of the forest—north, east, south, or west—did they finally emerge, and how long did it take from the moment they were lost until the moment they got out? How many full bags of peanuts did they have left?

42

STUDENTS IN school often use Venn diagrams to categorize things. Venn diagrams can clearly show relationships among different categories. But you can also use Venn diagrams to solve problems. Venn diagrams fall into the major category of spatial organization. They serve to organize information in a particular way that is very hard to see without a Venn diagram. You can draw Venn diagrams using closed circles, loops, rectangles, or, occasionally, blobs. Two loops can intersect, be entirely disjoint, or one can be completely inside the other. Each of these pairs of loops represents different types of relationships between two categories.

You will often encounter the three words "all," "some," and "no" in various problems. Using a Venn diagram can help you interpret the meaning of these three words in the correct way.

The word "all" could be used in a statement such as, "All roses are flowers." (Several words of caution: We are talking about principal, common understanding of words here. For example, you may have known a woman named Rose, but that is not the principal, common understanding of the word rose. Don't waste time looking for obscure meanings or interpretations that will render everything false.)

"All roses are flowers." A Venn interpretation of this statement follows.

This diagram shows "flowers." Anything inside is considered to be a flower. Anything outside the rectangle is considered to be "not a flower."

Flowers

◀ *When you recycle, you separate recyclable materials from other trash, then further sort these materials into subsets like aluminum, glass, and paper. Venn diagrams are helpful in problems involving objects that can be sorted into different categories.*

Add in the roses detail.

```
┌─────────────────────────────────┐
│ Flowers                         │
│                   ┌─────────┐   │
│                   │         │   │
│                   │ Roses   │   │
│                   └─────────┘   │
└─────────────────────────────────┘
```

"Roses" is an entirely enclosed subset of flowers. Every member of the group called "Roses" is also a flower. Inside the rectangle marked "Roses" are the items that are classified as roses, such as white roses, red roses, damask roses, and rugosas. Anything outside of that region is considered "not a rose."

Think of some examples that are "not roses." Pink carnations, tiger lilies, apricot blossoms, hamburgers, lawn mowers. Not a single one of these items is considered to be a "rose." (Unless, of course, the lawn mower is manufactured by a company called "Rose Garden Products, Inc." But remember, we are going by the principal, common understanding of these terms, in which case a rose is a rose is a rose.)

Some of these "not roses" items are flowers. They can each be placed in the diagram someplace. Label the regions A and B as shown.

```
┌─────────────────────────────────┐
│ Flowers                         │
│                   ┌─────────┐   │
│  A                │ B       │   │
│                   │ Roses   │   │
│                   └─────────┘   │
└─────────────────────────────────┘
```

Region A: Flowers, but not roses.

Region B: Flowers, in particular roses.

The characterization of the outer loop applies to everything within the loop, including other loops. The characteristics of a region are those of its principal loop minus the characteristics of any smaller, wholly enclosed loop.

Specifically, a pink carnation is a flower (as characterized in statement A) but it is not a rose. So pink carnations would be placed in region A, because they lack the characteristic necessary to place them in region B. Lawn mowers, on the other hand, would be placed outside of both regions, because lawn mowers are not flowers. You should figure out where each of the other "not roses" items should be placed.

Here is another example of a Venn diagram. This example involves two loops: a loop that contains students taking math and a loop that contains students taking chemistry.

Notice that the word "some" is key in both of the following statements.

1. Some math students are also chemistry students.

2. Some chemistry students are also math students.

This is the Venn diagram for the math students and the chemistry students.

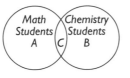

In this diagram, the two separate loops intersect one another. The math student loop is labeled A, the chemistry student loop is labeled B, and the intersection of the two is labeled C.

What are the characteristics of these regions?

Region A: Math students who are not taking chemistry.

Region B: Chemistry students who are not taking math.

Region C: Students who are taking both math and chemistry.

The overlap section has the characteristics of both loops. This was also true in the case of the flowers and the roses: the overlap (which was the inside loop) had the characteristics of both regions.

This diagram also has the option of including a large rectangle around the two loops. This rectangle is considered the universal set. In this case, the universal set could be assumed to be students. A student who is taking neither math nor chemistry could be placed outside of both of the loops in region D. This diagram is shown below.

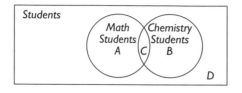

There are other cases where the two regions do not overlap at all. Consider these two statements:

1. No Buick is a mushroom.

2. No mushroom is a Buick.

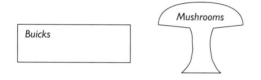

Note that a universal set really makes no sense here because Buicks and mushrooms really couldn't be related with one category. The mushroom loop is one example of a loop in the form of a blob.

There is no overlap either conceptually or in the diagrammatic representation. The diagram serves to illustrate and confirm our belief that no Buicks are mushrooms.

Earlier we produced a couple of overlapping loops with the following two statements:

1. Some math students are also chemistry students.

2. Some chemistry students are also math students.

The key in both of these statements and in many other statements is the word "some." The word does not, however, automatically produce overlapping loops. Consider the statement:
"Some flowers are roses."

This statement can actually be illustrated with the same two loops shown earlier for the statement "All roses are flowers." Recall that one loop was entirely enclosed within the other.

You need to look carefully at statements involving the word some. The Venn diagram may have overlapping loops, or may be one loop inside another.

BASIC RELATIONSHIPS

Draw Venn diagrams that represent each of these statements. Your understanding of this process is critical to understanding the problems that are presented in the rest of the chapter. The correct diagrams follow the problem.

1. Some birds are pets.
2. All accountants are college graduates.
3. No dogs are sheep.
4. All poodles are dogs.
5. Some dogs are poodles.

Work these problems before continuing.

The correct answers to the problems are shown below. If you haven't drawn the Venn diagrams yourself yet, do them before reading on.

1. Some birds are pets.

Animals — Birds, Pets

2. All accountants are college graduates.

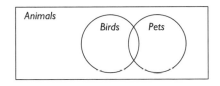

People — College Grads, Acntnts

3. No dogs are sheep.

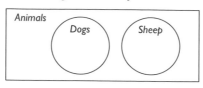

4. All poodles are dogs.

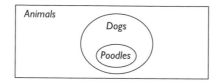

5. Some dogs are poodles.

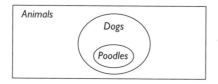

Note: In problems 4 and 5, the large rectangle could have been dogs, with only one circle inside of it representing poodles. The large rectangle is called the universal set, and it is up to the person drawing the diagram to decide what that universal set should be.

THREE CIRCLES

In how many ways can three circles be drawn? They can be inside each other, intersect in some way, or not intersect at all.
Work this problem before continuing.

This problem is relatively difficult. You have to be somewhat systematic in drawing the circles, to avoid leaving any out or repeating yourself. The solution shown started with the three possibilities for two circles: one inside the other, intersecting, and disjoint (not intersecting at all). The third circle was then added. It started out containing the two circles, and gradually moved to a position disjoint with the other two.

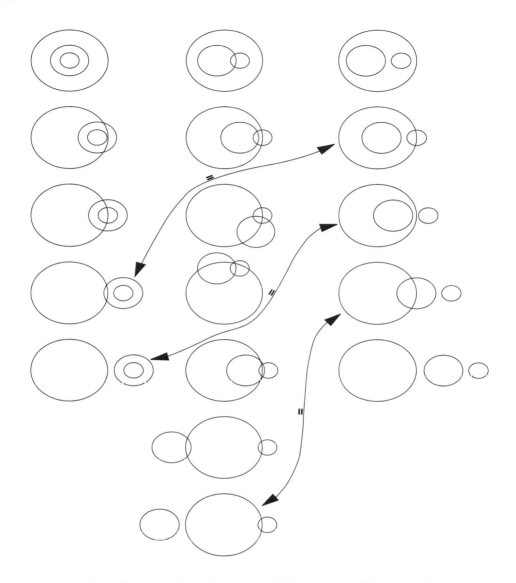

Now that you have drawn the different possibilities for three circles, consider the following problems. In each one, draw a Venn diagram that shows the relationships between the categories given. One of the categories describes the universal set, and the other categories describe the various loops inside the universal set. The universal set is not necessarily listed first.

1. Household pets, dogs, animals, cats.
2. Living things, lizards, apes, chimpanzees, reptiles, dogs, mammals, terriers, dachshunds.
3. Place of birth, USA, Canada, Miami, Florida, Orlando, Montreal, Missouri.
4. Colleges, private school, state school, Yale, Kent State, Notre Dame.
5. Trumpet, piano, musical instruments, clarinet, violin, trombone, brass, woodwinds.
6. Water vessels, submarines, war boats, sailboats, battleships, ferries.
7. Cows, brown, black, white, dairy, old. (These cows can only be one color.)
8. Hamburgers, with cheese, double, homemade.

Work this problem before continuing.

Are your Venn diagrams equivalent to the examples below? If not, how does your interpretation of the relationships differ?

1. Household pets, dogs, animals, cats.

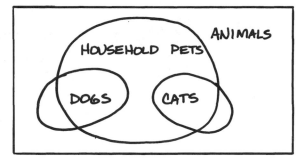

2. Living things, lizards, apes, chimpanzees, reptiles, dogs, mammals, terriers, dachshunds.

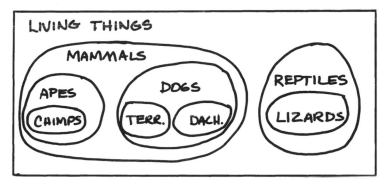

3. Place of birth, USA, Canada, Miami, Florida, Orlando, Montreal, Missouri.

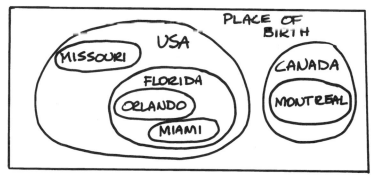

4. Colleges, private school, state school, Yale, Kent State, Notre Dame.

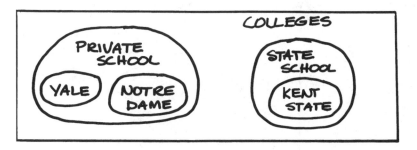

5. Trumpet, piano, musical instruments, clarinet, violin, trombone, brass, woodwinds.

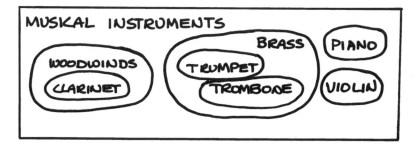

6. Water vessels, submarines, war boats, sailboats, battleships, ferries.

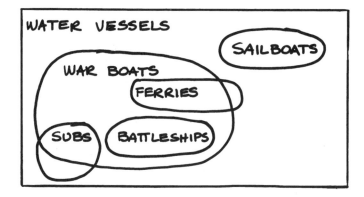

7. Cows, brown, black, white, dairy, old.

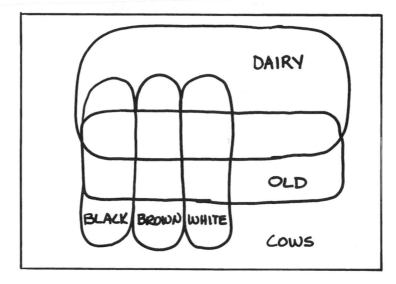

(You might wish to spend a few weeks of your life trying this problem allowing for multicolored cows.)

8. Hamburgers, with cheese, double, homemade.

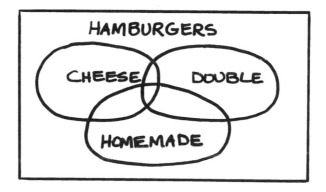

Now you are ready to solve some problems using Venn diagrams. Draw the diagrams, and then put the numbers in as they fit.

In a group of students, 12 are taking chemistry, 10 are taking physics, 3 are taking both chemistry and physics, and 5 are taking neither chemistry nor physics. How many students are in the group?
Work this problem before continuing.

Bryndyn and Toi were working together on this problem.

Bryn: Man, this problem is so easy. There are 12 in chemistry, 10 in physics, 3 in both and 5 in neither. So that is a total of $12 + 10 + 3 + 5 = 30$ students in all.

Toi: Yeah, that sounds right. But wait a minute. Aren't we supposed to be drawing some sort of a diagram to solve these problems? Isn't that what our teacher said.

Bryn: Oh yeah, a Penn diagram. The ones with the circles drawn in pen.

Toi: A Venn diagram, V-v-v-venn, not a Penn diagram. And we can draw the circles in pencils, I mean venncils, if we want. Let's try that.

Bryn: Okay, I guess we need one loop to represent the students that are in chemistry, and another loop to represent the students that are in physics.

Toi: Should the circles overlap?

Bryn: I'm not sure, what do you think?

Toi: I think they need to overlap, and the spot where the circles come together, the inter …

Bryn: Intersection.

Toi: Yeah, the intersection will represent the students who are taking both classes. Yeah, but where do we put the students who aren't taking either class?

Bryn: I guess they should go outside of both circles. Maybe we should draw a big rectangle around the whole thing.

Toi: Yeah, the universal set. That can be students.

Bryn: Okay, let's try drawing this thing. You draw it, I draw lousy circles.

Toi: They don't have to be circles. They can be blobs.

Bryn: Like "The Blob That Ate New York." I saw that movie, it was pretty gnarly.

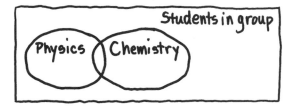

Toi: Okay, here is our Venn diagram. Now what do we do with these numbers?

Bryn: Well, let's see, let's put the 12 chemistry students in the chemistry student loop and the 10 physics students in the physics student loop.

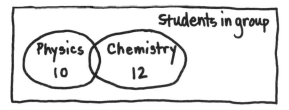

Toi: And put in the three students who are in both classes and the five that aren't taking either class.

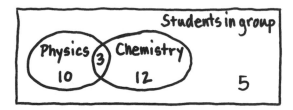

Bryn: Now let's see. That is $10 + 12 + 3 + 5 = 30$ students altogether. And that's what we got before so it must be right.

Toi: Great. Wait, wait, wait a minute, something's wrong here.

Bryn: What? It looks fine to me.

Toi: Aren't we counting the people who are taking both classes twice? From the looks of this diagram, there are 13 students taking physics and 15 taking chemistry.

Bryn: How do you figure that?

Toi: Well, look at the physics circle. Those three students in the intersection are taking physics right?

Bryn: Yeah, so what?

Toi: Well, that means we have 3 students in the intersection taking physics and chemistry, and 10 students in the outer portion of the physics circle taking physics and not taking chemistry. That means we have 13 students taking physics.

Bryn: Oh, I see what you mean. And by the same logic, we have 15 students taking chemistry.

Toi: So what can we do about this?

Bryn: Maybe we better start over. Or we could ask for help.

Toi: Help! No way, we can figure this out. We're a couple of smart people.

Bryn: Okay, let's see here. I think our original diagram is fine. So let's work with the numbers again.

Toi: Yeah, let's start by putting in the three students who are taking both courses in the intersection of the two circles.

Bryn: That sounds like working backwards that we just learned.

Toi: Yeah, it does. Okay, of the 12 students taking chemistry, three of them are taking both chemistry and physics. This leaves nine students taking chemistry but not physics.

Bryn: So let's fill in 9 in the section of the chemistry circle that is outside the physics circle.

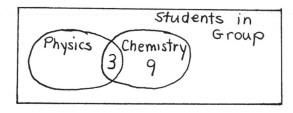

Toi: Yeah, that looks great. Now let's do the same thing for the physics loop.

Bryn: Of the 10 students taking physics, three of them are taking both chemistry and physics. This leaves seven students taking physics, but not chemistry. So fill in 7 in the section of the physics loop that represents physics only.

Toi: Great. Now put in the five students taking neither course outside of the two loops.

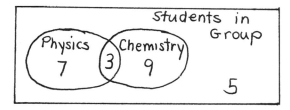

Bryn: Now let's answer the question. The question asks for the number of students in the group. So 7 + 3 + 9 + 5 = 24 students.

Toi: So before, we were counting those students who took both classes three times. Once in the physics category, once in the chemistry category, and once in the both category.

Bryn: You're right. It did seem too easy the other way. These Venn diagrams really help. Let's see if she's got another one for us to do.

In a poll of 46 students, 23 liked rap music, 24 liked rock music, and 19 liked country music. Of all the students, 12 liked rap and country, 13 liked rap and rock, and 14 liked country and rock. Of those students, 9 liked all 3 types. How many students did not like any of these types?

Work this problem before continuing.

This time there are three categories, so there need to be three loops. Since it is obviously possible to like two or three types of music, the three loops must intersect as shown.

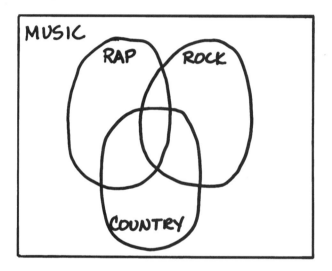

Tony worked on this problem. He succeeded in drawing the three loops, but after that point he was stuck. Maria joined him.

Tony: I can't figure out what to do with this diagram.

Maria: Well, let us figure out what each section represents. I will label each section with a letter.

(You may not need to do this when you are solving problems, but be sure you know what each section represents.)

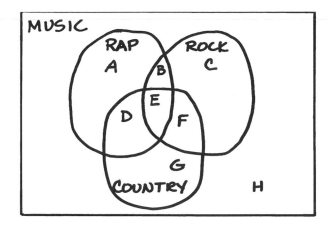

Before reading on, figure out what type(s) of music each section represents.

Maria: The sections represent students who like the following types of music.

A = rap only, but not rock nor country

B = rap and rock, but not country

C = rock only, but not rap nor country

D = rap and country, but not rock

E = rap, country, and rock

F = rock and country, but not rap

G = country only, but not rap nor rock

H = none of the three types of music

(This time, intermediate diagrams will not be shown. If you were unable to solve this problem yet, draw this diagram on another piece of paper, and fill in the numbers as Maria and Tony go through their explanation. The completed diagram will be shown at the end.)

Tony: Okay, I get that. So now what do we do? How do we put the numbers in?

Maria: Remember the strategy we learned last week?

Tony: You mean, working backwards?

Maria: Yes. So let's work backwards starting with the last clue. There are nine students that like all three types of music. This was region E in our Venn diagram, so enter 9 in region E.

Tony: Okay, I get that too. So now we should consider the students who like exactly two types of music. There are 12 students who like rap and country. But how do we put that in the diagram?

Maria: This encompasses regions D and E, since region D is students who like rap and country and not rock, and region E is students who like all three types of music, which of course includes rap and country. We already have nine students in region E. This leaves three students (12 − 9) in region D.

Tony: This is starting to make sense. Let me do the next one. Thirteen students like rap and rock. This encompasses regions B and E. We already have nine students in region E, so this leaves four students for region B.

Maria: Great, you're catching on. There are 14 students who like rock and country. This encompasses regions F and E. Since we still have nine students in region E, this leaves five students in region F. But I'm not really sure what to do next. This is as far as I got before you came over.

Tony: Well, let's keep on working backwards. Now we have to consider the students who like only one type of music. Region G is the students who like country only. We were told that there were 19 students who like country. So far we have 17 students who like country and something else. The country circle encompasses regions D, E, F, and G. Region D has three students, region E has nine, and region F has five. This adds to 17. Since there are 19 students who like country, we have 2 students left who like country but none of the other types. Therefore, put 2 in region G.

Maria: Okay, I see. Let me do one. The rock circle encompasses regions B, C, E, and F. We already have four students in region B, nine in region E, and five in region F. This adds to 18. Since we were told that there are 24 students who like rock music, we have 6 students left over (24 − 18) that just like rock music. So put 6 in region C.

Tony: Great. The rap circle encompasses regions A, B, D, and E. We already have four students in region B, three in region D, and nine in region E. This adds to 16. Since we were told that there are 23 students who like rap, this leaves 7 students (23 – 16) who like rap only. So put 7 in region A. And now we're done.

Maria: No we aren't. We haven't answered the question.

Tony: Oh yeah, what was the question?

Maria: How many students didn't like any of the three types of music?

Tony: Maria, Maria, Maria, how are we going to answer that?

Maria: Well, let's add up all of the numbers in the regions we have so far.

$$7 + 4 + 6 + 3 + 9 + 5 + 2 = 36 \text{ students}$$

Tony: But wait, there are supposed to be 46 students because that's what it said. We're off by 10. We messed up.

Maria: No we didn't. This just leaves 10 students (46 – 36) who do not like any of these three types of music. So put 10 in region H.

Tony: Okay, I see. Now we can answer the question. How many students do not like any of the three types of music? This is region H. There are 10 students who do not like any of these three types of music.
    The final diagram appears below.

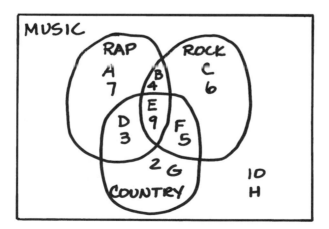

There are 23 students in a homeroom. Eighteen are taking math and 15 are taking science. Six students are taking math but not science. How many are taking neither subject?

Work this problem before continuing.

This problem is similar to the problem Science Courses. It again involves two circles, one labeled "Math" and one labeled "Science." The circles intersect since it is possible to take both subjects. The region outside of a circle represents not taking that subject. Debbie's diagram is shown below.

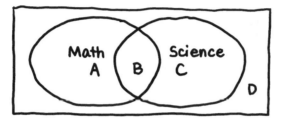

"I get really confused by these problems, so I decided to label the regions." The regions labeled A through D represent students that:

A—are taking math but not science

B—are taking both math and science

C—are taking science but not math

D—are taking neither math nor science

Again, we will not show intermediary diagrams, so follow along on another sheet of paper. The complete diagram will appear at the end.

Debbie went on, "Once I had the regions labeled, it didn't seem that hard. The problem states that there are six students who are taking math but not science. So put 6 in region A. The problem states that there are 18 students who are taking math. But I already have 6 in region A, and the students who are taking math are all contained in either A or B. So there must be 12 students (18 – 6) in region B. These 12 students are taking both math and science. There are 15 students who are taking science (and may or may not be taking math), so this leaves 3 students (15 – 12) who are only taking science in region C. There are supposed to be 23 students in the group. I added up the numbers in the diagram so far (6 + 12 + 3) and got 21. This leaves 2 students (23 – 21) for region D. The question asked was, 'How many students are taking neither subject?' This is region D, so the answer is 2."

The final diagram is shown below.

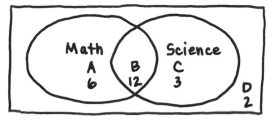

Frank Robinson, former manager of the Baltimore Orioles baseball team, looked over his roster at the beginning of spring training one season. He noticed the following facts. Every outfielder is a switch-hitter. Half of all infielders are switch-hitters. Half of all switch-hitters are outfielders. There are 14 infielders and 8 outfielders. No infielder is an outfielder. How many switch-hitters are neither outfielders nor infielders?

Work this problem before continuing.

This problem is quite different. It is not obvious what the Venn diagram looks like. Start with the outfielders and switch-hitters. The problem states that all outfielders are switch-hitters. This means the outfielder circle is completely contained within the switch-hitter circle. So draw two loops, with the outfielder loop inside the switch-hitter loop as shown. In the diagram, switch-hitters will be abbreviated SH, outfielders will be abbreviated OF, and infielders will be abbreviated IF. This could qualify under the easier related problem strategy, especially if the categories were rather nonsensical. (You might notice one such problem in the problem set.)

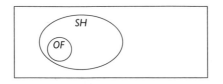

Now consider the infielders. The problem states that half of all infielders are switch-hitters. This means that the infielder loop must intersect the switch-hitter loop. The problem also states that no infielder is an outfielder. So while the infielder loop intersects the switch-hitter loop, it does not intersect the outfielder loop. The diagram is shown below.

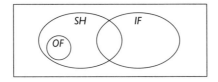

Now consider the numbers given in the problem. It says there are 14 infielders and 8 outfielders. Of the 14 infielders, half of them are switch-hitters. Therefore 7 of the 14 infielders are switch-hitters. This means that 7 of the 14 infielders are not switch-hitters. So put 7 in the intersection of the infielder and switch-hitter loops, and put 7 in the infielders-only part of the infielder loop. Also, put 8 in the outfielder loop, because the problem states there are 8 outfielders.

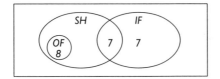

Finally, consider the statement, "Half of all switch-hitters are outfielders." Since the 8 outfielders represent half of all of the switch-hitters, there must be 16 switch-hitters. So far, the diagram has eight outfielders, and seven infielder-switch-hitters. This adds to 15 switch-hitters. So there must be one more switch-hitter. This switch-hitter is neither an outfielder nor an infielder (maybe he is a catcher). So he must go outside of the outfielder and infielder loops, but inside the switch-hitter loop. The final diagram is shown below.

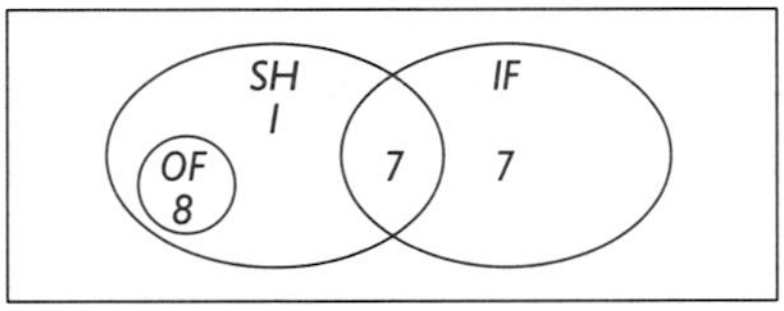

Now answer the question. How many switch-hitters are neither outfielders nor infielders? A quick look at the diagram shows the answer to be 1.

The next problem features a combination of Venn diagrams and guess and check.

THE COMIC BOOK COLLECTORS

Bruce and Clark went to the comic book store to buy some classic comics. They found that they could buy a Batman and a Superman for $18. They also found they could buy a Batman and a Flash for $16, and they could buy a Superman and a Flash for $22. How much did each of the comics cost separately?

Guess what? You should do this problem before continuing on! Solve it using a Venn diagram in conjunction with guess and check.

Mark solved this problem by a combination of Venn diagrams and guess and check. He drew loops to represent each kind of comic book, as shown. In the intersection of two loops, he wrote the price for those two comic books together.

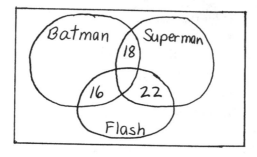

Then he tried using guess and check. "I guessed a price for the Batman comic book and then I followed that guess around the diagram. First I guessed that the Batman comic cost $10. I wrote 10 in the Batman only circle. This forced the Superman comic to be $8 since the Batman and Superman together cost $18. If the Superman cost $8, then the Flash must cost $14 since the Superman and Flash cost $22 together. But that means the Batman and Flash together cost $24, which contradicts the given information, which says the Batman and Flash together cost $16."

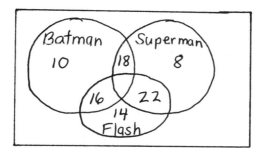

"I tried another guess. I knew I should make the Batman comic cost less, because on my last guess, the Batman and Flash together cost too much. So I tried $4 for the Batman comic and followed it around to the Superman and Flash comics."

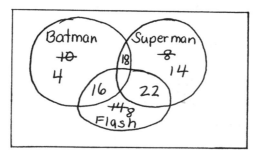

"This time the Batman and Flash together cost $12, so the guess of $4 was too low. I then tried $8."

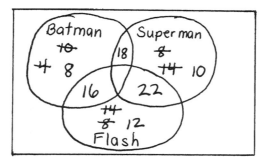

"That didn't work either, so I tried $6 and that worked. So the Batman comic cost $6, the Superman cost $12, and the Flash cost $10."

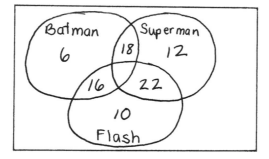

Suresh tried this problem with a similar strategy, but managed to do it with just the Venn diagram and without guess and check.

"I drew a Venn diagram just like Mark had done. But I also figured out that if you added up 18 + 16 + 22 − 56, this would be twice as much money as the comics cost, because you would be adding the cost of each book twice. So I put 28 in the intersection of the three circles."

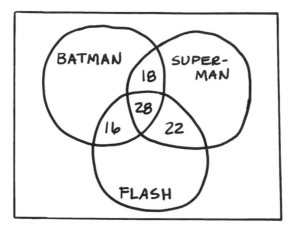

"Then I just had to figure out how much each book cost. Since the difference between the Superman/Flash and Superman/Batman was $4, I knew that Flash cost $4 more than Batman. So I needed two numbers that were different by 4 and added up to 16. So Flash must cost 10 and Batman must cost 6. After that it was a simple matter to put in the cost of the Superman at $12."

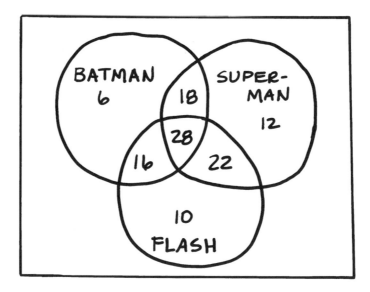

Thelma solved this problem similarly to Suresh, but she finished it a little differently.

"I put in 28 in the intersection of the three circles, just like Suresh did.

"Then I figured out that all three comic books cost $28, while just the Batman and Superman cost $18. So the difference of $10 must be the cost of the Flash comic. Similarly, the Batman comic costs $6 (the difference between $28 and $22) and the Superman comic costs $12 (the difference between $28 and $16)."

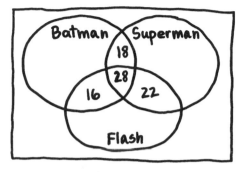

Venn diagrams can't be used on many problems. But they are very effective on those problems where a Venn diagram is appropriate. The diagram organizes information spatially and enables you to consider many different pieces of information at the same time. They are usually quick and easy to use, and can often solve problems that are very confusing when worked another way.

Problem Set A

1. **SENIOR CLASS**

   There are 100 students in the senior class. Twenty-five are on the mathletes team. Forty students are on the football team. Ten are on both teams. How many are on neither team?

2. **HAMBURGERS AND HOT DOGS**

   Of 900 people interviewed, 254 said they liked only hamburgers. Four hundred sixty-one said they liked only hot dogs, and 140 people liked both hamburgers and hot dogs. How many of the people interviewed didn't like either?

3. ROCK BAND

In a third-rate rock band, three play guitar, four sing, and two do both. Six have no talent for singing or guitar, so they do something else. How many members are in the rock band?

4. EATING VEGETABLES

The staff at "Tiny Little Cherubs" (abbreviated TLC) day-care center observed their 64 students' eating habits during several lunches. They observed that 59 children ate green beans, 56 ate cauliflower, 60 ate broccoli, 55 ate green beans and cauliflower, 54 ate cauliflower and broccoli, 56 ate green beans and broccoli, and 53 ate all three. How many children did not eat any of these three types of vegetables? How many children ate green beans but not cauliflower? How many children did not eat broccoli? How many children ate only cauliflower? And how many children ate exactly two types of vegetables?

5. THE FIELD TRIPS

The Unicorn class, the Radical Dog-Star class, and the Kitty class (all first- and second-graders) were talking about their favorite field trips during the school year. One of the teachers, Ms. Solomon, turned it into a math lesson, and the students conducted a survey. Each child was to write on paper which trip was his or her favorite. (Note that many children named more than one field trip as "favorite.") The survey revealed that 52 wrote down the trip to the river, 50 indicated the trip to the police station, and 44 included the trip to the hardware store. Nineteen papers showed the police station and the river. Thirty-two ballots included both the river and the hardware store, and 25 children had the police station and hardware stores on their papers. Seventeen students included all three and one did not write down any of the three trips. How many children were surveyed?

6. FAMILY REUNION

At one family reunion, every niece was a cousin. Half of all aunts were cousins. Half of all cousins were nieces. There were 50 aunts and 30 nieces. No aunt was a niece. How many cousins were neither nieces nor aunts?

7. JUST WHAT ARE THESE THINGS, ANYWAY?

All DERFS are ENAJS. One-third of all ENAJS are DERFS. Half of all SIVADS are ENAJS. One SIVAD is a DERF. Eight SIVADS are ENAJS. There are 90 ENAJS. Draw the Venn diagram. How many ENAJS are neither DERFS nor SIVADS ?

8. BLOOD LINES

Human blood comes in four types: O, A, B, or AB, depending upon whether it contains no antigen, A antigen, B antigen, or both A and B antigens. A third antigen, called the Rh antigen, is important in human reproduction. Blood is said to be Rh-positive if it contains this Rh antigen, and Rh-negative otherwise. So for instance, blood is type A^+ if it contains the A antigen and the Rh antigen. Blood is type AB^- if it contains the A and B antigens but does not contain the Rh antigen.

In a hospital this data was recorded.

Twenty-two people were either type A or type AB, 16 of which had the Rh antigen.

Twenty-seven were either type B or type AB, 18 of which had the Rh antigen.

Eight were type AB, two of which were AB^-.

Thirty-five were type O, five of which were O^-.

How many patients are listed here?
How many patients are type B^+?
How many patients are type A^-?
How many have exactly two antigens?

9. MANY PENNIES

Jason, Matt, and Critter were counting their pennies. Jason and Matt together had 31. Matt and Critter together had 19. Jason and Critter together had 24. How many pennies did each boy have?

10. BOTTLE CAPS

Rick collects bottle caps from root beer, orange soda, and cola. Seventy of his caps are not from root beer. Eighty of his caps are not from orange soda. One hundred are not from cola. How many bottle caps does he have, and how many of each kind?

11. WRITE YOUR OWN

Make up a Venn diagram problem.

Problem Set B: A Family Holiday

These problems all concern the Family family holidays.

1. HOLIDAY PASTRIES

Every year as part of the Family family traditions during the holidays, the whole family bakes something to give to their friends and relatives. This year they decided to make some special pastries. Mama Family was very careful to make sure they baked plenty so there would be plenty to give away. If there was anything the family liked better than baking, it was eating what they baked. So during the night, Papa got up and ate one-third of the pastries. As he started back to bed, he noticed his dog looking very hungry, so he gave one pastry to the dog. Ed was the next to get up. He planned to eat one-fourth of the pastries, but when he separated them into four piles, he found there were three pastries left over. He fed those three pastries to his dog and then ate one-fourth of the remaining pastries. Lisa then got up and ate one-third of the remaining pastries. As she was heading back to bed, her dog whined, so she gave it two pastries. Judy was the last to get up, and she consumed eight pastries but then gave one-eighth of the remaining pastries to her dog. When Mama went into the kitchen the next morning, she found a lot of crumbs, ants, and only 14 pastries. Mama sighed, realizing that again this year they would have no pastries to give away. She ate two, gave two to her dog, and then split the remaining pastries evenly for her family to have for breakfast. How many pastries did the family bake originally, and how many pastries did each person consume?

2. PRESENTS, OH BOY!

The Family family had two of the kids' cousins, Gail and Randy, over for holiday gift giving. The Family kids are, of course, named Ed, Lisa, and Judy. The Family parents bought presents for all five kids, but they forgot to buy wrapping paper. Consequently, the gifts were wrapped in strange ways, although every gift was wrapped in something different. One of the gifts was wrapped in a towel. Interestingly enough, the kids' heights were exactly three inches apart—their heights, in no particular order, were 59, 62, 65, 68, and 71 inches tall. From the clues that follow, determine the height of each child, the gift received, and the strange way in which it was wrapped.

1. The one who received a set of Legos is three inches shorter than the one who received a gift wrapped in a pillowcase.

2. The child who received shoes is not 59 inches tall but is shorter than the child who received the picture.

3. Randy is shorter than the child who got the belt and one other child, but he is taller than both Gail and the child whose gift was wrapped in a plastic bag.

4. Ed is taller than the one whose present was packaged in a box.

5. The child who received a gift packaged in newspaper is shorter than both Lisa and the child who received candy.

6. The child whose gift was wrapped in a pillowcase is not in the same immediate family as the child who received the belt.

3. LEGO MY PYRAMID

Of all the presents, the biggest hit was the Legos. None of the kids had played with Legos for years, and they all took turns building things. One of the really great structures built was a sort of pyramid built out of square Legos. It began with a single two by two square Lego. Then four squares were attached underneath it, so as to leave a strip of one bump showing all the way around the outside. This was continued for a total of ten layers. Although the pyramid could have been built by just putting Legos on the perimeter, they filled in each layer on the underside of the pyramid. How many bumps were showing and how many Legos were used to make the pyramid?

4. THE HOLIDAY PARTY

After opening up all the presents, the Family family went to Grandma and Grandpa's house for the big Family family holiday party. There were always lots of people there. Judy, who was interested in statistics, went around asking questions of everyone and recording their responses. She collected the following data. Every nephew was a cousin. Half of all uncles were cousins. One-third of all cousins were nephews. There were 30 uncles and 20 nephews. One-sixth of all uncles were nephews. She herself was a cousin but not a nephew nor an uncle. Judy wanted to know two things. She wanted to know how many cousins were neither nephews nor uncles. She also wanted to know how many uncles were also cousins but not nephews. Can you help?

5. HOLIDAY DINNER

The whole Family clan went out to dinner. The menu read as follows.

First course: chicken vegetable soup; shrimp salad, fruit salad.

Second course: shrimp, vegetable casserole, beef, chicken.

Third course: apple pie, carrot cake, ice cream.

Papa wants everyone to order a different meal. (Note: Soup, beef, and pie would be different from soup, beef, and cake.) Papa wants to know if there are enough different meals available that consist of one item from each course. However, he does not want any of the meals to have the same kind of food more than once during the meal. Example: If Ed ordered shrimp salad, then he could not order shrimp for the second course. You may assume that the items containing vegetables contain carrots, and the fruit salad contains apples. How many such meals are possible?

43 **algebra**

WE SAVED ALGEBRA for nearly last on purpose, but maybe not for the reasons that you think. Our reasons are as follows.

- Algebra is already the most familiar problem-solving strategy to students who have taken any typical high school math class.

- Algebra is emphasized as a problem-solving strategy in many texts. In fact, most texts have "five steps" in their problem-solving process, which are roughly: read the problem, choose a variable, write an equation, solve the equation, check the solution. This "process" (it's not really a process) gives the impression that all problems that will ever be encountered can be solved algebraically (with an equation). This emphasis also helps people feel dumb if they can't come up with the equation. Students will often say, "I can solve the equation once I have it, but I can never set it up. Can you help me set it up?"

- Algebra alone is not *the* problem-solving strategy. While it is a tremendously powerful tool, many problems cannot be solved algebraically. Many problems can be solved much more effectively when some other problem-solving strategy is used in conjunction with algebra. There are few problems (and these are usually found in algebra books) that should be solved with algebra to the exclusion of all other strategies.

◀ *An accountant must enter algebraic formulas in a spreadsheet to automatically perform calculations on variable data.*

- As a student advances in the study of mathematics, finding physical representations of problems becomes increasingly more difficult. Other problems are direct adaptations of real-life problems, such as the rate of flow of water through a pipe, but the complexity of the model forbids a reasonable representation. Therefore, as a student progresses through mathematics, he or she needs to become increasingly capable of changing problems posed into mathematical equations. This is a necessary skill. However, since most people in the world will not study or use math at a level where models are difficult, this skill is superfluous to their problem-solving experience. That is why the other strategies in this book are so important. They have been underemphasized (speaking historically) in mathematics education, but they are greatly needed in the world at large. A person solving a problem in real life is more likely to have to draw a picture than write an equation.

Algebra is a powerful tool. Like other tools, it reaches its peak of power when used in conjunction with complementary tools. This chapter will focus on using algebra in conjunction with the other problem-solving strategies presented earlier in the text. One of the things that was presumed at the beginning of the text was that you already have a working knowledge of algebra. Therefore, this book doesn't include algebra instruction. Instead, we offer instruction on melding algebra with other problem-solving strategies.

We will return to many problems from previous chapters, especially the Guess and Check chapter. We mentioned in that chapter that guess and check really helped to set up the algebra. In that chapter, the problems were solvable by guess and check alone. In this chapter we will use guess and check as a means to get to an equation. The goal will be the equation. The student quoted earlier mentioned the difficulty of setting up equations. Guess and check is a good way to accomplish this. Some of these equations will involve two variables and some will involve one.

Sandy held a garage sale during which she charged a dime for everything, but accepted a nickel if the buyer bargained well. At the end of the day, she realized she had sold all 12 items and raked in a grand total of 95 cents. She had only dimes and nickels. How many of each did she have?

See if you can recreate the guess and check chart for this problem without looking back at the Guess and Check chapter.

The chart from the Guess and Check chapter is reproduced here.

Dimes	Nickels	Value of Dimes	Value of Nickels	Total Value	Rating
5	7	$.50	$.35	$ .85	low
8	4	$.80	$.20	$1.00	high

The chart ends before the right answer is reached. The objective is now to set up an equation. Two students, Mike and Pat, each solved this problem algebraically after first setting up a guess and check chart.

Mike used the following reasoning. "Sometimes guess and check takes too long. I'm usually pretty good at it, but I tend to get bored. So I made a couple of guesses, and then I tried to set up the equation. Since I was guessing the number of dimes, I decided to call the number of dimes 'd.' So I wrote down d in the dimes column under the 8."

Dimes	Nickels	Value of Dimes	Value of Nickels	Total Value	Rating
5	7	$.50	$.35	$ .85	low
8	4	$.80	$.20	$1.00	high
d					

"Then I tried to figure out what to put in the nickels column. I noticed that in my guesses so far, the dimes column and the nickels column added up to 12. So the difference between 12 and d should be the number of nickels. So I wrote down $d - 12$ in the nickels column. I was working with my friend Amy, and she pointed out that $d - 12$ was wrong. For instance, if $d = 8$, then $d - 12$ would be $^-4$ and that doesn't make sense. She said it should be $12 - d$. I checked that with the two guesses I had already made, and it made sense because $12 - 8 = 4$ and $12 - 5 = 7$. So I put $12 - d$ in the nickels column."

Dimes	Nickels	Value of Dimes	Value of Nickels	Total Value	Rating
5	7	$.50	$.35	$ .85	low
8	4	$.80	$.20	$1.00	high
d	12-d				

"Again I looked back at my guesses. Where did I get the amount of money in the value of dimes and value of nickels column? I realized right away that they came from the number of dimes times 10 cents and the number of nickels times 5 cents. So all I had to do was multiply d times 10 cents and $12 - d$ times 5 cents. So I did that."

Dimes	Nickels	Value of Dimes	Value of Nickels	Total Value	Rating
5	7	$.50	$.35	$ .85	low
8	4	$.80	$.20	$1.00	high
d	12−d	(.10)d	(.05)(12−d)		

"This seemed like it was working really well. Finally, I figured out that my total value column came from adding up the value of dimes and value of nickels columns. So I wrote that down. Then I realized that this total value was supposed to be 95 cents. So I set the total value column equal to 95 cents, and I had my equation. While I was writing this, I decided that it would be easier to do the thing in cents instead of dollars, so I changed the algebra to cents by taking away the decimals."

Dimes	Nickels	Value of Dimes	Value of Nickels	Total Value
5	7	$.50	$.35	$ .85
8	4	$.80	$.20	$1.00
d	12−d	10d	5(12−d)	10d+5(12−d)=95

"Of course, solving this equation was really easy."

$$10d + 5(12-d) = 95$$
$$10d + 60 - 5d = 95$$
$$5d + 60 = 95$$
$$5d = 35$$
$$d = 7$$

"It's funny, but when I used to solve equations in algebra class, I would always write down the answer to the variable for the answer to the question. So I would write down $d = 7$ as the answer. But guess and check really helps me to answer the question. The question asks, 'How many of each does she have?' I've only figured out dimes so far, so I go back to my chart and figure out that the number of nickels she has is five because $12 - 7 = 5$. So the answer is she has seven dimes and five nickels."

Pat solved this problem in a similar way, but she decided to use two variables instead of one. So where Mike used $12 - d$ to represent nickels, Pat used n to represent nickels. Her chart looks like this.

# of Dimes	# of Nickels	Total Coins	Value of Dimes	Value of Nickels	Total Value	Rating
5	5	10	$.50	$.25	$.75	low-low
2	14	16	$.20	$.70	$.95	high-right
8	4	12	$.80	$.40	$1.20	right-high
d	n	$d+n$	$10d$	$5n$	$10d+5n = 95$	

Pat came up with a system of two equations and two variables. One equation is obviously $10d + 5n = 95$. But what is her other equation? It comes from the third column. The total number of coins is $d + n$ and is supposed to be 12, so the other equation is $d + n = 12$.

Solving:

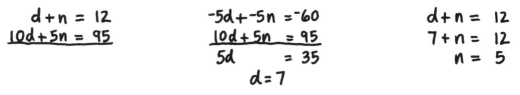

$$d + n = 12$$
$$10d + 5n = 95$$

$$-5d + -5n = -60$$
$$10d + 5n = 95$$
$$5d = 35$$
$$d = 7$$

$$d + n = 12$$
$$7 + n = 12$$
$$n = 5$$

So again, the answer to the problem is seven dimes and five nickels.

Farmer Jones raises ducks and cows. She tries not to clutter her mind with too many details, but she does think it's important to remember how many animals she has, and how many feet those animals have. She thinks she remembers having 54 animals with 122 feet. How many of each type of animal does Farmer Jones have?

Again, recreate the guess and check chart. Then set up the equation(s) to solve the problem algebraically.

Imogen used the guess and check chart below. She guessed the number of ducks and the number of cows. Actually, she didn't guess the number of cows: she simply subtracted the number of ducks from 54, since there were 54 animals altogether. She easily figured out the number of feet for each kind of animal and checked to see if there were 122 feet.

Ducks	Duck Feet	Cows	Cow Feet	Total Feet	Check
20	40	34	136	176	high
40	80	14	56	136	high
50	100	4	16	116	low
d	$2d$	$54-d$	$4(54-d)$	$2d+4(54-d)$	

Since the total feet column is what Imogen is checking, and she knows it must be 122 feet, the equation is right there for the taking: $2d + 4(54 - d) = 122$. When setting up an equation, you need to find two things that are supposed to be equal to each other. Solving this equation gives the solution 47 ducks and 7 cows.

~~~~

When you move from guess and check to algebra you must do exactly what you did before. In the above example, you got from "ducks" to "duck feet" by simply multiplying by two. The first guess had 20 ducks, so the number of duck feet was $2 \times 20 = 40$. This seems very simple, yet some students make this more difficult by being too afraid to proceed. Ask the question: "What did I do to get this number?" Whatever the answer is, the procedure is still the same for the algebraic guess as it was for the arithmetic guesses.

The next thing to do is to write the equation. An equation is simply two expressions connected with an equal sign. If the two expressions are supposed to be equal, then you have a valid equation. The actual equation usually jumps out of the last or next-to-last column. In the case of the cows and ducks above, it was the last numeric column, and there was a known amount that was supposed to equal the total feet.

ALL AROUND THE PLAYING FIELD

The perimeter of a rectangular playing field is 504 yards. Its length is 6 yards shorter than twice its width. What is its area?

Set up the guess and check chart for this problem and then write the equation.

Sheri's chart is shown below.

WIDTH	LENGTH	PERIMETER	
100	194	588	HIGH
60	114	348	LOW
80	154	468	LOW

Sheri was guessing the width, so she decided to let that be her variable, call it w. Now, where had she gotten the length? "The problem says that the length was 6 yards shorter than twice the width. For instance, $100 \times 2 = 200$, would be twice the width. The length is 6 yards shorter than that, so $200 - 6 = 194$. So if I'm letting w stand for width, then length must be $2w - 6$. The perimeter is twice the sum of the length and width. So it's 2 times the quantity $w + 2w - 6$. It is supposed to be 504 yards.

WIDTH	LENGTH	PERIMETER	
100	194	588	HIGH
60	114	348	LOW
80	154	468	LOW
w	$2w-6$	$2(w+2w-6)=504$	

The most difficult thing is being careful enough to get the equation set up correctly. Sheri used only three columns on this problem and had little difficulty changing over to the algebraic representation. Those who use few columns on guess and check are asking for trouble. If it works, fine, but if you get stuck you really need to habitually set up more columns. This problem could have been guess and checked as follows.

WIDTH	2x WIDTH	LENGTH	PERIMETER	
100	200	194	588	HIGH
60	120	114	348	LOW
80	160	154	468	LOW
w	2w	2w−6	2(w+2w−6)= 504	

The second column is only meant to help the problem solver. If you find that you are a little bit confused by a problem, it is better to use more columns. The people who have trouble with understanding their own charts tend to be those who try to do the problem without enough columns.

Solving this equation is now fairly simple:

$$2(w + 2w - 6) = 504$$
$$2(3w - 6) = 504$$
$$6w - 12 = 504$$
$$6w = 516$$
$$w = 86$$

So length is $2(86) - 6 = 166$.
Check the perimeter: $86 + 166 = 252$ (and $252 \times 2 = 504$).

So the length is 166 yards and the width is 86 yards. But the question asked for area. The area of the field is 166 yards × 86 yards = 14,276 square yards.

A group of exchange students from Japan went to a convalescent home to sing songs for the seniors and to demonstrate origami (Japanese paper folding). As it turned out, there was either one Japanese student at a table with three seniors, or two students at a table with four seniors. There were 23 students and 61 seniors in all. How many tables were being used to demonstrate origami?

Work this problem before continuing.

Manmeet solved this problem. "I started out using guess and check because the problem really confused me. I guessed the number of each kind of table, and then figured out how many students and how many seniors were at each one. I checked by figuring out the total number of students and seniors and compared it to 23 and 61. I used 1|3 to stand for tables with one student and three seniors, and 2|4 for the other kind."

1|3 tables			2|4 tables			Total		
# of tbls	# of stud	# of snr	# of tbls	# of stud	# of snr	# of stud 23	# of snr 61	Rating
10	10	30	10	20	40	30	70	high-high
5	5	15	5	10	20	15	35	low-low
8	8	24	8	16	32	24	56	high-low
5	5	15	9	18	36	23	51	right-low
5	5	15	10	20	40	25	55	high-low

"At this point, I was really frustrated. I was guessing two things, but I wasn't sure how to get closer to the right answer. I also thought that my first two guesses meant that the right answer was somewhere between 10 and 5 for each kind of table. But that didn't seem to work either. So I gave up guess and check and used algebra. I called the 1|3 tables x and the number of 2|4 tables y. Then I just did the same thing to x and y as I did to the number guesses."

| 1/3 tables | | | 2/4 tables | | | Total | | |
#of tbls	#of stud	#of snr	#of tbls	#of stud	#of snr	#of stud 23	#of snr 61	Rating
10	10	30	10	20	40	30	70	high-high
5	5	15	5	10	20	15	35	low-low
8	8	24	8	16	32	24	56	high-low
5	5	15	9	18	36	23	51	right-low
5	5	15	10	20	40	25	55	high-low
x	x	$3x$	y	$2y$	$4y$	$x+2y$	$3x+4y$	

"Then I knew that the total number of students had to be 23 and the total number of seniors had to be 61, so I just wrote two equations and solved them."

$$x + 2y = 23$$
$$3x + 4y = 61$$

$$\Rightarrow$$
$$\Rightarrow$$

$$2x + 4y = 46$$
$$\underline{3x + 4y = 61}$$
$$x = 15$$

$$x + 2y = 23$$
$$15 + 2y = 23$$
$$2y = 8$$
$$y = 4$$

"There were 15 tables that held one student and three seniors and 4 tables that held two students and four seniors. I checked this too. There are $15 \times 1 + 4 \times 2 = 23$ students and $15 \times 3 + 4 \times 4 = 61$ seniors, which works out."

Cloe is two years less than four times as old as Zeke. Cloe is also one year more than three times as old as Zeke. How old is each?

Solve this problem using guess and check to set up the algebra before continuing.

The guess and check chart from Chapter 6 is reproduced below. Following that, *b* is placed in the Zeke's age column to represent

ZEKE'S AGE	4 X ZEKE	CLOE'S AGE 4X ZEKE −2	3 X ZEKE	CLOE'S AGE 3X ZEKE +1	RATING
1	4	2	3	4	WRONG
2	8	6	6	7	CLOSER
4	16	14	12	13	HIGH (3RD COL. HIGHER THAN 5TH)
b	4b	4b−2	3b+1		

Zeke's age.

Cloe's age is represented by two things, $4b - 2$ and $3b + 1$. In the guess and check version, the problem was finished when column 3 and column 5 were the same. Again, dealing with the concept of two equal expressions, this means we need to set $4b - 2 = 3b + 1$ in order to set up the equation.

$$4b - 2 = 3b + 1$$
$$b - 2 = 1$$
$$b = 3$$

So Zeke is 3. This means that Cloe is 10, since $4(3) - 2 = 10$ and $3(3) + 1 = 10$.

As you work a problem using guess and check, you begin to understand it better. Then, you can easily convert it to algebra.

Augustus is trying to make chocolate milk. So far he has made a 10% chocolate milk solution (this means that the solution is 10% chocolate and 90% milk). He has also made a 25% chocolate milk solution. Unfortunately, the 10% solution is too weak, and the 25% solution is way too chocolatey. He has a whole lot of the 10% solution, but he only has 30 gallons of the 25% solution. How many gallons of 10% solution should he add to the 25% solution, to make a mixture that is 15% chocolate (which Augustus is sure will be absolutely perfect)?

Work this problem before continuing.

The guess and check combined with subproblems solution from the Subproblems chapter is shown below.

Gal of 10% Sol	Gal Choc in 10% Sol	Gal of 25% Sol	Gal Choc in 25% Sol	Total Gal of Choc	Total Gal of Mix	% Choc in Total Mix	Rate
5	.5	30	7.5	8	35	22.8%	high
30	3	30	7.5	10.5	60	17.5%	high
50	5	30	7.5	12.5	80	15.6%	high
g	.1g	30	7.5	.1g + 7.5	g + 30	$\frac{(.1g + 7.5)}{(g + 30)}$	

Although the expression for the last column looks complicated, it is easy to see where it came from when you break it down into parts: It is simply a ratio of the numbers in the two preceding columns. That is, the numerator is from the column called "total gallons of chocolate" and the denominator is from the "total gallons of mixture" column.

The algebra was arrived at in the same way the guess and check was done. Do the same thing to g as was done to all of the other numbers. The final equation comes from the chart and from knowing that the guess is supposed to produce 15% as a result. So 60 gallons of the 10% mixture are required.

$$\frac{(.1g + 7.5)}{(g + 30)} = .15$$

$$.1g + 7.5 = .15(g + 30)$$
$$.1g + 7.5 = .15g + 4.5$$
$$-.05g = -3$$

$$g = \frac{-3}{-.05}$$

$$g = 60 \text{ gallons}$$

Note: If Augustus wanted his mixture to be 14.65% chocolate, guess and check would have taken a long time, but algebra would have been as quick as it was when he was looking for 15% chocolate. Guess and check is very useful in setting up the algebraic equation. That doesn't mean you have to use guess and check to set up the algebra, but it is not a bad idea, and could save you a lot of grief. If you are at all unsure of the equation, then set up a guess and check chart first.

Here is another mixture problem with which to exercise your newfound skill.

? SALT SOLUTION

A pet store sells salt water for fish tanks. Unfortunately, recently hired Flounder (a character from the movie Animal House) *mixed a salt solution that was too weak. He made 150 pounds of 4% salt solution. The boss wants a 7% salt solution. Help Flounder out by giving him two options for reaching the 7% solution.*

a. Add some salt. How much?
b. Evaporate some water. How much?

Work this problem before continuing.

Steve, Brenda, and Gil worked on this problem.

Steve: I hate mixture problems. Poor Flounder, this one sounds tough.

Brenda: Come on, guys, we can do this. Let's set up a guess and check chart. What do we know and what do we need?

Gil: We have 150 pounds of solution. And it is 4% salt. How much of it is salt, then?

Steve: Sounds like a subproblem. Four percent of 150 is 6. So there are 6 pounds of salt and, therefore, 144 pounds of water in the original solution.

Brenda: Which part should we do first?

Gil: It probably doesn't matter. Let's do part a. Here's my guess and check chart. I guessed the salt added. The first three columns never change.

Lbs. Soln	Lbs. Salt	Lbs Water	Salt Added	Total Salt	Total Soln	% Salt
150	6	144	1	7	151	7/151 = 4.6 %
150	6	144	10	16	160	16/160 = 10 %

Brenda: I think I follow this. You guessed the salt added. Then you added that to the 6 pounds of salt you already had in the solution to get the total salt column. How did you get the total solution column?

Steve: Oh, I get that. You're just pouring more into the solution, so you need to add how much you put in to how much was already there. He added the salt-added value to the 150 pounds of solution that was already there. That gave him how much total solution there was.

Brenda: Okay, I get it. Then he divided the amount of salt by the total-solution amount to get the percent salt. Of course, it comes out as a decimal so he changed it to a percent.

Gil: Right. And the correct answer has to be in between 1 and 10 gallons added.

Brenda: I think we ought to use algebra. Guessing could take forever. It's probably some nasty decimal answer anyway.

Gil: Okay, let's use algebra. How do we do that?

Steve: Easy, just guess a variable. Put x in the salt added column and do the same thing to x that you did to the numbers.

Brenda: So the total salt column would be $x + 6$. The new solution column is $x + 150$. And the % salt column is their ratio. Just like with the numbers.

Lbs. Soln	Lbs. Salt	Lbs Water	Salt Added	Total Salt	Total Soln	% Salt
150	6	144	1	7	151	7/151 = 4.6 %
150	6	144	10	16	160	16/160 = 10 %
150	6	144	x	$x + 6$	$x + 150$	$(x+6)/(x+150)$

Gil: But where do we get the equation?

Brenda: Easy. The % salt column is supposed to be 7 percent, right? So set $(x + 6)/(x + 150)$ equal to 0.07. Then solve it.

Gil: Are you sure? This seems too easy for this kind of problem.

Brenda: Try it. It works.

$$\frac{x + 6}{x + 150} = 0.07$$

$$x + 6 = .07(x + 150)$$
$$x + 6 = .07x + 10.5$$
$$.93x = 4.5$$
$$x = 4.5/.93$$
$$x = 4.84 \text{ POUNDS (ROUNDED)}$$

Gil: That wasn't so bad. So he needs to add 4.84 pounds of salt. That's a lot of salt. Maybe he would be better off evaporating some water.

Brenda: Well, let's try that one. Set it up by guess and check again. I'm not going to bother writing down the first three columns like last time. I'll guess water evaporated.

WATER SUBTRACTD	WATER TOTAL	SOLUTION TOTAL	% SALT
4	140	146	6/146 = 4.1%
20	124	130	6/130 = 4.6%

Steve: Wow, this is taking forever. Let's try algebra.

Gil: Okay, put x in the water subtracted column.

WATER SUBTRACTD	WATER TOTAL	SOLUTION TOTAL	% SALT
4	140	146	6/146 = 4.1%
20	124	130	6/130 = 4.6%
X	144−X	150−X	6/(150−X)

Brenda: So we want $6/(150 - x)$ to be 7% or .07.

$$\frac{6}{150-x} = .07$$

$$6 = .07(150 - x)$$
$$6 = 10.5 - .07x$$
$$-.07x = -4.5$$
$$.07x = 4.5$$
$$x = 4.5/.07$$
$$x = 64.29 \text{ POUNDS}$$

Brenda: Wow, that's a lot of water to evaporate. Poor Flounder. It's going to be tough, whatever he does.

Again, as Gil, Brenda, and Steve found out, guess and check and algebra in combination can be a very powerful weapon in attacking problems. Guess and check can also be very tedious. If the answer to the problem is not an integer, guess and check could literally take all day. Abandoning guess and check for algebra in these situations is the best way to solve the problem.

The next problem is different. It is not a typical Algebra I problem.

THE SEASON'S STATS

Franny, Carl, and Amichung compared their season statistics during the post-season banquet for their high school baseball team. Franny had three times as many singles as Carl. Carl had four times as many doubles as Amichung. Each of them had exactly the same number of hits. None of the three had any hits besides singles and doubles (they were slap hitters). The three of them as a group had exactly as many singles as doubles. Added together, the three of them had fewer than 200 hits in all. How many singles and how many doubles did each of them have?

Work this problem before continuing.

Rick approached this problem this way. "I was really confused by this problem, so I decided to use guess and check. I started by guessing the number of singles that Carl had. First I guessed Carl had two singles. It says that Franny had three times as many singles as Carl, so Franny had six singles. Then I was stuck. I looked at the problem again and saw that Carl had four times as many doubles as Amichung. So I guessed Amichung had 5 doubles, and this meant that Carl had 20 doubles. My chart looked like this so far. Columns with asterisks were the ones I guessed."

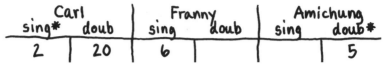

Carl		Franny		Amichung	
sing*	doub	sing	doub	sing	doub*
2	20	6			5

"Then I was stuck again. I didn't know how to check the guess. I reread the problem and found that they had fewer than 200 hits altogether. That didn't seem to help much. Then I read that each player had the same number of hits. That helped a lot. Since I already had both of Carl's types of hits filled in, I saw that Carl had 22 hits (for this guess). So Franny and Amichung must also have had 22 hits apiece. Since Franny has 6 singles, she must have 16 doubles. Since Amichung has 5 doubles, he must have had 17 singles. I filled this in on the chart."

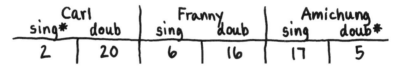

Carl		Franny		Amichung	
sing*	doub	sing	doub	sing	doub*
2	20	6	16	17	5

"Now, what? I still didn't know if this was right. It was definitely less than 200 hits altogether (66 to be exact in this case) but so what? There were lots of possibilities that would give less than 200 hits. Then I read that the three of them as a group had exactly the same number of singles as doubles. So I needed another column on my chart. I added it up and got 25 singles and 41 doubles."

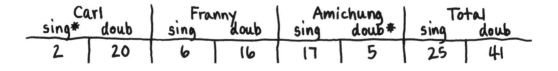

Carl		Franny		Amichung		Total	
sing*	doub	sing	doub	sing	doub*	sing	doub
2	20	6	16	17	5	25	41

"Now I could see that this was incorrect, but it gave me something to check. I knew this might take forever, but I went on anyway. I decided that it would be easier if I left one of the guesses the same, and changed the other one. I left Carl with two singles and changed Amichung to six doubles. So Franny had six singles (three times as many as Carl) and Carl had 24 doubles (four times as many as Amichung). So there were 26 hits in all, which gave Franny 20 doubles (she already had six singles) and Amichung 20 singles (he already had six doubles). The total number of singles was 28 and the total number of doubles was 50. This seemed to be getting worse, so in my next guess I gave Carl more singles."

| Carl | | Franny | | Amichung | | Total | |
sing*	doub	sing	doub	sing	doub*	sing	doub
2	20	6	16	17	5	25	41
2	24	6	20	20	6	28	50
3	24	9	18	21	6	33	48

"At this point, I decided to use algebra. I was guessing Carl's singles, so I made that x, and Amichung's doubles I made y."

| Carl | | Franny | | Amichung | | Total | |
sing*	doub	sing	doub	sing	doub*	sing	doub
2	20	6	16	17	5	25	41
2	24	6	20	20	6	28	50
3	24	9	18	21	6	33	48
x					y		

"With the numbers, I had tripled Carl's singles to get Franny's singles. So Franny's singles must be $3x$. I had quadrupled Amichung's doubles to get Carl's doubles, so Carl's doubles must be $4y$."

| Carl | | Franny | | Amichung | | Total | |
sing*	doub	sing	doub	sing	doub*	sing	doub
2	20	6	16	17	5	25	41
2	24	6	20	20	6	28	50
3	24	9	18	21	6	33	48
x	$4y$	$3x$			y		

"Now it got weird. The thing I did next with the numbers was to add up the total number of hits for each player, and then make the other players have that many hits. So Carl has $x + 4y$ hits. So far Franny has $3x$ hits. If her doubles were d, then $3x + d$ = total hits = $x + 4y$. Solving for d, I got $d = 4y - 2x$. So Franny must have $4y - 2x$ doubles. Notice that total hits which is right because that's what Carl has.

"I did the same thing for Amichung. So far he has y doubles. If I let him have n singles, then $n + y = x + 4y$ total hits. So $n = x + 3y$ singles."

Carl sing*	Carl doub	Franny sing	Franny doub	Amichung sing	Amichung doub*	Total sing	Total doub
2	20	6	16	17	5	25	41
2	24	6	20	20	6	28	50
3	24	9	18	21	6	33	48
x	$4y$	$3x$	$4y-2x$	$x+3y$	y		

"Then I looked back at what I did with the numbers. For each guess, I figured out the total number of singles and the total number of doubles and looked to see if they were the same. So adding the singles and doubles I got:

singles: $x + 3x + (x + 3y) = 5x + 3y$

doubles: $4y + (4y - 2x) + y = 9y - 2x$

Carl sing*	Carl doub	Franny sing	Franny doub	Amichung sing	Amichung doub*	Total sing	Total doub
2	20	6	16	17	5	25	41
2	24	6	20	20	6	28	50
3	24	9	18	21	6	33	48
x	$4y$	$3x$	$4y-2x$	$x+3y$	y	$5x+3y$	$9y-2x$

"Since I wanted total singles to equal total doubles, I set the number of singles equal to the number of doubles. I had two variables, so I wasn't sure what would happen. I decided to get the x's on one side and the y's on the other side."

$$5x + 3y = 9y - 2x$$
$$7x = 6y$$

"I realized this would be true if x was 6 and y was 7. I also realized it would be true if x was 12 and y was 14. Anytime the ratio of $x{:}y = 6{:}7$, there would be a solution. So I decided to guess $x = 6$ and $y = 7$, or to put it another way, Carl has six singles and Amichung has seven doubles. Then I tried giving Carl 12 singles and Amichung 14 doubles."

Carl		Franny		Amichung		Total	
sing*	doub	sing	doub	sing	doub*	sing	doub
2	20	6	16	17	5	25	41
2	24	6	20	20	6	28	50
3	24	9	18	21	6	33	48
x	$4y$	$3x$	$4y-2x$	$x+3y$	y	$5x+3y$	$9y-2x$
6	28	18	16	27	7	51	51
12	56	36	32	54	14	102	102

"It worked for $x = 6$ and $y = 7$, giving a total of 102 hits. When I guessed $x = 12$ and $y = 14$, it gave 204 total hits. But the problem said the number of hits was less than 200. So the first solution must be the only solution. So the answers are Carl had 6 singles and 28 doubles, Franny had 18 singles and 16 doubles, and Amichung had 27 singles and 7 doubles. Whew!"

~~~~~

Algebra is a powerful strategy in certain situations. It is very useful in combination with diagrams or guess and check. You will find that many problems cannot be solved algebraically. However, much of mathematics is based on equations and algebra, so it is worthwhile to learn how to set up and solve equations.

The next two problems use diagrams in conjunction with algebra.

? THE SHADOW

A man 6 feet tall is walking away from a street light that is 15 feet tall. How long is the man's shadow when he is 10 feet away from the light?

Work this problem before continuing. Note: Guess and check doesn't really help here, but a diagram helps a lot.

Suzanne drew the diagram shown below. "I drew the picture, and saw where the shadow would be. I labeled the length of the shadow x."

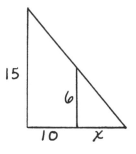

"It looked to me like the triangles were similar. The ratio of the height of the pole to the height of the man should be in the same proportion as what? Comparing the big triangle to the little triangle, the vertical side of the big triangle compared to the vertical side of the small triangle should have the same ratio as the bottom side of the big triangle to the bottom side of the small triangle. So I set up an equation."

$$\frac{15}{6} = \frac{10 + x}{x}$$

"Solving this equation I got this."

$$15x = 6(10 + x)$$
$$15x = 60 + 6x$$
$$9x = 60$$
$$x = 60/9 = 20/3$$

"So the man's shadow is $20/3$ or $6\,2/3$ feet long."

WORKING OUT

Brian is supposed to run around the basketball court inside the gym at the beginning of each day's volleyball practice. The court measures 70 feet by 120 feet. Brian is rather lazy, however, and cuts off each corner as he runs around. When he is 6 feet from the end of the court, he runs diagonally to a point 6 feet from the side of the court. He does this on each of the four corners. How many feet does Brian cut off one lap?

Work this problem before continuing.

This problem obviously needs a diagram of the court. This diagram shows the court and the four corners that are cut off.

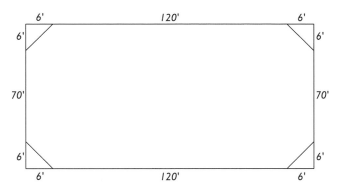

The problem breaks down into subproblems. First, find the length of the diagonal of one of the triangles. Find the difference between the diagonal and going around the corner. Then multiply the answer by 4 to find the total savings.

The length of the diagonal can be solved with algebra.

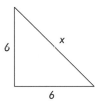

To solve this, you need to know the Pythagorean Theorem. The sum of the squares of the legs of a right triangle is equal to the square of the hypotenuse.

$$6^2 + 6^2 = x^2$$
$$36 + 36 = x^2$$
$$8.48 \approx x \qquad \text{(Take the square root of 72.)}$$

So Brian runs about 8.5 feet instead of running around the corner, which is 12 feet. This results in saving 3.5 feet on each corner. Multiplying by the four corners gives a savings of 14 feet for each lap. So Brian is cheating himself out of 14 feet of running. Instead of running the 380 feet around the court, he is only running 366 feet.

Algebra is a very effective strategy in some situations. You should not believe that it is the only strategy (as some algebra books would have you believe), but it does have its place and is therefore worth learning. When algebra is used in conjunction with other strategies, it becomes easier to use and more powerful. Don't be afraid to use it.

Problem Set A

1. **ALGEBRA THIS TIME**

Go back to Chapter 6 Problem Set A or any Problem Set B problem on which you used guess and check. Write equations for three of those problems.

2. **MORE COINS**

Bill has $3.25 in nickels and dimes. He has eight more nickels than dimes. How many of each does he have?

3. **SUPPLEMENTS**

The larger of two supplementary angles is 6 degrees more than twice the smaller of the two angles. What is the measure of each angle?

4. **BIKE RIDE**

Blaise rode his bike to his friend Elroy's house, which was 15 miles away. After he had been riding for half an hour, he got a flat tire. He walked his bike the rest of the way. The total trip took him 3 hours. If his walking rate was one-fourth as fast as his riding rate, how fast did he ride?

5. **CHAMPIONSHIP GAME**

A group of students were transported to the championship basketball game using buses and vans. When one bus and two vans unloaded, there were 55 students. A few minutes later, two more buses and one van unloaded. This time there were 89 students. In all, three buses and eight vans drove students to the game. How many students went to the game?

6. FISHING POLES

Daniel and Gary are fishing. They each have several fishing poles, and each pole has several worms on the line. Daniel's poles each have six worms on their lines. Gary's poles each have 11 worms on their lines. Between the two of them, Daniel and Gary have 103 worms. How many poles does each boy have?

7. CAR WASH

Alyse and Jeremy are washing their father's car. Alyse can wash the car by herself in 20 minutes. Jeremy can wash the car by himself in 30 minutes. How long does it take them to wash the car if they work together?

8. INTEREST

Lakeitha earned an extra $12,000 in her accounting job last year. This year she decided to invest the money split between two different savings accounts. One account was a certificate of deposit that paid

7.25% annual interest. The other was a money market account that paid 5.4% annual interest. At the end of one year, she had made $730. How much did she invest in the money market account?

9. CHEMISTRY

A chemist mixes two solutions. One is 24% acid (the rest is water) and the other is 41% acid. About how much of each solution does she need to use to produce 50 gallons of a solution that is 31% acid? (Answer to the nearest hundredth of a gallon.)

10. LADDER

A woman is working in her backyard. She wants to fix part of the gutter on her roof. Therefore, she wants to put a ladder against the wall and climb up to fix the roof. The gutter is 14 feet above the ground. Unfortunately, there is an 8 foot high retaining wall standing 3 feet away from her house. The ladder can't be placed between the retaining wall and the house, so it must be placed on the outside of the retaining wall. The ladder will go over the retaining wall (it can touch it) and then up to the roof. How long a ladder does she need?

11. INTERVIEW

Interview a professional who uses algebra on the job.

Problem Set B

1. ALL IN THE FAMILY

People of Hispanic culture traditionally have two last names. Both names come from their parents. The first one is from the father, and the second one is the mother. For example, a woman named María Sanchez Jones would have had a father with the last names Sánchez XXX (the other last name is irrelevant for this discussion) and a mother with last names Jones YYY.

Suppose a man named José García Lopez marries a woman named María Sanchez Jones. She would then drop the Jones and become María Sanchez de García, adding on her husband's name after the word "de." So she is now María Sanchez, "wife of García."

If that couple then has a child, the child will use the last names García Sánchez. Regardless of whether that child is a boy or a girl, the name that is passed on to his or her offspring is García. The sample family tree below illustrates that:

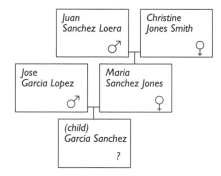

Jones is crossed off from María's name as she marries, and the "de García" is added on.

Write the names of these people in the correct places on the family tree below. Notice that some people have been listed twice: once with their maiden names and once with their married names.

1. Dolores Lara Baez (F)
2. Alberto Rodijo Saenz (M)
3. Marisela Saenz de Rodijo (F)
4. Consuelo Baez García (F)
5. Rafael Lara Echeve (M)
6. Dolores Lara de Rodijo (F)
7. Ana Luísa Rodijo Saenz (F)
8. Marisela Saenz Vaquero (F)
9. Concepción Rodijo Lara (F)
10. Juan Carlos Rodijo Gomez (M)
11. Consuelo Baez de Lara (F)

The F indicates a female and M indicates male.

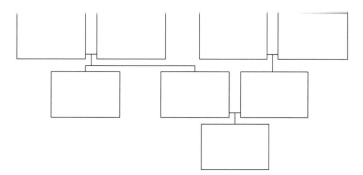

2. HOW MANY ZEROS?

The expression $n!$ means $n(n-1)(n-2)(n-3)(n-4)(n-5) \dots (3)(2)(1)$. It is pronounced "$n$ factorial." Thus 6! means $6 \times 5 \times 4 \times 3 \times 2 \times 1 = 720$ and 10! means $10 \times 9 \times 8 \times 7 \times 6 \times 5 \times 4 \times 3 \times 2 \times 1 = 3{,}628{,}800$. Notice that 6! ends with one digit of zero, and 10! ends with two digits of zero. How many digits of zero does 5000! end with?

3. VALLEY SPRINGS

Valley Springs Winery bought some grapes to make wine. One variety of grapes, called Zinfandel, costs $500 per ton. The other grapes, called Valdepeñas, are used to make regular red wine, and cost $200 per ton. The buyer ended up paying an average of $280 per ton for the grapes. What is the ratio of tons of Zinfandels to tons of Valdepeñas?

4. FORMING PENTOMINOES

Pentominoes are figures formed by connecting five squares so that they share a common side. (See illustrations of valid and invalid pentominoes below.) How many different pentominoes are there? (Reflections and rotations are not considered to be different.)

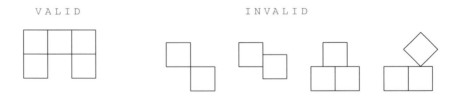

VALID   INVALID

5. WHEN I'M SIXTY-FOUR

This is a new game. Two people alternate taking turns by choosing a whole number from 1 to 8. Keep a running total. (For example, if you pick 2, and your opponent picks 6, the total is now 8, then maybe you pick 5, so now the total is 13, and so on.) The object of the game is to make the score exactly 64 on your turn. (If it was your turn and the running total at that point was 62, you would say 2, making the score 64, and you would be the winner.) You are going to choose the first number. What number should you pick in order to guarantee a win for yourself, and what strategy should you follow?

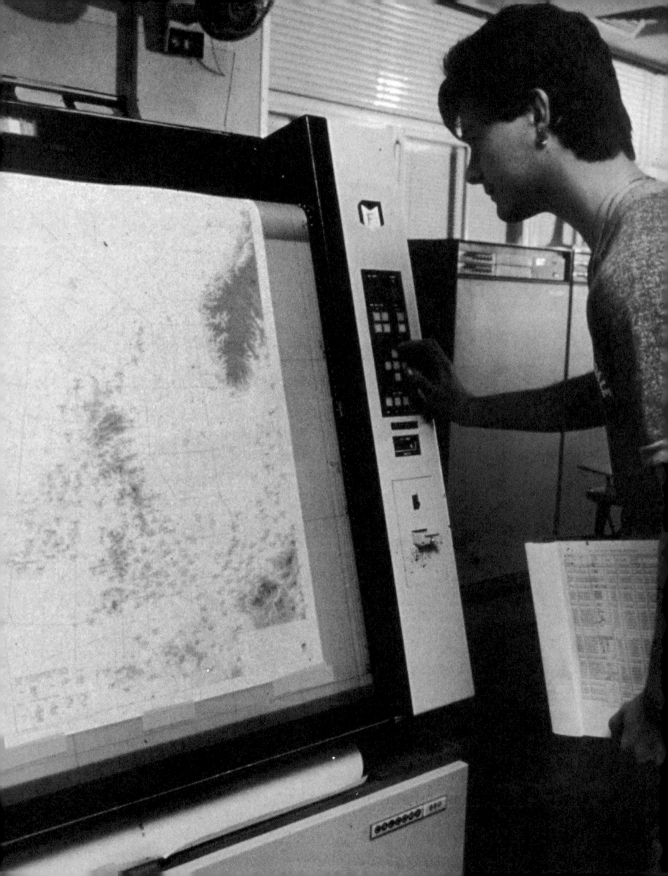

finite differences

THE STRATEGY of finite differences ties together many of the strategies previously discussed. It is a very powerful way of organizing information, and often leads to equations that can be used to solve problems. Recall the problem below.

? HOW MANY SQUARES?

Find a formula for the number of squares on a checkerboard that has any number of squares along each side. (This is an n by n checkerboard.)
Set up a pattern for this problem before going on.

This problem was first introduced in the Solve an Easier Related Problems chapter. At that time a chart was set up to determine the number of squares in a one by one square, a two by two square, and so on, up to an eight by eight square. This problem asks you to find a formula for an *n* by *n* square. The chart from Chapter 9 is reproduced below.

Size of Whole Square	Number of Squares
1 by 1	1
2 by 2	$4 + 1 = 5$
3 by 3	$9 + 4 + 1 = 14$
4 by 4	$16 + 9 + 4 + 1 = 30$

◀ *Meteorologists study differences in temperature and barometric pressure at various places at different times in order to establish a weather pattern that can aid in their predictions.*

Angie and Isaac were having a discussion about this problem, and they conjectured that there might be a formula for problems such as this. This chapter is about finding such formulas.

The chart above can be expressed in a slightly different way, and can also be expanded, as shown below.

Side of Whole Square	Number of Squares
1	$1 = 1$
2	$5 = 1 + 4$
3	$14 = 1 + 4 + 9$
4	$30 = 1 + 4 + 9 + 16$
5	$55 = 1 + 4 + 9 + 16 + 25$
6	$91 = 1 + 4 + 9 + 16 + 25 + 36$
7	$140 = 1 + 4 + 9 + 16 + 25 + 36 + 49$
8	$204 = 1 + 4 + 9 + 16 + 25 + 36 + 49 + 64$
9	$285 = 1 + 4 + 9 + 16 + 25 + 36 + 49 + 64 + 81$
10	$385 = 1 + 4 + 9 + 16 + 25 + 36 + 49 + 64 + 81 + 100$

The pattern mentioned in Chapter 9 is to add the next square number to each previous answer.

So $1 + 2^2 = 5$
$$5 + 3^2 = 14$$
$$14 + 4^2 = 30 \qquad \text{and so on.}$$

This chapter will explore this pattern in great detail, and you will learn how you can use what you notice about this pattern to figure out a formula or equation for the chart.

To begin with, consider the following input-output charts (usually called functions). Find a pattern in each problem and predict the output for inputs of 5 and 137. The input value is called x and the output value is called y.

x	y		x	y		x	y
0	3		0	-2		0	-4
1	7		1	5		1	1
2	11		2	12		2	12
3	15		3	19		3	29
4	19		4	26		4	52
5	?		5	?		5	?
137	?		137	?		137	?

*Find the pattern in each function and then fill in the y values for the x
values 5 and 137.*

Fazal worked on this problem. "The first function wasn't that hard
to figure out. I quickly saw the pattern that each y value increased by 4.
I decided to write this into the chart, putting $^+4$ between each set of
numbers. Doing that made it quite obvious that the output for $x = 5$
was $y = 23$."

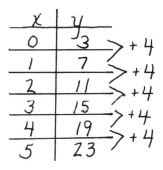

"But I got really stuck trying to figure out the output for $x = 137$.
"I decided to go on to the next problem. On this problem I could see
that the y values increased by 7 each time. So it was no problem figuring out that the y value for $x = 5$ was $y = 33$. But again, I had no clue
on $x = 137$."

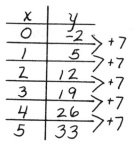

"The third problem was harder. I looked at the differences between successive y values again, but this time it wasn't quite so obvious what was going on."

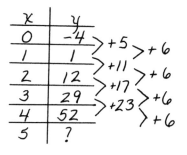

"After staring at it for awhile, I noticed that the differences were going up by 6. So I made another column of the differences of the differences. I wasn't sure this would help me, but I did it anyway."

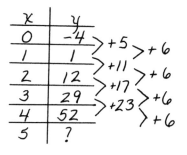

"I decided that if that worked, then the difference between the y value of 52 and the next y value would have to be 29. This was because the difference of 23 had to go up by 6, which would make it 29. Using this, I calculated the next y value to be 81. But I still didn't know how to get the y value for $x = 137$."

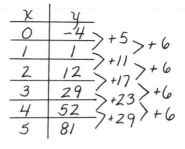

Finite differences can help Fazal with the problem of determining the y value for a particular x value. Fazal already found the key patterns in each of the problems. The strategy of finite differences allows him (and you) to use those patterns to find an equation for the function—an equation that relates the input to the output. Finite differences will work for functions that are polynomial in nature. It will not work for exponential functions, trigonometric functions, or other functions that are not polynomial. Just what are finite differences? Consider the two functions below.

The function on the left is the first problem Fazal worked on. The function on the right is an easier problem related to the one on the left. What is the equation for the function on the right? In other words, what equation relates the value of x to the value of y? Write your equation as $y = ?$.

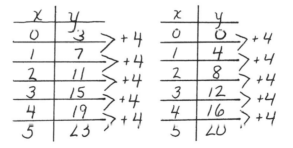

Reasonably quickly, you should see that the y value is always four times the x value. This relationship can be expressed with the equation $y = 4x$. What does that have to do with the function on the left? If you compare the y values term by term, you should notice that the y values for the function on the left are always three greater than the corresponding y values for the function on the right. This means that the equation for the function on the left is $y = 4x + 3$.

Suppose, however, that you don't figure out the helpful easier related problem when you are working on finding the equation. What, for example, is a useful easier related problem on the third function Fazal was working on? Is there another way to get the equation?

The answer, of course, is yes, or there wouldn't be much purpose to this chapter. The way to find equations for functions of this type is to use the strategy of finite differences.

The previous equation, $y = 4x + 3$, can be expressed in general form as $y = fx + e$. In algebra class, this equation was called the slope-intercept form of an equation of a line, and the letters m and b were used instead, as in $y = mx + b$. The exact letters used are not terribly important. (Note: It was important in algebra class to use m and b for linear equations in slope-intercept form. It was also important to use a, b, and c for the quadratic formula. However, the use of b is inconsistent between those two, even though they are taught in the same class. To avoid whatever you think b is or b should be, we are avoiding using b. We chose to start with e and f.) We used f first and then e for reasons that will become clear after a while. You can actually use whatever letters you want and it won't make any difference at all.

Look closely at the equation $y = fx + e$. Using different values of f and e, make up some equations and then fill out the values in a function chart, letting x be all integers between 0 and 5. For example, if $f = 4$ and $e = 3$, the equation would be $y = 4x + 3$, which would generate the function chart we have been working with. Make up some values of f and e and create the chart for three different functions before reading on.

~~~~~

Earvin made up these functions.

$f = 3$ $e = 1$	$f = -2$ $e = 9$	$f = 1$ $e = -4$
$y = 3x + 1$	$y = -2x + 9$	$y = 1x - 4$

x	y		x	y		x	y
0	1		0	9		0	-4
1	4		1	7		1	-3
2	7		2	5		2	-2
3	10		3	3		3	-1
4	13		4	1		4	0
5	16		5	-1		5	1

Now examine each of these functions using the differences that Fazal used earlier. You should also do this on the functions you made up yourself.

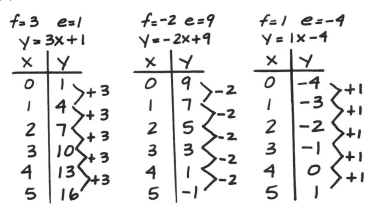

$f = 3$ $e = 1$
$y = 3x + 1$

x	y
0	1
1	4
2	7
3	10
4	13
5	16

(+3, +3, +3, +3, +3)

$f = -2$ $e = 9$
$y = -2x + 9$

x	y
0	9
1	7
2	5
3	3
4	1
5	-1

(-2, -2, -2, -2, -2)

$f = 1$ $e = -4$
$y = 1x - 4$

x	y
0	-4
1	-3
2	-2
3	-1
4	0
5	1

(+1, +1, +1, +1, +1)

You should notice that the second function features y values that decrease and hence the differences are ⁻2. What do the differences have to do with the original equations? You should see right off that the value of f (the coefficient of the x term in the original equation) is the same as the difference. The other thing you should notice is the value of e is the same as the y value when x is zero.

What is the equation for the chart below? This was the second problem that Fazal was working on earlier.

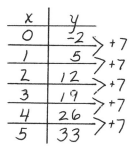

x	y
0	-2
1	5
2	12
3	19
4	26
5	33

(+7, +7, +7, +7, +7)

Did you notice that the common difference is 7, so the value of f must be 7. The y value for $x = 0$ is $y = ⁻2$, so e is ⁻2. Therefore, the equation is $y = 7x - 2$. This can easily be checked. For example, when $x = 5$, $y = 7(5) - 2 = 33$, which is correct.

Fazal tried to figure out the y-value when x was 137. Now that he knows the equation, this is easy to do. $y = 7(137) - 2 = 957$.

Does this work every time? Why? Consider the general equation $y = fx + e$.
Make a function chart for this equation using the values 0 through 5 for x.
Do this before reading on.

$y = fx + e$

x	y
0	e
1	$f + e$
2	$2f + e$
3	$3f + e$
4	$4f + e$
5	$5f + e$

Next, compute the differences between successive terms as we did before. This time, you have to algebraically subtract the upper one from the lower one. For example, the first two y values are e and $(f + e)$. Subtracting the upper from the lower gives $(f + e) - e = f$. The next difference is $(2f + e) - (f + e) = f$. It turns out to be f every time.

This general chart shows that the common difference will always be the value of f, and the value of e will be given by the value of y when x is 0.

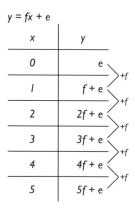

$y = fx + e$

x	y	
0	e	
		+f
1	$f + e$	
		+f
2	$2f + e$	
		+f
3	$3f + e$	
		+f
4	$4f + e$	
		+f
5	$5f + e$	

Now look back at the third problem Fazal was working on earlier.

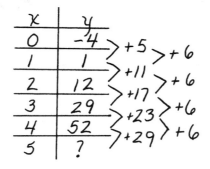

This problem had a common difference, but it didn't show up until the second set of differences. This didn't happen for equations of the form $y = fx + e$. So the general form for this equation must be different. Do you ever recall seeing a function that behaved this way—a common difference the second time? A well-known one is shown below. What is the equation for this function?

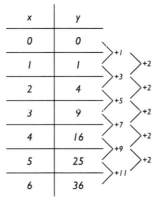

This function should be recognizable as $y = x^2$. So you might suspect that this type of function, where the second difference is a constant, would come from some sort of quadratic equation.

The general form for a quadratic function is $y = gx^2 + fx + e$. As before, by substituting x values from 0 through 5, make the general function chart for this equation. (You might notice if $g = 0$, this chart would be the same as one for $y = fx + e$.)

Do this before reading on.

$y = gx^2 + fx + e$

x	y
0	e
1	$g + f + e$
2	$4g + 2f + e$
3	$9g + 3f + e$
4	$16g + 4f + e$
5	$25g + 5f + e$

Now compute the first set of differences. This involves a little bit more algebra than in the chart for $y = fx + e$. For example, consider the values of y for $x = 2$ and $x = 3$. You must subtract the upper value from the lower value, so $(9g + 3f + e) - (4g + 2f + e) = 5g + f$. Be careful to do this consistently. You should notice that in each difference, the e term drops out. Here is the chart with the first set of differences filled in.

$y = gx^2 + fx + e$

x	y	
0	e	
		$g + f$
1	$g + f + e$	
		$3g + f$
2	$4g + 2f + e$	
		$5g + f$
3	$9g + 3f + e$	
		$7g + f$
4	$16g + 4f + e$	
		$9g + f$
5	$25g + 5f + e$	

These differences are not constant, so you must subtract again. This time take the difference of the differences.

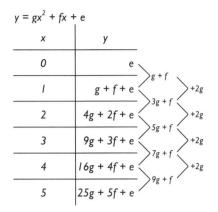

$y = gx^2 + fx + e$

x	y
0	e
1	$g + f + e$
2	$4g + 2f + e$
3	$9g + 3f + e$
4	$16g + 4f + e$
5	$25g + 5f + e$

(first differences: $g + f$, $3g + f$, $5g + f$, $7g + f$, $9g + f$; second differences: $+2g$, $+2g$, $+2g$, $+2g$)

This time, the second difference turns out to be $2g$ every time. This is the constant we were seeking. In the third function Fazal worked on, the second difference was constant. The second difference was also constant in the chart for $y = x^2$. We can use this master chart to figure out the equation for any function where the second difference is constant. First, compare the master chart with the chart for the function $y = x^2$.

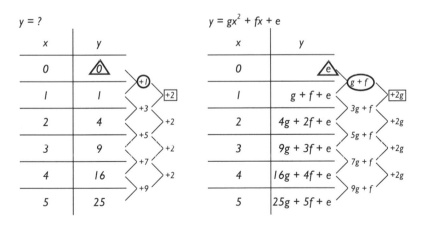

$y = ?$

x	y
0	0
1	1
2	4
3	9
4	16
5	25

(first differences: +1, +3, +5, +7, +9; second differences: +2, +2, +2, +2)

$y = gx^2 + fx + e$

x	y
0	e
1	$g + f + e$
2	$4g + 2f + e$
3	$9g + 3f + e$
4	$16g + 4f + e$
5	$25g + 5f + e$

(first differences: $g + f$, $3g + f$, $5g + f$, $7g + f$, $9g + f$; second differences: $+2g$, $+2g$, $+2g$, $+2g$)

The key to the strategy of finite differences is comparing the general chart with the problem you are working on and matching up places in the chart that are the same. Here you should notice that the second difference is always 2. In the general chart, the second difference is always $2g$. Equating these two (as they are in exactly the same place on the two charts) gives $2g = 2$ which means $g = 1$. So far we have the equation for this function is $y = 1x^2 + fx + e$. We now need to determine the values for f and e.

Again, compare two sections of the chart that are equivalent. For example, the difference between x values of 0 and 1 is 1 on the problem chart and $g + f$ on the general chart. So this gives $g + f = 1$. To solve this, remember that we already know that $g = 1$. So $1 + f = 1$, which gives $f = 0$.

We could have instead matched up the differences between $x = 4$ and $x = 5$. In our problem chart, that difference is 9. In the general chart, that difference is $9g + f$. Equating these gives $9g + f = 9$. Again, remembering that $g = 1$, gives us $9(1) + f = 9$, so $f = 0$. This is the value we got before.

Caution, however. Be sure the parts of each chart you are comparing are exactly the same. You wouldn't want to compare the differences between $x = 2$ and $x = 3$ on one chart with the differences between $x = 3$ and $x = 4$ on the other chart. That would lead to an incorrect value of f.

Finally, determine the value of e. In the problem chart, when $x = 0$, y is also 0. In the general chart, when $x = 0$, $y = e$. Therefore, e must be zero.

The values of g, f, and e respectively are 1, 0, and 0. Therefore, the equation for this function is $y = 1x^2 + 0x + 0$, or just $y = x^2$. This is what we got before.

Now consider the third problem Fazal worked on earlier. Compare it with the general chart and figure out the equation for the function.
Do this before reading on.

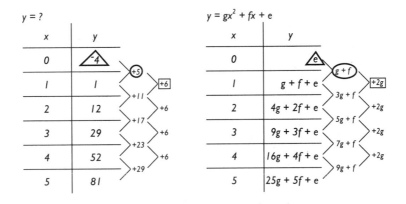

$y = ?$

x	y
0	⁻4
1	1
2	12
3	29
4	52
5	81

+5, +6
+11, +6
+17, +6
+23, +6
+29

$y = gx^2 + fx + e$

x	y
0	e
1	$g + f + e$
2	$4g + 2f + e$
3	$9g + 3f + e$
4	$16g + 4f + e$
5	$25g + 5f + e$

$g + f$, +2g
$3g + f$, +2g
$5g + f$, +2g
$7g + f$, +2g
$9g + f$

Compare parts of the chart that are the same. It's a good idea to find the value of g first, then f, and then e. The last column (second difference) is 6. This matches up with $2g$ on general chart. So $2g = 6$, which means $g = 3$.

The difference between 0 and 1 is 5 which matches up with $g + f$ on the general chart.

$$g + f = 5 \qquad \text{Recall, } g = 3.$$
$$3 + f = 5$$
$$f = 2$$

Finally, when $x = 0$, y is ⁻4, which matches up with e on the general chart. So $e = ⁻4$.

The equation is therefore $y = 3x^2 + 2x - 4$. Check it by substituting in $x = 4$. When $x = 4$, $y = 3(4^2) + 2(4) - 4 = 52$, which is correct.

Finally, you can use this equation to find the value of y for any x. In Fazal's problem, he needed to find y when $x = 137$.
So $y = 3(137^2) + 2(137) - 4 = 56{,}577$.

Find the equations for the two functions below. Then use your equation to find the y value for the other x value listed in each table.

x	y
0	-5
1	-2
2	5
3	16
4	31
5	50
48	?

x	y
2	14
3	11
4	8
5	5
6	2
7	-1
82	?

Work these before going on.

Sarah, Michele, and Iram worked on this problem.

Sarah: This problem looks like a tough nut to crack. What should we do? And we've got a pair of them.

Michele: Let's figure out what the differences are.

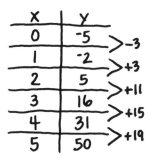

Iram: Wait a second. You have the first two differences wrong.

Michele: I do? What is wrong with them?

Sarah: I see what Iram means. From ⁻5 to ⁻2, it goes up three, not down three. So it should be ⁺3. That would have been a real lemon if we had blown that one.

Iram: Right. And from ⁻2 to 5, that goes up 7. Think of owing someone two dollars and then earning seven dollars. You would pay off the person you owed and still have five dollars. So ⁻2 + 7 = 5.

Michele: Okay, I see. (She changed her chart to this one.)

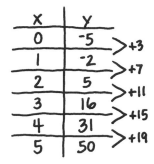

So it comes out constant on the second difference. That means it's a quadric equation?

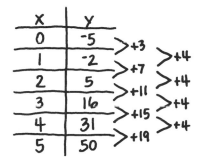

Iram: Quadratic equation. So the general equation is: $gx^2 + fx + e$.

Sarah: So we need the master chart for a quadratic—who wants that plum job?

Iram: Wait, I think I have it in my notebook someplace.

Michele: Don't bother looking, Iram. It's much better if we just create it from scratch. I'm not into memorizing stuff. I just know how to create it.

Sarah: I agree. I'll do it. This is pretty peachy. (This is the chart Sarah created.)

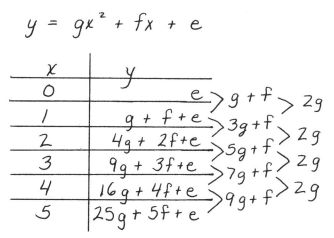

$$y = gx^2 + fx + e$$

Michele: Now what do we do, again?

Iram: Compare the master chart with the chart on the problem we are doing.

Michele: Oh yeah. (She put the problem chart next to the master chart.) Okay, 2g matches up with 4 in our problem.

Iram: Right. So 2g must equal 4 and therefore, g = 2.

Sarah: No problem. The next one is a little trickier. You have to make sure you are comparing apples to apples.

Michele: What? Come on, Sarah, forget the food and be serious.

Iram: I know what she means. The difference between 0 and 1 is $g + f$ on the master chart. On our problem it is 3. So $g + f = 3$.

Michele: Cool. I get it. We wouldn't want to match up $g + f$ with 7, because 7 is the difference between $x = 1$ and $x = 2$.

Sarah: Right. That would be comparing apples and oranges.

Michele: Got it. Anyway, $g + f = 3$ and we already know that g is 2, so f has to be 1.

Iram: Right. And e is obviously ‑5, because that is the y number when the x number is 0.

Michele: So the equation is $y = 2x^2 + x - 5$. We better check it.

Sarah: That's a good idea. Let's use $x = 4$. There is less risk of making a mistake there. Mr. Herr said something about not checking things with $x = 0$, 1, or 2, because it might turn out right and really be wrong. I don't remember. Anyway, using $x = 4$ is safe; 4 is a square, and you know what a square Mr. Herr is and I could sure use a square meal right now. Anyway, I don't care, because I've got a calculator. Okay, so $y = 2(4^2) + 4 - 5$ which is 31. I can even do this without a calculator. And 31 is what it is supposed to be.

Michele: Okay, now we need to know what y is when x is 48. So $y = 2(48^2) + 48 - 5 = 4651$.

Sarah: You know, these problems are fun. I know people who don't care at all about problems like this.

Iram: Yes, Sarah. Now look at the next one. It's different.

Michele: It doesn't start at $x = 0$.

Iram: Right. But I guess we can find the differences anyway.

(This is what Iram calculated for the differences.)

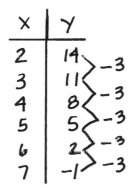

Michele: How come those are ⁻3 and not ⁺3?

Iram: It's just like in the last problem. The numbers are going down, so it's ⁻3.

Michele: Okay, got it. It came out constant the first time, so it must be an easy one. Aren't these called linear equations?

Sarah: Yeah, they are. I don't know why, though. What I know about vocabulary doesn't amount to a hill of beans.

Iram: So let's compare this with the master chart for $y = fx + e$. I think I can generate it, even though I'm sure I have it in my notebook somewhere. (This is what Iram wrote down next to the problem.)

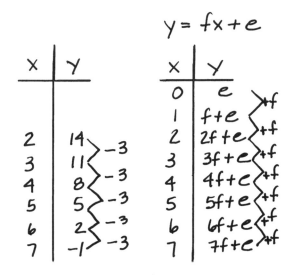

Sarah: I may be a vegetable, but I don't see why you wrote down the master chart like that.

Iram: I was trying to follow your advice about apples and oranges, Ms. Pineapple. I am trying to show the comparison between two things that are the same.

Michele: Good idea. But how should we handle the holes in the problem chart?

Sarah: I worked with Mel on a problem like this. We were really confused about those missing y values, too.

Iram: Well, either we don't worry about them, and just compare the similar parts of both charts, or we could work backwards and figure out the values for $x = 0$ and $x = 1$.

Sarah: Or we could meet halfway and do both. I suppose it doesn't really matter. Let's do it both ways and see if we get the same answers.

Iram: Compare similar parts of the two charts first. That gives us $f = {}^-3$. And opposite $x = 2$ we have $14 = 2f + e$.

$$14 = 2({}^-3) + e$$
$$14 = {}^-6 + e$$
$$e = 20$$

So the equation is $y = {}^-3x + 20$. This checks when $x = 6$ because ${}^-3(6) + 20 = 2$.

Michele: If we work backwards on our chart, we have to add 3 to go up the chart, since we subtract 3 going down the chart. We get $e = 20$ anyway since that is the number opposite zero. And f would still be ${}^-3$, since that is the common difference. So it must be right.

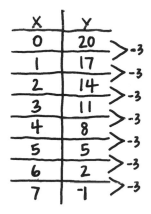

Sarah: Now we need y when $x = 82$. So $y = {}^-3(82) + 20$ which is ${}^-226$. That seems right since it really starts going down. Grape job, girls!

Iram: That was a berry good job, wasn't it?

Michele: You're starting to sound like Sarah. See ya later. I think I'm going to go have lunch. As they say in England, "Cherry-Oh!"

It seems that the trio did a good job on the problem. Notice that they were careful to compare similar parts of their master chart with like parts of the problem chart, even when some of the intermediary values for x and y were missing. They also checked their equations after they finished.

At the first meeting of the House of Representatives, all 435 members shook hands with each of the other members. How many handshakes took place? Work this problem before continuing.

Kowasky worked on this problem. "This problem sounded really hard. When I get a hard problem, I always want to make it easier. So I figured, suppose only one representative showed up. Then there wouldn't be too many handshakes. If two showed up, there would be one handshake. If three showed up, call them Ashanti, Ray, and Tina. Then Ashanti shakes hands with Ray, and then with Tina, and Ray shakes hands with Tina. That's three handshakes.

"When I got to four people, I drew a diagram. I counted lines in the diagram which represented handshakes. That was six handshakes."

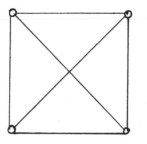

"Then I started making a chart and looked for a pattern."

People	Handshakes
0	0
1	0
2	1
3	3
4	6

"I figured I had better do five people. It was getting harder to make a diagram, but then I thought if there were four people there, they made six handshakes. If a fifth person came into the room, he would shake hands with the four people that were there already. So that would make ten handshakes. Then a sixth person would shake five hands, so that would be 15 handshakes for six people.

"I added this to my chart and looked to use finite differences since it would take forever to extend this pattern all the way to 435."

People	Handshakes
0	0
1	0
2	1
3	3
4	6
5	10
6	15

+0 +1
+1 +1
+2 +1
+3 +1
+4 +1
+5

"I saw that the constant difference happened the second time. That meant that the equation was quadratic of the form: $y = gx^2 + fx + e$.

I generated the master chart for that equation. I could have looked it up, but it's kind of fun to generate and I'm really too disorganized to find my old stuff anyway. I compared it with my chart for this problem."

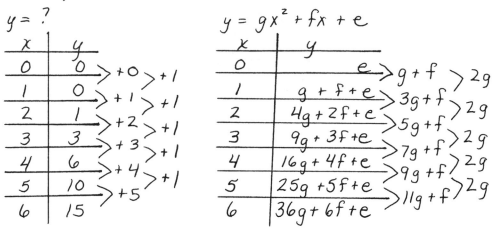

"Then I just had to compare similar parts of the two charts. The second constant difference is 1 which is equal to 2g. So if $2g = 1$, then $g = \frac{1}{2}$.

"Then I wanted to figure out what f was. The difference between $x = 2$ and $x = 3$ was 2 and that equals $5g + f$. I used these because I wasn't sure this problem made sense for fewer than two people."

$$5g + f = 2 \qquad \text{remember } g = \frac{1}{2}$$
$$5\left(\frac{1}{2}\right) + f = 2$$
$$2.5 + f = 2$$
$$f = -\frac{1}{2}$$

"Finally I wanted e. The y value for $x = 3$ was 3. In the master chart the value was $9g + 3f + e$."

$$9g + 3f + e = 3 \qquad \text{recall } g = \frac{1}{2} \text{ and } f = -\frac{1}{2}$$
$$9\left(\frac{1}{2}\right) + 3\left(-\frac{1}{2}\right) + e = 3$$
$$4.5 - 1.5 + e = 3$$
$$3 + e = 3$$
$$e = 0$$

"I noticed that I would have gotten the same value of e if I just used the value next to $x = 0$ in the chart. So my equation was $y = (1/2)x^2 - (1/2)x$, where x represents the number of representatives and y represents the number of handshakes. I checked this with six people."

$$y = (1/2)x^2 - (1/2)x$$
$$y = (1/2)6^2 - (1/2)6$$
$$y = (1/2)36 - 3$$
$$y = 18 - 3$$
$$y = 15, \quad \text{and that's what I got before.}$$

"Finally, I needed to find the number of handshakes for all 435 representatives."

$$y = (1/2)x^2 - (1/2)x$$
$$y = (1/2)(435^2) - (1/2)(435)$$
$$y = (1/2)(189225) - 217.5$$
$$y = 94612.5 - 217.5$$
$$y = 94395$$

"There will be 94935 handshakes. That's a lot of handshakes. I think there would be a lot of tired hands. And if the senators were there too, wow!

"This problem used a lot of strategies. I started with an easier related problem, then a diagram, then a pattern, and finally, finite differences. A lot of these strategies seem to work in concert really well."

~~~~~

Now look at the squares problem again that was presented at the beginning of the chapter.

Find a formula for the number of squares on any size n by n checkerboard. Set up a pattern for this problem before continuing.

When we last left this problem, the chart below had been developed. Angie and Isaac are back to discuss this problem.

SIDE SQRS	# OF SQRS
1	1
2	5
3	14
4	30
5	55
6	91
7	140
8	204
9	285
10	385

Angie: I think we can use finite differences to figure out the formula for this problem.

Isaac: I agree. Let's go for it. First find all the differences.

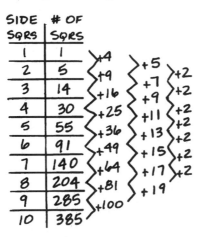

Angie: Wow, I've never seen one that took three differences to come out a constant.

Isaac: Yeah. I wonder what we should do. It can't be linear or quadratic.

Angie: Huh?

Isaac: You know linear is $y = fx + e$ and quadratic is $y = gx^2 + fx + e$.

Angie: Oh yeah. Because those take one difference and two differences. So what does that mean, does it have to be a cubic equation?

Isaac: I guess so. It's got to have an x^3 in it. I wonder what that looks like?

Angie: Probably $y = x^3 + x^2 + x + e$

Isaac: Don't we need some coefficients in there?

Angie: Yeah, okay. How about $y = hx^3 + gx^2 + fx + e$?

Isaac: Sounds good. Let's try and generate the master chart for it.

CUBIC MASTER CHART

Generate the master chart for $y = hx^3 + gx^2 + fx + e$.
Do this before continuing.

Angie: Okay, I think I've got it.

Isaac: Me too. Let's compare.

$$y = hx^3 + gx^2 + fx + e$$

x	y
0	e
1	h + g + f + e
2	8h + 4g + 2f + e
3	27h + 9g + 3f + e
4	64h + 16g + 4f + e
5	125h + 25g + 5f + e
6	216h + 36g + 6f + e

First differences: h+g+f, 7h+3g+f, 19h+5g+f, 37h+7g+f, 61h+9g+f, 91h+11g+f

Second differences: 6h+2g, 12h+2g, 18h+2g, 24h+2g, 30h+2g

Third differences: 6h, 6h, 6h, 6h

Angie: Wow, we got the same thing. I think we really understand this stuff.

Isaac: We do. Now let's compare this master chart with our chart.

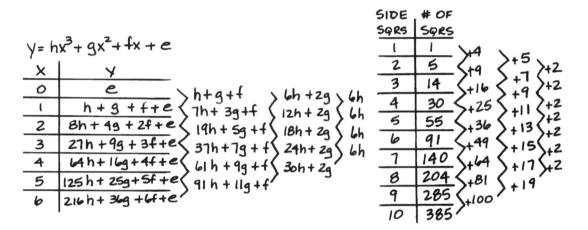

Angie: Okay, let's start with the last column. In our chart, the last column is 2. In the master chart, the last column is *6h*. So if *6h* = 2, then *h* is 3.

Isaac: No it's not. It's one-third. $h = \frac{1}{3}$.

Angie: Oh right, sorry, I divided the wrong way.

Isaac: Now let's compare the third columns. The top number in our chart is 5. The top number in the master chart is *6h* + *2g*. So *6h* + *2g* = 5.

Angie: Wrong. *6h* + *2g* is opposite the *x* = 1 value. But we never had *x* = 0 in our chart, so we need to compare 5 to *12h* + *2g*.

Isaac: Oh, I see what you mean. We need to make sure the spots in the two charts are in exactly the same place. Okay, so $12h + 2g = 5$.

$$12h + 2g = 5 \qquad h = 1/3$$
$$12(1/3) + 2g = 5$$
$$4 + 2g = 5$$
$$2g = 1$$
$$g = 1/2$$

Angie: Great. Now let's go to the second column and make sure we are comparing the same things.

Isaac: Okay, $7h + 3g + f = 4$ Those are the differences between $x = 1$ and $x = 2$.

Angie: Right. I can solve that for f.

$$7h + 3g + f = 4 \qquad h = 1/3, \quad g = 1/2$$
$$7(1/3) + 3(1/2) + f = 4$$
$$7/3 + 3/2 + f = 4$$
$$23/6 + f = 4$$
$$f = 1/6$$

Isaac: Great, even though we had to use fractions. I'm sure glad my calculator does fractions.

Angie: Me too. Okay, now what is e? Isn't it just the top number in the y column?

Isaac: It would be if we had a value for $x = 0$. It should be zero, since with no squares you wouldn't have any squares. But let's compare:

$$h + g + f + e = 1$$
$$1/3 + 1/2 + 1/6 + e = 1$$
$$1 + e = 1$$
$$e = 0$$

Angie: You were right, *e* is zero. Okay, so what's our equation?

Isaac: It's $y = (^1/_3)x^2 + (^1/_2)x^2 + (^1/_6)x$ where x is the number of squares on a side and y is the total number of squares in the figure.

Angie: Great! Let's test it. Suppose $x = 8$. We know that answer is supposed to be 204.

$$y = (^1/_3)x^3 + (^1/_2)x^2 + (^1/_6)x$$
$$y = (^1/_3)8^3 + (^1/_2)8^2 + (^1/_6)8$$
$$y = (^1/_3)(512) + (^1/_2)(64) + (^1/_6)8$$
$$y = 512/3 + 32 + 4/3 = 204$$

It checks.

Isaac: All right. So for a checkerboard that is *n* by *n*, there will be $(^1/_3)n^3 + (^1/_2)n^2 + (^1/_6)n$ total squares on it.

Angie: These finite differences are pretty cool. I think I could even figure out an equation that started with x^4 if I had to.

~~~~~

The strategy of finite differences is very powerful for finding equations that are polynomial in nature. It is really useful when used in conjunction with easier related problems, patterns, and sometimes diagrams. It organizes the information in a new way, and leads quickly to equations. But be careful; it doesn't work on all equations. Consider the chart to the right.

This problem was created by the function $y = 2^x$. Watch what happens when it is evaluated with finite differences.

x	y
0	1
1	2
2	4
3	8
4	16
5	32
6	64
7	128
8	256
9	512

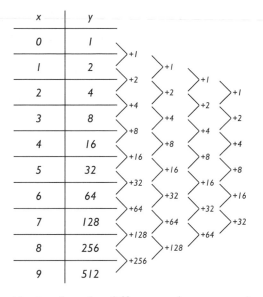

Notice that the differences keep repeating themselves. This type of a pattern is very typical of exponential function. You might investigate the pattern that arises from attacking the function $y = 3^x$ with finite differences. Be sure you consider x values up to at least 9. The repeating pattern that shows up here does not occur, but something else interesting does happen.

There are other booby traps in finite differences. Consider the problem below.

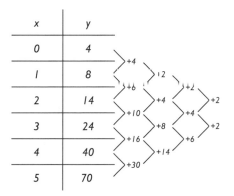

While it appears that there is a constant difference of 2 in the fourth column (indicating that the equation is 4th degree), there are only two values present. This should not be enough information to convince you of the validity of the pattern. If it is a problem where you generated the data—such as the handshake or squares problem—then you should generate a few more pieces of data. In this way you will have a better idea of whether or not your pattern is correct. No pattern is guaranteed to last forever, so be careful.

Another potential difficulty is when you make a mistake in a chart. Mistakes completely mask any patterns that are present, and the mistakes compound themselves as you go to more columns. Any common difference that is supposed to be present will disappear because of one mistake. See the problem below.

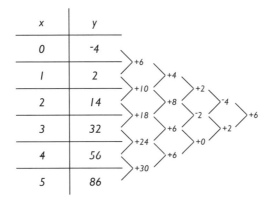

A simple subtraction mistake leads to all kinds of chaos. Be careful, especially when dealing with negative and positive numbers. Used accurately, finite differences is a great strategy. It ties together many strategies presented previously. (By the way, did you find the subtraction mistake?)

Problem Set A

1. **EIGHT FUNCTIONS**

Find the equation for each function.

a.

x	y
0	6
1	13
2	20
3	27
4	34
5	41

b.

x	y
0	6
1	12
2	20
3	30
4	42
5	56

c.

x	y
0	4
1	3
2	6
3	13
4	24
5	39

d.

x	y
0	5
1	1
2	-3
3	-7
4	-11
5	-15

e.

x	y
0	-2
1	3
2	20
3	55
4	114
5	203

f.

x	y
4	10
5	16
6	22
7	28
8	34
9	40

g.

x	y
2	3
3	10
4	19
5	30
6	43
7	58

h.

x	y
0	1
1	-1
2	9
3	43
4	113
5	231

2. **TRIANGULAR NUMBERS**

Find a formula for the triangular numbers.

3. **PENTAGONAL NUMBERS**

Find a formula for the pentagonal numbers.

4. **DIAGONALS**

How many diagonals are there in a polygon with n sides?

5. **THE GREAT PYRAMID OF ORANGES**

A very bored grocer was stacking oranges one day. She decided to stack them in a triangular pyramid. There was one orange in the top layer, three oranges in the second layer, six oranges in the third layer, and so on. Each layer except the top formed an equilateral triangle. How many oranges would it take her to build a pyramid 50 layers high?

Problem Set B

1. **CELEBRATION TIME**

Luke and Dicey decided to celebrate. They didn't know what they were celebrating, but it sounded like fun. They started with dinner. It cost them one-third of their money, plus $4.50 more for a tip. Then they spent $3.75 each on admission to the county fair, and they immediately saw that they could buy tickets for an open-air concert for half their money plus one more dollar. They bought a bottle of Alka-Seltzer with $2.50 of their remaining money, and then spent one-third of what they had left on the trip home. At this point, feeling sick and exhausted, they had only $5.00 left. How much money did they spend on this "celebration"?

2. **WILSHIRE BOULEVARD**

Ardith, Burris, Chris, Dawn, and Eartha all live on Wilshire Boulevard, which is a very long street. Ardith lives at one end of the street. Driving down the street from Ardith's house, you would first get to Burris's house, then Chris's, Dawn's, and finally Eartha's. The five of them had lunch one day and discussed the distances between their houses. The number of blocks between each pair of houses was different. These ten numbers, arranged in numerical order, are 15, 21, 27, 36, 42, 48, 63, 69, 84, and 111. If Ardith lives closer to Burris than Dawn lives to Eartha, determine the distances between each pair of adjacent houses.

3. FIVES AND ONES

Monica, Jurmaii, Carol, Andy, and Tomás each have some $1 bills. Monica has one of them, Jurmaii has two, Carol has three, Andy has four, and Tomás has five. Each person may also have a $5 bill. None of them has any other kind of money.

At least one person has more money than Jurmaii and less money than Tomás. Monica does not have less money than both Carol and Andy. Tomás does not have more money than both Monica and Jurmaii. The person with the most money has six dollars more than the person with the least amount of money. How much does each person have?

4. REGIONS IN A CIRCLE

A circle can be separated into seven different regions by three straight lines across the circle. The regions will not be the same size. You should be sure that you can draw a circle and cut it into seven regions with three straight lines before you go on.

What is the maximum number of regions that will be formed by drawing 100 straight lines across the circle? (Some of these regions will be very small!)

5. CUBS WANT PETS

A Cub Scout troop went to a very large pet store. The troop leader wanted to find out how much the pets were, because some of the scouts said they wanted one. He noticed some signs at various places in the store. The sign above the fish tank said, "Buy sixteen fish and eight cats for the price of seven dogs." The sign above the cat cage said, "Buy eleven cats and seven dogs for the price of nine fish." The sign above the dog cage said, "Buy three dogs and nine fish for the price of eight cats." The troop leader ended up helping one of his scouts buy a fish and a dog. The fish cost $42 less than the dog. At this time, the troop leader discovered that exactly one of the three signs was incorrect. Which sign was wrong, and how much did a cat cost?

other ways to organize information

A T T H E California State Fair in Sacramento, there are two types of tickets. Adult tickets cost $6 and children's tickets (ages 5–11) cost $4. Kids under five are free. The manager of the fair realized that with the number of people crowding into the fair when the gates opened at 10 a.m., the time it would take the cashiers to add up the price of the tickets for each group would slow down the line. So the manager devised the matrix shown below to speed things up. All the cashier had to do was ask each customer how many adults and how many kids. Then the cashier would read the number of adults on the top, and the number of children down the side, and find the appropriate dollar amount in the matrix. Look in the chart below to determine the cost for five adults and seven children.

ADULTS

CHILDREN	0	1	2	3	4	5	6	7	8	9	10
0	0	6	12	18	24	30	36	42	48	54	60
1	4	10	16	22	28	34	40	46	52	58	64
2	8	14	20	26	32	38	44	50	56	62	68
3	12	18	24	30	36	42	48	54	60	66	72
4	16	22	28	34	40	46	52	58	64	70	76
5	20	26	32	38	44	50	56	62	68	74	80
6	24	30	36	42	48	54	60	66	72	78	84
7	28	34	40	46	52	58	64	70	76	82	88
8	32	38	44	50	56	62	68	74	80	86	92
9	36	42	48	54	60	66	72	78	84	90	96
10	40	46	52	58	64	70	76	82	88	94	100

◀ *Baseball statistics are organized in a wide variety of ways so that fans, players, and coaches can evaluate different aspects of a player's performance.*

With the ticket information organized in this way, the cashiers are able to save a lot of time in figuring out what each family owes for its tickets. Did you get $58 for the family described above? How much would admission for your family cost?

~~~~~

Earlier in the book, you saw a number of different techniques of organizing information. Systematic lists, eliminate possibilities, matrix logic, patterns, guess and check, unit analysis, algebra, and finite differences all organize information in some manner. There were also elements of organizing information in the changing focus strategy of working backwards. When you organize the information presented in the problem in a meaningful way, the problem is usually much easier to solve. This chapter will explore more ways of organizing information.

This problem first appeared in the Algebra chapter.

THE SEASON'S STATS

Franny, Carl and Amichung compared their season's statistics during the post-season banquet for their high school baseball team. Franny had three times as many singles as Carl. Carl had four times as many doubles as Amichung. Each of them had exactly the same number of hits. None of the three of them had any hits besides singles and doubles (they were slap hitters). The three of them as a group had exactly as many singles as doubles. The three of them had fewer than 200 hits in all. How many singles and how many doubles did each of them have?

Do this problem before continuing on.

In the Algebra chapter, Rick's solution started out like this. He mentioned that he had kept the singles the same and changed the number of doubles. Ryan continued this line of reasoning a little further. (The * columns are the numbers that were guessed.)

Carl		Franny		Amichung		Total	
sing*	doub	sing	doub	sing	doub*	sing	doub
2	20	6	16	17	5	25	41
2	24	6	20	20	6	28	50
2	28	6	24	23	7	31	59
2	32	6	28	26	8	34	68

Ryan noticed many patterns. "If you read down each column, some patterns show up. In Carl's doubles column, the numbers increase by 4 each time. The same thing happens in Franny's doubles column. In Amichung's singles column, the numbers increase by 3. In the total singles column, the numbers increase by 3 and in the total doubles column, the numbers increase by 9. I wanted to see if this would keep happening, so I started over with three singles for Carl, and returned Amichung to five doubles."

Carl		Franny		Amichung		Total	
sing*	doub	sing	doub	sing	doub*	sing	doub
3	20	9	14	18	5	30	39
3	24	9	18	21	6	33	48
3	28	9	22	24	7	36	57
3	32	9	26	27	8	39	66

"The same thing happened. I also noticed that the difference between the total singles and doubles started here at 9 (from 39–30) and went up to 15, then 21, and so on—a difference of 6. In the previous chart, the difference started at 16 (found by subtracting 41 – 25) and went up to 22, 28, and so on, also a difference of 6. I realized that if I could make this difference 0, I would solve the problem. I looked for a better way of organizing the information.

"Since I had two variables to work with, I decided that a two-dimensional array might be useful. I set one up, with the numbers running down the outside left-hand column being the guess for Carl's singles, and the numbers running across the top row being the guess for Amichung's doubles. The numbers in the array are the difference between the total number of singles and the total number of doubles. The first four numbers in the first two rows are from the two charts above. The rest of the numbers in the chart (the circled numbers) are from the observed patterns."

AMICHUNG'S DOUBLES

CARLS SINGLES	5	6	7	8	9	10	11	12	13
2	16	22	28	34	(40)				
3	9	15	21	27	(33)				
4	(2)	(8)	(14)	(20)	(26)				
5	(-5)	(1)							
6									
7									
8									

"I noticed that there were some neat patterns here too. Going across each row, the numbers increase by 6. Going down each column, the numbers decrease by 7. If you go diagonally down to the right, the numbers decrease by 1. So I knew that I would reach 0 very soon. I didn't bother finishing the whole chart, I just continued until I reached a 0."

AMICHUNG'S DOUBLES

CARLS SINGLES	5	6	7	8	9	10	11	12	13
2	16	22	28	34	40				
3	9	15	21	27	33				
4	2	8	14	20	26				
5	-5	1	7	13	19				
6	-12	-6	0 bingo						
7	-19								
8	-26								

"So Carl must have had six singles and Amichung must have had seven doubles. These numbers go into the chart, giving us the same answers that Rick got." (See the Algebra chapter.)

~~~~~

You first encountered the next problem in Problem Set A of the Eliminate Possibilities chapter. You probably solved it with a combination of systematic list and eliminate possibilities. In this chapter, we will look at a different way to organize the information.

Three cousins, Bob, Chris, and Phyllis, were sitting around watching football on TV. The game was really boring, and so they started talking about how old they were. Bob (the oldest) noticed that they were all between the ages of 11 and 30. Phyllis noticed that the sum of their ages was 70. Suddenly, Chris(the youngest) burst out, "Gee, if you write the square of each of our ages, all of the digits from 4 to 9 will appear exactly once in the digits of the three squares." How old was each person? See if you can organize the information in a new way.

Do this problem before continuing on.

This solution was contributed by Ed Migliore, a mathematics teacher at Monterey Peninsula Junior College. It uses eliminate possibilities as well as a new way to organize the information.

"First, I made a list of numbers from 11 to 30 and their squares. I didn't bother to include numbers like $11^2 = 121$ since there are repeated digits, which obviously was not allowed."

AGE	SQUARE	AGE	SQUARE
13	169	23	529
14	196	24	576
16	256	25	625
17	289	27	729
18	324	28	784
19	361	29	841

"I set up a chart on graph paper. The numbers on the top row are the digits 1 through 9. The numbers down the side are the numbers between 11 and 30 that are to be squared. I just checked off the digits that appeared in each square."

NUMBER	1	2	3	4	5	6	7	8	9
13	X					X			X
14	X					X			X
16		X		X	X				
17		X						X	X
18		X	X	X					
19	X		X			X			
23		X		X					X
24				X	X	X			
25		X			X	X			
27		X					X		X
28				X			X	X	
29	X			X				X	

Ed went on. "The only 3's appear in the squares for 18 and 19. So either 18 or 19 must be in the list. Assume it is 18 (an example of seeking contradictions). This means that 3, 2, and 4 all appear in 18^2 and therefore can't appear in any other number. So eliminate all of the numbers that have 3's, 2's, or 4's in them. This eliminates 16, 17, 19, 23, 25, 27, 28, 29."

NUMBER	1	2	3	4	5	6	7	8	9
13	X					X			X
14	X					X			X
~~16~~		X		X	X				
~~17~~		X						X	X
18		X	X	X					
~~19~~	X		X			X			
~~23~~		X		X					X
24					X	X	X		
~~25~~		X			X	X			
~~27~~		X					X		X
~~28~~				X			X	X	
~~29~~	X			X				X	

"The only number left with a 7 is $24^2 = 576$, so 24 must be one of the ages. But 576 also contributes a 5 and 6, and the only remaining ages of 13 and 14 have squares that both contain 6's. So the assumption that 18 is one of the ages proves false, so 18 may be crossed off. This also means that 19 is one of the ages for sure, since it is the only other number whose square can contribute the 3. Now I had a bunch of crossed out values from my false assumption. I had to clean up my chart before I could proceed."

NUMBER	1	2	3	4	5	6	7	8	9
13	X					X			X
14	X					X			X
16		X			X	X			
17		X						X	X
~~18~~		X	X	X					
19	X		X			X			
23		X			X				X
24					X	X	X		
25		X			X	X			
27		X					X		X
28				X			X	X	
29	X			X				X	

"This means that the digits 1, 3, and 6 are contributed by 19² and I can cross off all of the other numbers whose squares contain 1, 3, or 6. This eliminates 13, 14, 16, 24, 25, 29."

NUMBER	1	2	3	4	5	6	7	8	9
~~13~~	✳					✳			✳
~~14~~	✳					✳			✳
~~16~~		✳			✳	✳			
17	X							X	X
~~18~~		✳	✳	✳					
19	X		X			X			
23		X			X				X
~~24~~				✳	✳	✳			
~~25~~		✳			✳	✳			
27		X					X		X
28				X			X	X	
~~29~~	✳			✳				✳	

"The only number left that contains a 5 is 23². So 23 must be one of the ages. I circled it and eliminated the other numbers that contained 2's, 5's, and 9's. This eliminated 17 and 27. The only number left in the list was 28, so it must be in the final list also. So the ages are 19, 23, and 28."

NUMBER	1	2	3	4	5	6	7	8	9
~~13~~	✳					✳			✳
~~14~~	✳					✳			✳
~~16~~		✳			✳	✳			
~~17~~		✳						✳	✳
~~18~~		✳	✳	✳					
19	X		X			X			
23		X			X				X
~~24~~					✳	✳	✳		
~~25~~		✳			✳	✳			
~~27~~		✳					✳		✳
28				X			X	X	
~~29~~	✳			✳				✳	

"So Chris (the youngest) is 19, Phyllis is 23, and Bob (the oldest) is 28."

Notice that each digit in a square appears in only one column. It is also interesting that Ed never used the clue that the ages had to add up to 70. This clue is superfluous to solving the problem. The way that Ed organized the information presented in the problem made the solution very easy to reach. This approach is somewhat similar to the matrix logic grids used in that chapter.

~~~~

The high schools in and around Sacramento participate in a series of monthly math competitions called Mathletes. Each Mathlete team consists of five members, and each member must take three of the five tests. The tests are given in Arithmetic, Algebra II, Algebra I, Trigonometry, and Geometry. Each test is taken by three team members.

Ken was the coach of the Mathlete team at Luther Burbank High School for many years. When he started, he made up the schedule for each event like this:

Arith	Alg II	Alg I	Trig	Geom
John	Hoa	Khanh	Hoa	Hoa
Julie	Khanh	Julie	Khanh	John
Dahlia	John	Dahlia	Julie	Dahlia

The advantage of this schedule was that each person on the team could look at the schedule at the beginning of each test to see whether or not to take the test. However, each team member could not immediately see which tests he or she would take. In addition, Ken had a hard time figuring out whether each person was taking three tests.

Another Mathlete coach showed Ken a matrix that she used. It is easy to see which test is being taken by which person. It is also easy to immediately see which three tests each person will take. For the coach, it is evident that each person is taking three tests, and each test is being taken by three people. It is also really easy to change if necessary.

	Arith	Alg II	Alg I	Trig	Geom
Hoa		X		X	X
Khanh		X	X	X	
John	X	X			X
Julie	X		X	X	
Dahlia	X		X		X

～～～

In Problem Set A from Chapter 2 there was a problem about rectangular sheds. You were asked to find all possible sheds that could be made with panels of length 8, 10, 12, and 15 feet. Michelle did the problem like this. Each X represents a side panel. (Note: Since opposite sides are the same, she only used two X's instead of four.)

8	10	12	15
XX			
X	X		
X		X	
X			X
	XX		
	X	X	
	X		X
		XX	
		X	X
			XX

8 X 8
8 X 10
8 X 12
8 X 15
10 X 10
10 X 12
10 X 15
12 X 12
12 X 15
15 X 15

～～～

Another common way of organizing information is with a tree diagram. Tree diagrams were illustrated in Chapter 2. You may have used a tree diagram to solve some problems in this book. One place where tree diagrams show up in life is in the scheduling of tournaments. The NCAA basketball tournament and all tennis tournaments use an organization scheme that looks like a tree diagram. This type of tournament often features seedings. The best player in the tournament is seeded number 1, the next best player is seeded number 2, and so on. The schedule is set up so that the best player plays the worst player in the first round, the second-best player plays the second-worst player, and so on. It is also set up so that the number-1 and number-2 seeds cannot meet until the final round. A typical tennis tournament diagram for eight players appears below.

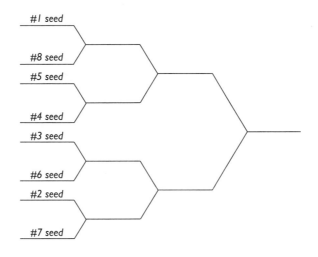

There is often more than one way to organize information, as many of these examples demonstrate. Experiment with different methods of organization as you do the problems in the problem set. Don't be afraid to throw out what you have and start over.

Problem Set A

1. COFFEE STAIN

At an amusement park, the cashiers all had a matrix containing the ticket prices, similar to the matrix described at the beginning of this chapter. Toward the end of one day, entries to the park were getting rather slow. The manager closed down all entry gates except one. Unfortunately, the cashier spilled coffee on his matrix. All he could read were the numbers shown below, and he wasn't even sure that they were all right, although he figured most of them were. Recreate the matrix, changing the fewest numbers possible, and determine what the prices are for adult tickets and for children's tickets. Also

ADULTS

	0	1	2	3	4	5	6	7	8
0									
1				59					
2				58					110
3		34				99			
4			57			93			
5				74				126	
6		55							
7						114			
8									

(rows labeled CHILDREN)

determine which numbers in his matrix are incorrect.

2. THE OTHER THREE SQUARES

Three other cousins of the three squares we met before noticed that their ages were all under 40, and the squares of each of their ages contained all of the digits from 0 to 9 exactly once. What were their ages?

3. TWO BILLS

I once met a father and a son, both named Bill. Bill senior said, "I moved to Florida in 1965." Bill junior said, "I was a sophomore in high school when my father moved to Florida." Bill senior said, "Bill turned 16 in his sophomore year." The conversation took place in 1991. What were the possible ages for Bill junior?

On a recent airline flight, six people from the same company were seated in rows 1, 2, and 3. Each had booked the flight at different times, so they were all charged different amounts. The people in the window seats had fares that were $5 apart (like 14, 19, 24). One person in an aisle seat had a fare equal to her seat partner's. Another person in an aisle seat had a fare that was one and a half times her seat partner's. The third person in an aisle seat had a fare that was twice her seat partner's. The total fare for all six was $1025. All fares were whole dollar amounts. How much was the second most expensive fare?

The Mathematical Association of America sponsors a high school math contest every year called the American High School Math Exam. The contest consisted of multiple choice questions with five possibilities in each question. The scoring system for the 30-question test was, for many years, as follows: Each right answer was worth four points. Each wrong answer was worth ⁻1 point. Each question unanswered was worth 0 points. Each participant started with a score of 30 points. Thus, for a person who got 6 right, 3 wrong, and left 21 unanswered, the score would be $30 + (6 \times 4) + (3 \times {}^-1) + (21 \times 0) = 51$ points. To qualify for the second round of competition, a person had to score 95 points.

Around 1988, the scoring system changed. The new scoring system is as follows: 5 points for a right answer, 0 points for a wrong answer, 2 points for no answer, and each participant starts with 0 points. Thus the example of 6 right, 3 wrong, and 21 unanswered would result in $(6 \times 5) + (3 \times 0) + (21 \times 2) = 72$ points.

To qualify for the second round of competition, a person had to score 100 points.

Analyze these two different scoring systems and discuss which system you think gives a person a better chance for qualifying for the next round.

For each system, decide on the best strategy of reaching the second round, given that you are sure of the answers to 10 questions, and have narrowed down 10 other questions to two choices.

6. **TWO-INPUT FUNCTION**

The following is a function with two inputs. The first input is x, and the second input is y. What is the rule for calculating the output?

Input	Output	Input	Output	Input	Output
2,3	17	1,5	29	7,4	44
4,1	17	9,2	40	1,4	20
3,7	61	0,5	25	2,5	33
4,3	25	5,2	24	4,2	20
3,9	93	2,4	24	3,8	76

Problem Set B

1. ALGEBRA AND FRENCH

There are 53 students in the freshman class.

1. Twenty students are enrolled in both algebra and French.

2. Seven students taking language are not taking math.

3. Two-thirds of all language students are taking French.

4. The number of algebra students not taking language is one-third the number of math students not taking language.

5. Three-fourths of all math students are taking algebra.

6. There are 42 language students and 33 algebra students.

7. Ten algebra students are taking a language other than French.

8. The number of French students not taking math is three less than the number of math students not taking language.

How many students are taking a math class other than algebra and a language class other than French?
How many students are not taking a math class?

2. LOTSA FACTORS

Including 1 and itself, how many positive integral factors does 1,746,360,000 have?

3. DICEY DIFFERENCES

You are playing a new dice game. You roll two regular dice and then subtract the smaller number from the larger number. (If the dice show the same number, then, of course, it doesn't make any difference which way you subtract.) What is the answer most likely to occur?

4. MOVIE THEATER

Five adults and their five young children went to a movie. The adults all sat together and the children sat together with one empty seat between the two groups. As the lights dimmed and the movie began, the children realized they had sat behind a basketball team, and asked the adults to trade places with them. However, to be considerate to the people behind them, they decided to follow these principles.

1. They could move into the next seat if it were empty.

2. They could leapfrog over only one person into an empty seat.

3. Nobody would backtrack. All moves had to be toward their new seats.

How many moves will be necessary for the two groups to switch places?

5. AREA AND PERIMETER

Find the dimensions of all rectangles that have area equal to twice the perimeter, where both the length and the width are whole numbers. (Ignore units.)

46 other ways to change focus

Y OU HAVE thus far learned many problem-solving strategies in this book. The strategies were separated into three major categories: organize information, change the focus, and spatial organization. The last three chapters of the book explore other ways to use these three strategies.

This chapter concerns the strategy of changing focus. Some problems are best solved by looking at the problem in a completely different way. For example, subproblems focus your attention away from the question that is asked and onto lesser subgoals. Easier related problems require you to temporarily suspend your work on the original problem and concentrate on easier versions of the same problem. This chapter explores three other ways of changing focus. We call the three ways: Change Your Point of View, Solve the Complementary Problem, and Change the Representation.

Movie and TV directors often use a changing focus strategy in filming a movie or TV program. The old TV show *Mission: Impossible* used this technique quite often. The camera would focus on someone in the foreground, and then gradually change to focus on someone in the background that the person in the foreground was unaware of. If you have ever looked through a window on a rainy day, you probably experienced a similar sensation. While looking out the window, you don't see the raindrops on the window unless you focus your eyes on them.

◀ *Like the correct path through a maze, the solution to a problem can often be seen easily just by changing your point of view.*

Section 1: Change Your Point of View

Some conflicts may have risen in your life that you and your family could not resolve. Possibly you went to seek the advice of a friend or a family counselor. This person was able to bring a new, fresh, and objective point of view to your situation and perhaps was able to help you resolve your conflicts. Sometimes people can solve their own problems by adopting a similar strategy. If you can look at your situation the way someone else sees it, you may be helped in finding a solution.

Similarly, in problems presented in this book, changing your point of view may help you solve a problem that you thought to be impossible. You may have seen the following problem before. It is a good illustration of this strategy.

NINE DOTS

Without lifting your pencil from start to finish, draw four line segments through all nine dots.

```
•     •     •


•     •     •


•     •     •
```

The solution, by the way, has nothing to do with how wide the dots are or that possibly the lines determined by them are not parallel. The dots are mathematically defined—they have no width, and they determine sets of parallel lines.

Work this problem before continuing.

The solution to this problem is very simple. Finding the solution, however, is not easy. Generally people feel constrained to make the solution fit within the confines of the square determined by the nine dots. The key here is to be flexible enough to allow your thinking to diverge out of the zone indicated by the dots. You must change your point of view away from the structure of the square and allow yourself to draw outside it. The answer can be found on the last page of this chapter.

~~~~

A computer could be used to solve the next problem. That, however, is taking a sledgehammer approach. This chapter is about creative ways to look at problems differently. Think creatively as you solve this problem.

THE HUMAN FACTOR

Mayra is a human computer. She has appeared on talk shows with her amazing ability with numbers. One of the problems that Mayra is very adept at is the following: A person from the audience will give Mayra a number and Mayra will immediately be able to tell how many one-digit factors that number has. For example, if you were in the audience and you said 50, Mayra would say three, because 50 has three one-digit factors (namely 1, 2, and 5). One day, Mayra was on a well-known talk show, and some wise guy in the audience asked Mayra to tell him how many one-digit factors the numbers from 1 to 100 had. The answer was not nine, since Mayra had to count every factor as it appeared for a particular number, and sum that with the number of factors for each of the other numbers from 1 to 100. So for instance, even though the factor 5 appears in 50, it also appears in 45, and so must be counted each time. Mayra quickly "programmed" her brain to give her the answer, and she had it in a few moments. What was her answer?

Work this problem before continuing.

This problem encompasses many strategies. One possible approach to this problem was taken by Arlene. "I decided to list all of the numbers from 1 to 100, and write down all their factors. Then I counted up the factors that were only one digit."

A portion of Arlene's list appears below.

Number	Factors
1	1
2	1, 2
3	1, 3
4	1, 2, 4
5	1, 5
6	1, 2, 3, 6
7	1, 7
8	1, 2, 4, 8
9	1, 3, 9
10	1, 2, 5, 10
11	1, 11
12	1, 2, 3, 4, 6, 12
13	1, 13
14	1, 2, 7, 14

At this point, Jessica joined her. As Jessica would say later, "It seemed like this was going to take an awfully long time. So I suggested to Arlene that maybe there was an easier way. We looked at her list together to see if we noticed something."

Arlene: When Jessica came over, I resented it at first. I mean, I had a perfectly reasonable way to do this problem, and I was doing fine. I knew it was going to take a long time, but I tend to be a very diligent, hard-working student [she was] and I figured I could do it. Sometimes, when I see a way that will work, I just continue with that method, even though it may take a while. It's better than not doing anything.

Jessica: I tend to be lazy (she was) so I wanted to find an easier way. I had a feeling that Arlene was a little bothered by my presence, and I thought about leaving her alone, but lots of times two heads are better than one. So I asked Arlene if she noticed anything about her list.

Arlene: After I recovered slightly from my resentment, I did as she asked. And of course, right away I noticed that I had written down 1 every time, 2 every other time, and 3 every third time, etc.

Jessica: After Arlene pointed this out, it seemed as though there was a really easy way to solve the problem. All we had to do was count up the number of 1's, 2's, 3's, 4's, 5's, 6's, 7's, 8's, and 9's that appeared in the list. But we didn't have to make the whole list to do that. There was obviously going to be 100 ones, and 50 twos.

Arlene: We had a little trouble with the number of threes. Then I realized that the last three would occur in the number 99, so there would be 33 threes.

Jessica: All we had to do was divide each number into 100. If it didn't come out evenly, we had to round down. For example, how many 6's are there? Well, $100 \div 6$ is $16\frac{2}{3}$. The last 6 therefore occurs as a factor of 96, and we can ignore the remainder, because the next 6 shows up as a factor of 102 and we weren't supposed to go that far.

Factor	Time It Appears
1	100/1 = 100 times
2	100/2 = 50 times
3	100/3 = 33 times
4	100/4 = 25 times
5	100/5 = 20 times
6	100/6 = 16 times
7	100/7 = 14 times
8	100/8 = 12 times
9	100/9 = 11 times
Total	281 times

Arlene: So there are 281 one-digit factors of the first 100 numbers. Jessica was right, there was an easier way.

Jessica: And it just goes to show that two heads are better than one.

Jessica and Arlene changed their point of view to solve this problem. They completely changed their approach to the problem after it became apparent that their original approach was going to take a long time. Instead of attacking the problem by checking each number to see how many factors each one had, they changed their focus onto the number of times a given factor appeared in the first 100 numbers. This method counted exactly the same thing, yet organized the count in a much more manageable fashion. This made the problem a lot easier.

≈≈≈

You must be "a little lazy" to use this strategy effectively. If you are willing to proceed with "the long way," you likely won't even look for an easier way. However, a little laziness is a good motivator in looking for the shorter way.

AVERAGE SPEED

Jacques left his home in Austin and drove to San Antonio. On the way there he drove 40 miles per hour (there was a lot of traffic). On the way back he drove 60 miles per hour. What was his average speed?
Work this problem before continuing.

Since 50 is the average of 40 and 60, the answer 50 miles per hour appears to be the answer. Unfortunately, this is incorrect. However, try changing your point of view. Instead of looking at speed, concentrate on the time and the distance. Notice that there is no stated distance in this problem. This causes some difficulty, so use an easier related problem. One way to make this problem easier is to make up a distance. What we learn from the easier problem could help us solve the original problem. Since you may not be sure this works, make up at least two distances and figure it out both ways.

A good distance to use would be 120 miles. One hundred twenty is the least common multiple of both 40 and 60. Hopefully, this will keep some of the other numbers in the problem simple.

Using 120 miles as the distance, Jacques traveled 40 miles per hour on the way from Austin to San Antonio. Unit analysis helps determine the time needed.

$$120 \text{ miles} \quad \times \quad \frac{1 \text{ hour}}{40 \text{ miles}} \quad = \quad 3 \text{ hours}$$

On the way back, he traveled 60 miles per hour. Unit analysis gives

$$120 \text{ miles} \quad \times \quad \frac{1 \text{ hour}}{60 \text{ miles}} \quad = \quad 2 \text{ hours}$$

The total distance traveled was 240 miles. It took 5 hours to travel that far. Use unit analysis to find the average speed.

$$\frac{120 \text{ miles}}{5 \text{ hours}} \quad = \quad 48 \text{ miles per hour}$$

You should verify this answer by using a different distance than 120 miles. The answer comes out the same. If you change your point of view away from speed and onto time, this problem becomes easy to solve.

Section 2: Solve the Complementary Problem

Some problems are more easily approached by a "comin' around the back" approach. Instead of solving the problem that is asked, try finding the opposite of what is asked. Consider a problem from probability: How many ways are there to roll two dice and have them sum to a one-digit number? Instead of answering this question, answer the opposite question: How many ways are there to get a sum of 10, 11, or 12? This is much easier to do. A 10 can be rolled (6, 4), (5, 5), or (4, 6). An 11 can be rolled as (5, 6) or (6, 5). A 12 can be rolled as (6, 6). So there are six ways to roll 10, 11, or 12. Therefore, since there are 36 ways to roll two dice, there must be 30 ways to roll a one-digit number.

This approach, known as solving the complementary problem, is another way to change the focus. You might be familiar with the word "complement." Not compliment (like "gee, your hair looks nice today") but complement, which means two things that are different, yet fit together. Some of Webster's definitions are:

1. that which completes or brings to perfection,

2. something added to complete a whole; either of two parts that complete each other,

3. in geometry, two angles that sum to 90 degrees,

4. in music, the difference between a given interval and the complete octave.

The key in all these definitions is the idea of two parts making a whole. In the problem with the dice, the sums of 2 through 9 complement the sums of 10 through 12 and vice versa, since the complete set of possible sums includes those from 2 through 12.

~~~~~

This strategy is another example of changing focus. Rather than solving the stated problem, instead solve the complementary problem (if it is easier).

Solve the next problem using this strategy.

BOOK REPORT

Seiko had to do a book report. She was supposed to read five books (in any order), then write an essay comparing and contrasting the books. She could choose from the list below. In how many ways could she choose five books?

Pride and Prejudice
The Scarlet Letter
Huck Finn
No Exit
Call of the Wild
Catch-22.

Work this problem before continuing.

Seiko was handy with solving the complementary problem. "I thought about making a systematic list of all the ways I could choose five books. But then I realized that each entry in my list would always contain five of the books and leave one out. Figuring out the number of ways to leave a book out is a lot easier to do. There are six books, and each of them would be left out one time, so there are six ways to choose five books. The complementary problem was much easier to solve."

~~~~

Complementary events come up in many different areas of life. A baseball manager attempting to determine which of his pitchers will be relievers must first determine who will be starting. Mechanics can figure out what is broken by noting what is working. Head counts are used on field trips because the point of counting heads is to determine if anybody is missing.

Other strategies or problems in this book used the idea of complementary situations. When solving a matrix logic problem, you know that each person either is or isn't matched up with something else. Your objective is to determine the matchups, and you often do this by eliminating the complementary possibilities. The salt solution problem in the Algebra chapter required the pet store employee to raise the concentration of salt in a solution. This could be accomplished by either of two complementary actions: adding salt or evaporating water.

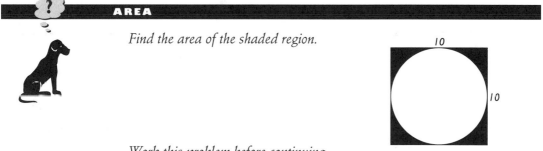

AREA

Find the area of the shaded region.

Work this problem before continuing.

The shaded area is a complement of the circle when viewed as parts of the square. This section focuses on complementary problems, and this problem clearly illustrates the concept of two problems that fit together well as complements. Nobody in his or her right mind would try to find the area of the shaded section directly (though it can be done). Instead, it is far easier to take the subproblem-complementary problem approach to it. It is much easier to find the area of the regions that are *not* shaded and then subtract from the square, rather than find the area of the regions that are shaded.

In this case, the area of the square is 100 square units. The area of the circle is approximately 78.54 square units. The complementary problem here is the area of the circle. It complements the area of the shaded regions. By subtracting, we find that the answer is approximately 21.46 square units.

OFFICE COMPUTER

I hate our office computer system. It seems to be "down" more than it is "up." Take the last eight days since I came back from vacation, for example. I work an 8-hour shift, but the computer works less. The first three days back were fine. It was working the whole time I was. But the fourth day, it was down for the first half-hour of my shift, and then went down again 15 minutes before I left. The next day I had to wait a half-hour longer than I had to wait the previous day for it to come up, and it went down 15 minutes earlier than the day before. The computer almost seems to have a brain. The sixth day it did the same thing: It came up half an hour later than on the fifth day, and went down 15 minutes earlier. That same pattern carried on to the seventh day. How many hours total was the computer operational during my last seven shifts?

Work this problem before continuing.

You could solve this problem by calculating how much the computer was operational each day, and adding it all up. But there is an easier approach. Say the magic words, "Solve the complementary problem." In this case, it is easy to calculate the amount of time the computer would have been working if it had been working during the person's whole shift for seven days:

8 hours/day × 7 days = 56 hours

Now figure out how much time the computer was "down." On the fourth day, it was down for a half hour in the morning and for 15 minutes in the afternoon. So it was down for 45 minutes on the fourth day. The next day, it was down for half an hour more in the morning, and fifteen minutes more in the afternoon, so it was down 45 + 45 minutes on the fifth day. This pattern continued on the sixth day: 45 + 45 + 45, and again on the seventh day: 45 + 45 + 45 + 45. Therefore, the computer was down 10×45, or 450 minutes, which is 7 $1/2$ hours. Subtract 7.5 from the 56 we originally calculated, leaving 48.5 hours. It was much easier to find how much time the computer was down and subtract from the 56 hours than it was to calculate how much time it was functional.

A big regional tennis tournament in New Orleans drew 378 entries. It was a single elimination tournament, where a player is eliminated from the tournament when she loses a match. How many matches must be played to determine the champion?

Work this problem before continuing.

Simon solved this problem by a diagram and easier related problems. "I looked at this problem and wanted to scream. It was way too hard. So I changed it to only two people in the tournament. That was a much easier problem and it had an easy solution: one match. Then I used three people. This was a little harder. If the players were A, B, and C, I figured A could play B while C had a bye. Then the winner would play C for the championship. That would be two matches. Four players seemed harder. I decided to make one of those elimination charts like they use in tennis tournaments and the NCAA basketball tournament."

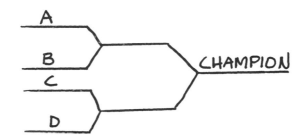

"From this I could see that there would be three matches. I suspected that the number of matches needed was one less than the number of players, but I really wasn't sure. That's when LaVonn came to help me."

LaVonn picked up the solution. "I saw that Simon had a good pattern going, but it seemed like he would never really be sure if he was right. It suddenly occurred to me that maybe we could look at the complementary problem. Instead of determining the number of matches necessary to determine a winner, I figured out how many matches were necessary to determine all the losers. Since there is only one winner, everyone else must lose. Each match produces a winner and a loser. The winner goes on, but the loser is eliminated. When the tournament is over, all players but one have lost. So there must be exactly that many matches: one less than the number of players in the tournament. So in a tournament that has 378 players, there must be 377 losers and therefore 377 matches to determine a champion."

Section 3: Change the Representation

Change the representation is a strategy that combines changing focus with another strategy. Generally, you will use diagrams when you change the representation. In your work in the third section of Chapter 10, you changed into manipulative form some problems that may not have seemed like manipulatives problems. You were essentially working with the strategy that we call change the representation. A problem may seem to lend itself to a particular strategy, or it may seem hard to approach with any strategy. Such problems may be good candidates for change the representation. If you can represent the problem in some other form, you may be able to solve it more easily. Again, a little laziness is helpful.

You may have solved the famous problem about cards in an earlier problem set.

You have ten cards, numbered 1, 2, 3, 4, 5, 6, 7, 8, 9, 10. Your task is to arrange them in a particular order and put them in a stack, hold the stack in your hand, and then do the following. Put the top card on the table face up, put the next card on the bottom of the stack in your hand, put the next card on the table, put the next card on the bottom of the stack, and so on, continuing to alternate cards that go on the table and under the stack, until all 10 cards are on the table.

That, of course, is really easy to do. The trick is to lay the cards on the table in numerical order. In other words, the first card you put on the table will be the 1, the next card you put on the table will be number 2, the next card you put on the table will be number 3, and so on, until the last card placed on the table will be number 10.

In what order should the cards be arranged in the original stack so that this will happen?

See if you can represent this problem in a completely different way (we used a diagram) and solve it more easily.

Work this problem before continuing.

You probably originally solved this problem with a physical representation in conjunction with working backwards. This problem can also be easily solved by changing the representation. Make 10 lines in a circle as shown below. Label one of them the first card in the stack. Write the number 1 on that line.

Top Card

        __|__

    __   __

  __   __

  __   __

    __   __

        __

Then go to the next line (this solution will proceed in a clockwise direction, but you could just as easily go counterclockwise). This represents the second card in the stack. This card will be put under the stack, so skip this line. The next line will be the third card in the stack. This will be card number 2. Label this line 2. Skip the next line as that card will go under the stack. Label the next line 3. Skip the next. Then label 4. Skip the next, then label 5. Skip the next.

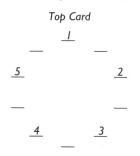

The next line you come to is line number one, but this line represents a card that has already been put on the table, so it would no longer be in the stack. The next empty line will be card 6. Skip the next empty line. Continue in this way until reaching card 10.

The final order is from the top (card 1) proceeding clockwise to the last card (card 8). So the order is 1, 6, 2, 10, 3, 7, 4, 9, 5, 8. Try it. Note that completely changing the way the problem was represented made the problem much easier to solve.

Ed also used change the representation on this problem, but he used a different representation. "I wrote down ten blanks in a row to represent the ten cards. Then I numbered the first blank 1, the third blank 2, the fifth blank 3, and so on. The second, fourth, sixth, etc. blanks I labeled A, B, C, D, E."

1 A 2 B 3 C 4 D 5 E

"The cards numbered 1–5 would be the first five cards laid down on the table. The cards labeled A–E would be the five cards put under the stack. So I drew arrows to show them being put under the stack."

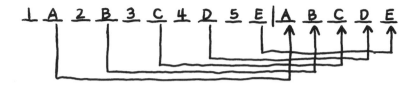

"After card E, the next card should be the 6. That means that card A should be 6. Then card B goes under the stack again, card C becomes 7, card D goes under the stack and card E becomes 8."

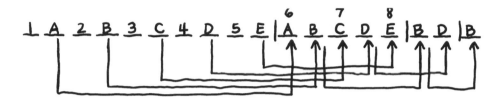

"Then card B goes under the stack again, and card D becomes 9. So card B is 10."

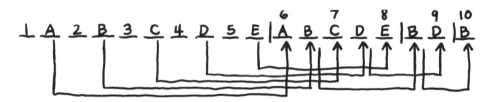

"Finally I went back into the original list and labeled A–E with the numbers they turned out to be. So now I knew the order of the cards."

1 6 2 10 3 7 4 9 5 8

Changing the representation is another way of changing the focus. It can be a very good strategy, though it may be difficult to apply to most problems.

The three strategies in this chapter all require insight, imagination, or creativity. You must be able to see the problem in a different perspective. The result of changing the focus is that the problem becomes easier to solve in its new form than it was in its old form. If a problem seems too difficult, and an easier related problem doesn't seem to help too much, then try changing your focus to a different approach in order to solve it.

By the way, here's the solution to the problem that opens the chapter.

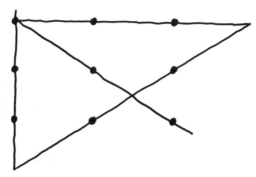

Problem Set A

1. MORE DOTS

Without lifting your pencil from start to finish, draw six line segments through all sixteen dots.

The solution, by the way, has nothing to do with how wide the dots are or that possibly the lines determined by them are not parallel. The dots are mathematically defined as points—they have no width, and they determine sets of parallel lines.

```
•     •     •     •

•     •     •     •

•     •     •     •

•     •     •     •
```

2. FEARLESS FLY

This is a famous problem. Two bicyclists, Frances and Fred, rode toward each other. Each traveled 20 miles per hour and they started off 10 miles apart. A frivolous fly flew furiously fast at 50 miles per hour from Frances to Fred. The fly started on Frances's handlebars as Frances and Fred started riding. It flew to Fred's handlebars and then back to Frances's and back to Fred's, always following the bike path (No self respecting fly flies a bee line.) It continued in this way until Frances and Fred reached each other. How far did the fly travel?

3. TOOTHPICKS

Using six toothpicks, make four triangles of the same size.

4. PERFECT SQUARES

How many perfect squares are there between 2000 and 20,000?

5. COMPLEMENTARY EVENTS

Given a situation. What is the complementary event?

a. You roll a die one time and get a six.

b. You roll a die one time and get an odd number.

c. You roll a die two times and don't get any sixes.

d. You roll a die five times and get six every time.

e. There are 40 people in the same room and they all have different birthdates.

6. PAY DAY

Marissa recently got a smaller than usual weekly paycheck. She normally works 8:00 a.m. to 5:00 p.m. with an hour for lunch, five days a week. Her pay is $7.50 per hour, but she only gets paid for the hours she works. On Monday, she left at 3:30 to go see her son play softball. On Tuesday, she was 45 minutes late getting back from lunch because she got a flat tire. On Wednesday, she left at 2:15 to go to her night class. On Thursday, she had a doctor's appointment in the morning and didn't get to work until 10:30. On Friday, she took a three-hour lunch break to pick her brother up at the airport. Then at 4:10, she left early to beat weekend traffic. How much did she get paid for the week?

7. THE LIKELIHOOD OF BEING LATE

The airline you're flying on has an on-time rate of 98% for the route you are taking. The bus from the airport to the convention center has an on-time rate of 95%, but if you are late, of course, you will miss the bus and be late arriving at the convention. What are your chances of being late?

8. ANOTHER CARD ARRANGEMENT

This problem is similar to the card-arrangement problem in the chapter. Start with all the cards in one suit in the deck: ace, 2, 3, 4, 5, 6, 7, 8, 9, 10, jack, queen, king. Arrange the cards in a particular order in your hand. Then spell the name of each card putting one card on the bottom of the stack for each letter in the name of the card. So for an ace, you would say "A-C-E ace," putting three cards on the bottom of the stack and laying the fourth one face up on the table (which will be the ace). Then continue by saying, "T-W-O two," putting three cards on the bottom of the stack and laying the fourth one (a two) on the table just as you say "two." Continue in this way all the way through jack, queen, and king, each time ending the spelling by saying the card you just spelled as you lay it face up on the table. What order do the cards have to be in originally for this to all work out?

9. KNIGHT MOVES

This problem comes from our friend and mentor Tom Sallee. Suppose you had chess knights on a 3 by 3 chess board as shown below.

White Knight 1		White Knight 2
Black Knight 1		Black Knight 2

A knight's move is one space in any direction (horizontally or vertically) then two spaces in either perpendicular direction. (That's equivalent to two spaces then one space in the perpendicular direction—knights can jump over pieces in their path.) Two knights may not occupy the same space at the same time.

a. How many moves does it take for the white knights to change places with the black knights?

b. How many moves does it take for White Knight 1 to change places with Black Knight 1?

Problem Set B

1. COMPUTER ERROR

A computer was printing a sequential list of positive integers, but due to a glitch in the software it neglected to print any numbers that were integral powers of integers (the powers were larger than one). Thus the list began 2, 3, 5, 6, 7, 10, 11, 12, 13, 14, 15, 17, …

How many numbers in this list had fewer than four digits?

2. THE AMAZING RESTIN

The Amazing Restin is a psychic. She can figure out anything anybody is thinking, as long as she is lying down. She gives performances all over the country. One of her favorite gimmicks involves words. Her assistant thinks of a five-letter word. Then the Amazing Restin proceeds to guess five-letter words, and her assistant tells her how many letters the word he thought of shares with the word she guessed. One day, she guessed five words and he told her that each of her words shared exactly two letters with the word he had in mind. The five words she guessed were:

BLUNT   VOTER   SPICE   BUOYS   MADLY

What word did the assistant have in mind?

3. BOAT TRIP

A man who lives in the South Pacific is planning a rowboat trip. His rowboat will hold him plus enough food to last three weeks. By a strange coincidence, there are small islands about one week's rowing apart. He plans on rowing to the fifth island, which is a large island with stores similar to the main island that he is on now. The four small islands in between, however, have no stores and he will not be able to buy any food on those islands. So he realizes that he will have to row out to an island, store some food, and return to the main island for more supplies. Show how he should organize his food supplies so he can get to the fifth island. How many weeks will it take altogether?

4. **PALINDROME CREATOR**

   How many three-digit numbers have the following special property? Take a three-digit number. Reverse the digits to create a new three-digit number (this number may be the same as the original number). Add the two numbers together. The result is a palindrome (a number that reads the same backwards and forwards). Neither the original number nor the new number can start with 0.

5. **MULTIPLES**

   Place the digits 0 through 9 into the circles below, subject to the following rule. Each pair of digits that are joined by a line must form a two-digit number (in either order) that is divisible by either 8 or 13. So, for example, the digits 4 and 8 could be connected with a line since 48 is divisible by 8. (Note that 84 is not divisible by either 8 or 13, but that doesn't matter—as long as it works in one of the orders it's okay.) There are two solutions, but they are basically the same, just two digits are switched.

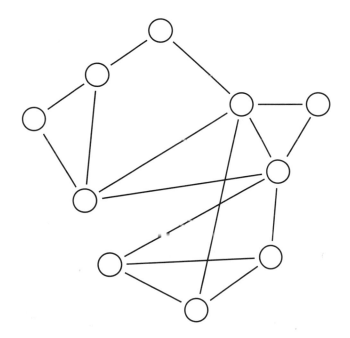

ANNUAL SALES

(Quarterly Basis)

47

other forms of spatial organization

W E H A V E already discussed several strategies that relate to spatial organization. Draw a diagram, physical representations, and Venn diagrams are all strategies that employ spatial organization. This chapter will explore two other strategies that fall under this category: graphs and scale drawings.

Section 1: Use a Graph

Some problems can best be represented with a graph. You see graphs everywhere. The newspapers are full of all different types of graphs. Graphs can clearly show the relationship between variables in a way that is difficult to see without a graph.

◀ *A graph can be a dramatic and persuasive way to show that a product is earning a profit or losing money.*

A local fast-food vendor sells chicken nuggets for the following prices.

SERVING SIZE	PRICE
6 nuggets	*$2.40*
10 nuggets	*$3.60*
15 nuggets	*$5.10*
24 nuggets	*$7.80*

Draw a graph of this information. Then answer the questions below.

a. What is the equation for this graph?

b. What is the slope for the graph?

c. What is the real-world significance for the slope?

d. What is the y-intercept for this graph?

e. What is the real-world significance for the y-intercept?

f. How much would it cost to buy a serving size of 50 chicken nuggets?

g. Another restaurant sells 13 nuggets for $4.25 and 20 nuggets for $6.75. Use the graph to find out whether these are good deals compared to the restaurant above. Then use the equation to check yourself.

A group of students worked on this problem.

Betty: This is impossible. How are we supposed to answer all these questions?

Nancy: Oh, come on, Betty. That's what you always say, but then you're the first one done. We can do this.

Betty: Okay, where do we start? I guess we should draw the graph. But what should we put on the *x*-axis?

Shauna: I think we should put the price on the *x*-axis.

Shelly: No. The price depends on the number of nuggets purchased. You're always supposed to put the dependent variable on the *y*-axis and the independent variable on the *x*-axis.

Betty: Okay. So *x* is number of nuggets and *y* is the price. (She drew this graph.)

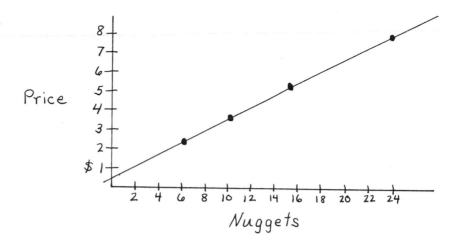

Barbara: What does the line mean?

Betty: It shows all possible combinations of number of nuggets and the corresponding price. So for instance, 8 nuggets would cost $3.00.

Barbara: I see. Let's try to figure out the equation for this thing. What do we need to do?

Shelly: We need the slope and we need the y-intercept. Then we can write the equation using $y = mx + b$.

Nancy: I can figure out the slope. It's just rise over run. So from 6 nuggets to 10 nuggets, the price goes up $1.20. A price change of $1.20/4 nuggets is $.30/nugget.

Shauna: That must be what the question means about real-world significance of the slope. It's just price per nugget. That's interesting. I never thought of that before.

Shelly: So the equation must be $y = .30x + b$. But how do we get b?

Barbara: Just look at the graph. It looks like it goes through somewhere around 50 cents.

Nancy: Let's work backwards. If it costs $.30 per nugget, then six nuggets should cost $1.80. But six nuggets really costs $2.40. That's an extra $.60, which is where the graph crosses the y-axis.

Betty: Or we could have plugged 6 nuggets and $2.40 into the equation that Shelly suggested and solve for b.

$$y = \left(\frac{\$0.30}{\text{nugget}}\right)(x \text{ nuggets}) + b$$
$$\$2.40 = \left(\frac{\$0.30}{\text{nugget}}\right)(6 \text{ nuggets}) + b$$
$$\$2.40 = \$1.80 + b$$
$$b = \$0.60$$

Wow, even the units work out.

Shelly: So our equation is $y = \$.30x + \$.60$. The slope is the price per nugget, but what is the significance of the y-intercept?

Nancy: Well, if you bought 0 nuggets it would cost $.60. That's what I was trying to say before. That's weird, how come it costs so much not to buy anything? You must be paying for something.

Shauna: Maybe you're paying for the privilege of buying your chicken nuggets there.

Betty: Or maybe for the forks and spoons and napkins.

Barbara: Or maybe it's just profit. Or the packaging.

Nancy: Okay, I get the message. There could be a lot of things you're paying for. I wonder if all restaurant food is priced like that.

Shelly: Probably. Question f asks for the price of 50 nuggets. We can figure that out with our equation or our graph.

Betty: I didn't use a big enough paper for the graph. But I think it would cost between $15 and $16.

Nancy: According to the equation it is $y = .3(50) + .60$ which is $15.60. That matches your estimate, Betty.

Barbara: How are we going to answer the last question?

Betty: Let's plot those points on the graph. The point (13, 4.25) is below the line and (20, 6.75) is above the line.

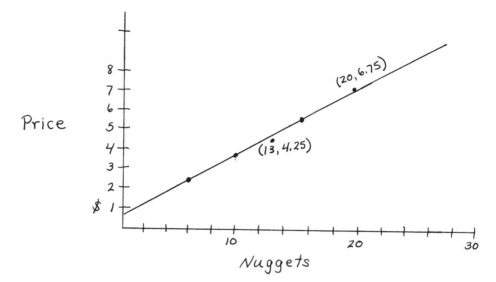

Barbara: What does that mean?

Shelly: Well, if the dot is under the line, then it costs less than it should, so it's a good deal. And if the dot is above the line, it costs more than it should, so it's a bad deal.

Barbara: That makes sense. Could we use the equation to figure that out?

Nancy: Sure, I think so.

Shauna: Yes we could. Use the equation to figure out how much 13 would cost. $y = .3(13) + .60 = \$4.50$. That means $4.25 is a good deal.

Betty: And 20 would cost $.3(20) + .60 = \$6.60$ which is cheaper than the other restaurant's price of $6.75, a bad deal.

Shelly: Wow, this was a really neat problem. The graph and the algebra together are pretty convincing.

   Either graphing or algebra could be used to solve the chicken nuggets problem. The combination of the two together provided a more sound and convincing solution. Part of the advantage of graphing was that you were able to represent the information visually. The saying "seeing is believing" was obviously coined in reference to this problem.

Work the following problem with similar methods.

PHONE CALLS

Lisa Family just got a new phone installed in her room. Her boyfriend, Ernie, loved to call her, and she needed her own phone because Ed was always monopolizing the Family family phone talking to his girlfriend, Candy. During spring break, Ernie went on vacation. Lisa was very sad, because she wasn't going to see him for five days. Fortunately, she could call him, although it was a long-distance call. During the five days that he was gone, she called him each day. The shortest call was 6 minutes, which cost $1.26. A 7-minute call cost Lisa $2.07. Here's a chart of the other three calls she made to Ernie:

Time (minutes)	Charge
11	$2.26
17	$4.57
22	$4.46

Determine the connect fee and the cost-per-minute for the two rate schedules she called under: day rate and evening rate. (A connect fee is the charge levied the instant a phone conversation begins.)

Work this problem before continuing.

In order to solve this, the graph is going to play a crucial, though not complete, role. Plotting the points on the graph produces:

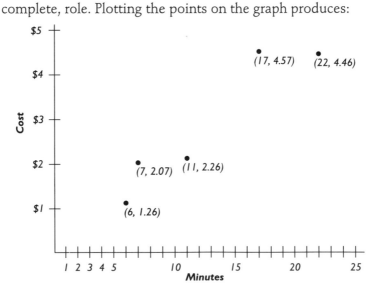

Since we know that Lisa called under two different rate schedules, we can reasonably assume that we need to determine the location of two linear functions.

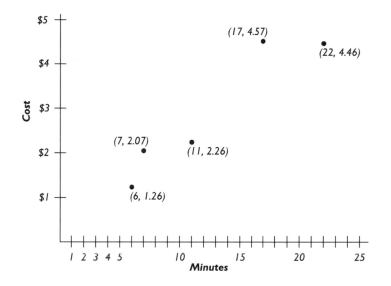

Three points in particular line up easily (the 6-, 11-, and 22-minute calls), and the other two also form a line, slightly steeper and slightly higher than the first. The steepness represents the cost per additional minute (in math terms, the slope). The higher location is caused by the higher connect fee (*y*-intercept in graphing parlance). Since day calls cost more than evening calls, we can assume that the higher and steeper line is for the day calls.

Now that the calls associated with the day rates and the evening rates have been identified, we can use finite differences to determine the exact rates.

Applying finite differences to two calls from the evening rate we compute:

Minutes	Charge
11	$2.26
22	$4.46

$$\left.\begin{array}{l} \$2.26 \\ \$4.46 \end{array}\right\} \$2.20 \qquad \left.\begin{array}{l} 11f + e \\ 22f + e \end{array}\right\} 11f$$

The coefficient f must be $.20 (this is the evening per-minute rate).

Applying
$$2.26 = 11f + e; \quad f = .20$$
$$2.26 = 2.20 + e$$
$$.06 = e$$

The connection charge itself is $.06, so the first-minute rate is $.26 and each additional minute costs $.20.

The equation for this is $P = .20m + .06$, where P is price of the call and m is the number of minutes talked.

For the day rate:

Minutes	Charge
7	$2.07
17	$4.57

$\dfrac{\$2.07}{\$4.57} > \$2.50 \qquad \dfrac{7d + c}{17d + c} > 10d$

This gives the equation:

$$10d = \$2.50$$
$$d = \$.25$$

Therefore,

$$7d + c = \$2.07$$
$$\$1.75 + c = \$2.07$$
$$c = \$.32$$

The cost for the day phone calls is $.25 for each minute, with a $.32 connection charge. The first minute costs $.57, with each additional minute at $.25. The equation for this is $P = .25m + .32$

The role the graph played was to allow us to see that there were two different rates being applied, with two calls on one linear graph and the other three calls being plotted on the other graph.

Besides using the graph to place items within one group or another, you can use a graph to extend the information to other data, not previously specified.

It should be noted that the linear model for this particular function is not entirely accurate. Phone rates do not actually correspond to linear graphs. Rather, they are examples of so-called step functions. The charge for Lisa's 11-minute call in the problem was given as $2.26. This would also be the charge for a 10-minute-and-1-second call, and a

10-minute-and-2-second call, all the way up to an 11-minute call. But as soon as the twelfth minute begins, the charge goes up to $2.46. The graph of this step function is shown below for the evening calls only. The line drawn as the original graph connects the right-hand endpoints of the steps.

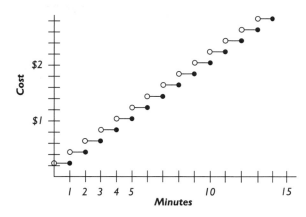

VACATION

The Family family wants to take another vacation. They have decided to take their van and drive to a destination that is 600 miles away. Plot a graph that shows various speeds on the x-axis and time spent driving on the y-axis. Work this problem before continuing.

Doug solved this problem with a systematic list, followed by a graph.

"I didn't really understand this problem at first. So I started making a list of possible speeds and times. I realized right away that if they traveled 60 miles per hour, it would take 10 hours of driving. And if they traveled 30 miles per hour it would take 20 hours of driving. I decided to make a systematic list of a lot of the possibilities. It wouldn't be all the possibilities, as that would take forever."

SPEED	TIME
1 mph	600 hrs
2	300
3	200
4	150
5	120
6	100

"At this point, I realized that I should try to put this information on a graph. But I knew I needed some more varied data, or my graph was going to be pretty dull. So I decided to skip some possible speeds."

SPEED	TIME
1 mph	600 hrs
2	300
3	200
4	150
5	120
6	100
10	60
20	30
30	20
40	15
50	12
60	10
70	8.57
75	8
80	7.5
100	6
120	5
300	2
600	1

"I realized that some of these pairs of numbers were a little ridiculous, like driving 600 miles per hour (although that could be reasonable for an airplane), but I didn't think my graph would be complete without them. So I drew my graph. I put speed on the x-axis and time on the y-axis, because the time it takes them depends on how fast they drive."

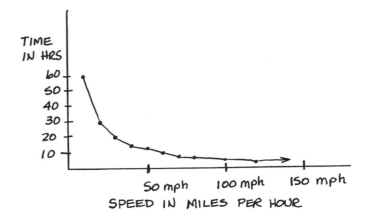

TIME
IN HRS

SPEED IN MILES PER HOUR

"The graph looks pretty neat, but I guess the whole thing is kind of dumb because anybody knows that the faster you drive, the sooner you'll get there. I suppose what would be more interesting is if you could somehow start adding in the time you have to spend waiting for policemen to write out your tickets if you were driving 90 miles per hour or the time you'd have to spend in the hospital if you were driving 250 mph."

FAT CONTENT

You may have seen ads for food indicating % fat or % fat free. For example: "Our burgers are 90% fat free," or perhaps, "Our lean hamburger is only 15% fat." A person reading these ads would probably assume that the percent of calories coming from fat is also only 10% in the first case and 15% in the second case. Unfortunately, this is not the case. The percentage of fat indicated in the ads is percent fat by weight, not by calories. Fat has 9 calories per gram. On the other hand, carbohydrates and protein each have only 4 calories per gram. So, for example, 10 grams of an apple, which is carbohydrates, is only 40 calories. Ten grams of butter (which is fat) is 90 calories. So a person will gain weight a lot faster by eating food high in fat.

Draw a graph that shows the percent fat by weight on the x-axis and the percent fat by calories on the y-axis. Then use your graph to find what percent of fat by weight gives 50% of the calories from fat.

Work this problem before continuing.

To draw the graph, it is easier to make up a weight for the food in question. Suppose you had 100 grams of food. (This is a good example of an easier related problem. When working with percentages, using 100 is often very easy.) Then change the number of grams of fat that the food contains. This will in turn change the number of grams of carbohydrates and/or protein the food has. So if the food has 5 grams of fat, then it has 95 grams of carbohydrates and/or protein. Since we chose 100 grams total, the number of grams of fat will also be the percentage of fat by weight.

Then we need to calculate the percentage of fat by calories. In the previous example, if 5 grams came from fat, that represents:

Fat

$$5 \text{ grams} \quad \times \quad \frac{9 \text{ calories}}{\text{gram}} \quad = \quad 45 \text{ calories}$$

Carbohydrate/Protein

$$95 \text{ grams} \quad \times \quad \frac{4 \text{ calories}}{\text{gram}} \quad = \quad 380 \text{ calories}$$

Since the food in question is made up of both fat and protein, there are 425 calories total in it: $45 + 380 = 425$.

Then figure the percentage of calories from fat out of the total calories.

$$\frac{45 \text{ calories from fat}}{125 \text{ calories total}} \quad = \quad 10.59\% \text{ fat}$$

Continue in this way, choosing a gram figure (which is also the percent fat by weight) and figuring out the appropriate percentage for calories. This information is summarized in the following table. Then draw a graph.

% Fat By Weight	% Fat By Calories
0	0.0
1	2.2
2	4.4
3	6.5
4	8.6
5	10.6
10	20.0
20	36.0
30	49.1
40	60.0
50	69.2
60	77.1
70	84.0
80	90.0
90	95.3
100	100.0

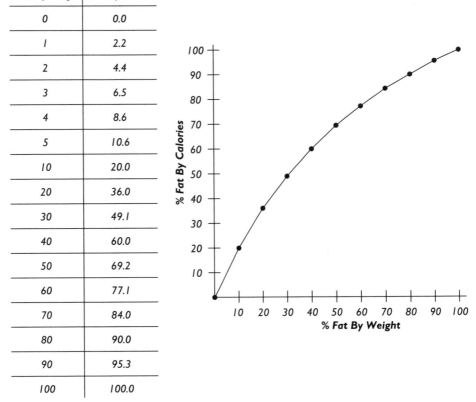

A look at the graph shows that with about 31% fat by weight, the food contains 50% fat by calories. The moral of the story is be a little cautious when you hear something is 90% or 85% fat free, because a lot more of the calories come from fat than you might expect.

The population served by the Roseville High School District has grown drastically. Roseville High School itself has grown quickly. The neighboring school, Del Oro High School, has also been growing. Here's the enrollment data for the two schools for the last several years.

YEAR	ROSEVILLE	DEL ORO
1986	1402	1718
1987	1462	1741
1988	1467	1745
1989	1548	1782
1990	1661	1765
1991	1801	1778

Use this to project the number of students for the next five years. Work this problem before continuing.

Shannon provided this graph and narration.

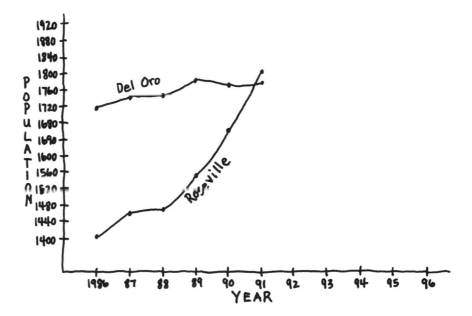

"One of the graphs probably provides a reasonable estimate of future enrollment. The other does not. The Del Oro graph shows a gradual amount of growth over several years. The growth is steady and appears to be approximately 12 students per year average over the last five years. Only one of the one-year changes was close to this average: 1990 to 1991. However, by examining the graph, we can see that the general trend of the points plotted clearly indicates a gradual, continuing growth. For an accurate forecast, it would be necessary to also check other factors influencing the population, such as housing and employment changes.

"The graph for Roseville High looks ridiculous. Growth there appears to be exponential, and an enrollment forecast based on the graph alone would give us around 2025 students in 1992 and some-where around 2400 in 1993. I can't believe that the school is really going to grow at that rate, because there has to be someplace that those students are living, and they are probably going to run out of housing in the Roseville area before the school gets much bigger."

As it turns out, the school district is building two new high schools, another neighboring district is splitting off its students, and the supply of land available for housing has decreased dramatically. Shannon's analysis for Roseville High is probably correct in that it cannot continue in the way the graph indicates.

The graph allowed us to extend growth into future data, and it also provided a visual picture that caused Shannon to doubt the very relia-bility of the forecast. In the case of Roseville High, the graph cast a doubt on the reliability of using the graph for forecasting, and yet in the case of Del Oro High, the graph strengthened the credibility.

DUCKS AND COWS

Farmer Brown has ducks and cows. The animals have a total of 12 heads and 32 feet. How many ducks and how many cows does Farmer Brown have? Solve this problem with a graph before continuing.

Eric solved this problem with a graph. "I set up two equations, one representing heads and the other representing feet. I let x represent ducks and y represent cows.

"My equations were:

$x + y = 12$
The total number of heads is 12.

$2x + 4y = 32$
The total number of feet is 32.

"Then I graphed each equation which gave me two straight lines. They intersected at (8, 4) which is 8 ducks and 4 cows."

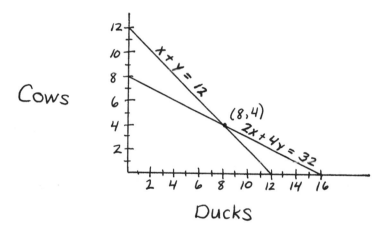

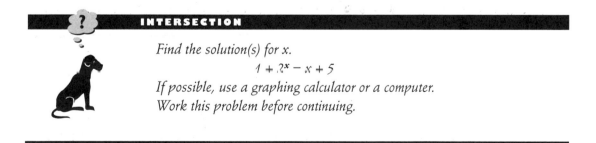

INTERSECTION

Find the solution(s) for x.
$$1 + .2^x - x + 5$$
If possible, use a graphing calculator or a computer.
Work this problem before continuing.

Using a computer or graphing calculator, draw the graphs of $y = 1 + 2^x$ and $y = x + 5$. The graphs can be seen to intersect twice, once between $x = {}^-4$ and $x = {}^-3$ and once between $x = 2$ and $x = 3$.

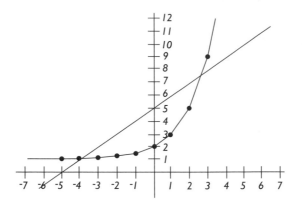

By zeroing in on the two points of intersection and altering the scale several times to zoom in on these points, the solutions can be found to be $x = {}^-3.934602$ and $x = 2.7562153$. (Note that it is somewhat difficult and time consuming to reach this degree of accuracy with a graphing calculator or with graphing software. On the other hand, it would be impossible to reach this degree of accuracy by hand. Approximating answers to the nearest tenth is reasonably easy, and to the nearest hundredth is probably sufficiently close within any application context.) Graphing calculators and computers can be an important tool in solving problems involving graphs.

MAXIMUM AREA

A farmer with 100 feet of fence to use wants to build a rectangular garden. What should the dimensions of the garden be in order to enclose maximum area? Work this problem before continuing.

This problem could be solved in any number of ways. Guess and check could be used, but you may not be sure you had the best answer. A systematic list could be generated, but again, you may not be sure of the answer. This problem could also be solved with calculus. In fact, calculus is a very good technique for solving problems such as these. However, this problem can also be solved with graphing.

One approach is to first set up the equation to be graphed. Do this by drawing a picture of the rectangular garden.

The total fence needed is 100 feet. One possible solution might be to have the length be 40 feet, and the width be 10 feet. You should verify this. So if the top and bottom sides are each x feet, then the left and right sides are each $(100 - 2x)/2$ feet. This can be written as $50 - x$.

The area of the rectangle is therefore $A = x(50 - x)$ square feet. By

hand, or with a graphing calculator or computer, graph $y = x(50 - x)$ or simply $y = 50x - x^2$

The y value represents the area of the garden. The x value repre-

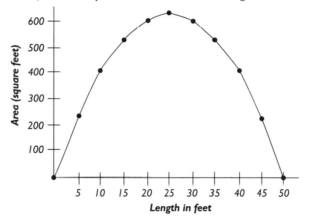

sents the length of the top side of the rectangle. Look for where the y value is at its highest point (called a maximum value). It appears that when x is 25 feet the area is a maximum at 625 square feet.

An equation is not necessary. You can also do this by making successive guesses and using the areas as the points to plot. The graphing process is then essentially the same: The *y* value represents the area of the garden, and the *x* value represents the length of the top side of the rectangle.

~~~~~~

Graphs are a very powerful visual tool for solving problems. A graph can give you a visual image of the situation that makes the problem easier to understand. We encourage you to use them often.

Section 2: Make a Scale Drawing

Consider the Ducks and Cows problem again.

DUCKS AND COWS

Farmer Brown has ducks and cows. The animals have a total of 12 heads and 32 feet. How many ducks and how many cows does Farmer Brown have? Read the following explanation of how to solve the problem with a special kind of scale drawing.

Melissa and Kevin each solved this problem with a type of scale drawing. This kind of scale drawing is called a "nomagraph." A nomagraph is a graph whose axes are parallel to one another instead of at right angles. Just as in a graph, corresponding values can be placed alongside each other in order to be able to illustrate proportions and relations. Melissa's nomagraph appears below:

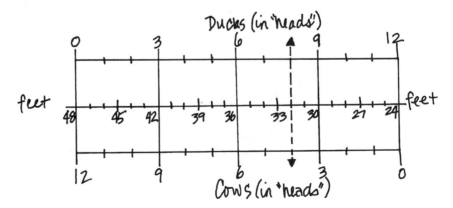

Melissa explained her diagram. "Because the total number of heads equals 12, the graph is set up so that a vertical line drawn anywhere in the graph will yield a solution of x ducks + y cows = 12 heads. The maximum number of feet possible (for 12 heads) is 48 and the minimum is 24; therefore the range of the feet units is between 24 and 48.

"To find a solution, move along the feet axis until the desired number is reached (in this case, 32). Draw a vertical line through that point and the corresponding numbers on the ducks axis and on the cows axis are the solution.

"The answer to '32 feet' is 4 cows and 8 ducks as shown above. Got it?"

Kevin took a similar approach to this problem. His solution uses a constant of 32 feet and he looks for the number of heads to add up to 12.

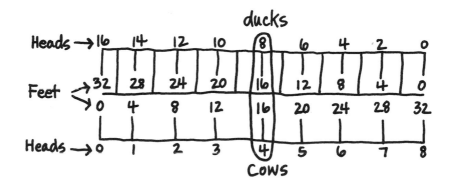

Kevin explained, "With this graph, I can locate the correct number of ducks and cows by finding which vertical line equals 12 heads because the feet for each line equals 32. Therefore, the answer is 8 ducks and 4 cows."

~~~~~

The previous two examples show a combination graph and scale drawing. In the first section of this chapter we dealt with drawing graphs to solve problems. The last part of the chapter deals with making scale drawings to solve problems.

Who uses scale drawings? Matt is a landscape architect. He frequently uses scale drawings to make the landscape plans for his clients. He makes a scale drawing of the area (backyard, park, office park) and places it on his drafting table. Then he draws in the various plants and trees on transparent overlays that he places on top of the main diagram. If he doesn't like the results, he just gets a new transparency and does not have to eliminate the main drawing. Matt draws all of the transparencies to scale and then checks for aesthetics, size of walkways, foliage density or sparseness, and so on.

Police investigators also make scale drawings of accident scenes. They use their scale drawing, along with some algebra, geometry, and trigonometry, as well as unit analysis and subproblems, to determine the original speeds of the cars involved. This helps in determining whether either driver was speeding, which in turn may indicate who was at fault.

A lot of scale drawing depends on unit analysis, as you'll see in the next problem.

MY PATIO

Make a scale drawing of my backyard patio. I have a rectangular patio that is 18 feet by 12 feet. On the patio is a rectangular lounge chair that measures 2 feet by 4 feet 3 inches and a circular picnic table measuring 5 feet 8 inches in diameter.
Make a scale drawing before continuing.

The first thing you must do is choose a scale. It is often easier to do scale drawings using centimeters, rather than inches, to represent feet.

Suppose you pick a scale 1 cm = 2 feet. You must do some unit analysis to convert real-life measurement to scale measurement. For example, the picnic table's diameter requires you to change 5 feet 8 inches into feet, and then scale to centimeters.

$$8 \text{ inches} \quad \times \quad \frac{1 \text{ foot}}{12 \text{ inches}} \quad \approx \quad .6666 \text{ feet}$$

$$5.6666 \text{ feet} \quad \times \quad \frac{1 \text{ cm}}{2 \text{ feet}} \quad = \quad 2.8333 \text{ cm}$$

So the 5.666-feet diameter table has a 2.8333-cm diameter in the scale drawing. Using an approximation of 2.8 cm should work well for this problem.

Note there is a difference between unit analysis and scaling, however. In unit analysis, the fraction that you multiply by has the value of 1 (for example, 1 foot/12 inches). In scaling, the fraction is not equal to 1 (such as 1 cm/2 ft). However, you choose to make 1 cm and 2 feet equivalent for the purpose of scaling.

The drawing of my patio is shown below. The table and lounge chair, of course, could be placed anywhere.

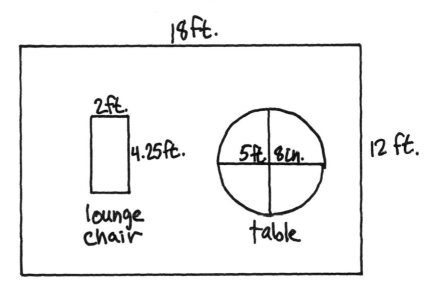

"Mayday, Mayday!" the call came in. It startled Ned in the Coast Guard office. He immediately got on the radio. "Coast Guard here. What is your position? Over."

"I'm not sure. We left the port at Miami at 7:30. We sailed due southeast for 2 hours at 35 knots. Then we turned about 30 degrees to starboard (right) and sailed for 4 hours at 25 knots. Then we lost our engines and we have been adrift for about an hour and a half. We would have called earlier, but our radio was out. Can you send us some help?"

Ned replied, "I'll work out your position and send out a chopper right away. Over."

"Thanks a lot."

Ned knew that the current in the ocean at that time of day was approximately 5 knots due south. A knot, or 1 nautical mile, equals 1.151 land miles. The helicopter speedometer measures land miles per hour. The likely speed of the helicopter was 80 miles per hour (that is, land miles). In what direction should Ned send the helicopter and how many minutes will it take it to get to the stranded boat?

Make a scale drawing and solve this problem before continuing.

Ned solved this problem as follows. "I knew I could probably use trig for this, but I didn't remember any of it. So I made a scale drawing. I let 1 mm = 1 nautical mile. So the 2 hours at 35 knots is 70 nautical miles and the 4 hours at 25 knots is 100 nautical miles. I drew my scale drawing. First I put a dot to represent Miami and then measured a 45° angle in the southeast direction. I drew a line 7 cm long. I put a big dot at the end of that line. Then I extended it a little and drew in a 30° right turn. I drew that line 10 cm long. Then I measured due south and drew a line that was 7.5 mm long to represent the one and a half hours of drifting at 5 knots per hour, which would be 7.5 nautical miles.

"Finally I measured the distance from the beginning of the journey to the end, and found it to be 17.1 cm, which stands for 171 nautical miles. The angle was about 64° south of east. To convert 171 nautical miles, I used unit analysis."

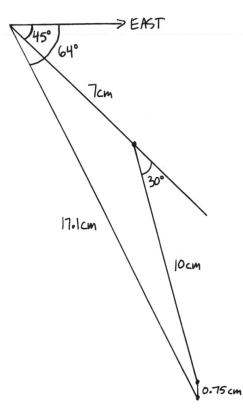

171 naut mile $\times$ $\dfrac{\text{1.151 land miles}}{\text{1 nautical mile}}$ = 197 land miles

"Then I figured out the time, given that the helicopter travels 80 miles per hour."

197 naut miles $\times$ $\dfrac{\text{1 hour}}{\text{80 miles}}$ = 2.4625 hours

0.4625 hrs $\times$ $\dfrac{\text{60 minutes}}{\text{1 hour}}$ = 27.75 minutes

"So it would take the helicopter about 2 hours and 28 minutes to reach the boat. Of course, in that time, the boat would drift a little further south, which means the helicopter will get to the spot and won't find the boat. It will have to turn due south at that point and look for the boat."

~~~~

All of the problems in this chapter can probably be done with a method other than graphing or scale drawings. However, we strongly advocate at least starting with a graph or scale drawing, then possibly using another strategy. Drawing has advantages over symbolic manipulation. The drawing brings your visual experience into the problem. Vision is the most highly developed sense in most people. Graphs enable you to meld the math with the visual, making for an effective, accurate problem-solving medium.

Problem Set A

1. REFRIGERATOR

Cher wants to buy a new refrigerator. She visits a store and finds two recommended models. The Major brand is $600 and is expected to cost $30 per month in energy cost. The Minor brand is $400 and is expected to cost $40 per month in energy cost. Which refrigerator would you advise Cher to buy?

2. SODA

There are two places that sell soda next door to each other. One is a hamburger restaurant, the other is a gasoline station/mini-mart. The prices they charge for their take-out sodas are shown on the chart.

Size (ounces)	Restaurant	Mini-mart
8	.59	
12	.69	
16		.57
20	.84	.72
32		.99

Each place is considering offering a 24-ounce size soda. What would be the probable price at each establishment?

3. LETTUCE

Fatima is the produce manager for a local grocery store. On information provided by the grower and shipper, she knows that iceberg lettuce will stay fresh for 21 days at 35 degrees, for 15 days at 40 degrees, for 10 days at 45 degrees, and for 1 day at 70 degrees. During a heat wave she knows that they will not be able to keep the produce as cool as she would like. How long can she expect the lettuce to last if they keep it at about 60 degrees?

4. APPLE ORCHARD

Ms. Pomme has an apple-tree orchard. If she hires 20 people to pick the apples, it will take them 6 hours. If she hires 30 people, it will take 4 hours. Draw a graph that shows people on the x-axis and time on the y-axis. Use the graph to estimate how long it would take if she hired 50 people, and how long it would take if she hired 6 people.

If you were Ms. Pomme, how many people would you hire? Why?

5. JEANNE'S ORIGAMI BOOK

Jeanne decided to make some money. She thought it would be nice to contribute something to society in the process. So Jeanne wrote a booklet showing people how to do origami. She then photocopied it (each one cost her $1.45 to copy) and sold the copies for $2.00 each. She bought a small ad for $24 offering her book for sale at $2.00 each. Not including any consideration for her labor, how many books would she need to sell before the endeavor turns profitable?

6. CUBIC EQUATION

Solve using a graph: $(^1\!/_2)x^3 - 2x^2 - 8x + 10 = 0$.

7. CHRISTMAS TREE LOT

A store owner wants to put up a Christmas tree lot in her parking lot. She wants to fence in a rectangular lot on three sides with 200 feet of fence, and on the fourth side use the wall of her store. What is the maximum area of the lot?

8. BOX

Take a piece of 8.5 by 11 inch paper. Cut a same-sized square corner out of each corner of the paper and fold the paper up to form an open-topped box. What is the maximum volume thus obtained?

9. JAWS

The movie *Jaws* was a big hit. It made $130 million. The producers decided that they would make a sequel. It didn't do quite as well, and neither did *Jaws III* or *Jaws IV*. Using the information below, draw a graph and predict how much money *Jaws V* might make if they filmed it. (They didn't.)

MOVIE	MONEY MADE (IN MILLIONS)
Jaws	$130
Jaws II	$50
Jaws III	$26
Jaws IV	$12
Jaws V	?

10. MORE PHONE CALLS

This is a list of several phone calls made during the day, the evening, and the night (each time period has different first-minute charges and subsequent-minute charges). Determine the first- and subsequent-minute charges for each time period.

5	$1.74
7	$1.86
8	$2.12
9	$1.66
10	$3.39
11	$2.90
13	$4.38
18	$3.28

11. BIG PROBLEMS

Both Allen and Jerry consider their weight a problem. Each one is trying out for the football squad, and wants to weigh more. Allen is eating, and working out, and has found he gains about 1 pound each week. At this point he weighs 180 pounds. Jerry, on the other hand, weighs 167 and is eating, working out, and eating. He is gaining about 5 pounds every 3 weeks. How long will it take for Jerry and Allen to weigh the same?

12. SAILING

Diane was sailing—she had been timing herself and plotting the average reported wind speed on a chart in order to determine what kind of times to expect if she were sailing a race. On five previous trips, she had the following times with the wind speeds.

WINDSPEED	TIME
20 knots	45 min
8 knots	112.5 min
12 knots	75 min
23 knots	39 min-8 sec
11 knots	81 min-6 sec

Today the weather report predicts an average wind speed of 17 knots. What time should she expect to have on the course?

13. YOUR BEDROOM

Make a scale drawing of your bedroom. Include all appropriate furniture. Choose a scale that allows you to fit your drawing nicely on a piece of paper, not so small that you can't see anything, and not so big that it runs off the paper. Label all interesting parts of the diagram with the real-life measurements.

14. TELEPHONE POLE

You wish to measure the height of a telephone pole. You measure a distance 40 feet away from the pole. Standing at that point, you measure the angle between the ground and the top of the pole to be 35°. How tall is the pole?

15. STADIUM POLE

You want to measure the height of a stadium light pole. However, it is on the other side of a fence and you don't care to test the trespassing laws. Instead, you stand at point A and measure the angle to the top of the pole and find it to be 40°. You then walk 50 feet directly away from the pole and measure the angle to the top again. This time it is 28°. How tall is the pole?

16. HOW WIDE IS THE RIVER?

Mai Khanh wants to measure the width of a river. She stretches a 100-yard string parallel to the river along the ground. (The river is completely straight for these 100 yards.) Directly across the river from one end of the string is a tree on the bank of the river. From the other end of the string, she sights to the tree and finds that the angle between the string and the line of sight to the tree is 35°. What is the approximate width of the river?

17. FRISBEE ON THE ROOF

Lisa is standing on the ground looking up at Judy in the second-story window. Ed is on the roof retrieving a Frisbee. From the point on the ground where Lisa is standing, the angle of elevation to Judy is 22°, and the angle of elevation to Ed is 40°. Judy is 12 feet above the ground. How far is Lisa standing from the building, and how high off the ground is Ed?

18. KITE STRING

It's Lisa's turn to go on the roof after the kite. It got stuck on the chimney. The string is caught on the chimney about 25 feet off the ground. Ed can sight Lisa at about a 15° angle from the ground. How long is the kite string from Ed to where Lisa is?

Problem Set B

1. SODA JERK

Larry took the job title "soda jerk" to heart. As a clerk at a soda counter he had to take orders, get the right-flavored soda in the right-sized cup, and get the drink to the right customer. On his first day on the job, not a single order was filled correctly. He did, however, get the flavor right on 13 orders, he also got the drink size right on 12 orders. He also managed to get nine drinks to people who'd actually ordered drinks; however, the size and/or the flavor were wrong. In defending himself to the manager he said, "At least there were 14 orders where only one thing was screwed up, and only once did I give the wrong soda in the wrong sized cup to a person who had not ordered a drink." It was true, but what is the minimum number of orders that Larry screwed up? What is the highest possible percentage of drinks that were salvageable (the right flavor in the right cup—they just needed to be given to the right person)?

2. LICENSE PLATES

License plates are issued systematically. In a state where the license plates are three letters followed by three numbers, the following sequence of licenses plates could have been issued: CMP998, CMP999, CMQ000, CMQ001, etc. The license plate that was just issued is AZY987. Notice this license plate has no repeated letters or digits. How many license plates must be issued following this one before a license will again have no repeated letters or digits?

3. KAYAKING

Darlene and Boris both live on the lake. To get to Boris's house by street, Darlene has to take Mountain View Road 2 miles south and then take Lakeshore Drive 3 miles east. Boris called Darlene and suggested they go watch a soccer game at the end of School Road. To get to the end of School Road, Boris simply needs to kayak due north across the lake. If Darlene kayaks directly from her house to the end of School Road, it turns out to be exactly the same distance that Boris has to go. How far is it from Boris's house to the end of School Road?

4. THE DIGITAL CLOCK AND THE MIRROR

If I look in the bathroom mirror while I'm shaving, I can see the reflection of my digital clock on my headboard in my bedroom. Sometimes the time that I see in the mirror (a reflection of the actual time) is the same as the actual time. How many times does this happen per day? (Ignore the colon because I can't see that anyway— the clock is too far away.)

5. THE LATTICE

Barbara and Archie are building a lattice out of wood. The lattice will be in the shape of a right triangle. The frame for the lattice measures 18 feet along the base and 12 feet high. They are going to put in vertical strips of 1-inch-wide wood every 9 inches connecting the base to the hypotenuse How many feet of 1-inch-wide wood will they put into the lattice?

CARTOON ILLUSTRATIONS
Dan Piraro
Dallas, Texas

COMPUTER ILLUSTRATIONS
Ann Rothenbuhler

STUDENT WORK ILLUSTRATIONS
Kerry Harrigan, Lisa DaValle, Ann Rothenbuhler

COVER AND BOOK DESIGN
Seventeenth Street Studios
Oakland, California

PRODUCTION MANAGER
Adam Ray

PHOTO CREDITS
Photos not acknowledged below belong to Key Curriculum Press.
Chapter 0 © Uniphoto; Chapter 1 © Steve Dunwell/The Image Bank; Chapter 2 © The
Image Bank; Chapter 3 © Uniphoto; Chapter 5 © The Image Bank; Chapter 6 © Uniphoto;
Chapter 7 © Bob Daemmrich/Unitphoto; Chapter 8 © Gary Gladstone/The Image Bank;
Chapter 9 © David Bownell/The Image Bank; Chapter 10 © HMS Images/The Image Bank;
Chapter 11 © Steve Dunwell/The Image Bank; Chapter 14 © Derek Berwin/The Image Bank;
Chapter 15 © Santi Visalli/The Image Bank; Chapter 16 © Gary Chapman/The Image Bank;
Chapter 17 © Gary Gladstone/The Image Bank. Cover photos; Michael Carr. Special thanks
to Alonzo Printing, Alan and Jesse Bond, Frankye Kelly, and Ann Williams for photo assistance.